Rose Scott

For Patricia White
and
Lyn Garton

Rose Scott

Vision and Revision in Feminism

Judith A. Allen

Melbourne

OXFORD UNIVERSITY PRESS

Oxford   Auckland   New York

OXFORD UNIVERSITY PRESS AUSTRALIA

Oxford   New York   Toronto
Delhi   Bombay   Calcutta   Madras   Karachi
Kuala Lumpur   Singapore   Hong Kong   Tokyo
Nairobi   Dar es Salaam   Cape Town
Melbourne   Auckland   Madrid

and associated companies in
Berlin   Ibadan

OXFORD is a trade mark of Oxford University Press

© Judith A. Allen 1994
First published 1994

National Library of Australia
Cataloguing-in-Publication data:
ALLEN, JUDITH, 1955–.
    Rose Scott.

Bibliography.
Includes index.
ISBN 0 19 554846 9.

1. Scott, Rose, 1847–1925. 2. Women social reformers
— New South Wales — Biography. 3. Social reformers
— New South Wales — Biography. 4. Feminism.
I. Title.

305.42092

Typeset by Syarikat Seng Teik Sdn. Bhd.
Printed in Hong Kong by Yau Sing
Published by Oxford University Press,
253 Normanby Road, South Melbourne, Australia

Contents

Preface and Acknowledgements

I remember when I first heard of Rose Scott. It was in 1976 in my third-year Honours Australian History seminar at the University of Sydney. One of my friends was doing a research essay on that most Australian of cultural practices — surf bathing. Mixed-sex surf bathing was illegal in Sydney until 1911. We laughed mightily at Rose Scott, the veteran woman suffragist of the 1890s who had fiercely opposed mixed-sex surf bathing. Moreover, she had also opposed the admission of men spectators to women's swimming carnivals — indeed, the presence of men at all when women used swimming pools.

What an embarrassment earlier women's movement activists like Scott were to young feminists in the 1970s. While in principle the idea of there being a long history of feminist activism was alluring, the more research that was done on women activists like Scott, the less possible it seemed to identify common ground with them. Despite the credit they were owed for fighting the good fight for a wide range of reforms, including female suffrage, their beliefs and attitudes, their representations of women, of men, and especially of sexuality, seemed to share more with anti-feminist women activists of the 1970s than with feminists. Anne Summers, the scholar who inspired a whole generation of Australian feminist historians, seemed to summarise the problem perfectly: women like Scott asserted not *feminist* consciousness, but female consciousness.

Yet if Rose Scott was so manifestly not a feminist by late-twentieth-century standards, why did she not receive some endorsement of her objectives from patriarchal governments of her day? A little digging showed that the one measure she prized above all — raising the age of consent from 12 as it stood in 1880 to 16 as it was in England from 1885 — took until 1910 to be enacted in New South Wales. Why did she think this reform was so critical, and what was the basis of the long opposition and resistance to it?

My questions about this woman, her context and feminism, began to snowball, and late in 1976 I began work on Scott's career, 1890–1925, for an Honours dissertation. With over seventy volumes and boxes of her personal papers, speeches, notes, journals, diaries, correspondence and printed material held in the Mitchell Library, Sydney (founded by her cousin, David Scott Mitchell), Scott's thirty-five years in public life seemed more fully documented than other women's rights activists of her time. By carefully examining the evidence, I hoped to be able to understand how Scott's work on behalf of women was 'radical' in its context, yet seemed so 'conservative' from the perspective of equivalent activists on behalf of women in the 1970s. I would be able to decide if it was appropriate to call Scott and others of her era feminists, albeit 'first wave' feminists, sharply differentiated from 'second wave' feminists of the late 1960s onwards.

I came to the conclusion, after a year's study, that Scott should indeed be classified as a 'feminist' after due consideration of her context, or what I understood of it. Why was it that she kept appearing among the most unlikely historical records of groups, activities, government departments and institutions? Why were her thoughts, speeches, and enthusiasms given such extensive press coverage? Was it true, as Australian writer Miles Franklin claimed in 1938, that Scott wrote over fifty letters a day and, on this account, persuaded the local municipal council to install a larger postbox at the bottom of her street? Why was she so eloquently, so earnestly, and so darkly concerned with the character of sexual relations, with what she saw as women's degradation to 'creatures of sex'? What transpired in this woman's lifetime to lead her to spend almost four of her five adult decades in unpaid public work, primarily in law and policy reforms affecting women's and children's conditions? Did her work make any difference, and by what criteria might it be evaluated? Moreover, what significance could the writings, the political lobbying, the relationships, the organisational roles, and the preoccupations of Rose Scott have for prevailing understandings of the history of feminism, and that of Australian culture and politics in this critical period?

After producing a conventional and rather celebratory account of the most public and worthy aspects of her career, I went on to explore other aspects of her context—in particular the history of the sexual practices and their outcomes, which were of such concern to her.[1] The themes of rape, seduction, illegitimacy, prostitution, marital violence, infanticide, abortion and babyfarming recurred throughout her papers. What was their Australian history? The study of crimes involving women since 1880 occupied my next decade, and forced me into a process of continuing re-assessment of Scott, and a recognition that I must, some day, fully document her career and its significance.

Rose Scott thus has had a place in my life for many years. A number of scholars, colleagues and friends have helped me write this book, and for this I should like to thank them. Since 1976, when I began researching Scott and Australian feminism, the staff of the Mitchell Library, Sydney, have been unstintingly co-operative, gracious and helpful, making the long hours deciphering the notorious and voluminous Scott handwriting more interesting than onerous. For assistance with photographic material and relics I thank Shirley Humphries and Paul Smith, especially for access to David Scott Mitchell's will; and I am grateful to Helen Yoxall for her herculean efforts in cataloguing the Scott Family Papers in 1978–79.

Heather Radi encouraged me to start this as an Honours dissertation in 1976 and then regularly urged me to persevere with a fuller study. When I moved to Brisbane in 1985 she afforded many kinds of practical assistance, including generous hospitality on my frequent research trips to Sydney and shrewd suggestions on ways in which my findings could be read. My childhood sweetheart, Dr Philip Graham, gave me warm hospitality during my research in the Newcastle and Region Public Library, for which I shall always be in his debt. I also thank the staff of the Newcastle and Region Public Library for their assistance with obtaining permission to reproduce some exquisite Scott and related family photographs.

Patricia White, Lyn Garton and Stephen Garton have discussed Rose Scott with me since 1977. I have benefited from their constant enthusiasm, memorable stories and support: their concern that Rose Scott should take her place in accounts of modern Australian history has inspired me. I also enjoyed many conversations with Jill Roe, my doctoral dissertation advisor, about Miles Franklin and Rose Scott; from her I have learned much over a very long time.

Louise Sweetland of Oxford University Press believed Rose Scott deserved a book and in 1986 persuaded me to write it. Griffith University Research Grants provided funding for travel and research assistance in Perth, Canberra, Melbourne and Sydney, while the Faculty of Humanities Research and Resources Committee assisted with funds for research travel and manuscript typing.

While I was in the processes first of imagining, then of devising the shape of the book, several colleagues responded positively to my in-progress papers on Scott or on aspects of the history of Australian feminism and its international counterparts. They gave me the opportunity to develop my readings and arguments in conferences and seminars, and in published articles and reviews. For this important support I thank: Marion Aveling, Barbara Caine, Dawn Emerson, Patricia Grimshaw, Elizabeth Grosz, Marilyn Lake, Marie de Lepervanche, Stuart Macintyre, Kathryn McPherson, Susan Magarey, Alison Prentice, Heather Radi, Patricia Roy, Susan Sheridan, Katie Spearritt, Catharine Stimpson, Veronica Strong Boag and Martha Vicinus.

Barbara Caine's commitment to the best possible understanding of the complexities and nuances of the late-nineteenth and early-twentieth-century history of feminism has provided me with a good professional and scholarly example; she has also been an unfailingly generous provider of comparative perspectives, criticisms and constructive solutions to interpretative problems. Her input as colleague, reader and friend made *Rose Scott* possible, in this form.

I have been fortunate over the years in the willingness of scholarly friends to discuss and debate various issues of interpretation raised by aspects of Rose Scott's life and I particularly thank Peter Bailey, Chilla Bulbeck,

Stephen Garton, Helen Hardacre, Rosemary Pringle, Janet Ramsey, Gail Reekie, Barbara Sullivan, James Walter, David Walker and Elizabeth Wood. They have also generously edited chapter drafts, thereby improving the manuscript in spite of possible shortcomings. In my year of research at Harvard University, the assistance of Wendy and Elizabeth Cowles, Nora Connell and Rose Darling was invaluable. I would like to thank the staff of the Arthur and Elizabeth Schlesinger Library on the History of Women in America, especially Dr Patricia King, Diane Hamer, Eva Mosley and Jane Knowles, for innumerable instances of generous advice, access to relevant resources and an environment conducive to excellence in feminist history. Many United States colleagues expressed interest and provided valuable comparative and theoretical discussions. In particular, I owe a debt to Margo Anderson, Nancy Cott, Ellen Dubois, Nancy Folbre, Laura Frader, Linda Gordon, Carole Pateman, Shulamit Reinharz, Susan Reverby, Gita Sen and Susan Cotts Watkins.

Janice Mitchell fearlessly tackled *Rose Scott* as text, producing her superb work rapidly and keeping me focused on the next phase or task. She has been much more to me and this book than her appointed role, and I hope she has some idea of the extent of my admiration and gratitude to her. My publisher, Peter Rose, has been unfailingly constructive and critical, setting me high standards of professionalism and care. Stephen Garton solved eleventh-hour matters, long distance, with his inimitable style, making everything possible. For her expert proofreading, and many much-needed laughs, Helen Hardacre has my special thanks, as does Maura Buckley of the Women's Studies Program at Indiana University, for her assistance with the index.

Finally, my involvement in contemporary feminism inflects my interest in its history and this amounts to a debt to the many theorists, activists, and cultural producers of the current women's movement in Australia and many other countries. If historical understanding can contribute to the forging of an effective future for feminism, the book will have some use. My various kinds of 'family', loved ones and friends have made it possible. They know they have my thanks and my love.

Judith Allen
September 1993

Abbreviations

ABS	Australian Broadcasting Commission
ADB	*Australian Dictionary of Biography*
AWS	*Australian Women's Sphere*
ECM	Edward Charles Merewether
ICW	International Council of Women
HSC	Helenus Scott Correspondence
MEA	Merewether Estate Archives
MFP	Miles Franklin Papers
ML MSS	Mitchell Library Manuscripts
MSRM	Miscellaneous Scott and Rusden Manuscripts
NCW	National Council of Women
n.d.	no date
n.p.	no pagination
NLA	National Library of Australia
NMH	*Newcastle Morning Herald*
NRPL	Newcastle and Region Public Library
NSWPD	New South Wales Parliamentary Debates
NUWSS	National Union of Women's Suffrage Societies
RS	Rose Scott
RSC	Rose Scott Correspondence
RSP	Rose Scott Papers
SAGL	Society of Australian Genealogists Library
SFP	Scott Family Papers
SMH	*Sydney Morning Herald*
SSC	Saranna Scott Correspondence
WFP	Windeyer Family Papers
WLL	Women's Liberal League
WLRL	Women's Liberal and Reform League
WLS	Women's Literary Society
WPA	Women's Progressive Association
WPEL	Women's Political and Educational League
WSG	Women's Service Guild
WSL	Womanhood Suffrage League
WSPU	Women's Social and Political League

Introduction

Rose Scott (1847–1925) was an 'elite', white, Anglo-Scottish Australian feminist social reformer who never married. A founder and associate of many feminist causes, including women's suffrage and citizen's rights, raising the age of consent, women prisoners, prostitution policies, working women's wages and work conditions, and women's access to higher education, the professions, civil service careers, and public office, Scott became a public figure of stature. Her biographer, writer Miles Franklin, said in 1951 that 'fifty years ago' Scott's name had been a household word.[1]

In constant correspondence with her overseas counterparts, Scott was an enthusiastic member of international feminist organisations. She understood feminism as being concerned with cultural as well as legislative change, and so promoted the work and critical reception of women writers, artists, musicians and actors. A key player in public controversies that constructed and contested gender meanings, Scott defended the much vilified performances of Ibsen's *A Doll's House* in the 1890s. Scott deplored the violence and what she called 'animalism' of warfare and imperialist subjugations around the world. She attacked British hostilities against the Boers and the imperialism that drew Australian soldiers into the Boer War, and later into the 1914–18 war. Refusing to appear as representative of 'woman', 'the sex', she made a scorching public critique of the pronatalism of the 1902–03 New South Wales government's Royal Commission into the Decline in the Birthrate. A warm patron of women's amateur swimming, she categorically opposed the early-twentieth-century move to admit men as spectators to women's carnivals and the new pastime of mixed-sex surf bathing. Scott identified English suffragette militancy as the expression of a bellicose spirit inimical to the interests of women and social reform.

In her notoriously unclear handwriting, Scott's vast private papers document the development of her feminism during the course of a forty-year public life. The intensity and darkness of much of this writing offer rare insights into the indignation that could motivate public feminist advocacy. Her writings also permit analysis of the prevalent terms and categories through which earlier feminists constructed the problem of sexual difference and gave their indignation cultural articulation and meaning.[2]

Pre-eminently, Scott maintained that women — and, most contentiously, for modern critics, *all* women — suffered 'degradation' as a sex in their relations with the 'other' sex. She advocated unflinchingly what Chantal Mouffe disapprovingly dubbed 'the man/woman antagonism'

1

as the central problem confronting culture and politics in her life-time.[3] Her cultural context mandated seeing sex as a fundamental organising divide, one more irrevocable than class. Sexual division seemed as salient for 'other' races and ethnic groups — including the Aboriginal peoples whose lands Scott's ancestors had seized — as for the Anglo-Saxon or Celtic majority of the population. Meanwhile, if difference constituted around sex had discursive, especially scientific, currency throughout Scott's life, the notion of sexual orientation as a site of legitimate difference between 'women' and 'men' was of the future, historically unavailable to her.[4]

Certain that 'women' and 'men' were unified and meaningful categories, with identifiable political interests and, partly as a corollary, unaware of their intersection by other modern categories, Scott's feminism forms an illuminating case study at this point in the international enterprise of writing histories of feminism. For in recent decades, feminist theorists and historians of feminism have become increasingly preoccupied by differences — of position, of experience, of representations, of history — which are seen as splitting the previously hegemonic and curiously persistent category of 'women' as a sex posed within feminism.[5] Its assertion by feminists as the fundamental prerequisite and political rationale for effective feminism is increasingly refused. Critics from many positions assail this traditional feminist claim as essentialist, biologistic, separatist, racialist, bourgeois or elitist, thus as silencing enquiry of this most unstable, fragmented type. Insofar as the historical record of earlier feminists like Scott prefigures such problematic claims, histories of feminism inevitably have become highly charged texts. Put plainly, the era of transition into the twenty-first century is not the most auspicious time for the discourses of feminists like Scott to interest feminist historians and biographers. Such forebears are easily judged unsound, misguided and myopic, with few redeeming qualities or achievements.[6]

Yet it is precisely her grim adherence to the unified category 'women', even in the face of evidence of its non-unity in practice, that makes the study of Scott's feminism instructive for contemporary feminist theorists and historians of feminism. Clearly, she and others like her did not see, or see as relevant to their feminist work, the divisions and differences that so trouble contemporary feminism. If simply demonstrating this fact, and denouncing earlier feminists as 'politically incorrect', satisfies some historians of feminism, it is arguably an insufficient and even ungenerous objective.[7] The confrontation here between past and present feminisms generates fascinating historical questions.

It is possible to put to the past a series of questions, in the light of earlier feminists' relative imperviousness to differences, other than those forged by sex. How was this imperviousness established and through what discourses was it maintained? Was adherence to the unified categories of 'women', 'men' and the proposition of their hierarchical antagonism, unchallenged and unqualified throughout the feminist careers of women like Scott? For all the condemnation of feminist forebears for 'exclusionary' formulations of feminist demands and arguments, is it possible that their unified categories may have 'challenged male supremacy', to borrow part of Linda Gordon's definition of feminism?[8] Did the 'essentialism' and 'elitism' of which we in the present can so easily (and anachronistically) convict those in the past actually generate forms of politics and resistance that would have been impossible had earlier feminists had their successors' sensitivities to different 'differences'? How was it that the proposition of a cross-class and cross-cultural state of subordination of women to men made sense for large numbers of nineteenth and early-twentieth-century white feminists, despite massive evidence of the political salience of differences among women?[9]

This study of Scott's feminism proceeds then from the full recognition that her beliefs and activities are substantially uncongenial to, and irreconcilable with, those of contemporary feminists, positioned in what DeLauretis terms 'the post-colonial moment'.[10] Despite this non-identification, and perhaps even because of it, much can be learned from the case study of Scott about some core qualities of the Anglophone feminism of her period, and its legacy. The appeal of the dream of a unity of women rightly troubles contemporary feminists, possibly over-troubling some in revealing ways. Many of the prolific theoretical writings of recent Anglo-American and Australian feminism resemble secular sermons, bursting with the language of prescription, exhortation and the exorcism of evil. The unresolved debates they advance, in turn, inflect the writing of the history of feminism and re-evaluations of the mission of women's history, with many favouring the reformulation of that mission as 'the history of gender'.[11] Coming to peace with feminism's past preoccupies the feminist present. Coming to *terms* with the history of feminism has proved no easy matter, particularly when the questions put to that past have been 'presentist' — that is to say, shaped principally by current and present concerns — and therefore profoundly decontextualising in character.[12]

Setting this examination of the Australian feminist social reformer Rose Scott in an appropriate context requires an evaluation of the enterprise of writing the history of feminism in Anglophone countries over the past two decades. This evaluation is indispensable, since a principal objective of this book is to explore the substantial change in Scott's feminism, marked by shifts in the terms, claims and categories she employed between 1880 and 1925. For Scott began public life speaking of the need to 'elevate the condition' of women, by enlarging their realms of effective agency. This would be achieved through challenging masculine dominance of public institutions and culture. In this quest, suffrage and citizenship were paramount. By the 1920s, she would put the matter in different, though no less significant terms. What was needed, she claimed, was women's 'real emancipation', a term connoting release or freedom from bondage and from paternal, masculine power. That shift of focus from 'elevation' to 'emancipation' signalled a fundamental change in Scott's vision for women. She always stressed the importance of seeing, of vision, in the formation of feminist analyses and strategies. By the 1920s, then, her vision had undergone major revision, apparent to the reader of her writings, even if not to their author. The ramifications of this revision within feminist thought, a shift which arguably facilitated the emergence of modern feminist preoccupations, require new investigation.

Questions of periodisation are important in any attempt to contextualise this revision in Scott's feminist world view, rendering comparison with studies of feminists and feminism not only in Australia, but also in New Zealand, Britain, Canada and the United States, especially useful.[13] Debates on the best ways both to characterise and periodise feminism are complex and have reached an impasse.[14] This book aims to illuminate the issues at stake in current historiographical debates on periodisation, from a perspective outside the two principal national traditions typically informing their content: those of Britain and the United States. The tendency of the history discipline to demand place and period specialisation generates analytic issues concerning feminism and characterisations of its historical forms, primarily within national boundaries and periodisations, as conveyed by titles like *Victorian Feminism*. Too few specialist historians read comprehensively outside their own national context, implicitly at least suggesting the uniqueness of the feminism of their place and period. Even if some recognition of the internationalism of late-nineteenth and early-twentieth-century feminism is recorded, the assumption of a determining character for the national framework in question is overwhelming. For instance, studies emphasise how feminism emerged from or can be seen as a side effect of British liberalism, or United States post-bellum Reconstructionism, or Australian nationalism of the 1890s, or the formation of the Canadian version of the welfare state, or New Zealand post-Depression political radicalism.[15]

Despite differences of national and local contexts, however, the similarities between the preoccupations, rhetoric and intellectual influences within feminism in Anglophone countries are remarkable. Why would it be otherwise? Nationalist historical frameworks can obscure the extent to which feminism from at least the late nineteenth century was an internationalist movement that built powerful transnational ties of culture and politics. Its leaders and members travelled, conferred, lectured, emigrated temporarily and permanently, wrote, read, emulated, boasted, exchanged crucial strategic materials, and sought and received advice, solace, criticism and support across national lines. Both individually and through organisations, Australian feminists had political and cultural exchanges with Britain, the United States, Canada, South Africa, New Zealand, India, Scandinavia and, to a lesser extent, countries of northern Europe. To move beyond the tendency to 're-invent the wheel' in the multiplication of parochial and particularist studies of feminist movements in local frameworks, historians of feminism would do well to follow their feminist forebears' interest in international comparison and exchange. Far from endangering our understanding of the features truly unique to each nation involved, we can accurately establish the unique only by identifying shared elements.[16]

In order to position this study of Scott's feminism, three elements of current debates arising within the historiography of feminism should be addressed. The first is how feminism should be defined and characterised in the past and the appropriate periodisations to be employed. The second is the problem of presentism and the different options proposed by historians of feminism for its redress. The third is the widely debated instability of analytical categories hitherto taken as self-evident by historians of feminism and practitioners of women's history. These three elements are interconnected and pose serious issues for the consideration of any study of feminism. Such consideration precedes a brief outline of Scott's various locations and contexts as a transitional figure across generations of feminists, as an internationalist activist, and as an Australian feminist of her place and period.

DEFINING, CHARACTERISING AND PERIODISING FEMINISM

Historians of women and of feminism from many countries debate definitions, characterisations and periodisations for feminism. Some, like English historian Rosalind Delmar, contend that while probably all feminists agree that 'women suffer discrimination because of their sex', and that only radical social change would secure women's specific needs, this agreement does not result in a shared understanding of 'why this state of affairs should exist or what can be done about it'. Analysis of the intellectual content of feminism, she writes, has been subordinate to chronicling the vicissitudes of feminism as a social movement in most published histories of feminism, women's suffrage and various women's rights campaigns.[17] It is those historians (who have turned their attention to the philosophical content of feminism and its political ramifications) who advance competing and possibly irreconcilable definitions and characterisations of feminism in history. Delmar declares the 'impossibility . . . of arriving at a shared definition of feminism'.[18] By contrast,the prolific historian of United States feminism, Nancy Cott, insists that we cannot proceed as if feminism, were elusive and indefinable. Her work, in some respects, currently defines the parameters of the matters in dispute.[19] These debates are of great importance to this book's attempt to situate Rose Scott's feminism.

Historically, feminism was necessarily Janus-faced, seeking to affirm and support women in conditions of sex-based oppression, and yet to eliminate those conditions and the inclusion of both women and men within them.[20] This conflicting political brief for feminism itself establishes the terrain for competing definitions according to the elements chosen for emphasis. That historians would dispute its meaning is hardly surprising. Cott observes:

> Feminism is nothing if not paradoxical. It aims for individual freedoms by mobilizing sex solidarity. It acknowledges diversity among women while positing that women recognize their unity. It requires gender consciousness for its basis, yet calls for the elimination of prescribed gender roles. These paradoxes of feminism are rooted in women's actual situation, being the same (in a species sense) as men; being different with respect to reproductive biology and gender construction from men.[21]

Historian of nineteenth-century English feminism, Barbara Caine, takes the paradoxes Cott identifies as defining characteristics of feminism. The need to reconcile 'underlying similarities between men and women with their equally fundamental differences' preoccupied not only the four Victorian feminists of her most recent study but is also, she argues, 'a problem which is integral to any form of feminism'.[22]

Recognition of this historical feminist concern with both the similarities and specificities of the sexes has meant that some historians characterise the history of feminism as permanently oscillating between equality and difference. Some distinguish 'real' feminism in the past by the extent to which rhetoric and activism were used to pursue women's equality with men, minimising the focus on sexual differences. Faced with earlier feminist preoccupations with women's specificities and special demands upon the polity, such historians as Sandra Holton, Linda Gordon, Ellen Dubois and Veronica Strong Boag deprecate them as ineffective, conservative or irrelevant tendencies.[23] Alternatively, others such as Karen Offen, Gail Brandt and Naomi Black take the focus on women's specificities and differences from men as the definitive core of feminism, and represent the aspirations of those egalitarian activists, focused only upon citizenship, paid work, public life and non-familial lifestyles for women, as unrepresentative of more typical feminist strands.[24]

Until relatively recently, these discrepant characterisations of the history of feminism co-existed with little dialogue. Under the influence of debates within feminist theory, however, particularly through the contributions of feminist philosophers and literary theorists, re-appraisal of the categories involved in prevailing characterisations of feminism began in earnest. The general tendency of Western thought to proceed through dualisms or radically opposed binarisms, in which one term was subordinate to the other (especially public/private, reason/emotion, mind/body, man/woman), engendered a reassessment of the equality/difference dualism evident in histories of feminism.[25]

In the light of feminist critiques of dichotomous thought, some historians attempt to dismantle the concentration on the first term of the dualism — equality — which they argue dominates representations of the history of feminism. They offer sympathetic expositions of feminism arranged around 'difference', ending its obscurity for the modern reader. Jill Kerr Conway labels such feminists as 'enhanced authority feminists', charging historians with neglecting their impact.[26] Many Canadian feminists describe this tendency within feminism as 'maternal feminism'.[27] Others subscribe to the term 'social feminism'.[28] Noting the limits of equality-oriented feminist campaigns like equal suffrage, which, as Dubois observed in 1978 'did not address the domestic side of the nineteenth century sexual order directly',[29] historians in many countries began exploring the ways in which earlier feminists acted politically upon their analyses of sexual difference. This re-oriented the focus from equal rights campaigns to their diverse cultural politics contexts.

Through this re-orientation, a vigorous body of work emerged, which set in historical context feminist concerns with prostitution, seduction of young girls, voluntary motherhood and conjugal sexuality, domestic violence, family life, women's health, dress reform, temperance, relationships among women, religion, and women's writing, art, music, education and sport.[30] Historians of these feminist issues noticeably by-passed definitions of feminism centered upon either equality or the equality/difference dualism. Susan Kent, for instance, ventures that feminists were those who sought 'recognition for their full and complete humanity and thereby [to] eliminate the reductively sexualized definition of femininity that threatened their integrity and dignity'.[31] Furthermore, from her study of Victorian feminists, Caine designates the objectives of feminism as women's autonomy and self-determination, along with a core belief 'that all women make up a single category, that they were oppressed on the basis of their sex. They fought to remove this oppression'.[32]

In view of the important insight that the two terms in any dichotomy are mutually interdependent for meaning — for instance, rationality/irrationality — historian Joan Wallach Scott urged historians of feminism to rethink the relationship between equality and difference. Since the problem for women of any given civil inequality arises only from the cultural meaning of subordination attributed to aspects of their differences from men, historians would do better to insist 'on difference as the very meaning of equality itself'.[33] This would seek to implode the polarity into something more like an interplaying continuum of feminist meanings for 'equality' and 'difference'.

It is perhaps ironic that Joan Wallach Scott's article, constructively suggesting a way out of an unproductive impasse, was first published just when a number of other publications in the history of feminism appeared to re-polarise characterisations of the history of feminism. There had always been a tension attached to uses of 'difference' by historians of feminism. The same word signified differences between the sexes, and differences between women. Cott contended that a theoretical and practical problem in the history of feminism has been 'the fact that women's gender identity is not separable from other factors that make up our selves: race, region, culture, class, age'.[34] From the beginning of the 1970s explorations of the history of feminism, historians showed an acute concern with differences between women. Dubois, for instance, characterised the United States women's suffrage movement as 'composed primarily of white, middle class women'.[35] Class was the dilemma at the heart of that movement. Its efforts to mobilise working-class women failed, she contends, 'due to the limited vision of middle class suffragist leaders'. Historically, Marxists defined feminism as a bourgeois deviation that could imperil working-class unity. In the women's movement of the 1970s, from which historians of feminism emerged, Cott recalls that those 'wedded (sometimes literally) to New Left or democratic socialist politics and class analysis' battled those 'who moved toward woman-centered theories'.[36] Identical dynamics in Australia resulted in historians' condemnation of earlier feminists as conservative agents of 'bourgeois hegemony' and puritanical advocates of biologistic sex antagonism.[37] In the late 1980s publications by Cott, Dubois and others might be read as reactivating and reasserting the egalitarian tradition in feminism, in response to the explorations of 'difference' feminism that they perceived as dominating histories of feminism.

Reservations about the posing of a unity of women based upon differences from men, combined with renewed sensitivity to the historical prominence of differences between women, culminated in marked historiographical innovation. In 1987, Cott published *The Grounding of Modern Feminism*, a text that took stock of both the state of the history of feminism and advanced a bold new argument regarding the characterising and periodising of feminism. For Cott 'feminism' was born in the 1910s, when usage of the term first became current in the United States. Its demands, advanced by 'mainly young and educated women', included: 'female individuality, political participation, economic independence and sexual freedom as a new challenge to the social order'. Feminists opposed sex hierarchy, believing women's situation was cultural, not natural, and therefore amenable to change, and perceived women as a social grouping.[38] Women failing to subscribe to these views did not qualify for the label 'feminist'.

Cott elaborates two corollaries: the first is to call 'the nineteenth century woman movement' all advocacy on behalf of women, undertaken prior to the birth of feminism in the 1910s. Activists of this earlier period spoke of women as a unified category, insensitive to differences among women. The feminist movement was born modern, and engaged with all the dilemmas of difference between women that still prevail today.[39] This re-periodisation creates a unity between feminism from 1910 until the present, but unhesitatingly excises women's activism before that date as pre-feminist or non-feminist. To continue to include the women involved in the mid-nineteenth-century ferment over the 'woman question' as feminists, she holds, is to commit the error of anachronism.[40]

The second strand of Cott's redefinition of feminism is her argument that the historical vocabulary available to describe women's involvement in politics is needlessly impoverished. Any venture of women into reform activity in any period is apt to be called 'feminism', a 'mistaken inclusiveness' removing all meaning and substance from the term. By expanding the vocabulary of women's political choices, it should be possible to distinguish 'feminism' — which challenges 'male domination' — from, for instance, 'female consciousness', a term defined by historian Temma Kaplan as, 'a mindset . . . socially constructed from women's common tasks'. This latter approach typically concerned women's demands on behalf of children, mothers and the home. For Cott these do not, or at least do not self-evidently, constitute feminist demands.[41]

Yet a year after the publication of Cott's book, historian of France, Karen Offen, advanced a new bipolar characterisation of 'individualist' and 'relational' feminism. Elements Cott identified as 'feminist' Offen designated as 'individualist feminism'. Meanwhile, those forms of women's politics which Cott excluded from the category of feminism, particularly home-centered assertions of women's interests, Offen termed 'relational feminism'. The Anglo-American feminist tradition (and its historians) has been dominated by 'individualist feminism', unfairly eclipsing, Offen contended, the more important relational strand:

> Relational feminism emphasised women's rights as women (defined principally by their childbearing and/or nurturing capacities) in relation to men. It insisted on women's distinctive contributions in these roles to the broader society and made claims on the commonwealth on the basis of these contributions.[42]

In Offen's view, relational feminism, with its 'couple-centered vision', appealed to more women than individualist feminism, which, in its public-sphere orientation and minimisation of sex differences, served the needs of single women in a male-defined world. Although classic feminist theorists, such as Mary Wollstonecraft and Elizabeth Cady Stanton, are usually characterised in terms that, by Offen's scheme, would make them 'individualist feminists', Offen demurs. From a reading of their texts, she finds their key articulations 'relational feminist in character'.[43]

Both Cott and Dubois took issue with Offen's argument, each publishing comments in 1989, to which Offen published rejoinders — all without reference to Cott's recently published book advocating major re-classification and re-periodisation within the history of feminism. In her comments on Offen's argument Cott implicitly refuses the label 'feminist' for those Offen calls 'relational feminists', since they were more striking for their 'acceptance of sexual dualism, belief in the complementarity of the sexes and reliance on the nuclear family as the basic unit of social organisation . . . the standard conservative status quo view of women's social position, rather than anything remotely feminist'.[44] Meanwhile Dubois, while conceding that Stanton did indeed make claims for women's differences from men, especially through motherhood and the perspective it accorded them, insists that 'it fundamentally misrepresents the totality of Stanton's thought . . . to characterize the essence . . . as a rumination on difference'.[45]

In any attempt to adjudicate these disputed readings, Joan Wallach Scott's helpful exposition of the interdependence of equality and difference within feminist thought seems eminently pertinent. Despite Offen's decrying of the unhelpfulness of the equality/difference dualism, her individualist/relational dualism inadvertently functions as a proxy for it. It is puzzling that the commentators did not examine Offen's new dualism more directly. Instead, in the characterisation and periodisation of feminism, we are still in an undeclared war of boundaries.

Were the implications of Cott's 1987 argument accepted, the exchange between Offen and Dubois over which feminism best encompasses Stanton would become very much beside the point. Stanton was dead before feminism was born. Stanton was not a feminist. Nor was Mary Wollstonecraft. Since 'feminism' obtained currency in other Anglophone countries at the same time as in the United States, its historians, especially those working on movements before 1910, owe Cott serious consideration and response. Some acknowledge her point about the anachronism entailed in retention of the term 'feminism', only to use it as before, without further defence. Those who published works using the term prior to Cott's book have been resoundingly silent in the face of her dramatic re-periodisation of feminism.

Barbara Caine is one of the few historians of feminism so far to engage with the strategy entailed in Cott's argument. Evaluating the issues at stake, she defends her use of the term 'feminism' in a study of Victorian England. She has no quarrel with Cott's insistence that historians recognise the significance of the early-twentieth-century introduction of the term 'feminism':

> But this recognition does not necessarily require one to jettison the term when dealing with the nineteenth century. Most political terms — including for example liberalism and socialism — are used retrospectively to apply to individuals, groups or ideas which have some . . . similarity with those for whom the term was originally used. But the history of both politics and political theory

would be impossible if we did not use these terms . . . [T]o jettison them would leave one without any signposts in a sea of chaos. [T]here have been significant shifts in the range of ideas of feminists . . . often indicated by changes in the language feminists use. [T]here were significant shifts in the outlook of British as of American feminists in the early years of the twentieth century, but these were changes within feminism rather than involving a change from something that was pre-feminist or non-feminist to feminism.[46]

The fact that the women in her study never applied the term 'feminism' to themselves does not deter Caine from describing them so, for no other term captures 'the intensity of their concern about the situation of women'. In fact, Cott's definition of feminism, including the opposition to sex hierarchy, the belief that women's condition was a matter of cultural constitution, and the perception of women as forming a sex-based social group, seems to Caine 'to apply to all these women and to state very well their central beliefs'.[47]

Periodisation is an important issue in Caine's defence of historians' use of 'feminism' in relation to the nineteenth-century theorists and activists. What Cott is effectively calling an early-twentieth-century ending of non-feminism, and the beginning of feminism, Caine re-reads as a change *within* feminism. Of her four mid-Victorian feminists, Millicent Garrett Fawcett, is for Caine a transitional figure between the mid-nineteenth and early-twentieth-century women's movements, exemplifying 'how and when Victorian feminism was supplanted by its twentieth century counterpart'.[48]

A similar theme of change within feminism is used by Susan Kent. She identifies three feminist generations — those born before 1850, those born between 1850 and 1870, and those born after 1870. Arguing that sexual issues formed the heart of British suffragist concern, an older generation, of which Fawcett was a member, focused on prostitution, venereal disease, marriage, and the legal and moral double sexual standard. These women 'shrank from much that for a later generation was part of the essential tissue of feminism'. Subsequent generations did not so much jettison the earlier generations' concerns as add to them the questions of succeeding ones, including menstruation, childbearing, sexual assault, incest, homosexuality, sexual pleasure for women, and birth control.[49]

On the question of how historians have characterised feminism in history, then, there have been several options. One has been to cast feminism as eternally polarised between opposed tendencies: equality versus difference, individualist versus relational, equal rights versus social. A second option is Cott's proposal to delimit radically the definition of feminism to those who first self-consciously embraced the term in the 1910s, and after, reclassifying all previous women's activism by other terms. This option rests upon a particular argument about periodisation and its significance in this case.[50] A third option is to retain the term 'feminist ' over a longer chronology than Cott favors, but to reject the dualistic and ahistorical tendencies of previous characterisations (now including Cott's own 'feminism' versus 'nineteenth-century woman movement'), and attend carefully to dividing change within feminism into periods and into the spectrum of discourses that might be present in feminism at any historical moment. Commenting on the necessary generality of any workable definition of feminism, Caine notes that 'designating someone a feminist does not of itself indicate exactly what they thought even about . . . women's oppression'.[51]

This book embraces this third option in its study of Rose Scott's feminism, though not without a serious attempt to apply Cott's argument and to explore the analytical advantages of categorising Scott and her Australian and overseas contemporaries as 'the nineteenth-century woman movement'. However, greater definitional clarity did not result, distinctions were difficult to draw, and the time-frame implied in this century-long designation did not allow the ready identification and characterisation of change. Born in 1847, the same year as Millicent Garrett Fawcett, Rose Scott could be seen as a transitional figure between generations of women in politics. It seemed unconvincing to cast her 1890s concerns, typical of late-nineteenth-century women's movement figures, as non-feminist or pre-feminist, but to portray the updated version of those concerns in the 1910s as 'feminist', simply because the word now had Anglophonic currency. This credibility problem was heightened by the unmistakable challenges to male dominance, and a belief in its capacity to be resisted and removed, evident in Scott's prolific personal writings, correspondence, public speeches and published articles and addresses three decades prior to the birth of 'feminism' in the 1910s. By the criteria of Cott, Gordon and many others, Scott was a feminist.

Although I cannot endorse Cott's final recommendation in this study of Rose Scott, her emphases, especially her insistence on clarity and precision in analytical terms employed by historians of feminism, have enormous importance. She is correct to urge that 'feminism should designate something more specific than women's entrance into public life or efforts at social reform. The very point of historians using the word *feminism* or *feminist* should be to distinguish among women's choices in reform'.[52]

'PRESENTISM' IN HISTORIES OF FEMINISM

The writing of the history of feminism has revealed problems of imprecision on the one hand, and dogmatism on the other, problems Cott critically addresses. Dubois comments, too, on historians' tendency to divide the past into 'good' feminism and 'bad' feminism, based on subjective judgements — a tendency that may be described as 'presentism'.[53] This is a problem that contributes to the intractability of dualism and dogmatic forms of labelling feminism in history, which too often obscure more than they illuminate. Existing studies referring to Rose Scott, and to Australian feminists and feminism, display this problem, as do studies of British, Canadian and United States frameworks.

If presentism can be a danger in any history writing, its risk is heightened when the topic is currently and openly part of the historian's life — that is to say, when it is not a topic remote and esoteric. When a historian of feminism holds feminist convictions, the risk of partiality is similar to that operating when historians of liberalism, for example, are themselves committed liberals. The historian of French feminism, Genevieve Fraisse, puts the problem well:

> it is clear that this historical subject, feminism, brings into play not just individual but sexual subjectivity. The historian is not forced to take sides in quite the same way by the working class, the peasants, the proletarians or the middle class, which are of course not neutral subjects, but which do not compel a radical and definitive recognition of difference, not to say opposition between the sexes. This kind of history thus becomes a dangerous game, for it is in itself a kind of commitment . . . The history of feminism certainly rules out indifference in analysis.

The remedy is not some specious search for objectivity, or an insistence that historians avoid topics with which they have sympathy. Presentism should be expected, identified, evaluated and self-consciously countered as far as possible by rigorous and faithful contextualising of the matter at issue. As in other fields, this has not always been done in the writing of histories of feminism.

The Women's Liberation Movement (WLM) of the late 1960s unleashed great interest in the history of women's resistance to male domination. The earliest investigations of foremothers caused serious unease. Since many members of the WLM began their political lives in the New Left and libertarian student movements of the time, earlier feminists could not fail to disappoint. No wonder women's liberation was needed, some concluded. The forebears had failed badly. They had tackled all the wrong questions. Imagine their thinking that suffrage would change the world. They were prudes and puritans, offensively moralistic on everything. Free abortion on demand, twenty-four-hour child care, free contraception, orgasmic equality, free love and open relationships seemed to be nowhere on the agenda of these mainly Protestant, bourgeois, teetotal, race-blind dinosaurs.

Indeed, many 1970s feminists refused the women of earlier women's movements the title 'feminist' at all. Yet many of these women secured important reforms and undoubtedly struggled to end inequalities in citizen rights, education, family law and labour and industry, even though many of their beliefs were anathema to WLM members. A paradoxical desire to affirm a historic link between these pioneers and contemporary feminists, and yet distinguish sharply between earlier and later feminist beliefs, aspirations and campaigns, especially with regard to sexual and reproductive issues, paved the way for the well-entrenched 'wave' metaphor. Earlier activists were dubbed 'first-wave feminists', as distinct from 'the second wave' of the 1970s.[54]

This metaphor implied peaks and troughs — a periodisation of lull between the waves — as well as establishing one of the first adjectival composite modifiers of the simple category 'feminism'. Both this periodisation and the modifiers reflected presentist criteria. Gradually, as more contemporary feminists undertook historical research during the 1970s, the repudiations built into the wave metaphor began to soften. Feminist historians contended that the vast difference between earlier and later feminists signalled the historicity of feminism. Rather than simply condemn past counterparts for failure by present standards, the more illuminating task was surely to probe the world those women inherited and attempt to grasp the options they saw as being available to them. In this way, the character of their feminist preoccupations might be rendered intelligible.[55]

This impulse to put 'first wave feminism' into context led in many directions. Some historians chronicled and analysed women's campaigns. Others wrote biographies of women's rights leaders and studies of movements, texts and theories.[56] Insofar as earlier feminists had worked with an entirely different rhetorical and discursive universe defining domesticity and womanhood in distinct terms, stills others went back to the seventeenth, eighteenth and early-nineteenth-century genealogies of gender relations in cultural texts and social conditions.[57] Cott's *The Bonds of Womanhood* and 'Passionlessness' are examples of this kind of work. The sexual ideas of earlier feminists began to receive a more sympathetic hearing with the gradual decline in naive adherence to belief in the essential progressiveness, for women, of 1960s sexual libertarianism. The increasing and often horrifying findings that emerged from feminist research into abusive aspects of contemporary male sexuality and power underscored this revision. From earlier repudiations, the interpretative cycle began to swing towards something like identification with first-wave feminism. This identification, as much as the earlier disavowal, was motivated by present concerns.[58]

Other contemporary concerns also stimulated enquiry into past feminism. Rifts quickly developed in the women's movement over the analytic weight to be accorded to sex relative to class, race, ethnicity and aboriginality within contemporary feminist theory and politics. As divisions between socialist and radical feminists developed in the 1970s, historians undertook research to discover past versions of similar tensions or divergences. This was driven by the 'contemporary need to categorize diversity within feminism'. The entrenchment of the labels 'radical feminist' and 'socialist feminist' led to much research identifying with past heroines or with present privileged topics and themes.[59]

A further consequence of the phase of identification with earlier feminists and the expansion of historical research into them was the development of doubts about the wave metaphor and the periodisation it implied. Evidence of the vigour of feminist activism in the 1920s and 1930s, and during the years of the Second World War and the immediate post-war period, led to titles like Dale Spender's *There's Always Been a Women's Movement This Century*. This called into question the supposed trough between the 1920s and the 1960s. It also provided an auspicious framework for historians struck by the continuities within feminist concerns and objectives. The sharp break between the feminism of suffragists and their post-suffrage successors seemed, certainly in some key areas, misleading.[60]

The same logic impelled scrutiny into women's resistance movements prior to the late nineteenth century, back at least to Wollstonecraft in the late eighteenth century. Some scholars contend that identifiable feminism existed in the eighteenth, seventeenth, sixteenth and fifteenth centuries, citing Christine de Pisan's now famous 1405 text, *The Book of the City of Ladies*, as one of the earliest feminist texts of the Western tradition. This manoeuvre in turn elicits controversy, with some contending that feminism only becomes possible in tandem with the Enlightenment, bourgeois individualism, suffrage-based citizenship, and industrialisation. The matter remains contentious, and a marked feature of debate on periodising earlier feminism is presentism in criteria employed for and against inclusion of figures like de Pisan in the feminist canon.[61]

If identification with past feminisms through present criteria began to fray both the 'wave' metaphor and prevailing periodisations of the origins of feminist thought and activism, it also produced a distinct focus on the study of women's culture in the past, especially relationships and friendships between women, and their place in the genesis of feminism.[62] This focus mirrored developments within contemporary feminism. The building of women's culture in both the creative and anthropological senses became a key objective within feminist studies.

However, the preoccupations influencing some feminist historians' identification with those called first-wave feminists constituted only one element of presentism in the writing of the history of feminism. Equally presentist were the concerns of those uneasy about what they saw as the privileging of culture over politics in the women's movement of the late 1970s and 1980s.[63] This unease was strongest among those socialist feminist historians who stressed class differences between women, and later race differences, which they believed aborted claims for a unified sisterhood of women, present or past. They also worried about the movement away from the optimism of libertarian sexual politics by many feminists, whose stances on issues like pornography seemed puritanical and, on rape, simplistic and insensitive to issues of class and race. The term 'cultural feminist' was coined to characterise the anti-pornography and frequently separatist politics of feminists who eschewed either intimate or working relationships with men. Sometimes these 'cultural' feminists came under criticism for elitism, essentialism and political pessimism through their demonising of male sexuality.[64]

Versions of the feminist past began to accord with this reading of contemporary wrong turns in feminist theory and politics. Historians offered the stories of feminist social purity campaigners who finally colluded in the criminalising of homosexual men, the regulation and sexual repression of teenage girls, and the stigmatisation of prostitutes as a professional group. Contemporary feminists unmindful of this historical lesson could reperpetrate an ignoble past. In view of the ubiquity and intensity of late-nineteenth and early-twentieth-century feminist critiques of marriage, prostitution, seduction, and rapacious male sexuality, the stage was set by contemporary debates in feminist theory for a new phase of repudiation of earlier feminists.[65]

This contemporary repudiation was not a helpful framework for this book. Scott was of her time on many of the most contentious issues dividing feminists today, if more than prescient on others. The development of her feminism in its context seemed to illustrate important options available to earlier feminists, and the ramifications of the choices that they made, especially in the Australian colonial framework. Although this study can provide such illustration, and analysis of Scott and her contemporaries' many texts is worthwhile for feminist historians of feminism, I acknowledge how contentious such a rationale has become within contemporary feminist theory.

CATEGORICAL INSTABILITIES

Given the long history of presentism in the writing of the history of feminism, the current preoccupation of feminist theorists with deconstruction, post-modernism, post-structuralism and anti-humanism is not surprising. The implications of the interaction between each of these intellectual positions and/or techniques and feminism are profound. The nature of this interaction has been described as 'corporate mergers' rather than one of the marriage or conjugal metaphors used to describe earlier Marxism/feminism or psychoanalysis/feminism relationships. Theorists analysing these mergers often observe the ways these positions/techniques destabilise, denaturalise, disrupt, or refuse the foundationalist categories of feminism. At this stage, observations of feminism having a comparable or reciprocal destabilising and transformative impact on these current theoretical approaches are somewhat fewer.[66]

By the terms of these mergers, no longer may the category 'woman', and therefore 'man', have fixed meanings in advance of their incorporation within particular discourses. So propositions hitherto axiomatic to feminism, such as the claim of women's oppression by, and in the interests of, men, become, to many proponents of mergers such as feminist anti-humanism, unacceptable and essentialist foreclosures of more worth while investigations.[67] It would be more useful to ask:

> how is 'woman' constructed as a category within different discourses? How is sexual difference made a pertinent distinction in social relations and how are relations of subordination constructed through such a distinction? [W]e no longer have a homogeneous entity 'women' facing another homogeneous entity men but a multiplicity of social relations in which sexual difference is always constructed in very diverse ways and where the struggle against subordination has to be visualized in specific and differentiated forms.[68]

This kind of anti-essentialism applied to feminism dates from the late 1970s and early 1980s, manifest in its most heroic forms on the pages of the British journals *m/f* and *Politics and Power*. Many of its proponents had earlier theoretical origins in Althusserian Marxism or other varieties of socialism. These theorists warmly promulgated the writings of Foucault, Donzelot, Kristeva, and critics of psychoanalysis such as Deleuze and Guattari, and critically engaged with the anti-humanist French feminisms of Irigaray and Plaza (who invariably turned out to be insufficiently anti-humanist). Though initially received without enthusiasm by theorists of the old New Left, greater agreement emerged by the late 1980s as the diverse stakes investing currently in destabilising the subject of feminism delineated themselves.[69]

Post-modernist critiques have powerfully undermined the claims of the Enlightenment philosophical heritage, which anchors Western scholarly and political truth claims, and into which earlier feminists like Rose Scott sought women's inclusion.[70] From the nineteenth-century women's suffrage movement to the current campaign for affirmative action, a persistent post-modernist reading portrays feminism as complicit in a defunct (and many would add 'racialist') Enlightenment rationalism. By this same portrayal, feminism would erroneously essentialise 'woman' and would offensively disregard the competing elements that constitute women's diversity of positions — their races, classes, ethnicities, ages and sexual orientations. A remedy is at hand, but only with the recognition that feminism 'cannot be grounded in cross-class antagonism between coherent categories called women and men'. As Haraway contends, 'an adequate feminist theory of gender must simultaneously be a theory of racial and sexual difference'.[71] Joan Wallach Scott also deploys this trope of simultaneity: by opening up the category 'women' (and all universal categories), it becomes possible 'to think about race, gender, sexuality etc. simultaneously rather than separately, competitively, hierarchically or exclusively'.[72]

Historians informed by this assertion of the instability of 'women' tend to redefine previous understandings of the mission of women's history, especially that of historians of feminism. In 1988 Denise Riley suggested, through a focus on deconstruction of feminist categories, that a number of dilemmas resembling inescapable double binds, faced earlier feminism:

> Feminism has . . . been as vexed with the urgency of disengaging from the category 'women' as it has with laying claim to it . . . twentieth century European feminism has been constitutionally torn between fighting against over-feminization and against under-feminization and especially where social policies have been at stake.[73]

Riley identifies the dilemma historically facing feminists, who claimed citizenship on the basis of common humanity (from which they were excluded), but then risked the gain of general humanity in the pursuit of their special needs.[74] 'Women' she depicts as inching towards humanity, 'but never entirely getting there'. Her essay would seem to exemplify the revised mission of women's history (or gender history) as advocated by exponents of the feminism and post-structuralism or post-modernism or anti-humanism 'corporate mergers'. Joan Wallach Scott, for instance, maintains that the task ahead for historians is to avoid describing what happens to groups of people already taken to be different.[75] In her view the moment the (feminist) historian subscribes to the mission of revealing the 'experience' of women as a distinct unified category — the manifest approach of most women's history — the more useful task of critically examining the workings of the ideological system which produces sexual difference is closed off. The historian of women in fact merely reproduces, and worse, naturalises, existing terms — the very terms that need scrutiny.[76] Scott recommends instead that historians of women focus on the production of difference through language.

Although Scott, Riley and historians of like persuasion have received wide citation and endorsement, they have been criticised as well. While class, race, ethnicity and sexual preference are posed as assembling for the historian such a field of difference around sex as to fracture any coherent unity, some feminist historians note how difference based on sex seems never to be accorded the status of destabilising the other differences in historical accounts. Although Dubois represents the intersecting class/race/gender framework as 'a feminist common place now',[77] critics like Judith M. Bennett contend that, in practice, the intersection often falls far short of dynamic interaction, exponents ranking gender beneath the other factors.[78]

In a forceful and eloquent plea for the uses of deconstruction for feminism, Judith Butler insists that feminism supposes that the term 'women' designates an undesignatable field of differences, one that 'cannot be totalized . . . by a descriptive identity category'. 'Women' therefore could be resignified, emancipating it from 'the maternal and racialist ontologies to which it has been restricted'.[79] Yet Kathleen Barry, the biographer of nine-teenth-century feminist Susan B. Anthony, sees this approach as the death knell for women's history. It 'usurps women's location in sex-classed power arrangements'. By an act of exclusion 'racism, classism and even heterosexism are treated as structures of power . . . but sexism is not'.[80] Meanwhile, socialist, feminist historian Elizabeth Fox-Genovese wor-ries that in the eschewing of both 'women' and 'experience' in favour of language and representation, socialist-feminist history risks 'floundering on the reefs of decomposing individualism . . . disembodied meanings with-out reference to specific conditions'.[81] Moreover, in her review of Joan Wallach Scott's *Gender, Politics and History*, historian Linda Gordon doubts that anything about deconstruction and 'linguistic analysis automatic-ally leads to questions about gender'.[82] Finally, historian Gerda Lerner observed that, in practice, as a feminist historian paying scrupulous atten-tion to the analytical intersection of race, class, ethnicity and gender, 'one seems to add endless variation to any problem without gaining greater analytical clarity: one drowns in illustrative detail'.[83]

Perhaps these disagreements are the early stages of discussion over new formulations of unquestionably important issues for historians of fem-inism. Resistance to what feminist theorist Linda Singer calls the 'attempts to frame or pursue feminist issues under the regulatory or strategic practices initiated by some other theoretical paradigm' has marked fem-inist debates for 'the last thirty years'.[84] This often-noted feature of rela-tions between feminism and other positions is sometimes portrayed as a deliberate attempt to 'delegitimize feminist commitment to acting from a collective identity of women', of which the current proposed 'corporate mergers' are just one more instance.[85] Despite reservations of estab-lished historians, feminist theorist Louise Newman urges transcendence of the current impasse of academic name-calling. She characterises his-torians of women as clearly organised around the problematic category of 'experience' and therefore able to be distinguished from historians of gender, who attend to representations and constructions of difference, informed by post-structuralist theory:

> the perspective afforded by post-structural theories no longer
> enables us to think of women's history as an accurate recon-
> struction of objective experience — 'experience' is produced and
> mediated through cultural forms that are not only gendered but are
> also represented through other ways of organising meaning
> through constructions of race, class, nationality, ethnicity, etc.[86]

If the outcome of this continuing ferment over the mission of feminist-inflected history remains unclear, the destabilising of foundational categories that feminist historians have worked with seems unquestionable. However, it would be a pity if, as a consequence, the historical study of women and men as sexes, in all their diversity and their philosophical and political engagements around sexual differences and meanings, was to be diminished. Such an outcome might vindicate or give credence to some of the more knee-jerk feminist responses to the deconstruction of 'women'. Many feminist exponents of the history of 'women', of feminism, even of 'gender', require proponents of the 'corporate' mergings of feminism and post-structuralism/post-modernism/deconstructionism/anti-humanism to address a series of reservations. Until this is done properly, these historians are unlikely to perceive such mergers as enhancing the analytic grasp of feminist discourse. Rather, they may concur with feminist scholar Kathleen Barry, sociologist Liz Stanley, historians Catherine Hall and Joan Hoff, feminist theorist Somer Brodribb and others in seeing 'old wine in new bottles', or worse, a misogynist impulse pursuing a disavowal of feminism as underlying this 'corporate merger' moment.[87]

In the context of unresolved reservations, definitions of 'feminism', such as Newman's — 'a consciousness of and attempt to escape the oppressions of living in a female body' — can elicit distinct unease.[88] Its implications as a post-structuralist feminist contribution stand in marked contrast to Gordon's fighting characterisation of feminism as the challenge to male supremacy with the will to change it and the belief it can be changed. By one reading at least, Newman's definition centres on femaleness as the problem, implying the preferred strategy as escape or transcendence of the feminine, rather than fighting to end oppressions inflicted upon female bodies. The corporeal focus of her terminology is in one sense welcome as an important corrective to disembodied tendencies in the more egalitarian strands of feminist theory.[89] Yet in the endeavour to avoid the polarised categories of 'women' and 'men', Newman leaves the matter of who or what might oppress these female bodies from which 'escape' is sought unspecified or, some might say, 'off the hook'. Clearly, the political purchase of such a definition is problematic.

In the historical study of feminism, and of feminists like Rose Scott, the instability of feminist categories could be considered as never being greater than it is now. Yet some historians react with irritation or bemusement to the suggestion, most explicit in Newman's account, that until the current wave of deconstructionist feminist historians, historians of women had ignored differences between women based on class and race, and failed to address theoretical and epistemological issues in their work. Feminist theorist Lise Vogel takes particular exception to this view, and to the periodisation from the darkness of the late 1960s to the enlightenment of the 1990s advanced by Newman. She recalls feminist historians as always engaged in vigorous debate over philosophical and epistemological issues. As for differences between women, it is difficult to identify a moment when feminists did not express anxiety about this issue, one way or another, as the merest glance at feminist journals and newspapers of the past twenty years reveals. Vogel warns us against amnesia and selling short the continuing, even permanent, state of engagement between feminist scholars and theoretical developments, as true a century ago as now.[90] The current deconstructionist/post-modernist turns in intra-feminist debate logically succeed longer contests over difference and competing categorical claims articulated throughout the 1970s and 1980s — contests which stimulated creative research and the marked theoretical sophistication now the norm in contemporary feminist scholarship. In this connection, Judith Newton decries the current feminist tendency mistakenly to attribute feminist breakthroughs to deconstruction and related non-feminist positions.[91]

If categorical instability is the diagnosis, the prognosis for feminist history still remains unclear. The exhortation to simultaneity in the historical analysis of sex, class and race has produced few role models that avoid subordinating the analytic centrality of sex. This is not to say that in principle it cannot be done; only that in general, it has not been done; thus producing the reservations of feminist historians such as Bennett and Lerner about its political and analytic purchase. Moreover, historians' desire for unity, comprehensiveness or totality seems to underpin their recommendation that historians must 'deal with' or 'treat' simultaneously gender, class, race and sexual orientation.[92]

A further reservation not yet dispelled arises from the deconstructionist/post-structuralist/post-modernist/anti-humanist contention that 'women' and 'men' have no fixed meanings apart from their use within particular discourses. Precisely how blank is the historical slate here? Is it as absolute as implied? Few feminist historians would deny the impressive variations in the meanings accorded to the fact of being a woman or man, not only between cultures, but also across different periods within any given culture, and even at any one moment across diverse sites or positions within any one cultural formation. Indeed, it is feminist historians whose work has built our knowledge of these diversities. A priori presumptions of the exact, detailed meanings of 'women' and 'men' will of course block their effective historical exploration.

Alongside the diversities of detail, however, feminist research establishes unquestionably a number of strikingly consistent patterns in the historical situation of women and men, and not only in cultures of European derivation. Examples abound in the modern histories of the (mainly) Anglophone cultures of Australia, New Zealand, Canada and the United States. In each 'new world', founded through the dispossession, attempted genocide and continuing subjugation of indigenous peoples, a number of historical patterns predict meanings for the categories 'women' and 'men'.

All four settlements had initially high numbers of males in their colonising periods and distinct 'frontier' regions with high rates of lifelong bachelorhood or late marriage for white men and, for white women, high rates of marriage, especially at young ages. Young frontier wives — especially the many with much older husbands — bore more babies at closer intervals, experienced more infant deaths, more maternal morbidity and mortality, and a shorter life expectancy than their urban counterparts in these settler colonies. They also had less education and less opportunity to enter paid work. They inhabited a world in which prostitution was a major, unexceptional result of men's sexuality, and itinerant work a common cause of breadwinner absence. Both indigenous and white women and girls worked as prostitutes. Often isolation from family, friends and medical services made ordinary childbirth, the termination of unwanted pregnancies, the management of venereal diseases, or family illnesses, extremely difficult episodes in the everyday lives of frontier wives.[93]

How open and unfixed were the meanings of the terms 'women' and 'men' in the frontier regions of these four countries across their colonising periods? Surely the distinct population patterns and features common to Anglophone frontiers in the eighteenth and nineteenth centuries justify some advance hypotheses on the part of feminist historians concerned with the dynamics of sex in history? Is it likely that meanings of sexual difference were so various that she or he will find, for instance, women changing places with men in marriage ceremonies, in which the former promise to honour and financially support, and the latter swear to obey, in rural Iowa in the 1850s or rural New South Wales in the 1870s? Will men be found primarily assigned to housework and childcare on the late-nineteenth-century Canadian prairies or New Zealand highlands? Will a double standard of sexual morality be discovered in the Dakota wild west or Queensland outback, which divided men into the virtuous and the fallen, stigmatising the latter, while condoning women's ventures into pre- and extra-marital sexual encounters? Will she or he find legislatures in which men were decreed *homme covert* upon marriage, unable to own their own property and without legal custody of their children, and where men were not permitted to vote or stand for political office, or be admitted to degree programmes in universities or enter the learned professions?

If these are unlikely possibilities, it is because plausible generalisations circulate about the significance Anglophone colonising cultures historically gave the fact of people being 'women' or 'men' — being sexed. These generalisations are based on cross-national research and permit predictions of the kind that stimulate viable new research. Such advance generalisations have not obstructed revisions or disruptions of prevailing wisdoms within the writing of feminist history. The disputed characteristics of feminism in the past are but one example of this. Working from the generalisation of the sexual division of labour prevailing on the western frontier, for instance, Glenda Riley and others demonstrate its frequent flouting by women entrepreneurs.[94] However, the interesting ways in which frontier conditions could destabilise its operation can just as readily highlight the normative significance of sexual divisions of labour, in giving meaning to the categories 'women' and 'men'. That all four countries had different points of discontinuity, tension and reconstruction of historical sexual divisions of labour, often through women's resistances, does not alter the centrality of such divisions in all of them for the marking of femininity and masculinity.

Therefore it is difficult to see that a feminist historian would be likely to proceed without some advance hypothetical notion of how people of the place and period under investigation gave meaning to the categories 'women' and 'men'. It is equally difficult to see how she or he could not do so, even if persuaded that it would be theoretically sound or desirable not to for other reasons. More simply, it is difficult to see what, in practice, the feminist historian is being asked to do, and how she can be expected to do it. The urging against advance meanings is delivered with considerable force by critics of the conventional mission of women's history. It is to be hoped that the outcome of lack of clarity concerning both the positioning of a feminist standpoint and the process of execution available will not consign would-be historians of 'women' and 'men' to silence.

One final and related reservation is about historians' tendency to polarise the investigation of 'experience' and that of 'representation' in much of the literature under discussion. The latter preference is, it seems, that of the 'historians of gender', the side of the angels. The former is posed as undertaken by the former, the epistemologically naive historians of women who naturalise the very differences that need de-naturalising, taking women's difference as given. They are asking the wrong questions.[95]

The history of women's history does not justify so polarised a reading. Simplified accounts of 'women's experience' have been little respected, while questions of representation, of how women and men have both constructed and articulated meaning for sexual difference, have been paramount in the most distinguished works of women's history since the 1970s.[96] Few historians engaged in the ferment over the purposes and limits of historical enquiry of the past few decades could imagine that their task was the unproblematic and unmediated revealing of the 'experience' of their particular subject. Since feminist historians have made some of the most insightful of the contributions to this ferment, this binary approach seems especially unhelpful for clarifying the issues at stake in any prognosis for women's history/gender history generally, and histories of feminism particularly.[97] Joan Wallach Scott is correct to observe that 'experience is at once always already an interpretation and in need of interpretation'.[98] This study of Rose Scott is guided by precisely this axiom, much of it devoted to how Scott constructed and articulated the problem of sexual difference, how she unified the category 'woman', and the ways in which the meanings she gave sexual difference altered and required new categories.

This examination of debates in the history of feminism discloses a pre-occupation with present dilemmas over differences between women, mainly centred on class and race, in the work of feminist historians of feminism. In their explorations of earlier feminists' thought and work, historians of feminism display current preoccupations in the analytic typologies applied to past feminist activists and movements. These include the varying emphases on equality versus difference; inclusive and exclusive definitions of what constitutes feminism and when it can be said to have begun; and cycles of repudiation of and identification with earlier feminists according to their match with changing contemporary priorities with regard to class, race and sexuality. The attempt to destabilise major categories of feminist positionings in mergers with post-structuralism/postmodernism/deconstruction/anti-humanism through advancing different terms and arguably greater rigour is continuous with a longer history of the scholarly reservation about the unitary category 'women' — and therefore 'men' — as basic to feminist analysis. Rosalind Delmar wrote in 1986 that:

> It is for example one of women's liberation's paradoxes that although it started on the terrain of sexual antagonism between men and women, it moved quickly to a state in which relations between women caused the most internal stress. Women, in a sense, are feminism's greatest problem.[99]

For Rose Scott, differences between women and men formed her feminist vision, even if she was forced to revise its terms during the course of her career.

LOCATING ROSE SCOTT'S FEMINISM

Rose Scott was born fifteen years after the first British electoral reform Bill, which enacted the initial exclusion from emerging citizen rights on the basis of sex. When Scott was 10 years old the Australian colonies obtained self-government and instituted universal manhood suffrage, which, she would later remind an audience, did not exclude Aboriginal men, but excluded Aboriginal and white women alike. When Scott was 19 a number of English women, represented by John Stuart Mill, petitioned the House of Commons to reverse the sex-exclusionary provision of the 1832 Act, so that henceforth the vote would be granted to women who met the same criteria of eligibility as men. This unsuccessful attempt led to the formation of the first British movement for woman suffrage.

If United States suffragists had worked before, during and after the Civil War with all those seeking the abolition of disenfranchisement on the basis of race and sex, that too changed dramatically in the later 1860s. The Reconstruction-era Republican party would countenance formal enfranchisement of freed black *men*, but not women of either race. The abolitionists took what they could, declaring it 'the hour of the Negro' — or at least, the males of that category. Abandoned by former allies, the movement for *equal* suffrage died, replaced by organisations for *woman* suffrage, in response to a constitutional specification of the eligible voter as a male.[100]

Thus the sexualisation of political rhetoric and notions of citizenship solidified internationally during Scott's early life. The 'woman movement' described by Cott, comprising campaigns attacking many areas of subordination of women on the basis of sex, was typically, rightly or wrongly, represented as epitomised by the demand for woman suffrage. The genesis of the demand for a sex-based suffrage was political contest over the competing claims of categories of difference. In each national context, difference was debated hierarchically, at the expense of the claims of sex. The white, British, enfranchised, male elite more readily embraced as citizen voters men of lower classes and 'other' races who met the gradually receding property qualifications for suffrage, than women of their own class and race, and women of all other classes and races. In the United States, the governing parties already admitted all white men to voting rights and, at the moment of so admitting African-American men (at least in theory), specified the exclusion of all women of all races. From Scott's Australian perspective, both national cases proved instructive: the franchise henceforth demarcated absolutely between the sexes, and no longer between races and classes (at least in the United States and Australia). Citizenship signified manhood.[101]

In Australia and New Zealand, this sexualisation of politics and citizenship had a particular clarity and elicited many forms of resistance by the newly excluded political category 'women'. The colonial context was smaller in scale than that of Britain or the United States. Feminists here did not face the political complexities of the inheritance of black slavery faced by their United States counterparts. This inheritance has always rendered United States feminist advocacy on behalf of women as a group a fraught undertaking. If one ventures that, surely, the dispossession of Australian Aboriginal peoples and of New Zealand Maori peoples posed a comparable complexity for white feminists in Scott's time, it is unquestionably the case that a land-based indigenous claim is politically and rhetorically utterly different from the former-slave civil rights claim of African-Americans. The closer parallel would be the claims of Native American and Native Canadian peoples, and these are rarely specifically included in the fundamental differences taken to fissure the unity of the category 'women' of the United States feminist deconstructionist. Nor was recognition of indigenous claims much in evidence in past feminist analyses in the United States, Canada, New Zealand or Australia.[102] So Scott came to Australian adulthood in 'the cause of woman' unfractured by questions of differences based on race. In this she was of her context.

Moreover, the particular forms of British class hierarchy expressed in property qualifications for suffrage did not prevail in Australia and so did not split the development of Australian feminism, especially with regard to suffrage demands, as they did in Britain.[103] While some property-based plural voting remained a target of late-nineteenth-century reformers, property did not substantially divide the Australian 'manhood' unified by suffrage. Meanwhile, women's involvement in philanthropy and temperance in such a pared down colonial context imparted a sense of working for, and often intimately with, 'less fortunate' sisters around feminist demands. Myopic as this angle undoubtedly was, it obstructed feminists like Scott's capacity to understand how elite the suffrage movement was and how it alienated working-class women.[104]

Thus the starkly sexed character of citizenship in Australia in Scott's early life was unmistakable. The gradual shift in politics from personal factions organised around fiscal philosophy to class-based parties, and from Australia as a continent of several British colonies to Australia as a self-governing federation, coincided with Scott's adult life. She was witness to economic booms, the 1850s gold rushes, the financial turbulence and depressions of the 1870s, 1880s and 1890s, the Crimean War, the American Civil War, the Boer War, and the First World War. She also lived through Australia's economic diversification from an intercolonial and imperial supplier of primary produce — especially wool and minerals — to the beginnings of its early-twentieth-century industrial and service sector expansion. From a rural childhood, Scott lived an urban adulthood, like all the others whose choice of city existence made Australia one of the most urbanised of the world's nations, notwithstanding the much-vaunted bush mythologising of its (chiefly male) cultural articulators. She applauded the attempt to erode the pervasive Anglophilia of elite Australian culture, never taking the obligatory trips to England typical of her class. Instead, she generously supported the efforts of Australian writers and artists to explore local themes, issues and sensibilities. Adoring the Australian landscape, she wrote often in old age of her longing for the lonely blue gum trees of her childhood, of a time and a world that was gone forever. Nevertheless, she was always acutely conscious of her status as an observer, excluded from participation on the basis of her sex, her womanhood.

An examination of Scott's feminism affords the opportunity to explore a key figure in one nation's feminist development, one whose work spanned the period before and after women's enfranchisement. British- and United States-dominated accounts represent feminism as strong and united around suffrage campaigns, then disintegrating in the 1920s with suffrage's enactment. The granting of state and federal woman suffrage by 1902 means that the period from then until Scott's death in 1925 permits close analysis of post-suffrage feminism two decades earlier than that studied in the British and United States contexts of the 1920s and 1930s. Furthermore, it permits some revision of periodisation conventions. Instead of asking 'why/how did Australian and New Zealand women obtain the vote so *early*?', one might as usefully explore how the study of feminism in the suffrage and post-suffrage decades in Australia and New Zealand could help to explain why/how women in the United States, Canada and Britain were enfranchised so *late* in history.

Scott's feminist career straddled the era of startling transition in the history of feminism discernible by the 1910s. As such her feminism provides an illuminating case study of the kinds of transformation reported by all major historians of feminism. However, Cott's argument for seeing this transformation as 'the *birth* of feminism' both overstates the discontinuities between earlier and later feminists, and impoverishes the history of feminism by confining its adherents to those who, from 1910, adequately foreshadow current feminist concerns with differences between women.[105] Nonetheless, the argument signals the vital and trans-national importance of cultural developments affecting early-twentieth-century feminism, especially its constructions of sexual difference, its representations of the key categories 'women', 'men' and the 'sexual'.

The reason for Scott's contemporary fame was her record of social reform work on behalf of women and children. First colonial, then state and federal, governments consulted her and were lobbied by her on laws and policies affecting women. In a period before women's access to public office and before the emergence of government ministers with responsibility for 'women's affairs' or 'the status of women', accompanied by the appointment of associated bureaucrats to formulate policy ('femocrats' as they are called in the Australian vernacular), Rose Scott performed some of these embryonic functions. She performed these functions through influence and personal contact, and through the work of voluntary women's organisations. Never facing an electorate, nor an appointment panel, she worked informally and without salary. Her power was perceived as sufficiently formidable to merit anonymous 'hate' letters.

Certainly 'a bit of a favourite', not only with newspaper editors, but with writers, artists, actors, singers, architects, academics, senior public servants, judges, lawyers and politicians, the other source of Rose Scott's contemporary fame was her role as the hostess of 'the only real Salon Sydney has ever known', at her home in Sydney's eastern suburbs on Friday nights. Her beauty was legendary, her bonnets were 'the delight of Sydney', and her lifelong spinsterhood, despite many worthy proposals, the subject of amazement and regret among the petitioners. Though never having the benefits of a formal education, Scott was remembered as charming, cultivated, earnest, quietly-spoken and merry. A patron of the arts, a philanthropist and social reformer, Scott has found a ready historical place as a late-nineteenth-century bourgeois worthy. She occupies a place alongside the early-nineteenth-century philanthropist Caroline Chisholm (satirised in Charles Dickens' *Bleak House*), who arguably performed some of the same functions for an earlier generation of women (and who, incidentally, Scott greatly admired).[106]

Nonetheless, Scott's portrait does not grace any note of Australian currency, as did Chisholm's, nor does it still grace the walls of the Art Gallery of New South Wales. Perhaps there is no great loss here. For by the time Scott's portrait was painted by Sir John Longstaff in 1922, as a silver-haired, bespectacled elder in black and lace, the public and worthy persona — partly the creation of the press, her friends and herself — so dominated all representations of her that a more risky, complex, disturbing portrait and certainly a more interesting one, was probably no longer possible. One simple fact about Scott, and its ramifications, remains undeveloped within portraits and accounts of her. The result is a puzzling bloodlessness, a life whose rationale and motivation can appear unconvincing, even allowing for the jaded lens of the late-twentieth-century viewer. Rose Scott was a feminist.

To date no full-length study of Scott's life and work has been published, so this book functions beyond any authorial intent as the redresser of a gap, presuming her significance, thus indicting previous neglect. For more than two decades exponents of women's history have charged the main-stream history discipline with a gender-blindness, a neglect of women that, of necessity, continues to justify the specialist area 'women's history'. At times scholars in Australian women's history have feared that both the discipline and the nation it serves exhibit an especially intractable misogyny. It is not my purpose to fully canvass the competing claims on each side of this case. The neglect of significant public figures like Rose Scott, however, might be taken to support the often desolate picture of Australian gender relations frequently drawn by white Australian cultural critics, to the fascination of international observers.[107]

It is true that most Australians grow up without hearing of Rose Scott, or of other women of her era and after who, like her, worked in the public domain to better the position of their sex — women like Louisa Lawson, Mary Windeyer, Maybanke Anderson, Vida Goldstein, Edith Cowan, Bessie Rischbieth, Emma Miller and many others. In this, Australians may resemble most citizens of the United States and Canada who grow up unaware of the work of women such as Sojourner Truth, Elizabeth Cady Stanton, Ida B. Wells, Charlotte Perkins Gilman, Nellie McClung, Flora McDonald Denison and Josephine Marchand Dandurand. In fact, with the possible exceptions of English suffragettes, Emmeline and Christabel Pankhurst, feminists of earlier generations may be as marginal to the educational and cultural legacies of British and European citizens as they appear to be in the newer worlds of the United States of America, Canada, New Zealand and Australia. The prevailing obscurity of Rose Scott is comparable with that of her local and international counterparts. It is not an especial neglect.

Yet one of the fundamental tasks of this book is to de-marginalise Western feminism and feminists of the late-nineteenth and early-twentieth-centuries, by advancing a case for their significance to our understanding of the historical transformations that have produced modern forms of masculinity and femininity — gender — as we currently (though contentiously) call it.[108] This task is executed through the case study of Rose Scott, whose story is at once her own and indicative of more general possibilities and constraints confronting feminists of her era. If the specifics of the story are mainly Australian, the implications translate to the consideration of other national contexts comprising the history of Western feminism since 1880.

While most historians of Australia probably know of Rose Scott, Louisa Lawson and Vida Goldstein, researches into the history of feminism could not yet be identified as a major priority of mainstream Australian historians. The history of socialism, liberalism, conservatism, racism, ethnocentrism and even environmentalism have fared considerably better, so it is quite possible to submit the Australian configurations and characteristics of these political/philosophical movements to historical comparison with their counterparts in other Western countries. It is difficult to trace the history of feminism through mainstream Australian political histories, which leaves the task, almost by default, entirely to exponents of women's history. Though brethren historians may consider this logical, the political history of feminism has never been simply 'about women' in a conceptual quarantine. Instead, its manifestations have been extensively about men — men as the problem or object of scrutiny, as biased legislators, as an interest group demanding particular sexed rights and conditions, and occasionally as allies and co-campaigners in feminist reform. The exculpation of the history of feminism from political history is an unwarranted narrowing of the politicised past.

Three main genres represent the bulk of the history of Australian feminism within women's history: biography, histories of political organisations and campaigns, and textual analysis of feminist cultural production. A modest quantity of illuminating work is in circulation. Arguably, only textual analysis has given priority to a primary scrutiny of feminism itself, as discursive position, political stance, philosophy. Despite what amounts to a rich collection of Australian case studies, the direction of work has been, at least until recently, towards neither the definitive interpretative monographs nor the interrogative anthologies of United States, Canadian and British historians. Instead, Australian work generally has a tangential quality, the scrutiny of feminism tending to emerge indirectly in the context of a larger discussion of something else. It is tempting to conclude that Australia's most insightful contributors to the history of feminism have circumnavigated it, peering at it obliquely.[109] This may warrant some explanation, in the context of this study of Rose Scott's feminism.

Viewed from feminist frameworks of the 1970s and 1980s, late-nineteenth-century Australian feminists may have had less interest for historians of women than their British or United States counterparts. In 1975 Anne Summers sharply disputed the longstanding belief that Australian women were handed the vote 'on a platter' without a serious struggle. Yet the record exposed an undeniably orderly woman suffrage movement that broke no windows, set no fires, and created few public scandals. Its leaders (including Scott) were judged energetic and vigorous, but eclectic and not original theorists. All commentators seemed to agree that whether due to peculiar colonial political circumstances or surprising frontier egalitarianism, Australian women were enfranchised *early*, before the heroic and at times violent struggles of British, European and American women. Whether because of progressive political culture or, conversely, because of the educational deprivation of the women and girls of Australia's relatively small colonial upper and middle classes, historians of women contend that the Australian women's movements produced no original feminist theory.[110]

The rapid changes in Anglo-American readings of past feminists discussed above may help to explain a certain hesitancy among Australian historians of women in tackling the history of feminism more directly during the 1970s and 1980s. At first sight, the band of primarily Anglo-Celtic bourgeois temperance advocates who substantially constituted the colonial women's movements appeared offensively prudish, racist, heterosexist, authoritarian, Protestant and hopelessly unselfconscious in claiming to speak for *woman* singular, despite their own absolute specificity. Moreover, as noted above, a certain Anglo-American hegemony understandably developed in the writing of the history of feminism. Australian and New Zealand women's history did not fit the mould. For fully half of the period currently designated 'first-wave feminism', Australian and New Zealand women had had the vote. This is a historical fact that provides a unique opportunity to test the dominant woman suffrage and women's-rights-centred interpretations in prevailing histories of feminism. To my knowledge, this opportunity has been neither recognised nor seized.

Instead, Australian women's history practitioners, well-read in comparative — if vote-centred — histories, may have felt justified in perceiving the feminists of Scott's time as outside the key time-frame defined in the literature and thus, as limited and uninteresting. This may have been confirmed by the first researches on the ideas, beliefs and political priorities of Australia's first-wave feminists. To Australian feminist historians of the 1970s and 1980s, engaged with international feminist theory debates centring on relationshipss between feminism and Marxism, on differences between women wrought by class, aboriginality, race, ethnicity, age, and disability, and upon the theorising of sexuality, sexual preference, pleasure and desire, first-wave feminists like Scott, Lawson, Goldstein, Windeyer and Rischbieth appeared rather retrograde. Further, engagements more recently between feminist theory and psychoanalysis, deconstruction, post-colonial theory, cultural studies, post-structuralism and postmodernism arguably deepen the gulf between the so-called first-wave and contemporary Australian feminism.

As Katie Spearritt understatedly notes: 'Historians expressed only modest interest in articulate, politically involved women', judging the contributions of the late-nineteenth-century women's movement at best inconsequential, and at worst puritanical and reactionary. The principal analytic framework through which earlier activists have been judged is class analysis, reflecting the vigour of Australian labour and socialist history. Women's labour history and, to some degree, their social history, attracts stronger institutional support. Hence Australian historians more promptly attended to the history of conflicts between past feminists and labour activists over working women's issues, for instance, than to the sequence and chronology of the woman suffrage campaign.[111]

As a contribution to a more recent rebalancing of effort towards fuller understanding of the Australian feminist past, this book is offered despite problems of genre and approach. It is not principally a biography. The examination of Scott's life and family is undertaken in order to situate the development and transformation in her feminism, rather than embraced in and of itself, for its own sake. I am aware that for many this may be an insufficiently expansive rationale. If present and future biographers of Scott find the study of service, a worthwhile outcome will be secured. While competing characterisations of Scott could engender biographies within various genres, it is to be hoped that this study establishes the salience of *feminist* biography in this case. That is to say, any full biography of Scott will be the biography of a feminist.

Having expressed this hope, it should be noted that biography has become one of the most debated and complex zones within contemporary feminist scholarship and theory. The genre of biography raises important problems that the framework of this book did not allow to be fully addressed. One such problem of feminist biography is the 'sole, singular woman' problem — a feminist reformation of the problem of contextualising biographical subjects among their peers. Some scholars, for instance, advocate the solution of group biography, as with Barbara Caine's *Destined To Be Wives*. Insightful psychoanalytic, post-colonial and post-modernist contributions to feminist theories of biography ensure that feminist biographies of Rose Scott, Vida Goldstein, Mary Windeyer, Maybanke Anderson, Louisa Lawson, Miles Franklin and many of the other feminists active between 1880 and 1925 will be very different from studies like this one.[112]

In order to explore directly the progress of Scott's development and transformations as a feminist thinker and activist, this book has adopted a chronological approach. Since few of her writings and speeches have been published, each chapter contains considerable verbatim quotation and citation of Scott's unpublished work and correspondence. The first two chapters explore biographical materials in order to situate the genesis of Scott's feminist concerns, and to place in context the choices and events that permitted her to devote the bulk of her adult life to reform work. Throughout the remaining chapters, focused upon key phases in that reform work, relevant biographical materials are included, insofar as developments in her family and personal life constrained or influenced some aspect of her feminist analysis and work.

The third and fourth chapters investigate Scott's work for woman suffrage and related reforms. Emphasis is placed not on the course and character of that political struggle, increasingly well explored by other scholars, but upon Scott's arguments, presuppositions, rhetorical style and lobbying for the vote. The fifth and sixth chapters undertake analysis of the erosion of Scott's initial vision of the causes of women's degradation. Her stress upon the systemic sexual degradation of women emerges as central to her sense of the mission of the 'cause of women'. After enfranchisement, Scott revised both her earlier objective of 'elevation' of the unity 'women', and the strategies she had envisaged for securing such 'elevation'. Her prediction of an effective, unified, non-party women's vote failed to materialise, leading her to revise her analysis in fundamental ways. This revision developed across the post-suffrage period, reaching a peak in the years just prior to and during the First World War. The impact of war upon women seemed to her unremittingly negative, enshrining the worst kind of masculinist agenda in the political system. The seventh chapter explores the ways in which Scott finally came to terms with shifts in her 'beloved cause' and with differences between herself and the younger generation of feminists determining the orientations of the movement, as she prepared herself for retirement, and for her impending death. The final chapter critically assesses prevailing representations of Rose Scott, tracing their sources and inflections, summarising Scott's relationships and her contributions to feminism of her period.

Chapter 1

Generations (1847–64)

Is baby to be the flower of the flock that you hint at the name of Rose? If she should not grow up a beauty in spite of your anticipations, altho' Mama's anticipations are seldom out in this respect, she might be called Scott's Rose which is rough, strong and dwarfish — not very pretty . . . Of a tomboy the Wild Rose; when in love the Rosemary? in complexion she might be Rosey, a white Rose, or a new variety of great curiosity, a black or dark Rose; if she tumbled into some dirty puddle . . . 'Rosewater,' if she were stiff and formal she would be named primrose . . . if troublesome they will wish her to be the Rose of Jericho.

Helenus Scott to Saranna Scott, 5 January 1848,
Helenus Scott Correspondence, Mitchell Library

Rose Scott was born to an immigrant Anglo-Celtic and Anglophilic family. Her father, Helenus Scott (1802–79), arrived in New South Wales in 1822, her mother, Sarah Anne Rusden (1810–96), a decade later, both accompanied by their families. For Rose Scott the marriage and childbearing of her parents, grandparents, uncles, aunts and siblings created not only her immediate family, but also several visions of her life options and those for women of her background. Both sides of her family espoused expectations of masculinity and femininity in its members which Rose Scott came to resist and later to subject to fierce criticism. It is therefore worth considering these family cultures, and the influence they had upon Rose Scott's feminism.

Often the family backgrounds of earlier feminists are examined as a source of *explanation* of the subject's feminism. This is not my intention. The same family experience did not generate feminist convictions in Rose Scott's mother, aunts (with one possible exception), sisters, cousins or nieces, nor in their male counterparts. It is unlikely that the emergence of Western political and philosophical movements can be satisfactorily attributed to the sum of individual family histories. Instead, as the study of biographies of advocates of these movements reveal, there are many routes to the same destination. In late-nineteenth-century Australia, as elsewhere, the women who first organised around feminist demands had a vast range of family circumstances and backgrounds, defying any search for common links in the genealogy of feminism.[1] The *origins* of feminism, or of that of an individual like Rose Scott, are not usefully pursued through family history.

Nonetheless, examination of Scott's family experiences provides an indispensable context for many of her characteristic concerns and assumptions about and approaches to the array of causes she was involved in between the ages of 42, when she began public work, and 75, when she ceased it. In addition, the rich sources of evidence of her family history provide significant insights into colonial women's history, the development of Australian masculinity and the history of pastoralism. The practical outcomes of the fortunes and misfortunes of the Scott and related families in the circumstances of Rose Scott's childhood certainly deserve some scrutiny. Her education, relationships with her siblings, and the experience of living away from them and her parents during periods of financial and emotional crisis were also formative influences. A final concern is the ways in which the Scott family's relocation to town life in Newcastle, a port town north of Sydney (when Rose was 11), in a period from resettlement to adolescence, created many of the choices and options that were available to her.

FORTUNES AND MISFORTUNES

Rose Scott was born amid a family storm of bankruptcy, the genesis of which lay in earlier generations. On both sides of her family, claims to gentility prevailed. Scott's mother, known as Saranna, was the eldest of 11 children born to Anne Rusden (née Townsend) between 1810 and 1827 in Somerset, England. Her father, Reverend George Keylock Rusden, was descended from a distinguished Cambridge clerical family, and was an amateur scholar of Asian language, mythology and culture. Anne Townsend and George Rusden married in 1809. When, in 1832, he was offered the chaplaincy of St Peter's Anglican Church at East Maitland in the Hunter Valley of New South Wales, they emigrated and moved their by then large family into The Parsonage, attached to the church.

Rusden included the education of his children within his schedule of parish duties. Through his teaching Saranna and her siblings developed enormous religious piety, a propensity for foreign languages, considerable skills in artistic representation and handcrafts, and enthusiasm for serious reading, especially history, geography, biography, orientalism and the classics. George William Rusden, the noted historian of Australia and New Zealand, was Saranna's younger brother. Another Rusden brother,

Henry Keylock Rusden, moved to Victoria to become Recorder of the Legislative Council. He was an intellectual and an atheist, to the horror of his parents and pious siblings.[2] Barred by sex from public and professional vocations, Saranna and her sisters obtained, nonetheless, an invaluable legacy from their education, with significant consequences for Rose Scott.

Five of Saranna's ten siblings remained unmarried, and of the five who did marry, two were childless and the other three bore large families of between seven and ten children.[3] Three options for adult women were thus displayed to the young Rose: spinsterhood and caring for parents and community; marriage without children and with service to family and community; and marriage with service only to immediate family, largely consisting of numerous children.

More is known about the Scott side of the family. Rose Scott's father, Helenus, was born in India, the son of Dr Helenus Scott , president of the Medical Board of Bombay and a distinguished research scientist who introduced the vaccination technique of his friend Edward Jenner into Indian medical practice. Since Dr Scott's father, David Scott, had been a modestly paid Scottish minister, his marriage to Augusta Maria Frederick entailed upward social mobility. Her wealthy family was descended from Sir John Frederick, the seventeenth-century sheriff of London and lord mayor. Upon retiring from a career in the British East India Company, Dr Scott resumed private practice at Bath. By then, he had one daughter and five sons to support, several of the latter of whom had received a military education in India. However, his health failed, and his friend Sir Joseph Banks persuaded him to migrate to temperate Australia. He died en route in 1821, and was buried at Cape Town.[4]

His sons Robert and Helenus, who had accompanied him, continued on to Sydney and were successful in obtaining two adjoining land grants in the Singleton region of the Hunter River Valley. They amalgamated them into a single holding they called Glendon after an ancestral Scottish residence. Eventually in 1830, Robert Scott returned to England to accompany their mother, and sister Augusta Scott, on the voyage to Sydney. Rose Scott never knew her paternal grandmother.[5]

Other Scott brothers joined the family. Alexander Walker Scott, who had followed in his father's scientific footsteps, was an entomologist. On his brothers' advice he applied for and obtained land grants in the Hunter Valley region in 1829. In 1834 the eldest Scott brother, Captain David Charles Frederick Scott of the Indian Army, arrived in Australia. He promptly obtained a land grant in the Hunter Valley near Muswellbrook. Finally, the younger brother, Patrick Scott, joined the others in 1844, also obtaining Hunter Valley lands in partnership with Helenus. Wishing to devote his life to writing poetry and cultural developments, Patrick Scott was a less-than-enthusiastic grazier and landholder. He passed the management of his colonial business affairs to relatives and returned to England to marry and raise a family of four children in the 1860s.[6]

The conjugal fortunes of the Scotts were largely formed by colonial circumstances. During the 1820s the young Scott brothers resided in a poor 'marriage market'. They concentrated their efforts on the demands of establishing their landholdings, living in tents, using convict labour and subsisting on a monotonous diet of kangaroo and salt pork. Shortages of basic necessities such as clothes, shoes, tools, utensils and household supplies produced a dependence upon their mother, and not only for material resources.[7] Helenus confided his matrimonial anxieties to her. In 1826 he wrote:

> I hope you will not scold me for writing to you so much like *a farmer*. I shall soon be able to write to you more like a gentleman when our new little cottage is finished. It contains two rooms and three small verandah rooms and one closet. We shall live in it for some years unless a Mrs. S. (Mrs. R. or H.) should interfere and say she must have a better house — we have nearly sufficient furniture for the cottage except for the principal ornament — the before mentioned Mrs. R. or H.[8]

He informed his mother that the young ladies in the colony 'are not so reserved as those in London and talk openly' of things that would be thought improper at home.[9] Upon receipt of two handsome candlesticks from her in 1827, he ventured that, when alight, they would 'add much to show off the beauties that inhabit this cottage at Glendon (I mean that are to be! When? I don't know)'.[10]

When separated, the Scott brothers wrote to one another, often discussing the women with whom they were acquainted — sometimes in terms similar to those used when buying pastoral stock. Dr James Mitchell of Sydney became their business partner and one evening took Helenus to a dinner party at Point Piper in Sydney. As well as reporting his adverse opinion of the political figure, Mr W.C. Wentworth, he wrote to Robert of the host and his wife, whom he did not think 'either pretty or ladylike', while noting that the solicitor, Mr Stevens, had daughters said to be very pretty.[11] Of their near neighbour's five unmarried daughters, he wrote that some of them were 'pretty good-looking girls'.[12]

When in 1830 Robert arrived in London to escort his mother and sister back to the colony, he wrote to Helenus of the matrimonial machinations of their English uncle, Sir John Young, and family, who were 'moving heaven and earth to make the youngest Miss Melluish, Mrs Young. They have £80 000 each now and probably £100 000 more at the father's death'.[13] Marriage settlements on this scale would have been rare in colonial New South Wales, which for Robert Scott would have been an obstacle to a colonial marriage. Yet he seems not to have seriously pursued a moneyed English bride.

The brothers prospered in the 1830s, expanding their landholdings, and diversifying their ventures. They were the pioneers of the thoroughbred horse breeding industry in the Hunter Valley, importing several important stud horses, the most famous of which was Dover. The Scotts were founders of the Hunter River sweepstakes.[14]

As an accompaniment of economic success, Glendon became a centre of social life in the Hunter Valley, the brothers respected as men of means, justices of the peace, and honorary magistrates. In the early 1830s Robert and Helenus visited the newly arrived Rusdens, possibly both with courting in mind. It is unclear whether Robert also had an interest in Saranna, then aged in her early twenties, or in 19-year-old Amelia, 18-year-old Grace or 16-year-old Georgianna. Robert was already over 30 years old.

The skewed age structure of the colonial marriage market in this period has received considerable comment: the majority of bachelors were a full generation or more older than most marriageable women.[15] Though this was primarily a consequence of convict immigration and the male dominance of indentured and free immigration, wealthier free landholders and entrepreneurs experienced a version of the same problem, often intensified by exclusionary class, ethnic and cultural expectations, ill-suited to the penal and colonial situation.

Men like Robert and Helenus's brother, Alexander, may have escaped the difficulties of colonial demography by unconventional conjugal choices. Shortly after arrival in the colony he became involved with the estranged wife of Captain Robert Stirling, known in Sydney as Harriett Calcott. Stirling returned to England in 1825, while Harriett and their daughter Frances remained in Sydney. In 1829 Robert Stirling died and in 1830 Alexander Scott and Harriett Calcott's first daughter, also called Harriett, was born. A second daughter, Helena, was born in 1832. Yet no marriage took place for a number of years, though there is no evidence of any legal impediment. The daughters and their mother lived with Alexander Scott on Ash Island near Newcastle, where he pursued his entomological interests and educated the girls in science, scientific illustration and art. His business ventures were unsuccessful compared with those of his brother and brother-in-law, and he finally pursued a political career as a Member of the New South Wales Legislative Council. In 1845 Frances Murdoch Stirling married the German merchant Ludwig Karl Kirchner, and in 1846 Alexander Scott and Harriett Calcott were married in Sydney at a ceremony witnessed by the newly-wed Kirchners.[16]

Rose Scott was to be close to their daughter, her cousin Helena Scott, at whose wedding in Newcastle in 1864 she was a witness. Helena married Dr Edward Forde, whom she accompanied as illustrator on a scientific expedition along the Darling River in 1866. He died suddenly from fever at Menindee; no children had been born. Helena's mother, Harriett

Scott (née Calcott), also died in 1866; and Alexander Scott, Helena Forde and Harriett Scott the younger set up house together in Double Bay, Sydney, in the late 1860s. Harriett married Cosby William Morgan in 1882 when she was 52 — a marriage that quickly ended in separation.[17]

Although Alexander Scott's marriage was delayed until the 1840s, his siblings Augusta, Helenus and David all married in New South Wales in the 1830s. Augusta married Dr James Mitchell in 1833 at the mature age of 35, her husband being 41. They lived in Sydney and had three children, Augusta Scott Mitchell, David Scott Mitchell and Margaret Scott Mitchell. Meanwhile in 1838 David C. F. Scott married Maria Jane Barney, daughter of a pioneer family, who bore three children. Also based in Sydney, David Scott worked as a magistrate, investor and real-tor, after his profitable period as a pastoralist, while Maria Jane Scott became a skilled landscape and seascape watercolour artist.[18] Her father, Colonel Barney, in collaboration with Governor Gipps's aide-de-camp, Edward Charles Merewether, led the 1846 expedition to establish the new colony of North Australia in what became northern Queensland, and which was abandoned shortly after.

Merewether, who was acquainted with the Barneys and the Scotts, soon became involved in business ventures with Dr James Mitchell, through his position as Commissioner of Crown Lands and General Superintendent with the Australian Agricultural Company from the 1860s. In 1860 he married Augusta and James Mitchell's daughter, Augusta Scott Mitchell, Rose Scott's cousin and 15 years his junior, who bore 10 children between 1862 and 1878. Merewether played an import-ant role in the Mitchell and Scott families, especially in the affairs of Rose Scott's siblings after the death of their father, Helenus Scott, in 1879.[19]

Helenus Scott married 25-year-old Saranna Rusden in 1835 at the age of 33. Correspondence among relatives attests to the romantic, affec-tionate and happy state of this union, yet Saranna's previous domestic life left her ill-prepared for the demands of being mistress of Glendon. There was no Mrs Robert Scott and would be none. If Helenus, who had long awaited the arrival of his helpmeet, had considerable hopes and needs, so did Robert. All three lived at the Glendon homestead, headquarters of a land-holding operation that by the end of the 1830s extended over vast areas of the Hunter Valley, Liverpool Plains and regions to the south-west.[20] Despite the accounts often spun in genealogical and celebratory family his-tories, pastoral life of the kind pursued by the Scott brothers was violent, rough, spartan, exploitative and constantly imperilled. What success they had was built upon convict labour, men referred to as 'the prisoners'. As Helenus explained to his mother: 'We need not give any wages but supply with sufficient meat, drink, clothing etc. but we prefer giving them their rations and £10 per annum as wages according to the old regulation; with £10 they supply themselves with everything except rations.'[21]

In her unpublished memoir, Rose Scott's niece, Annie Rose Scott Cowen, related a story told to her by an old man who was the son of convict prisoners born on the Glendon station. The overseer who organised the convict labour was cruel, and one day the convicts attacked and beheaded him. She retold the story to her mother, Alice Hamilton, the youngest of Helenus Scott's children, who claimed never to have heard of the incident.[22] There are indications that the Scotts had poor labour relations, a high turnover of servants, and that they regularly complained about labour shortages. Robert and Helenus Scott were among the 1842 petitioners for the introduction of 'coolie' indentured labour from India.[23] The cheap coolie labour still under contract in the late 1840s permitted survival of the enterprise even after bankruptcy was in train.

This source of wealth forged in the brothers, as in other pastoralists of the period, particular political stances and interests, not always consonant with those of what Connell and Irving term the emerging 'mercantile bourgeoisie'.[24] From the beginning of their landholding ventures, they reported to family members that the blacks in the vicinity 'have been very troublesome'.[25] In response to his mother's enquiries about Aboriginal language and customs, Helenus sent long accounts of examples of what he called the 'Anglo-blacko-lingo' that they all had to learn to speak. While his account observed accurately the great diversity of Aboriginal peoples, languages and customs in the district, he declared all members of local tribes to be useless as farm workers:

> they are by no means a fine race of people; their greatest recommendation is their good temper and are [sic] very inoffensive when kept in check and if they don't fear you they are apt to be treacherous — they have scarcely any ingenuity or art amongst them but like children with but little of their innocence.[26]

Robert Scott was even less liberal in his views. In 1826, for his part in the pursuit and capture of the convict bushrangers known as the Steele gang, he was honoured with the award of a silver tea and coffee set, bequeathed eventually to Rose Scott.[27] He was handy with weapons and not shy of direct action, and one can only speculate on the fates of 'troublesome' blacks perceived by him as a threat. In 1838 he called and presided over a meeting at Patrick's Plains in support of eleven whites who had murdered Aboriginal people in the notorious Myall Creek massacre. Furthermore, he led a deputation to Governor Sir George Gipps on behalf of the men convicted for this massacre. On the basis of these actions, Gipps had Robert Scott omitted from the new Commission of the Peace in December 1838.[28] Yet while Robert and Helenus pursued the continuation of plantation-style pastoralism, their brother-in-law, Dr James Mitchell, based in Sydney, was active in moves to end the transportation of convicts and to establish a free, waged labour force befitting a commercial capitalist economy.[29]

A biographer of Rose Scott, May Munro, offered a rather benign view of the Scott brothers, though conceded that there were problems: 'Robert who had less inclination for farming than his brother lived more the life of an English country gentleman and their home became the centre where writers, books and philosophy were discussed and debated.'[30] She contended that, ignorant of farm management, Robert lived at Glendon in a style that exceeded his income, entertaining clergy, explorers, early wine growers, artists and writers. Thus Glendon became a 'unique centre of culture'.[31] The memoirs of Rose Scott's niece include her mother Alice's anecdotes about the visits to Glendon of Ludwig Leichhardt, the famous mid-nineteenth-century explorer. She claimed her mother would converse with him in French, German and Italian.[32]

Rose Scott never knew her Uncle Robert. His untimely passing in 1844 was the end of an era. In his will, written shortly before, he stated: 'I think it would be wise for Helenus to concentrate his estate and have money in hand instead of the property being largely diffused. I have commenced with Helenus, continued with Helenus, made my money with him and Helenus is my heir.'[33] In fact what Helenus inherited were huge debts, a result of what an English cousin described to Saranna as Robert's lack of prudent and economical management, and his indulgence in foreign speculation.[34] The state of affairs disclosed by Robert's death inadvertently revealed the extent to which Helenus the farmer had unquestioningly deferred to his elder brother's judgement in all things. In a real sense, Robert had been his life's companion, and after his death Helenus felt abandoned and out of his depth.

However great was the culture and refinement of life at Glendon in the 1830s, its basis was the frontier penal and colonial expansion of white settlement, achieved at the expense of and resisted by the Aboriginal owners of the land. The impact of this on Saranna Scott in her early married life was enormous, especially in the context of frequent childbirth. Her first child, a girl, Saranna (known in the family as Fannie), was born less than two years after her marriage. After Fannie, she bore ten more children within fourteen years.[35]

By the time Rose was born in 1847 — the eighth child of the family — Saranna was not only caring for a large brood, but was also facing new and increasingly onerous demands. From 1843 the family finances had been in crisis. In 1844 Helenus wrote to Saranna while on a trip with the dual purposes of searching for domestic servants and filing the probate on Robert's will. The court fee of £16 for the latter alarmed him, but he reported that no one had yet pressed him for money 'and all retain some delicacy except the Commercial Bank, a heartless, greedy set, keen and mean in their acts'.[36] In passing he mentioned that William Manning had been appointed Solicitor General and that, as a magistrate with a vote in the matter of his appointment, he had been asked by Manning for his vote.

Helenus had refused, arguing that Manning's appointment would be 'without hope of success nor do I think he will be qualified for the situation'. Manning later became Attorney General and this refusal was to prove costly in a controversial public scandal involving the Scott family in 1869. Meanwhile, he wrote that: 'I am sorry my darling I cannot just now send you any money for the purposes you mention but I am in hopes of doing so soon by raising money on our wool, tallow or cattle . . . I hope . . . that I may not again be pressed so much for money.'[37]

The financial crisis left Helenus Scott insufficient liquidity to meet everyday costs such as wages. His letters to his wife over ensuing years give the impression of an emotionally manipulative and rather desperate man, floundering amidst events moving beyond his control. He demanded that Saranna on the one hand be responsible for obtaining money to pay 'the coolies', and yet, on the other, that she be cosseted with complete rest, since she was still exhausted and ill from Rose's birth. Perhaps humiliated by having insufficient funds to send her the hairbrush he had promised to buy her, he wrote rather harshly in March 1848 with reference to Saranna's continued indisposition and to her younger sister Amelia's breakdown after the death of a baby, her fifth birth: 'I hope you will take a caution by her bad example and not add another to your family — it appears only the other day that she had her baby in this colony and now we hear of another to be expected'. Clearly, he treated pregnancy as entirely Amelia or Saranna's responsibility. In this period 50 per cent of married women in the colony had nine or more births, higher than English family averages. Saranna Scott, then, was at the upper end of the average. Perhaps Helenus protested against the stress of so many dependants in this time of prevailing crisis, but such stress did not prevent him playing his part in the birth of three further children.[38]

Saranna also became distressed, at times unhinged, by these financial problems. By 1844 the rigours of six births within nine years of marriage, as well as of her responsibilities as mistress of Glendon and its extensive staff and dependants, had taken a serious toll on her physical and mental health. She coped only with the help of her unmarried sisters, who made extended stays with her to reduce the volume of work. In late 1840 her father, Reverend Rusden, responded to a call for help: 'Mama has shown me your letter and told me of your request for Emily's longer stay with you . . . [W]e readily assent . . . trusting that dear Emily amidst the delights of Glendon will not be averse to join her family circle again and her customary occupations.'[39] Since one of Reverend Rusden's pioneering activities in his parish was the operation of East Maitland's first bank, and Emily was the bank clerk, it did inconvenience him to part with her. Yet Emily was needed at Glendon again in 1845. As recompense, Rusden sought an exchange: Saranna's eldest son, Helenus, 'since he is such a good and clever boy at his sums'.[40]

By October 1845 Saranna was again pregnant and this time resting with relatives in Sydney. Her husband wrote her mournful letters, disappointed, expecting to hear more from her. Upon receipt of a letter, he wrote 'I feel now more happy; but your letter is not sufficiently minute about yourself'.[41] Saranna returned to Glendon, but the pregnancy continued to be difficult. The baby girl, Amelia Mary, born in July 1846, was frail and by September was suffering from whooping cough. But again financial troubles detained Helenus in Sydney. He wrote:

> My own dearest bedfellow, you do not know with what eagerness I seize your letters. I shake with pleasure and anxiety and every expression of love and affection from you delights me and I am disappointed when I do not get an abundance of them. You know I am a jealous miser of such treasures as your love and affection . . . [T]his is really distressing to see nothing prospering, my affairs at Glendon neglected and sickness in my house. I blame myself for being absent and yet I cannot help it.[42]

The baby died, Helenus came home, their troubles continued, and by February 1847 Saranna was pregnant again. It is unclear whether Helenus was present for Rose's birth, for Saranna spent her confinement at East Maitland with her parents.

On 1 January 1848, the directors of the Commercial Bank of Sydney demanded the speedy liquidation of three sums totalling nearly £10 000. This final financial blow spelt bankruptcy — though Helenus took considerable time to accept and adapt to it. From the New Year until well into 1848 he was away, again sending affectionate, demanding and morose letters. In one, of April 1848 — by which time it was generally accepted that the family would have to leave Glendon — he wrote, 'often, very often do I think of the poor little baby we lost. God grant that I may not lose another of my blessings'.

Anne Rusden tried to comfort her daughter as best she could, especially after the shocking news about having to leave Glendon: 'I can hardly bear to think that you had to receive it alone'.[43] The process was ugly; creditors took that which Saranna prized most of all — her books. Her mother had assumed they would not be able to keep the piano, but thought the books would be safe. She stressed that Saranna should not dwell on 'the idea that disgrace is attached to you by these unhappy events . . . Misfortune is not disgrace when guilt has not brought it upon us'.[44]

Ever practical, Saranna's mother pointed out some good consequences of the change of household, such as the reduction in household maintenance required. Saranna's intense anxiety about the disadvantage to her sons, Helenus, George, Robert and Walker, who would no longer be given the kind of private school education planned for them, worried her mother. In reassurance, Anne pointed out that 'their minds are certainly advanced beyond their years by being the companions of their parents and learning to be useful to them'. Saranna's father also sought to offer her comfort, though in rather different terms. He reminded her that:

> it is in adversity that female virtues shine forth in their brightest lustre, as flowers of exquisite fragrance flourish in the shade. Man, by education and habit is formed for bustle and toil; his energies are like the sun. Woman's gentler influence is like the Moon which, though she shines with lesser power, still shines brightest at the darkest hour. The frail drooping ivy will at last support the tree that formerly sustained itself.[45]

Glendon was leased and much of the property sold in stages between 1848 and 1851. During this period the remaining children were born and the older ones began the pattern of living with various relatives. In 1853 Helenus Scott senior began a new career, as stipendiary police magistrate, that would last until his death. For the first five years this was a migratory existence for him, serving first at Louisa Creek, Carcoar, then Patrick's Plains, Wollombi, and McDonald River. From 1858 he took up the position of Newcastle police magistrate.[46]

LEGACIES

Rose's father was absent during much of her infancy and childhood. Her mother was either absent or much preoccupied with family difficulties, further pregnancies and confinements. It was Rose's maternal grandparents who functioned as surrogate parents from the time she was just over a year old. In 1848 another baby was born, premature, but died soon after birth. It is possible that baby Rose remained with grandparents and her unmarried aunts and uncles through significant portions of time following this second death and yet another pregnancy, which resulted in the birth of Mary Ann ('Millie') in March 1849.

Saranna again needed her family's help. Augusta was aged 6, Walker 4, and Rose only 18 months. Probably the eldest Scott daughter, Saranna (Fannie), now aged 11, assumed considerable responsibility for helping her mother. She was educated at home, but no doubt the educational attention she received was less than that of her brothers Helenus, George and Robert, owing to family and social assumptions regarding the primary importance of education for male children. As well, Fannie was only 6 when the financial difficulties that so dramatically altered the family fortunes struck. Crisis dominated her childhood. By her adolescence the two Sarannas lived in some tension with each other. In 1855 when Fannie was 18, Saranna wrote to Helenus: 'Did I not speak of your letter to Fannie? It was excellent and I am happy to say I think it has had a good effect. I certainly think that she makes more effort to control her temper and is more ready to do as I wish.'[47]

Even with the help of this eldest daughter, Saranna could not manage the burdens of family and property in the frequent absence of

Helenus. Various children were sent to relatives. George and Helenus spent time with Frank and Alice Rusden, their childless uncle and aunt. In 1851 the birth of Alice, the youngest and last addition to the family, heightened this dependence on neighbouring relatives and family.

The marriage of Rose's aunt, Rose Rusden, to the future Anglican Dean of Newcastle, Edward Arthur Selwyn, in 1852 established a new household to assist with Saranna's childcare problems. Rose Selwyn was to remain childless and the couple was devoted to Rose, whom they regarded as a surrogate daughter, and she spent much time with them from the age of 5 years. The pattern of spending significant periods living with relatives was common in the mid-nineteenth century. Her aunts and uncles and grandparents provided Rose with education, sources of cultural enrichment and different models of life possibilities from those of her parents.

One consequence of these circumstances, however, was a heightened sentimentality about family life. Saranna occasionally took a break from the burdens of domesticity to visit Rose. She wrote enthusiastic letters to Helenus reporting on how their daughter was developing. She seemed particularly proud of Rose's curiosity and capacity to handle social relationships and new situations with skill and intelligence. The young Rose accepted nothing just on faith. She always asked how and why things were so, especially on matters relating to God, Aboriginal people, and sexual relations. Rose herself, and others who remembered her as a child, reported that she spent much of her time alone in the bush exploring and playing.[48]

As well as formal lessons, all of the households in which Rose stayed observed the practice of reading aloud as recreation. To one such reading occasion the elderly Rose Scott attributed her early conversion to 'the cause of women'. One night, when she was 7, Saranna read aloud to the assembled family group Shakespeare's *The Taming of the Shrew*. Scott claims to have been so enraged by this story of women's subjugation that she stamped about in the garden:

> It was with surprise that I contemplated Katherine at the bidding of her husband taking off her cap and trampling upon it (I w'd have thrown it in his face) and then her sermon (at the bidding of her husband) to her sisters and others upon the duty of wives to their husbands! . . . And when the reading was over I paced the garden in a secluded spot with clenched hands and fury in my heart. I pitied and blamed Katherine at first but now — the craven wretch to give in; in that servile manner and worse still, to turn the tables on her own sex! From that moment I was a rebel against injustice and wrong.[49]

This is of course a retrospective account, constructing a version of the self that will need scrutiny in analysis of the sources of Scott's feminism; but the memory does at least reliably reveal the process of informal education of girls through reading aloud.

In Scott's childhood, then, the legacy of the family misfortunes was considerable contact with the maternal side of the family. The Rusdens were genteel but hardly prosperous. They provided a model for coping with the reduced circumstances ahead for the Scotts. If Miles Franklin is correct that the New South Wales coastal town of Grafton, was the first proper town Rose Scott saw, in 1857, it would seem that the more Sydney-based paternal side of the family were distant figures during her first decade of life.

Arguably, the Rusdens demonstrated the viability of and satisfactions that could accompany life without marriage and childrearing. Several of the Rusden uncles and aunts remained unmarried and pursued intellectual, professional, cultural and philanthropic vocations. During Scott's childhood they were living with their parents. Scott's formative years clearly provided experiences that challenged the cultural expectation that in colonial Australia women *must* marry. Of the Rusden uncles and aunts who did marry, those who bore larger families lived far away — in Melbourne, Shanghai and England. The married Rusdens she was close to, especially Rose and Frank, were without children, so childless marriage was also a feature of her early experience.

In the Scott/Mitchell/Merewether side of the family, who certainly visited their rural relatives at times, there were different marital and reproductive patterns for Rose to observe. The patterns in this side of the family contrast with the Rusden side. There was less recourse to unmarried life. Half of Saranna's siblings remained unmarried, compared with only one of Helenus's five siblings — Rose's bachelor uncle, Robert. Whereas the Rusdens who married did so at the average age of 27, the Scotts tended to marry later. Helenus was 33, David over 40, Alexander 46, Patrick in his fifties and Augusta 35. Only the Helenus Scott family, with eleven children, resembled the reproductive pattern of the Rusden marriages. David and Maria Jane Scott had only three children, Alexander and Harriett Scott two, Augusta and James Mitchell three, and Patrick Scott and his wife four. These smaller family sizes were not typical of the period, and were produced by those Scotts who, despite periods of pastoral life, basically resided physically and culturally in towns and cities.

The Scott uncles and aunts also provided for Rose examples of adults whose lives were not totally occupied by childrearing. Even Aunt Augusta Scott Mitchell, whose life as the only woman among the siblings could be expected to be the most family-centred, had completed her bearing of three children eight years before Rose was born. The Aunt Augusta that Rose knew as a child and young woman had a life different from and with wider options than that of Rose's own mother, who was bearing and rearing young children well into Rose's adolescence. As well, the smaller family sizes of David, Augusta and Alexander Scott meant that because Rose was born eighth of eleven children, her few cousins from these marriages were considerably older than she — Harriett and Helena were aged 17 and 15 respectively when Rose was born, while cousin David Scott Mitchell was 11 and Augusta Scott Mitchell almost 13.

This family pattern produced a blurring of generational lines. For example, two first cousins from different sized branches of the family might be far enough apart in age as to be like parent and child. Edward and Augusta Merewether acted almost as parental figures for cousins such as Rose's youngest married sister and brother-in-law, Alice and Terrick Hamilton.[50]

Late marriage and small families were clearly the favoured pattern in the Scott family, with closely spaced births. The men were of that colonial professional class that often blended private landholding, a secondary industry enterprise, and public (often stipendiary) office. The women were of genteel education and accomplishment, with two earning considerable artistic achievement. If the young Rose Scott cared to absorb their example, then delaying marriage and reproduction into the thirties and pursuing knowledge, culture, accomplishment and urban social life were the indicated courses of action.

These circumstances meant that Rose Scott grew up under a particularly diverse range of daily influences. Some of her elder siblings seem not to have figured in her early life at all, especially Fannie and Helenus, who then lived with Frank and Alice Rusden. Rose seems to have been a great favourite with Grandmother Anne Rusden and with the Selwyns. Grandmother Rusden thanked Saranna for sending a lock of 'Rosey's' hair in 1854 'but I do not understand her extraordinary intrepidity in using the amputating instrument herself'.[51] Saranna delighted in her daughter's curious and adventurous approach to knowledge, reporting to Helenus on Rose's early progress with reading while staying with her grandparents:

> She is, however very well reconciled to stay a little longer and the merriest little cricket you can imagine observing, and commenting on everything. Aunt Rose was sitting on Selwyns knee the other day when Rose ran into the drawing room; after peering about some time she said 'What are you doing sitting in laps' to the great amusement of both . . . I put on my alpaca dress today and Rose observing it is a similar material to a dress of Grandmamas comes feeling and looking at mine with the air of a connoisseur saying 'Why Mama your dress is a little drop like Grandmamas'. She had accompanied us two or three times to the school which is now so well-conducted by its intelligent master and mistress that it is most interesting for anyone to witness. She looks about at all the children most attentively and once seeing several of the children give Aunt Georgianna their pennies she asked many questions and her aunt told her about the good bishop having asked the children to give some money to have the little black children taught to say their prayers. When she came home she wanted to tell me about it: 'The children gave Aunt

Georgianna their pennies.' 'What', I said, 'to get lollies?' She answered very emphatically 'No mama not lollies', then running and putting her head in my lap looking up with sparkling eyes and glowing cheeks 'for the little black children to be taught their prayers'. 'That Good Bishop' afterwards she said 'and when they come and all kneel down to say their prayers won't they give the money back again?''.[52]

In educating her younger daughters, Augusta, Rose, Millie and Alice, Saranna sought to compensate for the period of family hardship. Her aim was to have each of them reading between their third and fourth year through the combined instruction provided by herself, her parents and siblings. Just after Rose's fourth birthday in 1851, Saranna reported on her progress with reading, principally learned through reading aloud. Irritated at the rules of word formation, the child had evidently tried to subvert them and the religious training imparted by her mother:

'What word does s-t-z spell mama or t-m-p or r-t-t? Mama I know how to spell God — G-o-d. I had it in my lesson — oh mama and I had hell too. I know how to spell it — h-e-l-l — isn't it a frightful word mama. I know what it means. Its the place where naughty people go. Oh mama (crying) Millie pulled my hair — did God see her does he love her for that!' . . . Little Rose is full as usual of intelligent questions and conjectures.[53]

Saranna wrote to Helenus in 1854 with the happy news that her family had contributed £1000 to assist in their troubles. She sent Augusta (Gussie), Rose's elder sister, to stay with relatives. Returning after some months, Saranna described Rose's delight at Gussie's return in September 1855: 'Rosie was soon wrapt in the book which was her present and retired to bed with Augusta very happy to be together again'.[54]

Some new misery must have afflicted Saranna in 1858, for her father Reverend Rusden wrote to her 'My dear girl, my heart bleeds for you', a short note completed with an invitation that she urgently come to stay with her parents and tell them all about it.[55] It may have been something to do with Fannie, then aged 20, to whom any further reference from this period onwards disappears from family sources. Had she eloped or fallen from genteel expectations?

The 1850s was a decade of major readjustment for all members of Helenus and Saranna Scott's family. It is likely that Saranna had what would later be called a nervous breakdown, and there is evidence of concern among relatives and friends. In November 1858 her father wrote: 'We were grieved to hear that you were again unwell and hope that you are again recovering as we trust you may gradually do'.[56] He would be dead within the year, and Saranna's mother a year later, ending the most significant source of advice and support that had sustained her through the first twenty-five years of a difficult married life.

The year 1858 was notable for finality in many areas. In June, Helenus finally permitted the Glendon homestead to be put under the auctioneer's hammer. The newspaper advertisement listed for auction livestock, farm implements, dairy and kitchen utensils, household furniture, medicine chest and medicine, and a valuable collection of books. The proceeds no doubt reduced the remaining debt and permitted the establishment of the new household at Newcastle. But the scale of the move and the resulting slide down the social scale would have been inescapable. The Scotts became town-dwellers reluctantly, despite their daughters Augusta and Rose declaring to Grandmother Rusden that they were eager to begin town life.

Rose had been away with the Selwyns in Grafton during this time of great difficulty for Saranna. Her earliest extant letter is the one she wrote to her youngest sister, Alice, in October 1858. Thanking her for her letter and birthday presents, Rose observed that 'I will soon see you and Mary again, it is a year and six months since I have seen you; is that not a very long time? Have you got any mulberries at Newcastle?'[57] The family was to be reunited at Newcastle for Christmas. Saranna approached the reunion — specifically the return of Augusta and Rose — with some trepidation, and evidently confessed her anxiety to her sister Georgianna. In response, Georgianna declared Saranna's fears to be morbid, arising from 'your weak state following so immediately and so naturally upon distressing circumstances'. Presumably, she here referred to the same disaster of 1858 about which their father George Rusden had sympathised a little earlier. Her letter concluded with strongly worded advice, with special reference to young Rose.

> Your girls have been taught to regard you (and justly) as an able and efficient guide for them and it would be very injurious to them if you suffer them to perceive in your conduct toward them, this distrust of yourself . . . Augusta is now at that age when . . . the mind begins to satisfy itself that no human judgement is infallible — but that a *young* child should not doubt its parent's judgement is beneficial for itself.[58]

Saranna's fallibility should not be forced upon her child's mind, and Georgianna urged her not to indulge in or foster anxiety and distrust. The eldest Scott son, Nene (the family abbreviation for 'Helenus'), was offered and accepted the position of bank manager in New Zealand in late 1858, a development which, under the circumstances, Georgianna contended should 'cheer you'. It seems it did not, and Georgianna was sorry to learn how depressed Saranna continued to be.

RESETTLEMENTS

By Christmas 1858, the Scotts were reunited in their new residence in Newcastle, known as The Barracks, originally attached to the 41st Artillery Battalion (by then disbanded). The large house had been the commandant's residence. Town life generated new influences on Rose and her siblings. Newcastle was in the process of becoming an important centre of coal-mining, shipping, building and town development. Their relatives were in the forefront of its expansion and to this day, suburbs, streets and parks of Newcastle bear the family names. Dr James Mitchell fared well in the aftermath of the crash of the Bank of Australia and the depression that had so reduced the fortunes of his brothers-in-law. Land he had salvaged in the crisis had rich coal deposits. With the fortune he made establishing mining in the area, he invested in railways, shipping and manufacturing as well as housing and commercial properties. His partnership with Edward Merewether enhanced both their fortunes and brought them frequently to Newcastle. Merewether's marriage in 1860 to Rose's cousin, Augusta Scott Mitchell, led to their settling in Newcastle at The Ridge (now the Hillcrest Hospital).[59]

The social world of the Scott family of Glendon enlarged with the move and resettlement. Firm and regular contact was established with Newcastle and Sydney relatives. It became more possible for Helenus and Saranna's children to visit Sydney in the company of Mitchell, Merewether and Scott uncles, who regularly made the journey by steamship. Rose gained the friendship and company of her Newcastle cousins, Helena and Harriett, daughters of Alexander Walker Scott. She also became closer to her Scott Mitchell cousins, David and Margaret. With these relatives came their business associates and friends — including pioneer families such as the Blaxlands, the Wyndhams, the Wallaces, the Robertsons, the Hamiltons, the Stokes, the Barneys, the Tyrells, the A'Becketts and the Ranclauds.

The increasing role of the paternal side of the family was matched by a diminution of contact with the Rusdens. The death of Rose's maternal grandparents, and the marriages and migrations of various maternal uncles and aunts, left only Georgianna and Grace on Saranna's side of the family. In 1862, in view of Saranna's continuing anxiety about the education of the remaining children, Georgianna advised that their sister, Grace, would be prepared to take in Rose, Millie and Alice to educate them; otherwise she suggested that if their means would not stretch to a governess, Saranna and Helenus might consider a school for them. It does not appear that this advice was heeded. Instead, most family news of the Scott girls centred on the extent to which maturity permitted them to relieve their mother of domestic burdens. By 1865, Georgianna was living in Melbourne with Grace and her brother, George William Rusden, and wrote to Saranna that she was 'so rejoiced to see that your dear girls are exerting themselves to share your labours, making their own dresses . . . and making preserves so successfully'. The acquisition of a stand-up sewing machine, courtesy of their uncle, Dr James Mitchell, extended their seamstressing.[60]

With the continuation of informal education in her early adolescent years, Rose absorbed much from the new social world around her. The norms of colonial courtship, marriage and childbearing were prominent among her family and friends between 1858 and 1864. The business of the marriage market and its significance for women cannot have failed to impress itself upon her. A diary she and her sister Gussie kept on trips to Sydney during 1864 and 1865 displays clear preoccupation with the alliances, associations and social occasions of courtship. Gussie was by then 21 and in considerable favour with the young men of their social circle in Newcastle and Sydney. During stays with their Uncle David or their Aunt Augusta, 17-year-old Rose accompanied her to social events such as balls, concerts, public lectures and functions at the University of Sydney.[61]

Throughout the early 1860s, Saranna Scott's frailty continued, with consequences for her daughters. Their aunt, Georgianna, had nursed and acted for her failing parents and aunt until their deaths in 1858, 1860 and 1861; and a similar role was increasingly expected of 'the girls'. Initially these tasks fell to Gussie as the elder Scott girl. In 1861, Arthur Selwyn, Rose's devoted uncle, wrote to Saranna about his impending visit:

> I am sorry to see from Augusta's letter to Georgianna that you are suffering from illness . . . I hope Rosie and the younger ones will be at home. I much wish to see them. Many a time I have missed at home dear Rosie's merry, open pretty face. What say to devoting the cares of the household to Augusta and taking a sea trip to Grafton. I am afraid I shall have no success in trying to persuade Helenus to submit to such an empty home, but Rose declares our climate and garden would set you up for years so be prepared for an attempt to carry you off.[62]

Saranna's inability to manage became the chief area of filial duty for Gussie and Rose. It caused a significant blurring of boundaries as daughters acted for mother in many capacities. The reason for these responsibilities falling on the two girls, was the maturing of the elder siblings. Fannie was gone.[63] Helenus the younger left in 1858 for New Zealand, then Melbourne, and finally settled in Brisbane, where he became a bank manager.[64] George remained a bachelor in the Newcastle area somewhat longer, before working as a stipendiary magistrate in the New South Wales country towns of Tenterfield during the 1870s, and Deniliquin during the 1880s. At the age of 46, he married into the Boydell pioneer family by wedding Elizabeth Marianne Boydell, a 40-year-old spinster. The last of Rose's brothers, Robert, also remained a bachelor during the 1860s and 1870s, living at home and working as Edward Merewether's Newcastle agent. Then to the family's surprise in 1885, when he was 44, he married

Aimée Ranclaud, the 29-year-old daughter of the Newcastle Commissioner of Crown Lands.[65]

These late marriages meant that during the 1860s and 1870s, the Scott household consisted of three male breadwinners — Helenus senior, George and Robert — as well as Saranna and the four girls, plus servants. Arthritis afflicted Saranna (now aged in her fifties) more and more seriously, circumscribing movement and reducing her capacity for unaccompanied travel. These circumstances, added to the family's painful financial history, made the question of marriage a vexed one for the Scott children. A strong sense of obligation to their parents influenced their decisions and perceptions of their options. With the possible exception of Fannie, all of Rose's siblings who married did so relatively late, the men marrying women significantly younger than themselves, compared with other men and women in the Newcastle region.[66]

Later marriage ages correlated with higher colonial social class in the second half of the nineteenth century. It was the miners, farmers, and manual tradesmen who married young their even younger brides. The adolescent Rose inhabited a community in which most women were married by 24, many before 21, and bore children every other year, to make the characteristically large colonial families of the 1860s and 1870s. Yet, in her own milieu, perhaps the youngest bride whose wedding she attended was that of her cousin Augusta Scott Mitchell, who married Edward Merewether in 1860 at the age of 25. In 1864, the 17-year-old Rose is recorded as the witness to her cousin Helena Scott's marriage to Edward Forde — Helena was 32. The norms of young womanhood in Scott's social location involved living with parents, and easing their domestic burdens, well into the twenties. In this framework, the courting that might take place was closely supervised by the family. Depending on the number of other siblings, it might not be surprising to find that such family patterns permitted parents to depend upon their adult children in ways that discouraged or inhibited the pursuit of marriage by the latter.

Experiences of class location and profession might also have worked to discourage early marriage. It is not clear whether Police Magistrate Helenus Scott brought the content of his work home in dinnertime conversation. But Newcastle was a relatively small community, and it would be surprising if the more contentious and scandalous matters that came before his bench were not discussed openly. In the 1860s his papers are striking for the way in which they dramatise the vulnerabilities of women within sexual, if not always marital, relationships in the Newcastle region. Illegitimacy, desertion of spouses, domestic violence, alcoholism, suicide, masters' and servants' disputes, lunacy, vagrancy, sexual assaults, and charges against women for malicious damage to property, often of men, were all matters typically claiming the daily attention of Rose's father.[67] Since women of his own family were involved with the local community, especially through church-based charity, many of the same problems affecting women also entered family discussions through the female line. In view of Rose Scott's later career, such direct access to information about the circumstances of women considerably less fortunate than her female relatives may well have been formative.

Perhaps the most important legacies of the Scott patterns of marriage, and of Rose Scott's experience, as philanthropist and magistrate's daughter, of the problems of the working-class women in the Newcastle area, was her lifelong tendency to see the options of most girls and women in negative terms. So different were the lives of women married at 19 from her own, that Scott probably inevitably saw them as 'other', and as objects for scrutiny. Later, this would lead Scott to utterances, writings and initiatives that offend modern sensibilities. Despite this, it seems clear that as she grew to maturity in Newcastle, town life permitted her to 'see' aspects of the organisation of colonial sexual relations and sex-based power and dependencies that were to form in her an ultimately *feminist* analysis of culture and politics. Even as she came to represent the majority of women's lot as 'other', that 'lot' touched her or caused some point of identification in her that committed her eventually to the struggle for feminist reform. The life of her mother, Saranna's lot, and all that it revealed about the difficulties of women's positions constituted some of that identification. Town, then city life gave it a broader framework.

The fortunes and misfortunes of the Scotts and Rusdens, what they made of life in colonial New South Wales with the qualities and constraints of the English and Scottish ethnicities they embodied, left particular legacies for their colonial-born descendant Rose Scott. Arguably, the failure of the pastoral dream of her gentleman father and uncles, and the relative downward social mobility of her branch of the family, which led to resettlement, altered conjugal patterns and urban life, actually permitted Rose Scott wider options than might otherwise have been the case. She remained 'at home' with her parents during the 1860s, 1870s and 1880s. From the age of 18 onwards, she had many lessons to learn before she would join 'the cause of women'.

Chapter 2

'Home Lessons' (1865–90)

*For women who wish to live a quest plot, as men's stories
allow, indeed encourage them to do, some event must be invented to transform their lives, all unconsciously, apparently accidentally from a conventional to an unconventional story . . . usually
. . . in a woman's late twenties or thirties.*

Carolyn G. Heilbrun, *Writing a Woman's Life*, pp. 48–9

The year 1865 was Rose Scott's eighteenth year. From then until her
twenty-eighth year, the process of deciding the purpose and projects of her
life intensified, while her contact with urban life increased with extended stays
with Melbourne and Sydney relatives. The conflicts between self-
development, the prospects of courtship and marriage, and duties towards
increasingly needy parents, deepened and encroached in ways that confused
and at times depressed her. Her relationship with her elder sister Gussie was
to be critical in the course of the decades ahead. The sisters were close, Rose
the admiring younger one learning womanhood from the feted elder.
Though in 1864 and 1865 the two managed to be away from home together, staying with Uncle David and sometimes Aunt Augusta, increasingly, only
one would be away, leaving the other to care for Saranna, the younger girls,
and the men of the family. That burden at first fell more on Gussie, who
nevertheless stayed away as long as she could when she had the chance.
In 1867 she wrote to Rose, who was staying in Melbourne with her Rusden
aunts and uncles. She described the daily round of family activities — riding,
going to church, walking, evening reading, and visiting with women friends
of the family, amidst regular preparations of hot beverages for Uncle Arthur
Selwyn and their father. Gussie informed her younger sister that her harsh
judgement of a would-be suitor was unfounded: 'do you know he isn't half
as ugly as you made him out to be; his profile is really ugly but his full face
when he smiles isn't a bit ugly . . . He said he'd seen you in Melbourne.'

Other news included the arrival of the *English Woman* magazine, from
which Gussie had copied two dress patterns; and the information 'that

Emmie Parnell was married the other day to Alex McKenzie!' Gussie reported that the whole family had gone to the Stokes' household, where the large group assembled sang comic songs, 'then we had dancing. I had two splendid waltzes with Mr Stokes. Of course, there were all sorts of enquiries after you and when you were coming home. Everyone joins in thinking it is quite time you did so.'[1] Both young women were engaged in various forms of courtship, but by 1867 Rose was probably amidst her first serious encounter with romantic love. The fact that she chose as a love object a man who was, for a variety of reasons, inaccessible or unavailable to her, and maintained her focus upon him across the period in which women of her class secured fiancés and ultimately husbands, merits careful consideration. It was a relationship that had consequences for Rose's subsequent life.

In 1872, Gussie, aged 29, married the son of Robert Barclay Wallace, a prominent Newcastle shipping manufacturer and merchant.[2] Her husband, Edward Hope Wallace (known as 'Hope'), worked for Edward Merewether in Newcastle. This marriage left Rose as the eldest daughter at home and the person on whom everyone in the family increasingly depended. In the 1870s courtship of the younger Scott girls, Millie and Alice, under family supervision, was a feature of life in the Scott household. Alice married Terrick Alfred Hamilton, also an employee of Edward Merewether, in 1878 when they were both aged 26; while in 1880, 31-year-old Millie married the 50-year-old widower, Edward Bowyer Shaw, an Anglican Canon posted in Singleton.

By the time of this latter marriage, the family was embroiled in another series of crises and transformations. Rose, now in her thirty-second year, nursed her frail 77-year-old father until his death in April 1879. But another loss promptly dealt Rose a serious blow: her beloved Gussie died of typhoid fever in 1880. One consequence of these events was the adoption of Gussie and Hope Wallace's son, Nene, into Rose's household. Another was that Saranna, Nene, his father, Hope Wallace, and Rose moved to the eastern suburbs of Sydney later in 1880. The possibilities and significance of this move for Rose were enormous. One decade later, at 43, she was a public figure committed to 'the cause of women', about to become the foundation secretary of the Womanhood Suffrage League of New South Wales. But Scott's emergence as a public figure concerned with women's issues was not only a product of familial chance, but was also conditioned by her response to other significant events and choices that faced colonial women.

LOVING COUSINS

By the mid-1860s Scott included among her suitors a number of soon-to-be-prominent men of the professions, business and public office, including Ernest Docker, a future New South Wales judge. These relationships were overshadowed, however, by the complexities of the one she conducted with her cousin, David Scott Mitchell, the antiquarian who bequeathed the collection that became the Mitchell Library in Sydney.[3] There are few sources of information about the relations between these cousins apart from a handful of letters from Scott Mitchell to Scott between 1865 and 1875, and some poems, watercolour art and relics connected with Scott in Scott Mitchell's papers. None of Scott's letters to him survive and she did not refer to him in letters to others. Yet there are grounds for believing that he was one of her most enduring attachments and an important influence on the course of her life.

Scott Mitchell remains an enigmatic figure. The one well-known photographic portrait of him as a young man was obtained by the State Library from his cousin, Rose Scott. Commentators on Scott Mitchell's life note that Scott's photograph showed him to be a handsome, vigorous, athletic-looking young man with a characteristic thick curly beard of glossy black hair. The archetypal 'man about town', he was an eminently eligible young bachelor, beloved of hostesses, the life of the party. A keen cricketer and sportsman, he was also a renowned expert at the popular card game whist. He was among the first graduates of the University of Sydney in 1854, a contemporary of William Charles Windeyer, future New South Wales Supreme Court judge and husband of woman suffragist and social reformer Mary Elizabeth Windeyer (née Bolton).[4] Although trained in law, Scott Mitchell was reluctant to pursue a full-time career in this profession. His post-graduate years were spent in leisurely reading, entertainment, family duties, and the beginnings of book and manuscript collection. His father, Dr James Mitchell, kept tight control of the family finances; his son was not exactly independent.

David Scott Mitchell appeared to have a lively interest in women. In 1864, at the age of 28, he became enamoured of Emily Manning, daughter of Sir William Manning, the future vice chancellor of the University of Sydney. Their romance developed during 1864, with the quaint charm of a Victorian soap opera, replete with misunderstanding, uncertainty, jealousy and temporary estrangements. Two poems document one of their misunderstandings, which took place at a Sydney Yacht Club Ball on 18 October 1864. The first, written by Emily Manning and dated 22 October, dedicated to D. Mitchell, rebukes him for faithlessness in dancing with another woman, then for proceeding to get drunk. The second, dedicated to her by Scott Mitchell in November 1864, counters charges that his drinking was caused by seeing her dancing with another man — a naval officer — 'His coat of blue and buttons gold'.[5]

Early in 1865, Scott Mitchell wrote to Rose, thanking her for congratulations upon news of his engagement to Emily Manning:

> It is some more than three weeks since I became that queer beast
> an engaged man and even yet I can scarcely realise the promotion.
> I think you know very little of the young woman who is to make

me miserable but I hope you will find that she is not altogether
detestable. It will be a long engagement as I have to make up for a
good many ill years but the time will tell more on me than her as
I am twenty-nine and she is not yet twenty. I shall very likely see
you soon as I think that I shall be down at the Ridge in about a fortnight and then we can talk which is more satisfying than writing.

He concluded the letter by thanking her for the present of a bookmark on
his birthday (6 April):

It was very pretty and I shall stick to it forever and a day,
Your loving cousin,
David

PS. Write soon, there's a dear girl.

Rose visited him in Sydney in May 1865, and then in June he and Emily
Manning visited Newcastle. Afterwards, he wrote to Rose:

Emily is flourishing and sends her love. She took a great fancy to
you which speaks volumes for your fascination for I told her all sorts
of bad things of you but they seem to have had no effect. Write soon
and tell me all the little games you have been up to, to whom you
have dared write, talked to, flirted with, but I forgot, you *never* do
that . . . Goodbye dearest Rose ever your loving cousin,
David

Their correspondence and his visits, some with his fiancée, continued. His
letters were full of gossip — who was engaged to whom and many contained
apologies for the way social engagements delayed their correspondence.
The tone of his letters to her was often playful and teasing. In October 1865
he wrote: 'Abuse me to your heart's content: I deserve it and then when
you have exhausted all your venom there is some chance of your revert-
ing to your natural, angelic sweetness of temperament and bestowing upon
me full and free forgiveness.'[6]

He also discussed books with her, recommending authors she should
read. His social routine seemed to continue, despite his engagement,
which proved to be long indeed. In 1866 he wrote a poem called 'To My Pipe'.
In it he bemoaned the troubles that accompanied the relations of love and
friendship, concluding that the only reliable companion was his pipe,
Scott Mitchell's constant companion. The final verses read:

I tenderly fill her spacious bowl
Rimful of the fragrant weed
The smile that lights her honest black face
Brings comfort to my need.

And one may sing of his lady love
And one may sing of his trusty friend

But I will sing of the only one
Who is faithful to the end.[7]

This hardly seems the poem of a man eagerly anticipating matrimony. His visits to the Scott's continued, sometimes with, but more often without, Miss Manning. On a visit in November 1867, he, Scott and someone else (perhaps Gussie Scott or Emily Manning) took shelter from a storm in a cliff-face cave by the sea. The three entered and all lay on the cave floor together. Afterwards Scott Mitchell and Scott exchanged poems — his called 'The Grave of the Three Hearts' hers, 'The Cave of the Three Hearts'. He wrote 'I liked your "Cave of Three Hearts" very much . . . I was surprized not to find it a jovial turn as you complained of mine being melancholy. Have you been back to our cave yet?'[8]

Among Scott Mitchell's papers is an exercise book filled with watercolour pictures by an unidentified artist. The book is entitled *Mutum est Pictura Poema* and dated 19 March 1868. The title-page reads: 'Original High Art Kindly Composed For and Dedicated to DSM, BA. for the edification and special enlightenment of his mind during his sojourn in Tartarius by pitying beings in Elysium.' It consists of forty images. Almost half of them feature a cartoon-like representation of a bearded man with a pipe, often also with a book in hand; and in most cases he is engaged in some kind of scene with a woman with light brown ringletted hair. She appears in a rose-coloured dress in some of the pictures; in others a rose is lying in the foreground.

There is a sequence to the images. Most of them centre on a family composed primarily of girls, their balding grey-haired father, their lace-capped, dark-dressed mother, and various visitors and relatives. Activities dominated by the bearded hero and ringletted heroine in these illustrations include croquet games, balls, parlour singing, hunting parties, fancy-dress parties, card games with her parents, cricket games, and various romantic encounters between them in fields, gardens, on a balcony, and in other domestic spaces. Other images in the collection show women and girls of the family in a drapery shop, apparently buying dress materials, and also other community residents, including working-class women and children.

A new character enters halfway through the narrative established by the sequence of images. She is a rather delicate, black-haired woman, depicted in red or other bright colours. In one illustration, the bearded hero gives her flowers. A succeeding image shows her chased out of a field by a bull. Her face also appears at the end of an array of women's faces drawn in an image called 'The Dream'. This image depicts the bearded man lying on the ground in a field asleep, with a book and pipe beside him. Seven distinct women's faces loom in the sky above him, the light-brown-haired woman in the centre of them, the black-haired woman at the extreme far left. Brushed in miniature sepia in the back-ground of 'The Dream' is a series of images that culminates in the wedding of the beard-ed man and the light-brown-haired woman.

The wedding outcome is the final image in the book, executed in full colour. The minister performing the ceremony bears a remarkable resemb-lance to the figure in the card game, and in other images, who is the father of the family of girls. Three previous images of him are worth comment. One shows him apparently swimming in a river, staring in dismay as dogs on the bank tear his trousers to pieces, while in the background a hunt-ing party involving the bearded man is in progress. Another shows him lean-ing out of a lower-storey window, cutting a rope ladder being climbed by the bearded man, leading to the window of the light-brown-haired woman. And, in the earliest image of him, he is frowning at the sight of a naval officer giving the light-brown-haired woman flowers.[9]

Although the artist is unidentified, it may be reasonable to speculate that it was Scott. Executed shortly after the cave incident in late 1867, it may sig-nal that some acknowledgement of the attraction and attachment between Scott Mitchell and Scott had taken place, or else it may itself have been the expression of such an acknowledgement. To make such expression in this form might be taken by the late-twentieth-century viewer and read-er as embarrassing and excessive self-disclosure. Yet, if the artist was Scott, it may be well to recall that in 1868 drawing and painting were the only accessible means of visualising wishes, hopes, infatuations and passions, while poetry, diaries and to a lesser extent, letters, put them into language. Rose Scott was 20 at the time. Among the family duties of women of her age was general preparation for marriage, a task that could be fraught with frus-tration, intensity and ambiguity. Presuming that cousin David received the book in early 1868, from 'the pitying beings of Elysium', his further letters to Scott were playful and most interested in her social life. In May he replied to a recent letter from her: 'Dissipation indeed! A concert, two balls and Ernest Docker to read to you! Have you been able to settle down to everyday life?'.[10]

Scott's family duties constrained her pursuit of contact with Scott Mitchell, but perhaps also her elders acted with an eye to decorum in view of his engagement to Emily Manning. Scott's Aunt Grace wrote to Saranna that she was:

> very sorry you have had so much trouble in various ways — no one can regret Rosie's temporary disappointment; she will enjoy her trip the more when the time comes, which I trust it will. Tell her I envy her her usefulness which makes her presence so desirable in two or three places at once.[11]

But what had happened to David Scott Mitchell and Emily Manning during the long engagement? It is possible that she is the black-haired woman in the picture-book from the pitying beings, seen at various points in visits to the family of girls, generally in the company of the bearded hero with book and pipe. Emily Manning was nearly two years Scott's senior, born in 1845. A great-niece who never met her believed that her grandmother recalled that Emily was a tiny and delicate woman only four feet ten inches tall.[12] If the black-haired visitor to the family in the picture-book is she, then the scene of the bull chasing her out of the paddock, in particular, but also the general way she appears, may suggest a certain hostility on the part of the artist(s).

The engagement did not survive the crisis years beginning with the death of Dr James Mitchell in February 1869. In the first place, David Scott Mitchell was greatly distressed at the loss of his father. This was compounded by the scandal that erupted when the legality of his father's will was contested in May 1869 by his mother and uncle, Helenus Scott. In a challenge that took twelve full days of Equity Court hearings, 'certain private matters received sensational publicity which certainly gave great pain to the sensitive soul of David now a young man of 33 and hurt his family pride'. In 1849, Scott's aunt and Scott Mitchell's mother, Augusta, had been named executor of Dr Mitchell's will, along with her brother, Helenus Scott. Upon the death of Dr James Mitchell it was discovered that a new will had been signed on 5 January 1869 making a German business partner of Mitchell's, William Ernest Wolfskehl, the executor and significant beneficiary of considerable real property. Helenus Scott and Mrs Mitchell contested the validity of the new will in May 1869 before Justice Hargrave in the New South Wales Supreme Court in Equity. The Attorney General, Sir William Manning, father of Emily Manning and ostensibly future father-in-law of David Scott Mitchell, represented Wolfskehl, against Helenus Scott and his family — perhaps motivated by a long-held grudge at Scott's withholding of political support upon Manning's appointment as Solicitor General two decades earlier.[13]

This did not augur well for the projected marriage. It may indicate that by 1869 Manning no longer believed or wished that the union would take place, though a few months before he had written to Dr Mitchell expressing the view that it was high time the wedding eventuated. Another possibility is that, informally, David Scott Mitchell had dishonoured the commitment to Emily by 1868. Scott's relative, Sir John Young, saw Emily in September 1869 in London and he wrote to Mrs Mitchell that she was 'looking quite fit and handsome. David might do worse than marry her yet'.[14] Had the romance declined and Emily Manning's father packed her off to London, in view of his decision to accept the brief for Wolfskehl against the Mitchell and Scott families, to avoid possible embarrassment to her?

The case turned on the soundness or otherwise of Dr Mitchell's mind at the time that the second will was made. Another significant development was that Dr Joseph Docker, a relative of Rose Scott's suitor, Ernest Docker, testified against the family to the effect that Mitchell had been of sound mind.[15] The machinations became ugly, and the costs huge, especially since all assets were encumbered. Edward Merewether and Scott Mitchell were in almost daily correspondence over the management of the case in April and May 1869. On 7 April, David reported that 'The carriage and horses were sold today and brought £118', which was put towards legal fees incurred by engaging Sir James Martin, QC, to prosecute the challenge to the will. Eventually, their solicitor advertised their need for a loan in order to proceed. Scott Mitchell also reported news of D.C.F. Scott, Sydney police magistrate and realtor: 'my respected Uncle David may buy Orwell, Wolfskehl's property. It would be decidedly quaint if his money were to supply Wolf with the means of carrying on the war'.[16]

Eventually the decision was in favour of the appellants, Scott Mitchell and Helenus Scott. Bureaucratic obstacles placed before them thereafter, which may have originated with the defeated Attorney General, Sir William Manning, delayed the settlement of the property for a further three years, when a partial division was formulated. Not until 1874 was a legal partitioning of the estate finally achieved. It was divided among Margaret Scott Mitchell, by then Quigley (she married the solicitor William Bell Quigley), David Scott Mitchell and Edward Merewether, who was named heir instead of his wife Augusta. Although David Scott Mitchell's share eventually included Newcastle and Hunter Valley lands, including the coal-rich Rothbury Estate and parts of the Burwood Estate (investments from which ultimately funded the Mitchell Library collection), these were difficult years for him.

David Scott Mitchell's dearly loved mother died in the wake of this tragedy and scandal in 1871. At this point the conventional accounts of his life report that he retired from public life to become a recluse. Thereafter he ventured outside his Sydney house only to inspect books and manuscripts in pursuit of his antiquarian interests. Later, Bertram Stevens, writer and literary critic, described his life as 'blasted midway . . . I have heard D.S. Mitchell referred to as an eccentric and cynical old man'. In 1922 the state librarian, H.C.L. Anderson, recalled meeting him in 1895, his face looking 'old beyond his years, apparently disappointed with life without any pleasant recollections, no pleasures of anticipation, obsessed with only one hobby'.[17]

Was it only his family affairs that produced this outcome and was his identity as a recluse established by 1871 as the accounts claim? Certainly he was in mourning for his father and withdrawn from social life in 1869. In August that year he wrote lovingly to Rose Scott, noting that 'it is more than 8 months since we have met'. Yet he was soon writing his playful and affectionate letters to her again. He expressed also his gratitude for her support during this difficult period. They discussed the merits of Thomas Carlyle's historical works. Perhaps to attract his attention to her own romantic eligibility and desirability, she evidently wrote in 1870 asking his advice on the handling of an amorous suitor. His reply was open to interesting interpretation on the part of his cousin Rose, considering that *he* was conducting a correspondence with her, even though he was engaged to be married to someone else. Early in 1870 he offered the advice that:

> if you are not sure that liking may not some day glide into love, I can see no harm in your acceding to his request. But if you are certain that you can never care for him as he wishes do not dream of the correspondence. It would be a mistaken kindness to him as it would keep your image more constantly before him and, which is of far more consequence, it would be a wrong to yourself as not being a nice or delicate thing to do.[18]

The implication of the presence of other suitors in Scott's circle was apparent in later letters in 1870. In one Scott Mitchell asked 'Have you been following up your new profession of dancing mistress and which is your favourite pupil?'[19] Scott by this time was 23, and cousin David 34. His surviving letters to Scott are few, and it is difficult to map his activities in the years from 1871 to 1874. Bertram Stevens later reported that in the 1870s Scott Mitchell was offered the position of Attorney General, which he declined.[20]

In 1873 Emily Manning married Henry Heron, a solicitor. Her family's version of events was that Emily 'jilted' Scott Mitchell 'because Mitchell was only interested in books'. Her great-niece, having seen only later photographs of Mitchell, concluded he had not been a robust man, and always 'bookish'. Heron, by contrast, was a big, robust, handsome figure of a man who would, in her view, have been much more attractive to her great-aunt.

Emily Heron bore six sons and one daughter and also had a career as a journalist, writing under the pen-name 'Australie'. According to the great-niece, her husband was caught in 1890 embezzling from clients. Rather than face the public scandal of criminal proceedings, she claims that Sir William Manning used his influence to have Heron certified insane and incarcerated. Shortly after his committal, Emily died from pneumonia at the age of 45. Apparently, for reasons her great-niece never understood, the Heron family had financial expectations of David Scott Mitchell. He paid for the education of the eldest daughter, Helen, and the eldest son, Fred.

It remains uncertain whether Emily Manning's marriage was rejection or relief for Scott Mitchell. If he put his interest in books ahead of her, as claimed, the marriage to Heron may have been a case of constructive desertion. If so, the scandal over Dr James Mitchell's will and Scott Mitchell's relative impoverishment, offered ready justification for breaking the engagement. A version of the story appeared in the *Sydney Morning Herald* in March 1966, under the headline 'A Broken Heart Gave Us History':

> Somewhere in Sydney there should be a statue of Miss Emily
> Manning with an inscription gratefully commending her refusal
> about 100 years ago to accept the hand of a scholarly young man
> named David Scott Mitchell. For, crossed in love, Mitchell began
> collecting books, manuscripts, maps, prints and pictures for the rest
> of his life.[21]

Scott Mitchell was hardly a recluse in the period after her marriage,
judging from his letters on doings in Sydney. Rose Scott evidently teased
him about his propensity for gossip. He wrote to her in March 1875
reporting on an exchange at a social gathering: 'By the bye Mrs Barry asked
me if I had heard that you were engaged and when I said no she said she
had heard so. There's a bit of gossip about yourself as I cannot give you any
about other people'. Perhaps Scott was being seriously courted by some
unnamed man at the time, possibly the future Mr Justice Rolin, hence the
rumour. It is also conceivable that the continuing association between these
loving cousins had caused speculation for some time since Emily Manning's
marriage and that interested friends were seeking to divine the intentions
of the nearly 40-year-old bachelor by suggesting that Rose Scott might marry
another.

The cousins continued to visit and write, until a painful impasse
was reached in June–July 1875. The now 27-year-old Scott had come to
Sydney to visit Scott Mitchell. Evidently he suspended his usual activities
to be with her and escort her to social and cultural events. Her Sydney relatives interfered, approaching her and her parents, generating misunderstanding, accusations and emotional distress. The only evidence
that remains of this affair are his letters to her, leaving no reliable clues as
to *her* conduct and perceptions of it. The first letter is undated but was probably written in late June shortly after Scott's return to Newcastle. It is worth
quoting at length for several reasons, including the illumination of the difficulties of Victorian heterosocial relationships, especially the almost over-
wrought reading to which all exchanges were prone.

> My dear Rose,
>
> I have received pain from nearly every quarter that it could pos-
> sibly come from — now at last from one which I expected it
> least. To be accused of being untruthful and dishonest and by you
> . . . The only thing I see clearly is how little you can have cared for
> me. I do not in the least understand your letter or what prompted
> you to write it, so I will simply say that I am not conscious of any
> word or act of mine that has been untrue . . .
>
> 26th
>
> So far I had written and meant to send you in a day or two. I have
> since received your letter and am glad to see by it that the pain I had
> seemed to give you is passing away and even if you had not
> asked it I forgave you what you have caused me. And now I

should very much like to hear what Rolin wrote and all that
took place in your talk with your mother if it does not worry you
too much to tell.

Evidently she complied with his request; but this was not the end of it.
Another lengthy letter of 25 July provides some of the missing details of
what happened to produce this situation between them:

It was a mean and cruel thing of uncle David to write such a letter. Certainly I went to his house when you were not there but the
same thing occurred when your sisters were there. As to going for
you I would have offered to do the same for either of them if they
had come to Sydney by themselves. I could do so little for your
amusement I thought at least I might enable you to go where you
wished, which you might have been prevented from doing for want
of a proper escort . . . I regret that it should have induced you to let
your mother believe that there was an understanding between us
. . . And, there is none, none in any worldly or ordinary sense of
the word. I have told you already and I now repeat it that in all
human probability I shall never be able to ask anyone to share my
lot. I have never asked you to trust me, I have never told you I cared
for you, I have never asked you if you cared for me. I have never
intentionally done anything to make you do so . . . I could not understand nor can I now what there is to tell your parents . . . We are
not engaged, you are as free as air. If any other feelings exist it is
for ourselves, in our own breasts; time *may* affect it or it may not
and we are accountable for it to none but God.[22]

This was the last of this series of letters from Scott Mitchell to Scott. Whatever
the immediate consequences, by 1880 Scott Mitchell was again on affectionate terms with Rose Scott and other members of her family. He
offered Saranna legal advice on a Hunter Valley private boys school in which
she had proprietary shares. He received a Christmas card which read 'To
David, with Rose's love'.[23]

In January 1875, prior to the traumatic ending of whatever romantic hopes she had concerning Scott Mitchell, Rose Scott visited Madam Sibly,
Professor of Phrenology. The elders in her family had a keen interest in this
form of analysis and Scott had several readings done during her life
time. Madam Sibly used the 3–7 range method (low to high) and offered
a reading of Scott, annotated by the recipient in various revealing ways.
For instance, she wrote:

This young lady possesses a good deal of evenness in her tem-
peramental conditions but would be improved by rendering her
physical condition rather more robust, wiry and tough so as to bring
her vital temperament near to that of her motive and mental
temperaments.

To this, Rose Scott added 'I don't think *anyone* could be stronger than I
am'. Interestingly, the phrenologist contended that Scott was a 7 in the

orientation toward conjugality, parental love, love of home, secretiveness, emotional continuity, spirituality, but only a low 4 in her capacities for friendship, destructiveness, appetites for food or drink, self-esteem, ideality, love of music and constitutional strength. Madam Sibly ventured that:

> Her love for the opposite sex is very considerable but it is kept in complete subjection to her still higher conjugal affection and power of concentrating her affections on *one* person. As is frequently the case when conjugal and parental love are extremely high, she is low on friendship, so that she will have but few 'bosom friends' nor will she confide much of her inner thoughts to them.

If thwarted in matters of the heart, this young lady would battle 'manfully'. Her religious faith was flawed by a commitment to reason, while 'she is rather reserved, cautious and methodical, even in matters of amusement'. Scott responded to Sibly's remark that 'she would plan and organise a pick-nick [sic]' with '"How are the mighty fallen". This is my vocation in life — Pic-nics!' The final conclusion for Scott's future was that she would be an excellent dressmaker or milliner (to which Scott added 'No I would not, just the contrary') and that 'She will make a judicious housewife, a kind and affectionate mother and the best of wives'.[24] Scott added nothing to this final prognosis.

Although Scott Mitchell became increasingly reclusive from the 1880s, later reminiscences suggest that his relationship with his loving cousin was important in making this possible. Once Scott moved to Sydney after the death of her father in 1879, she mediated between him and the outside world. When he wished to meet public figures, especially writers of Scott's acquaintance, he requested that she bring them to his house. Alternatively, those who wished to meet Scott Mitchell had no direct access, but were screened by Scott. A housekeeper who had been with the Scott Mitchell family for over 40 years cared for David until his death in 1907. Rose Scott was the only guest the household received, apart from visitors approved by her cousin.

One such visitor was Bertram Stevens, who wrote a nineteen-page reminiscence of Scott Mitchell in 1917. Stevens met Scott Mitchell in 1900 on a Saturday afternoon, after an introduction by Rose Scott. By then Scott Mitchell was seriously ill. Since he seldom wanted to see anyone, Stevens was flattered to learn that Scott Mitchell wished to see him again. They talked of books and related matters, leading Stevens to conclude that on most things Scott Mitchell was deeply conservative. Moreover he 'relished a certain amount of skulduggery as most men do and he told me some amount of blue tales that had the saving grace of wit'. He ventured that the various versions of the reason for David Mitchell's bachelorhood and seclusion 'doubtless will become public some day'.

Stevens noted that Scott Mitchell had wished to leave his collection of Australiana to his cousin, Rose, and was only persuaded to leave it to the people of New South Wales as the Mitchell bequest to the State Library when she declined the offer. In his will he left £5000 to Scott, a pension to his housekeeper, and £30 000 to the library for the establishment of the Mitchell Library. Apart from some to charities for women and children of which Scott would have approved, he left no other bequests. He had been ill for a long time prior to his death, for years 'suffering horribly from eczema which covered his face with sores, and he had not even his first love to comfort him' according to the state librarian, H.C.L. Anderson.[25] Whom did he refer to as Scott Mitchell's first love?

Scott's cousin remained an emotional commitment in her life until his death in her sixtieth year. This was an age when married women of her generation could expect to be widows. Thereafter, rather as if she were his widow, Scott administered aspects of his bequests, including the ceremonial elements of the founding of the Mitchell Library.

This attachment influenced the course of Scott's life at a number of levels. If it was not her first, it was evidently her most intense and enduring experience of romantic love for a man. In the highly supervised and chaperoned context of high Victorian middle- and upper-middle-class social life, their relationship probably obtained more space and less supervision than it would had they not been family. Moreover, whatever the degree of the conventional intimacies they experienced, Scott developed with him an intellectual and emotional intimacy unusual for the average regional Australian debutante of the 1860s.

A dimension of their relationship was always pedagogic, most particularly when they were young. The marked intellectual asymmetry between men and women of their class was produced by the practice of publicly and institutionally educating the men, but not the women. This asymmetry was routinely extolled (by opponents of higher education for women) as enhancing the harmony of sexual relations by maximising the natural differences between the sexes, thereby increasing the attraction of opposites.[26] In practice this could mean that a man of intellectual and worldly passions could relate only to like-minded men, while should a woman be similarly disposed she had, in all probability, no like-minded women in her immediate family and social circles. Despite prescriptions, the experience of educated and intellectual men, expected to live intimately with uneducated women, could be alienation, frustration, loneliness and boredom. A collective and conventional masculine response to this dilemma has been misogyny. Individually, however, men resorted to forms of resistance and subversion of their situation. The attempt privately and informally to educate paramours, women relatives and friends was another option, a prevalent enough practice to become, romanticised, even eroticised, in nineteenth-century cultural production.

Scott, deprived of formal educational opportunities, welcomed tutelage and intellectual input from a range of men, relatives and friends, throughout her life. Her uncle, Henry Keylock Rusden, for instance, had no hesitation in evaluating the strengths and weaknesses of the woman suffrage arguments in the 1890s of his now middle-aged niece, referring her to principles of political philosophy, especially democratic and conservative theory relevant to the issue.[27] Unlike educated men, women daring to venture into such terrain were perceived by themselves, as well as others, as open to correction and instruction by the knowledgeable and usually older man.

Since most women of marriageable age in their circle would not have been engaged with intellectual matters, Scott was no doubt an interesting and responsive companion and student for David Scott Mitchell. His real achievements, talents and abilities as an intellectual would have been difficult to deploy in his relations with most women. The David Scott Mitchell who visited Scott was both intense and relaxed during their long walks and absorbing intellectual conversations. Scott had an esteemed place in his universe and affections, which may have been difficult for Scott Mitchell's paramours. He may even have unconsciously used his relationship with Scott to keep others at a distance as well as to fulfil safely some of his own needs, while escaping, or at least forestalling, the demands, duties and commitments of marriage. He certainly did not encourage Scott's marriage to anyone else.

'I shall never be able to ask anyone to share my lot' wrote Scott Mitchell in 1875. We can only speculate on the reasons for his bachelorhood and reclusiveness, but for the purposes of this study of Rose Scott and the development of her feminism, the key issue is the impact of these circumstances on his loving cousin.

The conventional reasons for her attraction to this handsome, eligible bachelor eleven years her senior may be clear, but he offered her more than other suitors. He gave her access to a world she was denied on the basis of sex. She learned to share his fascination for books and ideas, for collecting manuscripts, letters and objects. Indeed, her voluminous papers in the Mitchell Library are the tangible outcome. Of course, she read nothing in the same way that a man like Scott Mitchell could. For the more she knew, the more she understood the enormity of the cultural disenfranchisement of her sex. Meanwhile in the 1860s and 1870s, his intellectual companionship and the development he offered were incomparable gifts, shaping the critique of conventional sexual relations that was the foundation of her public career after 1890. The paradox was that he taught her what men were — 'the animal in man' as she called it — while subverting conventional manliness in his life choices and in his intellectual relationship with her. Her lifelong ideal of the sexes enjoying friendship was realised early in her life.

The contrast between this relationship and others available to Scott must have been extreme. Since other men of her acquaintance could not or would not offer her the qualities Scott Mitchell did, she could not countenance marriage with those who proposed. The relationship with Scott Mitchell unfitted her for conventional marriage to the men of her class, circle and generation. Her expectations had been raised. Yet within existing terms of sexual options they could not finally be met.

Scott Mitchell chose not to combine intellectual and sexual relationships. The possibility of women being intellectuals was, if not unknown, then unlikely, so that few men ever faced the combination as an issue. But Scott Mitchell had put years into forming Rose Scott as an intellectual companion. His investment was less a matter of challenging existing definitions of woman than of making *this* woman more like a man, more intellectually accomplished than her sex predicted, so that he could have an intellectual relationship with her. He could not do this if she followed the conventional path towards marriage and maternity. Ironically, then, his respect and affection for her prevented him from embracing a sexual relationship with her. For, in the context, this meant marriage, probably more than six children, and a life of hard work in the care of others — the end of her intellectual development. He could not wish this for her, nor could he wish himself to be the husband and executor of such an outcome. These sentiments were not nascent feminism on his part, for his general views of women were typically manly, worldly and conservative. He declined her evident romantic interest in him in 1875 in affection, not rejection. It was a decision to choose bachelorhood — the only state that would preserve their existing relationship. Whatever the other secret factors involved, by not marrying anyone else he remained emotionally and intellectually available to her.

Scott was undoubtedly disappointed, if not humiliated, by this outcome in 1875. It was painful to have to recognise that even this exceptional man could not or would not combine the intellectual and sexual in a single relationship. Marriage did, after all, have to be confined to 'the animal'. This would no longer have been possible for her, since it seems that in her love for Scott Mitchell, intellectual, emotional and sexual desires were fused and inter-dependent. This was a long-term impetus for her efforts to challenge the nature of heterosexual love relations and constrained definitions of womanhood and manhood. In the short term, however, she was forced to choose. It would have been a most unusual husband who would have tolerated the presumably platonic, but intense, relationship between his wife and her bachelor cousin.

In refusing her other suitors, Scott chose spinsterhood, and a completely different life from that imagined for her by her parents, or that destined by colonial demographic probabilities. Her choice was not related to a particular moment or event; rather, it can only be identified as a 'choice' in retrospect, even if not by Scott herself. However, remaining unmarried allowed the cousins to continue their friendship, and that friendship entered a new phase in 1879 when Rose Scott relocated herself in Sydney.

In the period of Scott's realisation that she and Scott Mitchell would never marry, her three sisters married. Gussie's marriage to Hope Wallace in 1872 left Rose the eldest at home, and much more responsible for household, parents and siblings. There is little indication of her opinion of her first brother-in-law, though decades later Annie Rose Scott Cowen described him as a pompous and ineffectual man.[28] Hope and Gussie Wallace quickly became part of the Merewethers' social set; then Edward Merewether helped Wallace obtain a position with the Bank of New South Wales in Sydney. Merewether regularly wrote to Robert Scott, Rose's brother, who was employed as his Newcastle agent, once the Merewethers resumed residence in Sydney in the later 1870s. Often there was news of Gussie in these letters. Rose Scott must have greatly missed her older sister, and Merewether noted her visits and stays in Sydney with the Wallaces in the late 1870s.[29] No doubt she managed a visit in 1878 when their only son Nene was born.

The other event of 1878 was the wedding of 26-year-old Alice to Terrick Alfred Hamilton, a new arrival in New South Wales, and a descendant of the English aristocratic family. Employed first as a property worker, then as an agent supervising several of Merewether's property holdings, it was through his employer that he met Alice, who was visiting her first cousin, Augusta Merewether, in 1876. The courtship was complicated, in part by distances imposed by Terrick's employment, and in part because of the difficulties he had in gaining his father's acceptance of his desire to enter into a colonial marriage and ensuring sufficient family financial assistance to establish a landholding of his own. Merewether, by then aged 56, did much to intercede for this employee, whom he treated as a son. The outcome was Terrick Hamilton senior signing over a property investment — the Tambo station, a large property on the Barcoo River in western Queensland — to his son. The wedding took place on 20 February 1878, in Christ Church Cathedral, Newcastle. The couple were married by Scott's uncle, the future Dean of Newcastle, Arthur Edward Selwyn. Scott and Edward Merewether were the witnesses.

In all of these family developments, including the courtship of her other sister Millie, Scott had become household manager. By 1878, her father's health had completely broken down, ending his career as police magistrate. The absorbing and demanding task of nursing him until his death in April 1879 may to some degree have forestalled reflection as she approached her thirty-second birthday. But the death of Helenus Scott began a period of change that set Scott the Sydney feminist reformer on course.

PASSAGES

Rose Scott and her mother appear to have decided to move to Sydney and establish a household there at least by mid-1879, if not before. It is not clear whether Millie had intended to be part of this move, or whether she was already engaged to the man who would become her husband, the widower Canon Bowyer Edward Shaw of Singleton.

For Saranna, a major rationale for the relocation was proximity to Augusta, and to the first grandchild of this branch of the family in New South Wales. As well, the Merewethers and Mitchells all now lived in Sydney, as did many of the families who had been close to the Scotts during their twenty years in Newcastle. In fact, Newcastle retained few of the ties that had made it a significant home town to the Scott siblings as adolescents and young adults.

The death of Gussie Wallace within a year of Helenus Scott's demise was a devastating blow to Scott and her mother. It also provided a sense of urgency for the move to Sydney. Saranna leased a house and the process of moving began. Amidst this upheaval, Millie Scott and Bowyer Shaw married at Christ Church Cathedral on 8 June 1880, with Scott again acting as the witness.[30] The home in Newcastle remained in the family for a time, with George and Robert Scott as its inhabitants. By the end of 1880, the new Scott household consisted of Saranna, now aged 70, a housekeeper, Gussie's son, Nene Scott Wallace, now aged 2, and Hope Wallace, Nene's father and Gussie's widower, aged 41. Scott 'kept house' for Hope until his death twenty-one years later and, more intermittently, for Nene, until her own death in 1925.

If all this was not enough by way of domestic obligations, Scott's Woollahra home became the Sydney base for other members of the family. Alice came to be cared for by Rose in her confinements, and often brought her children for breaks from the immense difficulties that were to punctuate her married life on the land, in the hot arid west of central Queensland. Indeed, aspects of her married life resembled Saranna's first decades of marriage at Glendon, although the Hamilton establishment was clearly less prosperous. Millie also came to stay, often for quite long periods, during the 1880s and 1890s.

Little of Scott's surviving correspondence or papers relate to the first years of her new life in Sydney — perhaps a testament to her full absorption in family duties. Glimpses of her life and that of her siblings emerge in letters sent by Edward Merewether to her brother, Robert. Though clearly fond of her, he perhaps found her a puzzling relative. On 7 May 1881, he reported the following incident to Robert Scott:

> We met Rose on Tuesday just at the turn off to Darling Point and she greeted us with 'I was going to swear at you for hiring the cab I wanted to take mother out for a drive' which I thought was rather strong language for the niece and pupil of the Revd — but she appeared ashamed and I trust therefore that the language she thought of using was not the result of habit.

Merewether hired a billiard table at his new family home at Trelawney Street, Woollahra, and Hope Wallace came almost nightly to play.[31] In June,

Alice came down from Queensland seven months' pregnant and with a sick son, to stay with Rose and Saranna. Shortly after, the family received news of the death in Brisbane of Scott's eldest brother, Helenus, at only 43, leaving a widow, Emily, and two small children.[32] Merewether remarked: 'You have had great trouble in your family in that way during the last two years and I fear that it is not yet over.' Within a few weeks, Alice was suddenly confined while visiting with the Merewethers. Merewether was sent out to fetch the nurse, but since the baby had not been expected for another month, her midwife was in attendance at another confinement in a distant suburb. This was Alice's third confinement since her marriage in February 1878, and apart from the drama involved in securing someone to come in 'the small hours', Merewether observed that:

> It was fortunate for your mother and Rose that Alice's trouble came on her here as their pretty housemaid was and still is very ill with dysentery and Rose had her hands full in attending to her . . . Rose was in a great state of excitement about the nurse and I believe told the cabman who took her out in search of one that she must find one or *die* in the attempt . . . incomprehensible to the male intellect.

In September, the burdens on Scott of her sick sister, mother, housemaid, new-born infant, and Alice's elder boy, Eddie, who had been diagnosed as dangerously ill, continued. Merewether noted that 'Poor Rose is backward and forward a good deal and must have a hard time of it'. As if to repeat her mother's earlier coping strategies, Scott arranged to stay with her sister, Millie, and her husband at Singleton for a break at the end of October. Merewether arranged to 'look after her and get her a slap of rum and milk upon our arrival at Newcastle'. There are some indications that her health broke down under the strain, and that she spent some time away.

A further strain was occasioned in June 1882 by some scandal involving Alice's husband, Terrick, which proved of great concern to Scott. Unfortunately, Merewether's rather eliptical letter to Robert is the only extant source on the matter: 'I should not be surprised if the yarn were in a measure true as I could not avoid the conclusion from what I saw myself and Allie let drop that his relations with the female were very questionable to say the least'. The matter continued and involved meetings between the women of the family. A few days later, Merewether reported to Robert:

> I have heard little more except that TAH only remained in Sydney a few days and then returned to Brisbane. You will also have heard from Millie Shaw that he has returned to the Station. Canon A.S. meddles as usual and will probably have done mischief . . . *we* do not believe that T. could be such a fool as to do what was reported but . . . I cannot help thinking that something is wrong in connection with that ill fated b . . . h.

Scott took the view that her brother Robert 'ought to interfere', but Merewether discouraged this course since Alice had made no such request. Evidently Rose and Merewether disagreed over her uncle, Arthur Selwyn. Merewether believed him a lying, rude, meddling parson. Upon hearing the rumour he would be made an Anglican Dean, he quipped 'the higher the positions rise in the ecclesiastical scale, the worse men become'. In February 1883 he was relieved that Rose cancelled a Newcastle visit to the Selwyns because of stormy seas: 'She is a good creature in all respects save her admiration and regard for the Canon and I should be very sorry if she came to grief by drowning or in any other way'. A few months later, he encountered her at the rooms of Dr Bowker, the Scott family physician, waiting to collect some 'physic' for a family friend, and 'yarned to her for half an hour'. A medical matter in connection with Terrick Hamilton soon came to their attention via Robert Scott:

> I have not before heard that Mr Hamilton was suffering from the complaint that you speak of but I always thought that his ailments were not wholly due to gout. I want to write to Alice and if I can manage it I will this week and mention the rumour without saying where it came from.[33]

Whatever the circumstances alluded to here, Alice's trips to Sydney became fewer after her confinements of the early 1880s. Her daughter Annie Rose Scott Cowen's reminiscences of first visiting her aunt Rose relate to the 1890s, probably when Alice was confined with her last baby in 1890, and after.[34] The Hamilton family lived in frugal and often difficult circumstances on the Tambo station and, even with the assistance of servants, the burden of domestic work generated by the mainly male workers on the property and the six children under 11 years of age took its toll on Alice. Until the children were older, her contact with her Sydney family was of necessity intermittent.

Saranna, resigned to less contact with her youngest daughters, at least clearly enjoyed the closer contact with the Merewethers that living in Sydney permitted. In 1882 she wrote to her brother-in-law, Patrick Scott, about them: 'The Merewethers are well . . . I must tell you what a very nice good girl their eldest daughter Augusta is. She is not pretty but everyone is charmed with her simple, natural, bright and affectionate dispositions. She reminds me a good deal of your sister her grandmother'. This account by Saranna of young Augusta Merewether was almost immediately contrasted with another of Annie Rose Scott Hamilton (later Cowen), Alice's eldest girl:

> a bright, pretty child everyone praises her beauty except Grandmama who is much too wise for that, for these dear little creatures soon find out and take advantage of personal praise and uncle Robert says of her that she is already a finished coquette. Alas, and she is not 3 years old yet.[35]

Evidently, the move of Saranna and Rose Scott to Sydney in 1880 had its impact upon Robert and George Scott, the remaining bachelors in the immediate family. George soon pursued his father's career as police magistrate, with a posting to Tumut, New South Wales, in 1881. That left only Robert, the eldest brother there and man of the family, in Newcastle. At times like Christmas, Robert as often went not to the Sydney family, but to Singleton to Millie and Bowyer Shaw. Merewether wrote to him in 1885 asking was he to be the best man at the Darleys' wedding. Then only a month later he learned that Robert was to be married, news which, he wrote, 'I must confess took me completely by surprize as I had not the slightest conception that you had any leanings towards matrimony'.[36] It was his sister Millie to whom Robert first wrote and told of his young bride-to-be: he was 44 and she 29. Harriett Aimée Ranclaud was the daughter of Anna Biddulph and Charles Boscowen Ranclaud, the Commissioner of Crown Lands, based in Newcastle. It seems that she was a deeply religious woman worried by her fiancé's general irreverence (which he shared with Merewether, his employer and friend). She wrote promptly to Scott, nine years her senior, confiding her agenda:

> Rose I feel sure that he will be very happy. I mean to try and make him so for he is a very good fellow. I know you will be glad to hear he has been to church with me the last two Sundays and has promised to go with me *always* but you must not speak of this to anyone but your mother . . . Yes I think Alice will be glad for she told me once she would like me for a sister.[37]

There is a hint of defensiveness in Aimée's address to her future sister-in-law, while Merewether asked of Robert: 'What will your mother and Rose say or have they been in on the secret?' The wedding took place on 1 June 1885. A further wedding on 19 June 1885 bound the Scotts and the Ranclauds more closely together: Scott's friend Isabel Bowker, daughter and sister of two generations of doctors who cared for the Scotts, married Jack Ranclaud, Aimée's older brother.[38]

Merewether, now aged 65, was pleased at all these marriages. As a wedding present to Robert and Aimée he paid for the refurbishing and renovation of the house that would become their marital home. Aimée was soon pregnant and 'out of sorts', and delivered of a girl, Aimée, in June 1886. Merewether, apt to the gruff jocularity that described weddings as 'the trouble' taking place, sent his congratulations with the rider that 'it would have been a greater success if the sex had been different'. He employed his eldest son, Ted Merewether, in the Newcastle office, who boarded with Robert and Aimée during this period. Ted reported that the baby was small 'but can yell like a much bigger one', and Aimée had problems nursing her.

Scott complained to Merewether that the Sydney household 'never heard' from Robert and Aimée, probably little realising the hardship they were confronting. The baby continued to be ill, and finally Merewether, who took an active interest in childbearing and rearing, organised the services of a wet-nurse in December 1885:

> We were told two months ago that your little girl was being starved and I think your various medicos ought to have seen it — the opinion however being expressed by women, mothers of families was sufficient in itself to lead to it being scoffed at. I hope the employment of a wetnurse is not too late.

It was. The baby died within days. Merewether tried to have the grief-stricken Aimée stay with them for a rest. She also stayed with Scott and her mother and thereby became closer to them. Later, Aimée would take charge of caring for Saranna, permitting Scott to take holidays, sometimes with her young nephew, Nene.

However, during the first year of Robert and Aimée's marriage, 7-year-old Nene and his grandmother, Saranna, both contracted scarlet fever, and again Scott became nurse. Only months later another tragedy visited the family: David Scott Mitchell's sister, Margaret Quigley, was badly burned in a house fire. At first it was thought to have been caused by lightning; but it emerged that the fire began in the upstairs bedroom. Merewether, who was Margaret's brother-in-law, confided to Robert Scott:

> I for one have my own ideas on the subject. Quigley can and does take too many and stiff caulkers. Dr Boyd's ability in that way you have some knowledge of and they are not the only ones in the family who like more than is good for them.

Margaret died a week later. She was only 47. Evidently there was some alienation between her and her two siblings and their families, since Merewether remarked that he did not think it likely that Margaret 'would desire to see any of us'. If there was estrangement, it may have originated from the final partitioning of Dr James Mitchell's estate, and some disputes over property. Margaret's death caused Merewether to reflect on the so-called 'Great Will Scandal' of 1869: 'Sir James Martin is dead, making the 5th of those who were prominently concerned in the Wolfskehl business including Dr Mitchell, Barker, Judge Hargreaves and Margaret. I probably shall be the next, but what's the odds?'

If the 1880s were years of rites of passage for Scott, surrounded as she was by marriages, births, a new home and a more senior identity within her family, they were also years visited by death. The deaths of her father and beloved Gussie were followed by those of her brother, Helenus, and her paternal uncle, David Scott, in 1881, bachelor uncle, Thomas Rusden, in 1882, uncle Alexander Walker Scott in 1885, uncle Frank Rusden and her cousin, Margaret Quigley, in 1886, her uncles, Alfred Rusden and Patrick Scott, in 1887. This meant that the entire previous generation on her father's side of the family was dead by 1887, while on her mother's side, four of her uncles and aunts were gone.

Nevertheless, the cycle of death was not finished. Robert Glendon Scott, Aimée and Robert's second child, was just eighteen months old when the Sydney family heard the news that Robert, now aged 49, had been killed in an accident in Newcastle in July 1890. This left living only Fannie, George, Rose, Millie and Alice of the original eleven Scotts. Lack of contact with Fannie made it effectively a family of four siblings, but only Scott lived in Sydney. Only Alice had children and that family lived far away. This meant that Nene was *the* child of the Sydney family, the centre of attention for the three relatives, the housekeeper and housemaid who resided together. While Scott clearly had a life dominated by family responsibilities, she also now had a degree of freedom in Sydney to diversify her activities.

One part of shaping a wider life for herself was buying a home. Scott's mother had leased the house at Point Piper Road in 1880. Saranna had difficulty gaining access to the full bequest from Helenus Scott's will; Merewether advised that any house be bought jointly by Rose Scott and Hope Wallace, Nene's father, acting in trust for his son.[39] Merewether had reported to Robert that Rose 'had her eye' on a picturesque cottage in Jersey Road, Woollahra, called Lynton, not far for Hope to walk for the nightly billiard games at Merewether's. The Sands Sydney Directory lists 'Mrs S. Scott, 294 Jersey Road, Woollahra', as the household head from 1885 until 1896, the year of Saranna's death. Thereafter, the householder became 'Miss R. Scott'.

Remaining photographs of the interior of Lynton show a gracious Victorian-style home, intricately decorated with original paintings, vases, ornamental statues, oriental fans, dark-wood furniture, wicker chairs, a *chaise-longue*, flowers, velvet cushions, lacework tablecloths, table lamps and bookshelves stacked with cloth-bound books. Annie Rose Scott Cowen later recalled that the parlour and dining-room (which led out to Scott's treasured garden) were partitioned by a folding panelled door which, when pulled back, made an agreeable and large space.

It was in these two rooms from the late 1880s that Rose Scott held her Friday night 'at home' gatherings, while on Saturday afternoons she developed a tradition of receiving visitors in her garden.[40] Scott's correspondence during this period suggests that she was involved in cultural and philanthropic activities, which led her to question aspects of public policy and regulations. She had befriended an artist, Mary Stoddard, whom she met through her future sister-in-law, artist Marianne Boydell, who married George Scott in 1886. Stoddard's life disclosed the difficulties women faced if they tried to pursue an intellectual or creative career, in addition to motherhood. In 1884, the artist's children had whooping cough and she reported her struggles to continue with her work: 'My greatest difficulty is to find time to paint. I am looking for a ladyhelp to take the management of household affairs and look after the children.' Evidently Scott tried to encourage her, reporting her enthusiasm for her exhibition, but Stoddard eventually moved to Moss Vale on the southern highlands of New South Wales to work there. She missed Rose and Saranna Scott, and she also missed England and found features of life in the Australian countryside hard to take:

> The days are so lovely that one feels it is a sin to stay indoors and directly you go out the flies attack you in such numbers that you are driven home. I wrote to Sydney for those open veils they use in the country for the flies . . . They keep the flies out certainly but garble everything one looks at in such a way as to make one choose which is the lesser evil.

Stoddard's career improved. In January 1890 she invited Scott to her new studio in Pitt Street, Sydney, where she had been painting the New South Wales premier, Sir Henry Parkes.[41] She was one of several women artists with whom Scott developed friendships in the 1880s. While anglophilia might be expected as a predisposition of friends and relatives of Scott, it was not universal. Caroline A'Beckett, daughter of the Hunter Valley family (whose father testified on behalf of the Mitchell and Scott families in the Great Will Case) wrote to Scott from London in 1888:

> I think the mental atmosphere of an old country is exceedingly depressing and I am so thankful my home is in a colony . . . There is so much luxury here it tires me to death because I have to visit in the midst of it and when the novelty wears off it is so boring . . . I hope you will not suppose because I so much prefer Australia that I am sorry I came.[42]

Scott's philanthropic activities at this time centred on work with the Girls' Friendly Society. Her aunt, Rose Selwyn, was a founder of its Newcastle branch and her sister, Millie, also was involved. The Society met unaccompanied immigrant teenage girls and found employment situations for them — generally in domestic service. In 1884 there was a dispute over Scott's role in organising placements for girls in England prior to their journey, which resulted in what the Bishop of Newcastle called 'undesirable publicity'.[43] On another front, Scott became involved in enquiries about the law governing inebriates and the possibilities of having an inebriate asylum established in New South Wales. Her uncle, Henry Keylock Rusden, recorder of the Victorian Legislative Council, offered advice in 1888 on the legal aspects of the inebriate problem and referred her to Dr Bowker for medical details.[44]

It is unclear exactly what inspired Scott's interest in the inebriate issue at this time, though it was just after the death of her cousin, Margaret Quigley, had been attributed darkly by Merewether to the drinking of her husband.

The Women's Christian Temperance Union was founded in New South Wales in 1884 and was gaining organisational strength. Louisa Lawson, woman suffragist and publisher of the women's journal, *The Dawn*, was a staunch and vocal temperance advocate. Her son, the poet Henry Lawson, was an alcoholic. Others in Scott's gradually enlarging social circle were also involved in the temperance issue. William Charles Windeyer, Supreme Court Judge, and his wife, Mary, were total abstainers, with much to say as to connections between habitual drunkenness, crime and the wretchedness of poverty confronting the philanthropist. But there may have been more immediate familiarity with a problem Scott saw very much as a masculine proclivity.

During the 1880s, despite a broadening of activities, Scott probably appeared to share much with married women. She was raising a young boy, and experiencing all the joys and tribulations that could entail. She was caring for an aged mother, a task that often fell to wives. If she was not the hostess of entertainments for her 'husband', she provided for many of the social and networking needs of her deceased sister's husband, and she clearly inherited a social world in part shaped by her father's, brothers', uncles' and men cousins' place in their professions and cultural institutions. What has been retrospectively romanticised as 'a salon' probably began as a case of upper-middle-class country hospitality encountering the complexity of urban networks. The contacts that began as the legacy of her male relatives certainly expanded in directions these men would never have anticipated, nor one suspects, approved of. The social circles Scott forged were partly the consequence of the opportunities of Sydney, partly permitted by the deployment of her personal qualities, and partly the outcome of several political crises and transitions of the 1880s, which often threw unlikely protagonists into contact.

The stories of Scott's Friday night 'salon' remain chiefly as reminiscences recorded at the time of her death or later. These have several features. Their authors invariably were younger, often considerably younger, than Scott and seemed to have felt honoured to be invited, thrilled to rub elbows with the great, the famous and the powerful. They all contend that the great questions of the day were debated there and that the course of politics, social reform and cultural mores was shaped by the deliberations transpiring in Scott's 'salon'. Legislation such as the 1898 Early Closing Bill was drafted on her rosewood dining table, they report, while politicians were confronted with the sufferings and injustices of women by Scott inviting, for instance, shopgirls and having them speak. Issues debated there included free trade versus protection, industrial legislation, socialism, taxation, Utopianism, nationalism and republicanism, capital punishment, public charities and their administration, temperance, Australian literature and literary criticism, Australian art and exhibitions, and urban social problems including slums, contagious diseases, prostitution, illegitimacy and juvenile delinquency.

The principal visitors in the 1880s were men and it remains unclear how typically their wives accompanied them. Of course, some key women connected with culture and reform certainly were included, but those most directly involved in these so-called 'great questions of the day' were men: politicians, judges, lawyers, public servants, academics, teachers, journalists, editors, publishers, novelists, poets, painters, composers and musicians, architects, town planners, clergymen, literary and cultural critics, philanthropists, businessmen and industrialists, as well as gentlemen of independent means and various interests. Many were university-educated. Many were married, or would be within a few years, and were members of the urban professional middle class.

Those who have written of Scott's 'salon' — among them Miles Franklin, Alex Chisholm, Maybanke Anderson, Mary Booth, Edith Fry, Mabel Forest and Sydney Ure Smith — mention a series of visitors who could have been met there, though most of these commentators were too young to have been among them in the 1880s. So, of those mentioned, only some were Scott's guests in the years before she published her first article in the *Sydney Morning Herald* — 'Home Lessons' in 1889. One of these guests was Sir Henry Parkes, the premier of New South Wales and 'the old fox of faction politics'. Another was Judge William Charles Windeyer, the centre of controversy twice in the 1880s — as judge in the infamous Mount Rennie gang-rape case, resulting in the conviction of six youths in 1886 and the execution of four of them in 1887; and as the judge who ruled in favour of the bookseller distributing a version of Annie Besant and Charles Bradlaugh's birth control pamphlet 'Law of Population' in 1888. Mary Windeyer, his wife, was a noted philanthropist who advocated the scheme of de-institutionalisation of child state wards by boarding them out to foster parents, who would be paid to care for them.

Bernhard Ringrose Wise, Chief Crown Prosecutor in the Attorney General's department in the 1880s, was another of Scott's guests, a protégé of Sir Henry Parkes and widely admired as the Oxford-educated intellectual giant of Australian liberalism. William Lane, author of *The Workingman's Paradise* and leader of the ill-fated Utopian community established in Paraguay in the 1890s, was probably a guest in the 1880s. Certainly four men involved in the administration of charity and government regulation of childcare became associates of Scott in the 1880s. They were Sir Arthur Renwick, chairman of the State Children's Relief Board established in 1881, Sydney and Edward Maxted, managers of the Sydney Benevolent Asylum, and George Ardill, evangelist and founder of the Sydney Rescue Society, administering a network of institutions for women and children in crisis. Scott's circle at this time may also have included Timothy Augustus Coghlan, the government statistician, Edward Woolcott Fosbery, Inspector General of Police, and J.C. Nield, legislative councillor and moral reformer. She had their friendship and support by the early 1890s when she began her first law-reform initiatives.

If men in key positions were at times Scott's guests in the 1880s, her 'salon' should not be represented as a 'kitchen' parliament convened every Friday night with the same influential cast and possessed of decisive, if informal, force in New South Wales government and public administration. That so many reforms Scott came to seek took so long to achieve, and required extensive public and extra-parliamentary campaigning, belies any such reading. The significance of these alliances for Scott, and her emergence into a public career in the 1890s, resides in the access they gave her to sources of information and avenues for lobbying, persuasion, or at least influence.

Perhaps as significant was their place in legitimising, and perhaps even glamourising, Scott for contemporary and later commentators. This might be likened to the representation of Gertrude Stein, shrewdly given by Catharine R. Stimpson. According to Stimpson, Stein becomes significant through the important men for whom her home was at times a salon — Marcel Duchamp, Guillaume Apollinaire, Ernest Hemingway, Pablo Picasso and so forth. The bestowal of their consortium upon her legitimised Stein's cultural forays, but also counteracted the effect that her manifest deviation from conventional femininity (especially her relationship with Alice B. Toklas) may have had on her cultural influence. Arguably, her 'salon', like Scott's, made her an 'honorary man' at one level, yet this male approval 'hetero-sexualised' her, removing unsettling doubts about her femininity.[45]

While overt lesbianism was not an issue in Scott's persona, half a century before Stein's, her overt spinsterhood was an issue for herself and her contemporaries. There can be no doubt that middle-class spinsterhood in Scott's time was more respectable and considerably less stigmatised than it was to become by the mid-twentieth century. Historians have attributed this decline of the respectability of spinsterhood to a 'sexualisation' of everyday life and to the propaganda of sexologists and early and vulgar Freudian psychoanalytic theorists. Chosen spinsterhood was soon cast as neurotic and perhaps symptomatic of sexual immaturity, frigidity, penis envy, fear of erotic abandon, or else just pathological, deviant lesbianism. Yet, there is a danger of exaggerating the contrast to the point that late-nineteenth-century spinsterhood is misrepresented as unproblematic and, compared to the difficulties of wives, as almost the 'easy' sexual option.

Mid-nineteenth-century English debate about the so-called 'surplus woman' problem was usually cast in economic and industrial terms. How were women in a poor marriage market, in which they outnumbered available husbands, to get their livings? However, it is clear from many sources, especially from diaries, letters and women's fiction, that spinsters endured many damaging cultural messages in social relations built around heterosexual norms. Notwithstanding the 'female world of love and ritual' sketched by United States historian Carroll Smith Rosenberg, the respectability of the middle-class spinster might be attended with various forms of enforced marginality and covert expressions of contempt, misogyny or pity by the married of both sexes. Her lack of experience of the 'natural' estate of her sex — conjugality, motherhood and grandmotherhood — deprived the spinster of authority to speak or represent herself and other women as a woman, while her exclusion, as a woman, from civil society and public life ensured she had no authority from which to speak on public issues, as a bachelor might. Nineteenth-century spinsters could suffer a pervasive sense of unreality, non-identity, shame, failure, guilt, anger and frustration — sometimes manifest in hysterical symptoms which some scholars have read as a form of corporeal speech refusing to be censored.

While in late-nineteenth-century English, north-eastern United States, and south-eastern Canadian history spinsters struggled with increasing legitimacy for access and authority in civil society and public life, which to some extent opposed their psychical oppression, Australian conditions, and especially local demography, did not authorise the same struggles. Although some women in cities lived in poor marriage markets, spinsterhood was perhaps less visible in Australia than in England, the eastern United States, or some Canadian provinces. Under these circumstances, the colonial spinster might be more of a social oddity than her overseas metropolitan counterpart. Thus public life, with any legitimacy or authority to speak, stood to be peculiarly difficult for Scott. For 'failing' to marry in Australia there could be no excuse or explanation other than the want of womanly charms.

In this context, the representation of Scott as hostess is most significant. All the reminiscences of her in this role stress her charm, beauty, tact, and diplomacy, advancing arguments with opponents not with aggression, but with alluring persuasion and reason. Alex Chisholm called her home a 'treasure house' of Australiana and she the 'Lady of the Treasure House'. Scott as salonière, then, is part of the 1920s representation — indeed celebration — of her as an intensely feminine, worthy lady, the grand old lady of social reform; old-fashioned, dignified, devoting herself unselfishly to nurturing disadvantaged women and children. She was motherly, caring, loving, loveable, aesthetic, decorative, and alluring.

Such representations of Scott, and the place of her 'salon' in them, need to be seen in the context of their construction, primarily the inter-war period and after — the height of the period in which contemporary historians like Faderman, Jeffreys and Vicinus detect the emergence of an anti-feminist crackdown on the spinster, which discredited her in sexual and psychological terms. It was also the time during which Cott argues that the distinctively 'modern' birth of feminism was taking place.[46] Commentators on Scott may have been trying to protect her from the stigma to which spinsters in the 1920s had become vulnerable. They might also have been critics of the new feminists of the 1920s, against whom they compared Scott favourably. The gentle, ladylike Scott perhaps was not as revered as she might be, although as her old friend Edith Fry, vice president of the National Council of Women, claimed in an obituary published in the *Sydney Morning Herald*, 'For nearly 50 years her name has been a household word'. A key part of the contemporary assessment of Scott's importance and effectiveness was the fact of her relationships with the important and the powerful, an achievement beyond most women of the time. Serious men took her seriously. Yet the acknowledgement of this achievement, almost always through mention of her as the salon hostess, instantly domesticated, maternalised and therefore re-feminised her at the very moment she threatened to become masculine — to cease operating as a normal woman.

The curious feature of Scott's representation as the centre of a sparkling and influential salon is the failure to recognise the personal or sexual politics implications of her position, and her use of this salon circle. Historians of salons integral to artistic movements, such as Impressionism, or to intellectual or political movements, such as the Enlightenment and French Revolution, have noted the critical role played by women in facilitating the very existence of these movements and in popularising their work. On the other hand, such movements and their cultures formally excluded women, regardless of individual ability, from full participation, leaving women of these milieux with only informal, apparently 'domestic' modes of interaction with 'the great questions' of their day. The salon might have been a crucial avenue for women's input into debates, issues and arrangements vitally affecting their position and conditions. If the manner of women like Scott was all beauty and charm, the game was deadly serious.

But what was Scott's game in the 1880s? Why should a genteel spinster in her thirties, with a mother, brother-in-law and nephew to care for, who had 'good' social connections in the city in which she made a new home, make herself the hostess of this much remembered 'salon'? In April 1889 she published 'Home Lessons' in the women's column of the *Sydney Morning Herald*. The article, her first ever published, was a criticism of the education system in general and homework in particular:

> [N]ow that muscular power is of use for little else than manual labour . . . our education has become almost exclusively mental . . . We do not yet realise the truth that . . . the physical underlies the mental, the mental must not be developed at the expense of the physical . . . In a thousand homes tired children with heavy eyes are learning their evening tasks worrying their poor young brains to say nothing of wearying their elders. They have been in school during the whole of the morning, and probably most of the bright afternoon hours and yet their work is not finished. Directly after tea they have to write out exercises, find places in the map by gaslight.[47]

Why was Scott moved to intervene, at this time, on this issue? Although she declined matrimony, surely 'Home Lessons' was penned by a parent, probably a mother? But every mother with views did not submit articles to the *Sydney Morning Herald*, and the mere value of opinions expressed did not ensure publication. Scott was indeed a 'mother.' At the time of the article, Nene was an 11-year-old Sydney schoolboy. Already his education was greatly different from that of his adoptive mother — enough for her to protest; and by 1889 after nearly a decade in Sydney, Scott believed her protest mattered and would be received.

A few months before 'Home Lessons', Scott took Nene to a new phrenologist, Charlotte Hadfield. The readings proved most influential on the course of things to come. Nene was identified as delicate, sickly, of poetic and artistic tastes, but highly patriotic and destructive, as well as cautious and anxious. Another phrenologist consulted later concurred, adding that the child had only little desire for marriage and was best adapted for a career as an architect or surveyor. His formal training and eventual profession was indeed architecture, though much of his youth in his aunt's lifetime was spent in pursuit of a career in acting.

As for Scott, Hadfield stated explicitly that: 'your motive power is manifested by your vigour, determination and efficiency. You are not afraid of work and generally enjoy it and you are best fitted for an active life, a public philanthropic career where your energy would have scope for the cause of humanity.' Having recommended in this way, Hadfield was nonetheless concerned about Scott's spinsterhood, which, on the face of it, was the ideal state in which to pursue this public life. In fact, the phrenologist was quite prescriptive and, once again, Scott left the parts of the report addressing sexuality and marriage without annotation. Hadfield noted that 'you are inclined to live too far above those whom you come into contact with . . . your facility of amativeness is not developed. Your degree of reproductive love is small and also your sexual love'. Conceding that Scott did not feel it disagreeable to live in the unmarried state, she insisted that she would be happier married. Interesting in the light of the future Scott would make for herself are some further remarks, as are Scott's annotations:

> You are not much elated by praise but you are deeply wounded by censure [(RS) I fear this is true]. You evince a good degree of self respect, dignity and self-reliance but you are greedy for power. You must be a leader and not a follower . . . You have eyes that see . . . With practice you could become a good speaker.[48]

A FEMINIST GENESIS

When Rose Scott was but a few months old, Elizabeth Cady Stanton and many other American women met at Seneca Falls to declare the rights of women. Scott reached her twentieth birthday in the year John Stuart Mill presented a petition praying that women be enfranchised on the same terms as men, to the British House of Commons. In fact, during the first thirty years of her life, unprecedented numbers of women in England and America staked the claim for women to have access to public life and civil society. In the areas of paid work, education, the professions, local government, family law and property law reform, women activists worked, wrote and were discussed in newspapers and journals. Scott's bookshelves and recollections contained many heroines: Elizabeth Blackwell and Elizabeth Garrett Anderson, who struggled to enter the medical profession; Florence Nightingale, who worked to establish the profession of nursing; and Frances Power Cobbe, author of 'Wife Torture in England', the 1878 article that resulted in the establishment of judicial separation on the basis of cruelty and violence in English law. The women who worked for the English Married Women's Property Act (1870), which permitted married women to own property, enter contracts and keep their own earnings, as well as those who sought women's access to higher education, also captured Scott's admiration. Perhaps her enthusiasm for no woman activist of the period surpassed that she felt for Josephine Butler, who worked from 1870 until 1884 for the abolition of the English Contagious Diseases Acts, which permitted the detention until cured of any woman taken into custody on suspicion of being a prostitute and found to have any venereal disease.

From 1850 'the woman question' emerged in public debate in Western countries, with particular intensity from the 1880s. There was a strong correlation between town or city life and the emergence of secular women's movements devoted to extending women's rights and protecting them from exploitation and abuse. In the city women came to see, for the first time, the situation of women across all classes and sub-cultural groupings. Many middle-class women only 'saw' prostitutes, prostitution and the issue of men's demand, by living in cities for the first time. Obviously, many kinds of rural conditions isolated women, confining their attention perhaps to the immediate household, family and local community. Some historians of the United States have argued that the sex antagonism prominent in new industrial cities was less evident in many rural communities, where companionate, co-operative and complementary interractions characterised relations between the sexes. Interdependency and common cause mitigated women's oppression in God-fearing, temperate rural areas with balanced sex ratios. The 'rising of the women' to demand equal legal rights, citizenship, education, paid work, and industrial and moral protection, centred on the big towns and cities.[49]

In 1889 the first women's organisation ever to meet at night in Sydney was founded. It was called the Women's Literary Society (WLS). Its members met on the first and third Monday evenings of each month at eight o'clock. Rose Scott was a foundation member, along with twelve other women of her acquaintance. The Society established various objectives. The first was mutual help in the study of general literature. More generally, it was decided that the work of the society:

> shall consist in searching out and bringing before the meetings such matters as shall be of interest and improvement to the members. Discussion upon important topics of the day, papers upon various matters of interest, criticism upon literary or artistic works or theories upon practical matters will be in order at the meetings.

These official objectives were instructively vague. Programmes of meetings across the first five years provide more details. Topics of papers, group discussion and debates included the following: 'Is Higher Education Conducive to the Cultivation of the Moral Qualities?', 'Socialism', 'Suggestions for the Improvement of Affairs as Regards Wage Earning Women', 'Dress — Its Influence on Women', 'Shakespeare's Women', 'George Eliot's Women', 'Carlyle's Life and Work', 'Matthew Arnold's Essays on Criticism', 'The Moral and Intellectual Influence of Literature', 'Mrs Gaskell's Works', 'Mary Wollstonecraft', 'Australian Poets', 'The Brontes', 'Evolution', 'Marriage as A Profession', 'Ibsen', 'Jude the Obscure', 'Olive Schreiner', 'Nursery Rhymes', 'Elizabethan Dramatists', 'A Plea for Womanhood', 'Ruskin', 'Mill On Liberty' and the 'Probable Influence of Women's Suffrage on Politics'.

By 1893 the WLS had 120 financial members.[50] These women engaged in a form of cultural politics. Like Scott, many of them had little or no formal education, but wished to influence the course of philanthropy and public opinion in ways that improved the position of women. They wished also to develop their intellectual and critical skills. Some were daughters, some spinsters, others wives and widows. This kind of reading, reviewing and public speaking group might readily be characterised as élitist, mild and irrelevant to the everyday struggles of the majority of Australian women of the time. It could be contrasted unfavourably with two other forms of women's organisation to emerge in the same period — women's temperance work and women's work for improved industrial conditions. Such an assessment, however, would underestimate the significance of women's cultural politics. The WLS continued, during the 1890s, and became the Women's Club in 1900, established for educated and professional women, only to transform again into the Feminist Club in 1914, an incarnation that survived until 1929 when internal dissension caused its voluntary dissolution.[51]

The implications of women's moves towards cultural politics require fuller analysis. The women who founded the WLS would normally have confined their public activity to various forms of philanthropy. Scott likened the typical public work of upper-middle-class women to cutting the heads off weeds without digging out and destroying their roots. She found philanthropic work futile, bottomless and unsatisfying, since it did nothing to address the causes of social problems. Women philanthropists did the housework of public life. Yet this work permitted such women 'to see' the situations of their sex sometimes in broad and striking terms — situations that, in the 1880s, stimulated women's movements in temperance and industrial militancy. Although women philanthropists across the nineteenth century had undoubtedly 'seen' the same cluster of problems, seeing had not always led to a commitment to women's rights. From the 1870s, however, in the context of the English ferment over 'surplus women', education, divorce law and woman suffrage, philanthropists more frequently became 'politicised' by their work and channelled it towards women's rights campaigns. It was, after all, in her work as a philanthropist involved in rescue work with prostitutes that Josephine Butler had encountered the effects of the Contagious Diseases Acts on women's lives.

While the Sydney of the 1880s was a small city, social problems affecting women encountered by philanthropic women in Scott's circle reached unprecedented intensity. Illegitimacy generally accounted for less than 5 per cent of Canadian births, slightly more of English and United States births. Yet in New South Wales, recorded births to unmarried women reached 14 per cent at the end of the 1880s. The main crimes for which women were tried in the Supreme Court were infanticide and related offences. Sydney did not have a foundling hospital, since authorities had reasoned this would be an inducement to vice. That babies were found abandoned in varying stages of ill-health was the predictable outcome of this situation, as were the significant numbers of illegitimate babies dying in infancy. Since unmarried mothers were often cast out by employers or their families, they had to seek shelter and sustenance in a punitive and inhospitable world. Lying-in homes operated by various charities were available for unmarried pregnant women. These women were generally required to work for the institution, usually in its laundry or kitchen, until their babies were born, and would continue working there after the birth until the child was weaned, or until they found a new job, or both. These institutions also provided shelter for unmarried mothers who had been sacked or who were unable to cope with paid work while suckling infants, in return for unpaid labour. Women philanthropists sat on the boards of these institutions, which usually interviewed applicants for admission, especially regarding the prospects of suing the men responsible for maintenance and for other contributions to the mothers' and infants' care.

Amidst the truly pathetic stories to emerge in this process was a disturbing composite portrait of the sexual behaviour of men in servant-employing households, and the peculiar vulnerability of young domestic servants, waitresses, shopgirls, laundresses, and workshop hands to sexual coercion and exploitation in paid work and accompanying living arrangements. Most of these philanthropist women would have resided in servant-employing households. Indeed, it was the work of servants at home that permitted them to perform their 'public work'. There could have been moments of uncomfortable recognition of commonalities and connections between the situations of middle-class wives and working-class servants, despite the conventional forms by which their differences were marked.

For philanthropists engaged in rescue work, the same recognitions might be presented. Girls' Friendly Society work was explicitly about preventing the 'lapse into vice' of girls who lost or failed to obtain respectable situations. Unmarried teenage mothers were likely to face prostitution as their best and at times their only livelihood option. Those attempting to 'reform' themselves would have to tell their stories to obtain admission to residential institutions, and again women philanthropists might have to 'see' not only the degradation of these women but also the place of men, as seducers, clients, 'bludgers' or profiteers from their 'shame'. They also learnt of the prominent place of married men among the clients of working prostitutes. Most women philanthropists of Scott's acquaintance were married.

If these women saw the fates of 'fallen', mainly unmarried, women through lying-in home and rescue work, other areas of philanthropy called into question any assumption that 'married women' were necessarily more fortunate. The Benevolent Asylum and smaller institutions offering outdoor as well as indoor relief to the needy, constantly confronted the hardships of wives and mothers whose breadwinners were drunkards, habitually violent, or who would not or could not adequately support their dependent women and children. The complexities of these situations emerged, particularly in the cases of 'semi-deserted' wives with young children and without supportive family or neighbourhood networks. Such women often could not take on full-time paid work without childcare and could not take legal action for maintenance because the man co-habited regularly enough to frustrate any claim of desertion. In the wake of periodic violence, the husband often could not be found to enable a summons to be served against him, should the wife decide to prosecute. Meanwhile, baby after baby would be born, exacerbating the hardships of the woman and her existing children. Once again, to the married woman philanthropist, these unfortunate wives might seem radically 'other', poverty marking a major gulf between their situations. Yet some of the difficulties and abuses permitted by the marriage contract were not confined to working-class wives. If philanthropists did not have to confess these publicly, their recognitions can be deduced from the work they increasingly undertook in 'the cause of women'.

The women's temperance movements of the late-nineteenth and early-twentieth centuries, the largest public political mobilisation of women in Western history, had a decidedly Anglo-Celtic character. In the United States, Canada, New Zealand and Australia this movement was an important basis for many key sexual politics campaigns. In Australia, while individual evangelists, Quakers and philanthropists had advocated the extension of women's rights, including woman suffrage, the women's temperance movement preceded the suffrage leagues in the colonies. Susannah Gale, Euphemia Bowes, Sara Nolan, Bessie Harrison Lee and Eliza Ward were prominent among women temperance activists working in the 1880s. Unlike mainstream temperance workers, who simply attacked the availability of 'the demon drink', these women drew connections between the power of the breadwinner to drink and the oppression and sufferings of women and their children. The cultural representation of a strong association between Australian masculinity and excessive, 'binge' drinking is longstanding, and has now reached legendary status.

The vulnerability of wives to poverty, eviction, poor nutrition and ill-health was one set of issues highlighted by women's temperance activists. Vulnerability to violence and sexual abuse was also addressed, cautiously but unmistakably, by these women. The appeal of temperance to large numbers of Australian women can hardly be cause for wonder. Since most women, as Scott observed, so clearly depended on men for their livelihood, they had only limited bargaining power in the event of men's heavy and habitual drinking. Usually they were in no position to leave, especially if they had several young children. Drunkenness accounted for over half of all arrests of men in the 1880s but, since the punishment was generally a fine or a couple of days' gaol, days on which the breadwinner would earn no money, dependent wives and children were hardly assisted by these outcomes.

If a spinster of independent means like Scott could attack men and their behaviour, most wives could not. Blaming the availability of alcohol could be an effective alternative target, a displaced object for the rage and pain experienced by so many women as a consequence of their weak position in the marriage contract and the masculinist cultural distribution of wealth, resources and labour. Many churches blessed and indeed organised temperance activity. It became a legitimate way for women to meet, and learn important political skills through working together, without being open to charges of aping men or 'unsexing themselves'. On the face of it, temperance advocacy was ladylike and respectable. However, the intensity of the fierce masculinist backlash against women's temperance during this period may suggest that it was, covertly, subversive of the domestic sexual status quo or, at least, of collective masculine fantasies of that status quo. Cartoons typically represented women's temperance activists as 'mannish' — tall, thin, angular, black-dressed, cross and 'spinsterish'. These 'wowsers' were out to stop a man having a bit of fun and had themselves clearly never had fun with a man. This was an interesting disavowal of the fact that it was wives who dominated the ranks of women's temperance organisations.[52]

Another kind of 'rising of the women' in the decade from the 1870s — women's industrial militancy — also warrants study. Again, women's attempts to organise increases in wages, work options and workplace protection emerged primarily in the urban context. If marriage was almost universal for Australian women at some time in their adult lives, the majority of women aged 15 to 30 were unmarried at the time of both the 1881 and 1891 censuses of New South Wales. Conditions, wages and access to paid work were most keenly issues for young women, though of course women of all ages could need or wish to secure paid livelihoods both inside and outside marriage, especially deserted wives, widows and wives whose husbands were injured, invalids, unemployed or underemployed.

Around the same time that Scott came from the country to Sydney, another woman also migrated there from a quite different situation and became a key activist on behalf of women workers. Louisa Lawson, working-class wife of miner and speculator, Peter Lawson, took her children from their hut in Mudgee, western New South Wales, and set about earning her living in Sydney. She worked as a seamstress, a boarding-house keeper, and in other various ventures before beginning work as writer, editor-publisher and printer of the women's monthly newspaper, *The Dawn*, published from May 1888 until 1905. In the city Lawson 'saw' the sweated labour of young women, and their over-supply and over-concentration in a few low-paid, officially unskilled trades, chiefly in the service, food and clothing industries. These areas were characteristically not unionised and were of little concern to the emerging trade union movement.

Lawson learned a bitter lesson about the sexual politics of the trade union movement in 1888 when she employed some women compositors on *The Dawn*. The union would not admit women, and when the women began work, the union blackbanned the newspaper. In a later memoir on her mother's life, Lawson's daughter, Gertrude O'Connor, recalled that all the women working on *The Dawn* 'had been taught by their fathers and as long as they worked for them no one troubled to interfere, but as soon as they began to work for a woman on the staff of a woman's paper, the opposition began'. Not only did male trade unionists forbid their wives and daughters to read *The Dawn*, but they also engaged in such a degree of harassment and personal violence towards the women workers that they were compelled to seek police protection. Most notoriously, unionists leased part of the building opposite *The Dawn* office and shone mirrors through the windows, blinding the women momentarily to prevent them from working. The implications of this 'incident at *The Dawn*' were grave and shocking, engendering fierce debate within and beyond the labour movement. It fundamentally challenged, or at least complicated, the previous loyalties of labouring women like Lawson to the labour movement.

Lawson founded The Dawn Club for working women. It was devoted to the extension of women's rights, including divorce law reform and woman suffrage. She maintained that women must first elevate themselves, then contribute towards the general elevation. This was to be achieved by club activities such as 'the reading and discussion of thoughtful papers which condense the onward marching thoughts and life of larger and older communities . . . absorb progressive teaching upon temperance, education, health, charity etc. We will find plentiful occasion to apply it to surrounding life.' Like Scott, Lawson was concerned about conjugal misery and the sufferings of wives, though only her public writings on these subjects remain. Scott wrote extensively on these topics, in private and personal forms. With few exceptions she never published them. The relative lack of private papers by Lawson, compared with Scott, could erroneously suggest that Scott had a more trenchant and pessimistic view of men's sexuality and marriage than Lawson did, but the bulk of remaining sources are not strictly comparable. Arguably their concerns had much in common.

This lack of personal papers, especially correspondence, of Lawson makes comparison between her and Scott on the subjects of marriage and sexuality difficult. Such manuscripts as exist on Lawson are written by her children and other descendants. Her family's papers appear to have the common rationale of claiming for Lawson the status of the first, the pioneer, suffragist. This is not necessarily the best way to make her life intelligible. What must have been a vast correspondence accompanying the publication of *The Dawn* seems to have vanished, while few drafts in Lawson's own hand of the more than 200 lead articles she wrote remain.

Despite being forced to rely on Lawson's published work, in particular her articles in *The Dawn*, for comparison of her feminist concerns with those of Scott, the exercise is worthwhile. If some of Lawson's references to problems of marriage and sexuality for women are oblique, others are direct and compelling. First, Lawson was preoccupied by the prevalence of loveless marriages in which women were instruments of men's pleasures and whims. Second, she also dwelt upon the overwork and exploitation of wives and mothers, and the condition of marriage that led to their acquiescence before their own ill-use. Third, she placed great emphasis upon publicly articulated misogyny — the defaming of women through derogatory claims, popular truisms and other cultural representations.

Lawson supported widened grounds for divorce favouring women because there was 'nothing sacred in binding a good woman to a sot, felon or brute'. The felon dishonours her, 'the brute bruises her flesh and perhaps breaks her bones, but the sot makes her perpetuate his ignoble race'. She portrays the drunken husband collapsed 'in abandoned beastliness upon the floor or conjugal couch', only to proceed to 'make the night hideous' for his wife. Women were expected to endure nightly 'this horrid ordeal'.

The marital bedroom is described by Lawson as 'the chamber of horrors', a phrase Scott also used repeatedly when discussing wives compelled to provide their husband's conjugal rights; and like Scott, Lawson took the view that women's endurance of abuse without resistance perpetuated it for all women.

> If she is pinched or bruised or injured, if things are broken in a fit of temper, she will swear it was not he, it was the result of accident purely. If he insults her by boasting of his connection with other women, she does not resent it, if he squanders the money, she works the later and the harder to replace it, if he drinks, she hides the fact and shelters him with lies and bears him dipsomaniac children. In time she does not own her own body or mind and her only morality is to be faithful to the marriage contract.[53]

Whereas men's wrongs in the strike-filled 1890s would be vented by public speakers, women endured wrongs in their homes in 'abominable seclusion'. Women, she declared, were 'weak, unorganised and isolated'. Over the dark records of men's drunkenness and cruelty, Lawson claimed, women laid 'a white sheet of silence'. The amount of routine misery among wives was 'incredible'; they were 'too helpless to even murmur' in the face of men's selfish, brutal animalism. The cause of all these abuses of wedlock, wrote Lawson, was the subordination of women to men.[54]

Lawson's published writings make interesting comparison with Scott's unpublished, private writings on marriage and sexuality. Scott's papers contain a series of mainly undated early diaries, notebooks and notes on the topics of marriage, spinsterhood, masculinity and sexuality. Some were perhaps written before the move to Sydney, others were written during the 1880s. Some seem to be written in response to interrogations by new friends and acquaintances about her marital status, and perhaps as responses to marriage proposals, which she rejected. It is worth examining this writing closely, since the kind of analysis Scott deployed here illuminates her decision to begin a public career, the motivations for her different concerns and the kinds of challenges and opportunities she encountered in the Sydney of the 1880s. The following undated passage appears in one such notebook:

> [M]en are as clay in our fingers and yet we do all we can to foster the lower and animal nature in them . . . Oh women, men are but as tepid sewerage or a drain under our house . . . Oh mothers of children . . . marriage without love is a degradation as great for them as for the poor women in the streets. Would that you would consistently warn your daughters against matrimony to help counteract their disgusting desire for it merely as a means to form a home and be a married woman. Warn them of its dangers, its pains, its perils.

This passage is an example that could be multiplied. In her preoccupation with loveless marriages she took particular issue with women submitting to conjugality with men they did not love, in exchange for a livelihood and the greater respectability of wifehood over spinsterhood. In such situations, men's love for their wives was, she contended, 'animal' only. 'To the highest type of man the highest consummation of love is the indulgence of an animal passion' and 'he does not and cannot love without them (physical manifestations).' Scott believed that conjugal misery was legion and the reason was that in sexual relations, women typically met men's selfishness and self-indulgence with self-sacrifice. Thereby 'souls' were conceived amidst misery and 'animalism'. So, despite lofty and romantic ideals, marriage too often was, in Scott's view, the most 'unsympathetic' of relations. Men's sexual behaviour in marriage worked to 'deteriorate rather than enhance' women's feelings. One of the stark perils of which daughters should be warned, thought this sister of four married women and daughter of a mother who bore eleven children, was the coercive husbandly exercise of conjugal rights.

Scott's writings certainly alluded to the extreme of the continuum of sexual coercion to which wives could be subject. She wrote of the marriage night, of the shock and violence which bridegrooms inflicted on virgin wives in the bridal chamber — the 'chamber of horrors'. Elsewhere her tone was poignant as she commented on the disbelief and sense of betrayal experienced by young wives forced to submit, and for whom thereafter physical relations became a repugnancy they felt compelled to tolerate. It is significant, though, that in this critique of men's sexual behaviour and the cultural endorsement of the notion that husbands had enforceable conjugal rights, Scott did not dwell upon rape. That is, she did not privilege the breach of consent as the key element. Rather, she saw the entire situation of a wife dependent on marriage for livelihood, identity and respectability as sexually coercive.

That so many wives had more children than they wanted was for Scott testament to their difficulties in negotiating marital sexuality in their best material interests. These issues were delicate ones of which to speak or write directly. Sometimes Scott dramatised her concerns in early attempts at novels and plays. In one undated play called 'The Verandah' a conversation takes place between Letty, a spinster, and her friend Mabs, a wife:

> *Mabs*: Not that I am unhappy. My husband is good to me and loves me and I love him and the children. Each one seems as dear as the first but oh Letty I sometimes wish I could have some rest and they did not come so fast. No time for reading, no time for anything — babies from morn to eve . . . Men say women's sphere is home, but I feel I deteriorate intellectually.

> *Letty*: Oh these men that talk that way! Would I could give them a week of nothing but babies' society from morning until night and often all through the night. When one is not torn to pieces with anxiety about their health, one is prostrate oneself from sickness.

Scott's closeness to her mother, who had eight surviving children, three infants who died, and possibly other stillbirths and miscarriages, may contextualise her sentiments. Her married sisters produced the smaller families beginning to be evident in the final decades of the nineteenth century; but even by 1900, average completed families were still in the vicinity of four children. As an unmarried adult daughter and sister, cousin and niece, Scott's assistance and support was available, and much called upon, by the women of her family and by family friends in late stages of pregnancy, confinement and early childrearing, when the needs and demands of a new baby conflicted with the ongoing ones of previous children and of husbands. Her knowledge of the problems that women faced in negotiating marital sexuality, frequent pregnancy, childbearing and rearing, amidst already pressing household responsibilities, was considerable.

The dialogue Scott constructed between Letty and Mabs was stilted and didactic. But, despite its somewhat frowsy pitch, by exposing the typical consequences for wives, it challenged the supposed 'naturalism' and ethical neutrality of the unconstrained exercise of husbandly rights. Scott was appealing to her audience's sense of liberal justice. In particular, she highlighted the prognosis that the intellectual development of the individual woman was rendered virtually impossible if she could not read. If unchosen, unchecked motherhood obstructed education, it was an unjust and undesirable state from which wives should be free to refrain. Yet nowhere, in law or official discourse, was any right to refrain, and to expect husbands to abide by such a right, acknowledged. Of course to varying degrees individual wives negotiated this right, but for Scott this was hardly an adequate solution, depending as it did on agreeable husbands or wives unusually empowered by birth, circumstances or personal attributes.

Perhaps the most distressing consequence of wives' lack of right to say 'no', and the frequency of pregnancies that resulted, was maternal mortality and morbidity. In mid-nineteenth-century Australia, death in childbirth was most prevalent in rural areas, where women were isolated from rapid access to medical help in the event of complications. Childbirth was sufficiently dangerous for every woman of reproductive age to know, or know of, someone in her immediate generation who had died, as well as a few others seriously ill and impaired in various ways, after the experience. Prior to the adoption of curettage into routine medical procedure in the last two decades of the nineteenth century (and then amidst considerable controversy), the ordinary hazard of normal childbirth — retention of placental matter — could prove deadly. Infection of the bloodstream (septicaemia) was a typical cause of maternal deaths, as was rapid haemorrhage upon expulsion of the placenta. Tearing and ruptures of the uterus, birth canal and labia continued to result in peritonitis, prolapsed uterus, pelvic damage and related conditions occasioned by the risk of infections, until the mass marketing of penicillin in the 1940s considerably reduced maternal mortality from such causes. In a period of high rates of unwanted pregnancy, in part because the process of ovulation was either unknown, or misunderstood as occurring close to the menstrual period, every instance of marital sexual intercourse might be perceived by women not wishing to be pregnant as dangerous. If a woman had lost another woman close to her in childbirth, she may well have found frequent husbandly sexual demands positively frightening. However, the perceived threat posed by childbirth was always probably far greater, exerting more force in women's lives, than the actual statistics of recorded deaths attributed to this cause retrospectively might appear to warrant. This would have been especially likely for women of rural origins like Scott.

Scott's writings on these subjects, from late-twentieth-century perspectives, undoubtedly sound puritanical — often shrilly so: 'Purity is the eternal law . . . Men as Protectors! Protect us from yourselves, from selfish instincts and brutal lusts'.[55] Women activists like Scott have often been criticised by contemporary feminists for prudery, puritanism, and for having scant regard for female sexual pleasure, orgasmic equality and so forth. They are characterised as myopic in their emphasis upon the dangers, at the expense of the pleasures, of sexuality.[56] On the basis of Scott's undated writings on marriage, wives, husbands and sexuality, she would be a most fitting target for such criticism.

To apply this criticism may, for some purposes, be useful. However, it is important to be clear as to the definition of those purposes, so that they could be weighed fairly, in relation to other relevant considerations. For, without due qualifications, such criticism of nineteenth-century women activists like Scott and Lawson is flawed by an (equally) myopic immersion in unexamined current forms of libertarianism and insufficient consideration of the details of the sexual context these women faced. 'Female sexual pleasure' cannot be a pre-given category for the historian. There is little basis for assuming a common meaning for, and universal endorsement of, this category, between Scott's lifetime and the present. Instead, there is some basis for arguing the converse.

How could the meaning and implications of sexual pleasure and sexual expression for women be identical between the late-nineteenth and the late-twentieth centuries? For women in the former period, sexual contact and reproduction were intertwined and at times fatally connected. Parturition presented risks unheard of a century later. Public discussion of artificial contraception was substantially suppressed, and knowledge and practice of such measures and techniques were, in popular culture, associated with prostitutes and brothels — hardly suitable options for any respectable woman. Set beside average birthrates, infant mortality and related debility, these facts cannot be ignored, since they were crucial aspects of the sexual context in which women like Scott lived, thought and wrote. Such facts shaped so absolutely the experience and meaning of sexual contact that comparison with late-twentieth-century experiences and meanings is spurious. Today Western cultures officially separate sexual contact and reproduction, and (at least) pedagogically stress companionate erotic egalitarianism. The event of unwanted pregnancy can be solved in various ways. Could 'sexual pleasure', in the current sense and with these preconditions, have any meaning at all in Scott's cultural and sexual context?

Moreover, Scott's cultural world was decisively pre-Freudian or pre-psychoanalytic. Terms through which sex acts, sexual preferences and fantasies and sexual identities came to be theorised were not current. That is to say, categories such as the unconscious, repression, child sexuality, hysteria, and the Oedipus complex were of the future. Caution may therefore be the best provisional response to the easy temptation to dismiss not just Scott, but generations of women before and of her period all over the Western world, for their 'puritanical' view of sexual contact with men. A number of historians have noted the strategic ways in which nineteenth-century women's rights activists deployed the popular religious and medical notions of women's 'passionlessness' as a means of distancing women from sexual 'degradation' and, especially, from husbandly demands. This use of 'passionlessness' was pitted against those prevailing hydraulic accounts of male sexuality as 'natural', driven, irrepressible and uncontrollable, which underpinned the condoning of the husbandly exercise of conjugal rights, by force if necessary.

Scott always counted herself fortunate that she could choose to be a spinster once it was clear that she and David Scott Mitchell would not marry. Despite some of her more stinging pronouncements, she recognised that most women were not so fortunate. Lack of options for a fully independent livelihood bequeathed by a discriminatory sexual division of labour, masculinist employment policies, and the exclusion of women from the necessary training and education, rendered marriage their best, often their only, livelihood option. Since marriage was the estate of the majority of her fellow Australian women, for at least some part of her adult life Scott's continual and intense focus on this institution and its consequences for women and children was entirely appropriate. Sometimes the near-universality of marriage among Australian women was, for Scott, the key symptom of their poverty of options; but it was also the practical fact that curbed her more Utopian dreams for altering women's position in her lifetime. In the decades ahead, the social division between married and unmarried women identified by feminist historian, Beverley Kingston, as being of critical significance in this period, would sting Scott.[57]

While temperance or industrial organisation might have provided an immediate series of strategies and objectives for solving some of women's problems, neither directly addressed the cluster of sexual dilemmas disclosed in philanthropic work with unmarried mothers, prostitutes and abused wives. That women of Scott's circle would want to formulate different analyses and strategies might be expected. A concern to find the causes, to find ways of accounting for women's situation — their 'degradation', as Scott termed it — could be the outcome of the philanthropic gaze. For that gaze, disclosing as it did sexual asymmetry, exploitation and discontent, permitted the kind of cross-class, cross-ethnic identification of women as a sexed group: in Cott's words, the 'we' requisite for the emergence of feminism.[58]

In Australia, the genesis of feminism in the 1880s entailed the recognition of women's disenfranchisement, economically, legally and culturally, in the major spheres and activities of their lives. The basis of women's disenfranchisement was their sex. It would be challenged by sexual politics, which could take many forms. One form of sexual politics embraced by women activists was the analysis of cultural production. To meet independently at night, to assert the right to do the intellectual work of reading texts, writing papers and reviews, and presenting lectures on the work of leading women thinkers, essayists and authors of the period was, moreover, to engage in sexual cultural politics. It involved the positive evaluation of women's contribution to cultural representation and criticism. It also could entail becoming familiar enough with contemporary discourses effective in women's subordination to subvert them with confidence. Consider the following Scott quips to subvert Social Darwinism: 'Old Maid: survival of the fittest' or, 'why are women's brains so light? Because they inherit them from their fathers'.[59]

The ladies of the WLS had learned their 'Home Lessons' well. How fitting that their first venture into public life should be with the minimal skill bequeathed by the education of parlour — literacy. Where else were they to begin? Soon they started writing letters to relevant authorities protesting many aspects of women's and children's conditions. This was the immediate context for Scott's 'Home Lessons', and the beginning of her new and public profile.

Chapter 3

'Why Women Want a Vote' (1891–96)

Oh if you knew how the wrongs of women and children have burnt into my heart and brain ever since I was a child. The very fact that you men cannot get up enthusiasm to battle for this freedom should show you how handicapped we are, how we need the vote, since you cannot represent us any more than we can you.

Rose Scott to M.C., n.d.,
SFP, Mitchell Library

Women's Literary Society activities led in early 1891 to the proposal to form a Womanhood Suffrage League of New South Wales (WSL). Though this proposal caused dissent, Rose Scott was eager to participate. Her salon now included many of the key parliamentary players in the struggle for the vote, which would dominate her first decade of public life. Scott's investment in woman suffrage, and its possibilities for women, becomes intelligible in the light of her past involvement in charitable activities. As well, her friendships included the liberal intelligentsia of Sydney and the earliest members of the Political Labor League, most of whom supported woman suffrage amongst a range of 'progressive reforms'.

Between the foundation of the WLS in 1889 and the establishment of the WSL in 1891, Rose Scott developed greater knowledge and confidence. Moreover, the exercise of reading, analysis, argument and public speaking led to her construction of a well-developed case for the recognition of women as a distinct political constituency, entitled to self-representation, in parliamentary and other politics. She argued this case eloquently during the 1890s, earning a reputation as an engaging and persuasive lecturer. Another consequence of her efforts during these three years was the experience of working with an ever-widening circle of Sydney women, refining secretarial and negotiating skills which would prove crucial in the coming decades.

Scott's extension of her involvement in public causes was done without the blessing of her family. In old age she recalled how her commitments at this time distressed 'her people', who were deeply conservative. Family demands remained at the core of her daily life in the early years of the woman suffrage movement. Her relatives were 'causes' to which she was as committed as she was to the cause of women. At times this caused her considerable conflict. In this context, her circle of friends and acquaintances became important sources of support for her courses of action.

The story of the Australian woman suffrage movement is one that frames Scott's thought and activities in the 1890s, but is not itself the foremost object of this book. Rather, scrutiny of Scott's woman suffrage speeches, her correspondence with politicians, and her alliances and interactions with women within and beyond the woman suffrage movement contributes to the larger picture that is forming about the significance for the history of the sexes, and of feminism, of the struggle for woman suffrage in Australia. Analysis of Scott's suffrage work reveals the interrelation she saw between this and other reforms in 'the cause of women', with her focus on suffrage, for a time at least, as a single issue. In Scott's work for this reform, we encounter the first evidence of a pronounced discrepancy between the character of her private writings and that of her public, 'strategic' utterances — her letters to key protagonists and her public speeches require analysis in tandem.

The connections Scott drew between the need for the political representation of women and the sexual exploitation of women and girls emerge as a particularly important dimension of her public work at this time. Although overseas suffragists also pursued the vote as a principal means to the end of challenging men's sexual behaviour and power, Scott articulated this connection fully, in a form clearly influenced by late-nineteenth-century conditions in Australia and the experiences of women of her circle.

It is also in the woman suffrage campaign that Scott emerged as a dedicated, tenacious committee woman. It was sometimes noted later that she, as a foundation member of the WSL, was the longest-serving member, retaining from 1891 until 1902 the office of honorary secretary. Her claim and position were not without contests and difficulties, examined here only insofar as they illuminate her approach to notions of 'sisterhood' and modes of working with other women. Scott both learned and taught many political lessons during the first five years of the WSL — which coincided with the final five years of caring for Saranna Scott before her death in 1896. However, her main task in the period was lobbying politicians. This meant getting to know or working with men and extracting commitments from friends and foes alike: a task that involved considerable and largely unforeseen complexities.

CAUSES

In the first years of the woman suffrage campaign, Scott became involved in causes including early initiatives to raise the age of consent for girls, the Little Wives of India (an international welfare organisation opposing child marriage), and the establishment of the Women's College at the University of Sydney. Furthermore, she became acquainted with new spiritual movements, including theosophy, through her friend Maybanke Wolstenholme (later Anderson), and with spirit contact through seances at the homes of mediums, in the company of her friends William and Mary Windeyer. Meanwhile, the Movement to found New Australia, led by William Lane, was of enormous interest to her, as were the personal and domestic reasons for its failure as communicated through friends such as Mary Cameron (who became Dame Mary Gilmore). She enjoyed the company and correspondence of young founders of the Labor movement, in particular Arthur Rae and Frank Cotton. Both men tried to influence her to their views of politics and class struggle. She was enthralled.

Her aunt, Rose Selwyn, emerged as an important family ally in these new endeavours. Scott had worked with her throughout the 1870s and 1880s in Girls' Friendly Society work. The advent of the suffrage cause led Rose Selwyn to bolder articulations about women's position. She wholeheartedly supported her niece's stance on seduction of young girls and the need for a higher age of consent, confiding to her by letter some pathetic and outrageous instances of seduction and abandonment of young pregnant women in the Newcastle area. One man, in perfectly respectable company, even boasted of his conquests without suffering peer censure:

> a wretch in Newcastle actually had other wretches, his friends, to dine with him to celebrate his having ruined his *hundredth* girl. This, one would hope, is too wicked to be true: but unfortunately it is not . . . In a suburb of this place, a child of about 13 or 14 when attending a P. School was disgraced by a pupil teacher — when the thing could no longer be hid, she was taken home by broken hearted parents, there to hide her shame. But the wretch went on teaching at the school.

Rose Selwyn admitted that her sentiments were unpopular in her social circle — others would rather turn a blind eye.

With her niece's encouragement, Rose Selwyn took a leading role in the Newcastle suffrage movement, presenting speeches and lobbying politicians and senior clergy. She probably could not have undertaken these activities without the support of her husband, Arthur Selwyn — himself no stranger to political agitation to secure desired outcomes. In 1895, she delivered the public lecture 'Should Women Be Jurors?', in which the answer was a resounding 'yes', on the basis of a thoroughgoing criticism of the unfairness of the criminal-justice system towards women. She argued that women were judged according to men's experience. Meanwhile, the special insights to be gained from women's experience were nowhere admitted into juridical processes.[1]

Rose Selwyn was Saranna Scott's youngest sister. In the 1891, the former was 67, the latter 81. Saranna disapproved of all this talk of women's rights. While her ethics, her cultivation, and her commitment to others offered crucial examples for the career of her daughter, her explicit political and social values were increasingly at variance with those of both Roses in her family. Annie Rose Scott Cowen, Scott's niece, recalls as a 12-year-old visiting Lynton on a Friday evening when the house was full of visitors, including members of the Labor Party. By that stage, Saranna's rheumatism and arthritis were so chronic that her quarters had been relocated downstairs, since she could not manage mobility about the house. She presided on a downstairs lounge, from which pain permitted little movement. This meant that she could not avoid hearing sentiments, uttered by her daughter's guests, which were anathema to her. Cowen recalls that she would drown out the republican conversations of Scott's radical nationalist guests by loudly and aggressively singing 'God Save the Queen' and other royalist and Anglophile songs, and by reciting patriotic poetry.[2]

While Saranna cared little for her daughter's new friends, Scott's brother-in-law, banker Hope Wallace, now aged 52, may have cared even less to find the parlour full of bohemians and labourites. Perhaps distaste for them was offset by the presence at times of various members of parliament, judges and other notables. But business credentials were not the basis of invitations to Scott's home. Odds are that Wallace would have been more comfortable going round to the Merewether's on Friday nights for billiards, beer and whiskey. Merewether would also have been decidedly lukewarm about many of the salon guests. They introduced ideas and beliefs into household discussion that might be a worrying influence on young Nene. The boy met artists and cultural figures of various kinds. Such role models may have influenced Nene's decision to pursue a career as an actor, at least for the first decades of his working life. This was hardly the choice his father and elder second cousin would have hoped for. Even the learned and cultured George William Rusden, Scott's maternal uncle, queried the way she raised the boy. Evidently Scott objected to compulsory competitive sports in boys' schools. Her uncle teased her for her pacifism and gentility, asking: 'What did you advise Nene to substitute for *sport*? Would you nurse native dogs etc.?'[3]

Two babies arrived in 1891 — Alice's last child, Alice May Hamilton, and Millie's first and only child, Mary Ann Scott Shaw (Mollye). Scott, now aged 44, was still assisting with confinements and with the other children. During this year, Emily Scott, her brother Helenus's widow, visited from Brisbane with her daughter Rosie, who was the same age as Annie Rose Scott Hamilton (later Cowen). These girls would play together happily.

Rosie Scott, who married Harry Windon and lived at Petersham in Sydney, was later remembered by Miles Franklin for her great beauty. Franklin was then a very young woman, as she related in a letter to Rosie Windon's cousin, Mollye, in 1952:

> I, the little girl from the bush thought her [Rosie Windon] marvellous and your aunt seeing that I had the wrong values and doted on such girls rather than on the doctors and lawyers and social reformers used to murmur in her gentle way that she feared Rose would be spoiled with so much admiration for her beauty, but she showed no signs of it.[4]

The Scott household at Jersey Road, Woollahra, was frequently expanded in the 1890s due to the regular stays of Millie Shaw and baby Mollye, Aimée Scott, widow of Scott's brother, Robert, and her infant son Robert Glendon, and Rose Selwyn. Other relatives visited less regularly, but often for longer periods when they did, including Alice Hamilton (and whichever of her seven children accompanied her from Queensland), the Melbourne Rusdens — the elderly Uncle George, Aunt Grace — and the large numbers of cousins who were the offspring of her Uncle Henry and Aunt Anna Rusden. Nene, in his early teenage years, was very popular with his cousins and it is easy to see how the household became the Sydney base for the wider family.[5]

There were also many Sydney relatives and friends at various times visiting, dining, or taking members of the Lynton household out to events and occasions. Scott's middle-aged cousins, Augusta and David, were in close contact with the family. Merewether often noted his wife Augusta's attentions to Saranna by taking her out for a drive in the trap. Most of his detailed knowledge of family doings came through his wife. Their children were great favourites with Saranna and other members of the family, and these younger Merewethers visited Lynton during the stays of their second and third cousins.[6]

David Scott Mitchell maintained a warm and evidently regular relationship with the Scott household, as he did with the Merewethers. His bond with Merewether, and with Gussie Scott, may have disposed him well towards her widower, Hope Wallace, Merewether's billiards partner. Despite the later representation of Scott Mitchell as a recluse from 1870, he managed to reach Scott's home for family events, such as birthdays. Saranna wrote the following poem on the occasion of her eighty-first birthday:

My Birthday Gifts 3 April 1891.

Rose brought embracement for my arms
Lace, lace collar for enhancing my charms
Nene for my hands brought black silk mittens
Hope not to lose them like the kittens
Then Emily with her children came.

> Dear Mary worked such dainty chiffers
> On half a dozen pocket slippers
> At dinner plates and dishes too
> of handsome patterns, all brand new
> From David such a useful present.
> And shared with the others makes it pleasant.
>
> At tea time Hope comes and mercy
> He brings a frame of Lady Jersey.
> And books with various fables rife
> Brings David too this evening
> Telegram from Alice
> My birthday. Yes, I'm eighty-one.[7]

Death claimed Merewether in 1893 at the age of 73. Scott wrote lovingly to Augusta Merewether in sympathy: 'I felt one great longing that I could have told him once and forever how gratefully we all kept him in our thoughts for all his years of kindness to dear old Bob' (her deceased brother Robert). She sent Augusta a wreath from the four Scott women of her generation — Millie, Alice, Aimée and herself.[8]

Saranna's continued deterioration brought Scott's uncle, George Rusden, into more frequent contact with her in this period. He was interested in Scott's involvement in the attempt to establish the Women's College at the University of Sydney, and generally more supportive than her mother of the direction of her activities: 'Assuming that your Woman's College is needed and desirable I warmly congratulate you on having succeeded in raising the required £5000. I do not know the Jersey's but I have heard that she is clever so that in her you have a strong helper for your college.'[9] Indeed, the enlisting of Lady Jersey, the colonial governor's wife, undoubtedly lent a respectability to the cause, which influenced George Rusden. While he never went as far as to theorise on the oppression of women as a sex relative to men, his historical work was not immune to the analysis of systemic disadvantage. He was one of the first historians of Australia and New Zealand to confront the history of the dispossession of indigenous peoples. So damning and damaging was his history of New Zealand perceived to be that the New Zealand government undertook to proceed against him legally. Annie Rose Scott Cowen claims that he was forced to pay £5000 in damages.[10]

Class analysis and class struggle, however, were anathema to Rusden, and Scott's new socialist and labour movement friends received his disapproval. He found her defence of the 1891 strikes absurd. While in London in November that year, he wrote to her: 'Your strikes are bad and foolish but they are not likely to be so utterly destructive as amongst denser populations where more misery exists without them than exists in young countries with numerous possibilities.'[11] If they disagreed politically, he nonetheless increasingly entrusted Scott with family confidences, especially with regard to bequests, financial arrangements and career planning

Sarah Anne ('Saranna') Scott
(1810–96), Rose Scott's mother.
(Mitchell Library, State Library
of NSW)

Portrait of Rose Scott,
possibly by Conrad Martens.
(C.E. Smith Collection,
Newcastle Region Public Library)

David Scott Mitchell (1836–1907), Rose Scott's first cousin.
(Mitchell Library, State Library of NSW)

Saranna ('Fannie') Scott (1837–1924), Rose Scott's eldest sister, who married John Wensley and disappeared from the Scott family. (C.E. Smith Collection, Newcastle Region Public Library)

Mary Anne ('Millie') Scott (1849–1913), Rose Scott's younger sister, who married Bowyer Edward Shaw and was the mother of Mary ('Mollye') Menken. (C.E. Smith Collection, Newcastle Region Public Library)

Rose Scott and her adopted nephew, Hope Helenus ('Nene') Scott Wallace, 1880. (Mitchell Library, State Library of NSW)

Augusta ('Gussie') Maria Scott
(1843–80), Rose Scott's elder sister,
wife of Edward Hope Wallace and
mother of `Nene' Scott Wallace.
(C.E. Smith Collection, Newcastle
Region Public Library)

Edward Hope Wallace
(1839–1901), husband of Augusta Scott.
(C.E. Smith Collection, Newcastle
Region Public Library)

'Nene' Scott Wallace (1878-1950), Rose Scott's adopted nephew.
(C.E. Smith Collection, Newcastle Region Public Library)

Alice ('Allie') Scott
(1851–192?), Rose Scott's
youngest sister, wife of Terrick
Hamilton. (C.E. Smith
Collection, Newcastle Region
Public Library)

Terrick Alfred Hamilton (1851–
1907), husband of Alice Scott.
(C.E. Smith Collection,
Newcastle Region Public Library)

Emily ('Rosie') Scott (b. 1879), daughter of Rose Scott's eldest brother, Helenus Scott, and wife of Harry Windon. (C.E. Smith Collection, Newcastle Region Public Library)

David Scott Mitchell's home library. (C.E. Smith Collection, Newcastle Region Public Library)

for younger generations of the family. Perhaps he was still not entirely easy with the direction of Nene's development. In 1895 he ventured to Scott: 'I hope you will find some avocation for which Nene has a liking and an aptitude but any highly reputable calling cannot be irksome to an upright lad.'[12]

Since financial difficulty confronted Scott from 1895, George Rusden provided funds for household renovations, in particular, expensive installations necessary for heating the upstairs room that was to become Saranna's last sickroom. His elder sister, Grace Rusden, died in March 1896, leaving jewellery and £100 to Scott and everything else to Saranna. In the event of Saranna's death, the bequest was to pass on to Millie Shaw. Millie suddenly became a widow, also in March 1896. Her husband, Canon Shaw had what newspapers described as 'a shocking buggy accident' on a Singleton road. Shortly after, Millie and her daughter moved into Lynton on an indefinite basis. These deaths coincided with Saranna's gradual decline. In the final months, Scott nursed her night and day, and was devastated by her death in July. When he learned of the passing of his sister, George Rusden sent his condolences:

> You must of course feel a great blank around you but that is inevitable. The shock must have come at some time and increasing infirmity might have exhausted even your mother's elasticity of spirits and her cheerfulness. No one who knew her could have wished for any such change as that pain or weakness should have subdued her. You were able to do all that humanly speaking could have been done and indeed you have devoted much of your life to the task . . . You will have to consult with David Mitchell and with your brother George and with good Dr Bowker I suppose about arranging affairs and you must have other friends who are not known to me. It will be irksome but as it will be a duty you will meet it and the performance of it will be salutory for mind and body. Millie also will be a comfort to you as you have been to her.[13]

In dealing with this major life transition Scott was surrounded by a full household and many obligations and distractions. Years earlier the phrenologist had noted that Scott would be unlikely to confide much of her feelings to others, even inclining towards secretiveness. There are few indications (in her own words at least) as to what she made of the loss of Saranna. She threw herself into intensive work in public causes and admitted little of the pain she was feeling. A letter of sympathy from the poet, Dowell O'Reilly, in September 1896 evoked a rare response from Scott: 'It is hard to write about my loss for it is to me so great a blank that I feel in a way I am beginning life all over again and as if the great object I lived for had gone . . . Your letter pained me.'[14]

Scott's developing interest in theosophy, spiritualism and the occult was first manifest in the early 1890s and remained for the rest of her life. Its proximity to so many deaths of loved ones may be significant. In 1896 an unidentified correspondent on other matters observed his or her shock at learning that Scott was an atheist. If this is how she represented herself at this time of early public political engagement, it would hardly have pleased the members of her pious family, especially the clergymen amongst them. Jill Roe, historian of theosophy in Australia, has argued that a serious crisis in commitment to the established Anglican Church, especially in its perceived lack of social mission, engulfed the liberal intelligensia of Australia in this period. Friends of Scott were prominent in this spiritual reassessment.[15]

William Charles Windeyer — 'The Judge' as his wife Mary called him in her correspondence with Scott — was committed to contacting deceased spirits through seances. He accompanied Scott to several 'contacts' in the early 1890s. His papers contain fascinating accounts of his spiritual experiences. In 1876 Mary Windeyer had borne an infant named Mena, who died. Their second child, Margaret, was sick in 1880, the year William Windeyer attended a Melbourne seance anonymously. The medium, without knowing anything of him or his circumstances, told him that Margaret would recover while Mena was content and living in the spirit world, in the company of Windeyer's former friend and mentor, Dr Woolley, Professor of Classics. Indeed, Mena reported that Woolley was teaching her classics. Windeyer was startled by another event. Shortly before his death in Sydney, Dr Charles Badham (Woolley's successor as Professor of Classics) and Windeyer had disagreed as to life after death, Badham putting the atheist view. At another Melbourne seance Windeyer attended, two months after Badham's death, a figure entered the room and wrote on a piece of paper 'Your friend Charles Badham lives in the spirit life'. The medium said that Badham was anxious to 'tell you that the opinions which he held when living were erroneous and that he lives in the spirit world'. Windeyer believed that 'the importance of the communication rested upon it being relative to a conversation which none knew except Dr Badham and me. . . Though I had been accustomed to spiritual phenomena for years I was profoundly impressed and startled by the communication.'[16]

Scott wrote an account of a seance she attended in 1893. The other participants were Lady Darley (Leila), May Gullett, Miss Woolley, Miss Windeyer, Richard Windeyer and his wife, Mrs Ralston, Mr and Mrs Tovey, Miss McCauley and Mrs Laidley, and Judge and Lady Windeyer. The medium, the controversial Mrs Mellion, entered a cabinet in the centre of the drawing-room and they all joined hands. Then: 'I heard what I know was the medium speaking in a clipt way with the accent of a negro . . . "Dat Lady over dere wid de nice white arms she . . . wondering what I am." This was meant for me . . . ' Scott concluded this from the fact that she was the only one present in evening dress. Judge Windeyer squeezed her hand sympathetically and said 'That's you and she's got good taste'.[17] After various other questions and messages for participants, the medium collapsed, exhausted. Her husband explained to Scott that she could only manage these experiences about once a fortnight. How often Scott attended such seances remains unclear, though her tone in discussing this one had an air of bemusement.

At about the same time Scott became interested in theosophy. Mrs Cooper Oakley, an English theosophist and suffragist lecturer, visited Sydney in 1893 and was guest of the WSL. Then, in 1894, the international celebrity theosophist, Annie Besant, made a brief Australian tour. Many elements of theosophical belief had particular appeal to women suffragists. Roe observes that theosophists offered a cyclical view of the spiritual realm attuned to representation of the feminine. Critical of the male-dominated priesthood and dogmatic theology, theosophists claimed that these two features of conventional Christian religions had resulted in a weakening of women. Many of the most charismatic and famous of theosophical leaders were superb public lecturers who fervently supported woman suffrage. This support made many suffragists at least receptive to controversial aspects of theosophical beliefs, including reincarnation and the workings of karma.[18]

Scott attended lectures and other theosophical 'events' at the Sydney School of Arts. She was encouraged by her friend and fellow suffragist, Maybanke Wolstenholme, who assured her that 'we do not try to make converts but we do wish to encourage enquiries and there is so much that you will like that I long to interest you'.[19] Her involvement did not escape the notice of her family. George Rusden had entrusted the social overseeing of a young relative of the Melbourne Rusdens, Miss Michie, to Scott, and he sent his rebuke of theosophy through a discussion of her:

> I don't know that you would have demeaned yourself to take notice of that coarse Blavatzky or that creature Besant (though I deplore that Miss Michie worships their theories) but as much I shrink from the plots to lower women from their proper place, I at once resort to you on your throne, not amongst a mob of anarchists, when I want help in doing Christian good to the fatherless.[20]

Scott's interest in movements challenging orthodoxies was not confined to the spiritual realm. She became greatly interested in socialism in the early 1890s, to the horror of her family. Befriending William Lane through her 'salon', she watched developments in the planning and establishment of the Utopian communities' 'New Australia' in Paraguay with great eagerness. But she also offered support to young socialist women who attempted to take their place in such organisations. One acquaintance who eventually joined the Paraguay settlement was Mary Cameron. William Lane was greatly taken with Scott, and she confided to Cameron in 1894 that Mrs Lane seemed considerably less amiable towards her. It is likely that Scott routinely encountered lukewarmness, distance and even hostility from the wives of famous men of her acquaintance. She may have judged correctly in this case or she may have been 'over-reading'. Cameron hastened to reassure her that:

> I think you were quite mistaken in supposing that Mrs Lane did not feel cordially towards you. She is apart from any other consideration one of those women who like whom their husbands like. And, from what Mrs Lane tells me, Mr Lane had the greatest confidence in you . . . Of course, I have not mentioned what you said to anyone.[21]

'New Australia' collapsed, amid charges, countercharges, and considerable bitterness. Lane kept in contact with Scott, attempting to draw on her support in several ways. She later recalled his complaint that she held back from full commitment to his cause. But despite the basic warmth she maintained towards him, events led her to judge his ethics and commitment to *her* cause in adverse terms. His gradual abandonment of feminist principles has been well documented by Australian historians, and is no doubt the reason he disappeared from Scott's correspondence shortly after his migration to New Zealand.[22]

Two young men of the early labour movement, Frank Cotton and Arthur Rae, were anxious that Scott understand their cause as fully as possible. Cotton sent Henry George's *Condition of Labour* in 1893, instructing Scott to 'study the book carefully and note any points with which you do not agree in order that I may discuss them with you'. He was particularly concerned that she should not be led astray 'by seemingly plausible "social reforms" which deal merely with effects and not causes'. In the early stages of the suffrage campaign these socialist friends were apt to characterise women's lack of citizenship and certainly the seduction of girls, illegitimacy and widespread prostitution in this way — as effects or symptoms. Yet Cotton also insisted that Scott should distinguish between social conditions that could be altered and 'the laws of nature which are unalterable'.[23] A disquieting portion of Scott's concerns seemed to them to be challenging the latter, an endeavour as futile as it was perilous, especially regarding men and sexual behaviour.

Cotton and Rae attempted to convert Scott for two reasons. First, she was unlike other women philanthropists of her class because of her willingness to have direct involvement with the working class. As Rae put it after Scott's early lecture at the Socialist Hall, 'to come among the workers and teach is a thousand times more useful than stand off and dictate; and that is as you have done tonight.' Another Labor friend of Scott's, J.D. Fitzgerald, wrote 'I wish I could tell Lady Dilke and her clever Miss May Abraham and Miss Routledge that a woman of their own station in society in New South Wales were [sic] working down among their poor working sisters.' The second reason was her political networks. As Cotton put it 'You hold a position of influence amongst an ever widening circle.'[24] This made her an important person to convert to socialist objectives.

Some reciprocity was generated. These men addressed women's issues that might otherwise have left them unengaged; while Scott delved further, not only into socialism, but labour movement issues and policies more generally. In 1893 she gave a lecture entitled 'On Socialism' to a meeting of the WLS. After beginning by exposing the extent of poverty and the exploitation and degradation of the poor, Scott declared that the charitable activities all too familiar to her audience were an inadequate response to the problem. She estimated that through these works they might 'manage to give some relief to about one in every hundred of those who are less fortunate than ourselves'. Why should anyone have to accept charity as a solution to economic inequality, she asked?

Widespread public condemnation of socialists was based on ignorance and she set about ending her audience's unfamiliarity with socialist principles and political objectives. She quoted Annie Besant, among others, in support of her conclusion that socialism had much to offer the majority of the population: 'I do not say that any perfect system of socialism has yet been evolved but I do say that as one who loves humanity no one should stand aloof from socialism and in ignorance abuse it or those who are struggling earnestly to bring it about.' She addressed no specific gender issues in this lecture, yet her graphic examples of industrial exploitation and degrading living conditions were primarily of wage-earning and elderly women.[25]

Cotton and Rae attempted to address the women's issues raised by Scott by supporting woman suffrage within the labour movement, encountering the arguments of working-class men opposed to the reform. Rae often tried to deny that women's legal disabilities were distinct in type or cause from those of other groups. For instance, criminals' and lunatics' exclusion from voting was just as much the product of 'our wrong social conditions as the fallen woman whom you yourself would give the franchise'. In 1892 he insisted that the main hurdle Scott must overcome was 'the workers' fear' that woman suffrage 'is a scheme to secure conservative reaction in the legislature by strengthening the hands of property holders with a large, additional female vote from their intelligent, educated relatives'.

Rae also addressed the common masculine objection to women's rights by means of dubbing its advocates embittered and deficient in womanly charms. When Louisa MacDonald was appointed as the first principal of the newly established Women's College (which he kept calling the Ladies College), he wrote to Scott about a photograph he saw with the newspaper story:

> she is no bluestocking but likes a fair share of the fashions and pleasures of her sex. I like that because it shows that women can be clever without ceasing to be as purely human as ever. I never doubted it but many do. I am glad that one who will wield much influence will probably show their fears to be quite groundless. Fancy

> a woman of that mental calibre being denied *one* vote while the so
> called National Association would give the retired publican or prize
> fighter *two*.

Rae developed more than a political interest in Scott. When frequently on
the road in party work, prior to his marriage in 1894, he would write to her
late at night in his hotel bed. He asked for her photograph for his album, as
well as for what he saw as its political uses in giving 'some of my
brutal sex a kindlier opinion of the leaders of what they sometimes so ungra-
ciously term the "shrieking sisterhood"'. He disagreed with Scott's advocacies on behalf of Aborigines, the Chinese and indentured Kanaka
labour. They conducted an intense correspondence on these issues, in which
Rae consistently asserted the prerogatives of the male Anglo-Celtic worker
claims above claims of any others. He ventured also to advise her as to
correct political strategies for her various causes. In May 1892 he wrote 'Ah!
Miss Scott there is a lot of fighting to do yet and you can't do it with lavender water.' Asserting always a masculine, and at times explicitly muscular,
view of politics, he made the interesting prediction later in 1892 that the
vote for women would not be successfully won through orderly means:

> You'll just have to break the law . . . I predict that some day
> you'll just march to the polling booth armed with brooms and other
> weapons and record your votes whether the returning officer likes
> it or not. What matter if your votes aren't counted. You will
> have broken the law by belting the returning officer for resisting
> your desire to vote and you might get the franchise. Not before. I
> know you hate shams and it is a sham to expect reform without
> force, and force a little more *real* than the force of love too.[26]

Scott's exchanges with socialist and Labor men of the 1890s disclosed the conditional basis on which their support for 'the cause of
women' was secured. Their concern was with working-class women, who
were notoriously difficult to involve in class struggle and formal political activity. Dinners had to be cooked, and meetings were held in public
houses at night with no childcare provided. Insofar as Scott addressed the
disabilities of working women — women politically hard to reach — the
socialist brotherhood welcomed her endeavours with enthusiasm.
Woman suffrage was a good and just issue around which working
women could, they believed, be mobilised.

Most of these men were content to attribute women's difficulties to
the development of capitalism, private property and the state, and
women's lack of citizenship as a symptom. There was no sense in which
these early socialists believed that woman suffrage would itself be a
weighty reform. Nor could they accept the notion that working-class women
might have real political interests distinct from, and even opposed to, those
of working-class men, interests based on the fact of their womanhood: if

matters appeared so in the present, they were short-term conflicts, to be swept away by a new order which could never come about unless men and women worked side-by-side in common cause. An intense degree of sex complementarity underpinned the socialist and labourite world view. This did not prevent support and collaboration between socialist and labourite adherents and workers in 'the cause of women'. It did obstruct, however, the fuller engagement between the various tendencies in these competing positions. The vision of working-class sex complementarity was imperilled by the egalitarian dimension of feminist discourses of the period (which might, for instance, threaten the sex division of domestic labour and public activity by a stress on the sameness or common humanity of the sexes). That vision might equally be at risk from the elements of those same feminist discourses asserting women's specificity and differences from men and demanding legislation, representation and cultural space for them.

While Scott undoubtedly worked at her alliances with the labour movement and socialists, she would never permit the displacement of her political adherence to 'the cause of women' as a sexed group. She met argument with argument, confidently and with erudition. A major reason for her analytical strength and focus was the work she and other women had been doing in the WLS since 1890. The society then functioned as a forum for the development of her analyses of women's position in relation to the 'great movements' of the day. Scott's contributions to proceedings included, as well as her paper 'On Socialism' in April 1893, a paper on the novel *Dinah Morris* in September 1893, the notes of which do not appear to have survived. In February the same year, she read a paper entitled 'Thoughts on Pictures in the Art Gallery', and in May another called 'Australian Poets'. She and Edith Badham, daughter of the late Dr Badham, were part of a panel discussion on different literary representations of the story of Tristram and Iseult. Other papers she presented in this period included the topics of Keats, American short stories by women (with a focus on Charlotte Perkins Stetson), evolution, and Ibsen's *Master Builder*.[27] Scott's newspaper clippings from the period reveal an intense interest in Ibsen, whose plays became controversial from the early 1890s, especially *A Doll's House*, staged in 1890, which caused considerable debate in the *Sydney Morning Herald*. The journalist who wrote under the pen-name 'Rosa Boheme' entered the fray on several occasions, with a defence of Ibsen 'from a women's point of view'. She noted that the supposedly disgraceful conduct of Nora Helmer in leaving her children 'has been mainly if not entirely discussed in print by men'. Scott clipped many of Boheme's press articles and no doubt endorsed her contention that the lesson of *A Doll's House* was that spiritual affinity was 'the sole basis for physical affinity between the sexes . . . The Helmerian school, to whom woman is but a charming toy is a rapidly decreasing majority and it only depends upon woman herself to convert it into a minority'.

The phrase 'charming toy', used in this sense, appeared often in Scott's speeches and private writings. Interestingly, Emily Heron, David Scott Mitchell's former fiancée, published an article critical of Nora Helmer under her journalist pen-name, 'Australie', in the *Illustrated Sydney News*. Moreover, the stinging attack upon Ibsen in the *Sydney Morning Herald* by 'Outis' in January 1895 moved Scott herself to pen a letter to the editor. She took exception to Outis's judgement that 'Ibsen is not a dramatist at all, but a writer of thin, incoherent dialogue', and noted that this was hardly the view of the great actresses touring as Ibsen heroines, Elizabeth Robins and Janet Achurch, both also suffragists and activists on behalf of the cause of women in their profession.[28]

Scott engaged actively in intellectual and cultural aspects of feminism. This is especially striking in view of her domestic responsibilities and difficulties in the early 1890s, and of the expanding requirements of public causes in which she was involved. Perhaps above all others, this intellectual dimension of feminist work sustained her through the often tedious and frustrating aspects of committee work and the traumas of personal life. As well, it enriched her formulations of 'the problem', in addressing 'Why Women Want a Vote'. Scott's increased appreciation of the importance of women's participation in higher education made the committee to raise funds for the establishment of the Women's College at the University of Sydney an important commitment for her. With the success of this initiative and the appointment of its first principal, Louisa MacDonald, women's higher education became a continuing cause for Scott. Her friendship with MacDonald was to be a crucial and enduring one.[29] However, Scott's lack of formal education led her into revealing political conflicts with MacDonald later in their friendship.

TOWARDS REPRESENTATION

An early extant speech delivered by Scott at the Sydney School of Arts on woman suffrage is dated March 1892. It is worth analysing this and her other early suffrage speeches in some detail, in order to understand how she combined her previous concerns with the issue of women's political representation. After commenting on the massive improvements in social conditions in Wyoming since the enfranchisement of women there, she quoted Frances Power Cobbe on the political significance of representation, beyond the mere right to drop 'a paper into a ballot box'. Scott asked a series of questions about qualifications required to represent:

> Could men of university education and noblemen and gentlemen in the past legislate entirely for the working man? However much they tried to do so, could they understand all their wants? And yet there is a far wider difference between men and women and their separate needs and points of view than there can be between any two classes of men. It is against every principle of Democratic

Government that men should legislate entirely for women or
that any class should legislate entirely for another class.

If her insistence that women were entitled to represent themselves
encountered a series of typical objections, Scott observed that they all
returned to the 'notion that women are men's private property and
should only act in accordance with his wishes and prejudices'. To socialist colleagues, who posed woman suffrage as a 'side issue' for socialism,
she retorted that 'all else is a "side issue" till men have given women the
right to speak on these momentous questions'. To men who charged that,
if enfranchised, women would neglect their domestic duties, she asked
whether men 'are dreadfully afraid their dinners will not be cooked, their
socks darned and their children will be neglected if women have votes?
. . . Does the vote ruin the carpenters, stonemasons and other workmen
and lead them to neglect their business?' And, to the claim that women
could not have the vote because they could not serve as soldiers and risk
their lives in the service of their countries, she pointed out that small, weak,
sickly men rejected by the military in time of war, were not disenfranchised.
Meanwhile, she argued, 'women jeopardise their lives in the service of their
native land in childbirth more than men, including soldiers or sailors'.

Dealing with such objections propelled Scott's speech towards a
combative phase, which was disquieting for men in her audiences. She
began softly on the issue of men's sense of honour and morality, by observing that few women would care to trust a man 'whose private life had been
dishonest, whose conduct towards women had been mean' with their parliamentary representation. She implied that this basis for distrusting
politicians was almost universal by admitting that 'men are not and
never can be sufficiently educated to represent women'. In the context in
which this opinion was set, 'education' meant changing men's moral behaviour, especially with respect to the seduction and abandonment of
women and their adultery in private life. To reinforce her point, she suddenly presented two more 'common objections' to woman suffrage,
holding them up for merciless rebuttal: first, that politics is not woman's
sphere; and, second, that if women were granted suffrage, immoral
women, including prostitutes, would have the right to vote along with the
virtuous — surely an undesirable outcome?

Although commentators accurately portrayed Scott's lecturing
style as charming, warm and persuasive, rather than forceful, considerable
force resided in her choice of expression and the way in which she positioned (at least the men in) her audience, especially those socialist men
addressing industrial issues like 'sweated' labour. It is worth quoting
comprehensively:

'Politics is not a woman's sphere' . . . and yet men will tell you that
it is the sphere of thousands of women to lead lives of moral

> slavery and degradation! Oh how many would be reformers, strain at a knat and swallow a camel! (Sweating more terrible than prostitution!) Most men are selfishly content to see thousands of women leading lives they would shudder to see led by their own sisters. And even that quality they most respect in women they love, Purity, is not by them desired for all women. It is but a garment in which women should be clothed or otherwise as suits man's pleasure or convenience! His relatives must be stainless fore- sooth but it matters little to him if millions of women are the reverse ... Yes, these bad women will vote. Vote, why not? Are they really any worse than the men whose demand for degradation creates a supply of degradation? *Man* should no longer be as he too often is the sole aim and object of woman's existence.[30]

The bedrock of Scott's case for woman suffrage was her critique of men's qualifications and capacities to represent women in view of the fundamental differences between them. Sex differences were manifest in ethics, behaviour and political interests, though Scott rarely ventured to search for the origins or grand theoretical explanations of these differences, confining herself to reporting on matters as she and other women observed them. It would be possible to read her descriptions of sex differences as presuming biological causation, particularly her representations of man as 'ruled by the animal', woman as the 'spiritual' sex. Certainly bio- logical determinist and hereditarian discourses were decidedly in vogue in this period, and the positioning of the sexes in radically dualistic terms was familiar and plausible for audiences and readers.

If Scott had consistently believed the prevalent biological determinist wisdom about the sexes, then she and other suffragists deployed an ingeni- ous rendering of this wisdom towards obtaining political rights. Politics was conventionally understood in terms of different interests representing them- selves and battling the various arenas of public life. Scott asked for noth- ing more than the recognition that conventionally understood sex differences made women a cohesive interest group that was unjustly excluded from political representation.

This argument involved a cogent challenge to those opponents of woman suffrage who contended that women did not need the vote because their interests were well enough represented by their husbands and fathers to render woman suffrage an unnecessary doubling of votes in the same pattern. This anti-suffrage position came close to implying a sameness of interests and characteristics between women and men, against the grain of scholarly wisdom and popular belief. Yet anti-suffragists deeply adhered to the view of innate sex differences when expressing dis- taste at the idea of women 'unsexing' and 'degrading' themselves by enter- ing the rough, public fray of the polling booth. Moreover, opponents of woman suffrage would often concede that women's political interests were indeed different from men's. Enfranchising women would lead to a crisis in domestic government — for instance, to political bickering over the dinner table, with women presuming to express opinions on matters for which they had no qualifications to speak, let alone hold power to arbitrate outcomes as voters. In the interests of social stability and family harmony, men must monopolise citizenship and women be guided by the wisdom and experience of their male relatives.[31]

Faced with such contradictory but recognisably patriarchal opinions, Scott's case for women's political representation adroitly probed their weak spots. She called the male electorate to account for the social policies, conditions and practices that were the outcome of masculine 'wisdom' and 'experience'. The culture was dominated by poverty, aggression, ruthless competition and exploitation of the weak by the strong. Politics was organised around party, class and nationalism. This was the wisdom of male voters and the legislating brotherhood they empowered. Scott declared: 'What a small and petty thing is that brotherhood which limits itself to a party, a class or even a country? . . . Why in the name of all that is just and good should masculine notions have a monopoly?'[32]

This was the crux of the matter. Woman suffrage was an anti-monopoly reform that entailed public, legislative recognition that what had hitherto passed as universal principles of government with outcomes of universal consensus, had in fact been 'sexed'. That is to say, they were masculine, for the most part protecting and serving the interests of men, only one of *two* sexes. Scott was not seeking woman suffrage in pursuit of abstract ideas of equality, nor was she seeking to make government, legal rights and public life sex-neutral. On the contrary, since the differences between the sexes were for her and her contemporaries more striking than the similarities, public life could only be sexed. The input of *both* sexes was the objective. This addition of women's input was premised on the assumption that women would constitute a new and distinct element in political life, mitigating some of the adverse effects of masculine monopoly. Scott's target, then, was what modern feminists identify as phallocentrism — the pretence that terms of representation, government, knowledges or whatever, are universally applicable, when in fact they apply to and serve the interests and express the experiences of only one sex — men.[33]

In this context, her strategy was effective and plausible, since the masculinity of public life was readily conceded by most protagonists in the woman suffrage debate. Arguably, it was more obviously identifiable and admitted in the 1890s than it is now, when the legacy of nearly a century of egalitarian discourses is a strong investment in the belief in the sex-neutrality of public institutions, offices and their practices. Alternatively, had Scott attempted egalitarian arguments in support of woman suffrage, stressing the sameness and equal capacities of the sexes, she probably would have had no impact on the anti-suffrage case. For the teachings of religion and science alike stressed sex differences, while the merest observation of social facts seemed to lend undeniable support to the proposition of immutable differences. Women were mothers, men were not. From infancy to the grave, the sexes exhibited incontrovertibly different natures and attributes. Commonly, these differences were represented as complementary, but sometimes were construed as the basis of a sex war or battle of the sexes, of which woman suffrage advocacy was, like women's temperance work, another symptom.

Whatever sex equalities or sameness of capacities Scott privately believed existed, egalitarian arguments had little purchase in the discursive context of the 1890s. Instead, a focus of the anti-monopoly element of her woman suffrage case was to use the commonsense sex complementarity beliefs that saturated both high and popular culture. Rather than threatening her audience with the prospect of woman abandoning her sphere of household, domestic life and motherhood, Scott stressed the happiness of women in their roles as wives and mothers, when carried out in joint and harmonious co-operation with their husbands, the fathers of their children. To be successful, domestic life needed the contribution of both sexes — it was therefore not only women's but men's sphere too. The different qualities the sexes brought to bear were both needed. Moreover, just as both sexes should contribute to private life, so they both had a vital part to play in public, civic and political life. The ill-health of the body politic was a consequence of its deprivation of feminine attributes. The key domains of politics and public life thereby were unnaturally skewed, distorted and imbalanced.

In practical terms, then, Scott's woman suffrage case advocated extending women's sphere of influence so that, like men, women participated in public as well as private life. Read superficially, woman suffrage here might resemble an argument for equality, equal rights and sameness of treatment. The stated rationales of suffragists like Scott, however, cannot usefully be characterised as egalitarian. They did not advocate equal citizenship for women to operate in public life on the same terms with the same mission and attributes as men did. It was not the acceptance of existing male norms of politics and citizenship that was in play here, but more precisely, the criticism and rejection of them, that was the basis of the woman suffrage claim.

Significantly, this claim was built not only on a critique of masculinity but also on a positive assertion of the value of womanliness. Scott asserted the distinct experience of childbirth and childrearing as a basis for insisting that women exhibited bravery, heroism and service to their country, justifying the demand for citizenship. Similarly, she speculated that the experience of women in bringing forth and nurturing new lives might well mean that in political and public life they would be particularly concerned with solutions to social problems, and might typically oppose ventures involving aggression, competitiveness, military coercion and war.

Perhaps they might also prove laggards in the cause of republicanism — she jibed cheerily that she for one rejoiced in having a woman monarch!

Scott's sex complementarity and sex specificity arguments at first seem to respect the separation between public and private spheres; but underpinning these claims were arguments which transgressed that separation and suggested the inextricable connections between the two spheres. The man dishonourable in his relations with women being an unfit parliamentarian was one example. Another instance was her argument that the disenfranchisement of mothers undermined the respect they were due from their sons:

> Can it be good for the boy of 21 to feel he has a voice in the government of his country and his mother has none? This mother, whom as a rule he cannot but feel is his superior in all else. Is it good for the boy to feel that because he is of the masculine sex therefore a government gives him a voice in making those laws which his mother and all other women must obey? His father teaches him to be manly, to strike back when he is struck by another boy, to compete with others in the struggle for life, to battle, to fight and to carve himself a place in the world; no doubt necessary teaching. His mother would teach him to cultivate his affections, to be unselfish, generous and moral. Is hers not the higher teaching — the teaching that develops his noblest faculties? Yet her influence in a practical way is solely confined to the home, and too soon the boy is taught by his country's laws and the ways of other men to despise and look down upon the woman's teaching and influence in all business matters and to think that his heart is meant only for the domestic circle.

Scott's suffrage speeches bear interesting comparison with the arguments and preoccupations in two of Louisa Lawson's speeches. The first was presented to the Dawn Club in May 1889; the second at the June 1891 public meeting of the newly formed WSL. In these speeches Lawson exhibited the same preoccupation with the sexual exploitation of women and girls and the understanding of the vote as the necessary means of challenging such exploitation. 'Here in Australia,' Lawson declared in the 1891 speech, 'it is considered more a crime to steal a horse than ruin a girl.' She held 'the tender age of 14 years' to be too young for girls to comprehend the advances that men made. By denying them the vote, men bound women's hands in the 'battle raging against intemperance, gambling and impurity'. Women's first business had to be securing their freedom as a sex and 'to get ourselves into a position of independence'. Lawson perhaps put matters more bluntly than Scott, explicitly linking suffrage and temperance, a link Scott avoided in public speeches. In general, though, their placement in a shared world of sexual politics discourse is undeniable.[34]

In the first five years of the WSL's work Scott gave various versions of her case for woman suffrage and rebuttals of the case against. The repertoire of issues and arguments she included widened as a consequence of discussions with various politicians, and of work with a larger range of women. Her style also became more trenchant and determined. The moment in her speeches when she would discuss men's morality and prostitution became almost fierce and frequently sarcastic. The 1892 passage quoted above bears illuminating comparison with a speech she delivered in May 1895:

> if men desire to be chivalrous let them reserve their sentimental speeches about women being torn from their homes and domestic duties for the sad-eyed woman who sells newspapers in the street, for the charwoman who leaves her children whether she is sick or well while she goes out to slave by the day and for the women in the clutches of the sweater . . . and when men feel inclined to shed their tears over the terrible prospect of women forgetting or not caring to fulfil their heaven born vocation of wife and mother let them remember the vocation of the women who without protest from them stand at night at the corners of the streets! Let such men look to their motives when they talk of women's work, whilst they reserve for themselves all the comfortable billets and positions of honour in Political and Municipal life.[35]

THE QUESTION OF VICE

A number of developments had hardened Scott's resolve on woman suffrage by 1895. Perhaps the most significant of these was the fate of the Vice Suppression Bill, tabled in 1892 by J.C. Nield and endorsed by Scott, who attempted to raise and publish a petition in support of it. The Bill proposed to make seduction with promise of marriage a criminal offence, the object of the unsuccessful Seduction Punishment Bill debated in 1887. In addition, the Bill proposed raising the age of consent from 14 to 16, and a number of other measures, in line with the English Criminal Law Amendment Act of 1885. Scott often recalled that the Bill was defeated amidst laughter and ridicule by members of parliament. In fact, it was referred to a select committee, which ultimately lapsed without reporting. Many members of the Legislative Assembly spoke vehemently against the Bill at its second reading, but perhaps none so effectively as B.R. Wise, Edmund Barton, Frank Farrell and W.P. Crick. All used their criminal law experience to argue that a higher age of consent posed a threat to the liberty of men as British subjects. It was, in their view, 'idle' to deny that girls were grown-up at 14. The gratification of instincts was 'natural' and to legislate on behalf of hysterical and fanatical interests, in a direction antagonistic to public opinion, would bring the rule of law into disrepute. Wise's interventions were acknowledged as those which stopped the Bill. The terms of his opposition bear examination:

> We must take human nature as it is. I am opposed to raising the age of consent at all . . . [M]any girls are so physically constituted that

they are diseased in their imagination and under the influence of physical conditions that medical men can explain. Under the influence of hysteria and physical conditions there is positively no limit to the recklessness and the wickedness of the charges which such girls will make. They will make under the influence of a diseased imagination the vilest charges with the greatest detail under circumstances which make it almost impossible to refute the charges . . . If any barmaid or shop girl under the age of 21 chooses to charge her employer whom she may see only once a month or once a week, with having had connection with her, he will be absolutely at her mercy . . . Under this act consent is no answer and the result may be as in the East End of London that you would practically close off the avenues of employment to all girls under 21.

At this point in Wise's speech, Crick, the 'man of the world' lawyer who specialised in defending men charged with rape, interjected most significantly: 'The same thing might happen with a domestic servant!'[36]

Quite so. The issue was very close to home, too close for it to be strategically wise for Nield, the Bill's advocate, to mention this most typical case of 'seduction'. Its mention evoked parliamentary disavowal of the entire issue. For Scott, it was the supreme example of men legislating in their own interests. She tried to organise deputations to politicians and to encourage suffragists and women philanthropists to sign a petition in support of the Bill, to be published in the *Sydney Morning Herald*.

In response, she encountered an avalanche of hostility. Parliamentarians, especially Labor men who had become her friends, offered fierce opposition. Arthur Rae rebuked her in the sternest terms for her stance on this issue. While Scott saw a raised age of consent as providing a disincentive to men who would seduce and abandon young teenage girls, leaving them with illegitimate babies and perhaps no option but prostitution, Rae, like his fellow politicians, saw the measure in 'man of the world' terms. Earlier in 1892 they had disagreed on the issue of seduction and Scott's view of women as sexually exploited. Since he was a member of the WSL and publicly associated with Scott, Rae took rare liberties in his criticism of her following a deputation to the Premier on the Bill:

I do not wish to dishearten you but my opinion is that all our liberties are won by the negation of law . . . I should like to add that I was sorry for the way in which your deputation approached the Premier. Your statements seemed to me beside the mark and calculated to excite ridicule and raise opposition. What for instance do you think you would do to abolish the social evils of drunkenness, streetwalking and seduction? Evils which your deputation evidently believed to be due to bad laws by wicked men . . . No matter how you would proceed it is sheer nonsense to suppose that you could effect complete reform at once. It is equally absurd and unfair to infer that men deliberately make bad laws out of the innate wickedness of their sex. They don't . . . What would women do? Probably repress all these vices by cast iron laws and thereby create huge numbers of despicable paid

> spies and informers . . . Why not instead discourage avarice by
> making it unnecessary? Why not keep women from selling
> themselves body and soul by giving them an opportunity to
> gratify honest love in an honest and natural manner.

Four days later, Scott received a similar letter from her friend, Labor Member
of the Legislative Assembly, Frank Cotton. He anticipated that his opposition to the Vice Suppression Bill would shock and pain her, but nonetheless declared that he had to be honest with her. He claimed that if men's
standard of morality was low, the fault lay with women who regulate social
life. He asked rhetorically 'now do you know any social circle into which
a man who was known to have been the cause of a girl's ruin would not
be admitted if he were otherwise eligible?' Women became 'ruined' by men
because they were trained from childhood to bargain themselves, not for
love, but for a good home and social position. He concluded by talking of
his own 'early and improvident' marriage:

> Had I waited until I was in a position to marry I should be what most
> men are; . . . there is no alternative, broadly speaking between
> . . . early and improvident marriages and what happens everywhere
> all round us . . . we're not iron and we're not ice; and after all it's
> no use shutting our eyes to the fact that the laws of nature are the
> laws of God.

Evidently Scott replied to this letter, though it is unclear in what terms. She
seems not to have dislodged his essentialist and hydraulic version of
(male) sexuality. His next letter to her, shortly after, apologised for his
newspaper article opposing the raised age of consent — but nonetheless he
declared 'You don't realise, you can't realise what the curse of "compulsory celibacy" means under existing economic conditions.'[37]

In letters such as these, the men with whom Scott was working in the
suffrage cause at least made clear their interests in opposing the age of consent measure. The opposition of women was more complex. Mary
Windeyer, first president of the WSL, declined Scott's invitation to attend
the meeting to support the Bill. She wrote, saying, 'I do not think any good
is to be done by raising the age. There are many serious reasons against it.'
Perhaps she did not want to see the suffrage issue tainted by association with
an even more unpopular and controversial measure. With the allegations that an enfranchised electorate of women would target men's pleasures, especially 'vice' and drink, Windeyer may have feared, at least at this
early stage, that suffragist support for the Bill gave such allegations credence.
Certainly the temperance women were strong supporters of the Bill. This
caused tensions within the age of consent movement, and at one point Scott
attempted to resign from the committee. But another campaign organiser,
Alice Wilson, refused to accept this, and wrote back to Scott: 'I have
worked hard that this deputation should not be wholly of the WCTU and

for you to stay away would work against what is the truest interest of the cause. So come.'

Besides suffrage and temperance women, Scott tried to involve those women philanthropists most directly working with unmarried mothers and prostitutes. One of them, Georgina Edwards, who had pledged her support, changed her mind on the day: 'I think it would be better for me not to go to the meeting this afternoon. I am in full sympathy with what you are trying to do, but it is better for me to work quietly among the girls.' Lady Manning also had been involved in the campaign, but when the decision was taken to send a petition to parliament and to publish it in the newspaper she withdrew:

> After due consideration I have decided that it is inadvisable for me to affix my signature to any petition to parliament. Therefore, while cordially agreeing with the laudable sentiments expressed in your letter to me re the Suppression of Vice, I am nevertheless obliged to decline to comply with your request that I should head the list of signatures.

Undaunted by the withdrawal and lack of co-operation of a number of key women, Scott pressed on. For some women in the campaign, sending a petition to parliament was one thing, but publishing it was quite another. Annie Kelly wrote to Scott begging her to reconsider. The terms of her appeal are illuminating:

> Would it not be a mistake when so many men have refused to let their wives sign on account of their dislike for the imaginary notoriety loving women? And I do think there is a good deal to be said on their side. It seems to me that if we publish the letter without the names it will have infinitely more effect on the general public. You might say that among those who signed were women connected with those societies and institutions — that would be quite enough for the public, and those who were afraid to give their signatures would be sorry they had not joined us. Please think it over well and remember that if we want to gain our point we must not stir up the men's prejudices. They have all the power still.

Scott ultimately did back down — the petition was published but not the signatures — at least for the time being. The episode was revealing on many levels, but most striking was the way in which women interested in the issue could be silenced, directly or indirectly, by the views of their husbands or other sources of masculine authority. For these women, their livelihoods, or at least the quality of their lives, stood to be threatened by earning male displeasure on so confronting an issue. Though many of these women supported woman suffrage, they could not manage broader sexual politics confrontations. Dora Montefiore, a founder of the WSL (who later went to England and joined the militant suffragettes), epitomised the position Scott reached as a result of this abortive affair, in a letter to her shortly afterwards:

> women will never get laws past [sic] to help the cause of purity *until* they have the suffrage. A vote means power and those who have power also have to be conciliated; witness all the legislation that is being carried on for the good of working men. 50 years ago no one troubled their heads about the working man and his wants, the same applies now to politicians and women. 50 years hence when women have a vote all such social questions will rest on very different footing.[38]

This assessment may have confirmed Scott's conviction that measures such as the raising of the age of consent would always be opposed until women were half of the electorate; but the episode exposed more than this. Would women having the vote have altered the tenor of the male hostility or the evasiveness of women on whom she had relied for support? The issue of seduction, and of punishing men for its outcomes, touched a raw nerve in Scott's circle and wider political circles. It signalled a level of confrontation over sexual mores and power that was not fully disposed of, or challenged by, the politics of representation entailed in women simply obtaining the vote. Arguably, the hesitation and withdrawal of her women colleagues on the issues of seduction and the age of consent highlighted issues Scott could hardly consider in public at this stage: women's complicity with men's views of women and sexuality; women's fears of challenging or exposing men's sexual practices; and possibly women blaming young women rather than (their) men in the event of seduction and carnal knowledge. It is important to recall that the majority of teenage unmarried mothers whom such women met in philanthropic work were domestic servants who had become pregnant whilst living in the homes of their employers. In public, however, Scott repeatedly explained the failure of the age of consent measure as a consequence of women's disenfranchisement. She used it as further evidence of the need for women to represent themselves. Thus it became part of the rhetorical repertoire by which she 'shamed' men opposed to woman suffrage.

In private, however, Scott's writings from the early to mid-1890s increasingly focused on the servility of women, especially married women, in their dealings with men, and its consequences in fostering seduction and ultimately the prostitution of other women. She stressed the issue of *vision* — the importance of women seeing the connections between these things. In some of her writings she blamed women for men's exploitative behaviour towards women. While this would seem to attribute great power to women, it was also an expression of her frustration at what appeared to her as a failure of 'sisterhood' between women. In some undated notes from this period she wrote:

> Women pride themselves on their unselfishness, but I maintain that
> we must have temperance in virtue. Women often cloak their weak-
> ness, their servile subjection to men under the cloak of noble
> unselfishness . . . Women are timid and strongly conservative and
> their fault lies, especially in their dealings with men, in the non-
> assertion of their individuality. They do what others do. They are
> (at any rate outwardly) what men expect them to be. How few men
> know anything about the real nature and thoughts of their
> wives, mothers and sisters. They are so busy asserting them-
> selves, and we are so busy sympathising with them and doing all
> we can to develop their selfish and animal nature that our indi-
> viduality is quite lost sight of and if it peeps out now and again in
> spite of ourselves men are startled and say who can understand a
> woman? . . . I am afraid that we women are chiefly responsible for
> the faults of men, for men are what women make them.[39]

Women's failure to 'see' the meaning of prostitution and homes for
unmarried mothers preoccupied Scott, who often quoted the *bon mot*: 'in
nature as in all else one must, if one wishes to understand, use not only
the microscope, but the telescope and one's own eyes as well'.[40] Prostitution
was the extreme symptom of what needed to be 'seen' and understood by
those who would work in the cause of women.

Scott's views on prostitutes, however, were not straightforward. At
times she represented them as victims of poverty and male lust, at others
she wrote in more punitive terms as if they, as much as the women reluctant to work for the age of consent measure, failed in loyalty to their own
sex by permitting themselves to be 'degraded'. Compare these two
passages:

> As for the poor woman who walks the street at night: She sells her
> soul partly for money and they buy it for money. She at any
> rate knows and feels that she is degraded and often to drown her
> thoughts she takes to drink. Whereas the man smiles in drawing
> rooms, talks in Parliament. Many is a fine girl whose hand he is not
> worthy to touch;

and

> It is for men that street women live and die. Oh would that
> some amongst them might strive to live and die if need be for
> women . . . if these words I could say could make man love
> woman for her own sake, could make woman as dear to woman as
> man now is dear to her.[41]

The inflections here about the individual prostitute as herself degraded and,
implicitly, aiding the wider degradation of women as 'creatures of sex' and
'a degradation to her intellectual and spiritual nature', would be disowned
unambiguously by contemporary feminists. As political theorist Carole
Pateman observes, the target of feminism is prostitution, not the

prostitute, just as for socialists the enemy is capitalism, not the individual worker.[42] Hence, in the most obvious confrontation with current feminist ethics, Scott can be read here as buying into the double standard of sexual morality of her period, which stressed the degradation of the 'fallen' woman. Her remarks on prostitutes can be thought, at best, a failure of the very vision or understanding she so commended to women and, at worst, a reneging on the 'sisterhood' fundamental to any recognisable feminism. On prostitutes, Scott was unsound, an embarrassment to her successors.

This judgement has a validity that can withstand any further scrutiny of the sexual context of Scott's writings and utterances on prostitution. However, for interrogating the preoccupations which informed Scott's case for the political representation of women, this judgement is a response that can obstruct such interrogations. If Scott stressed the need for vision, it is clear that the way she 'saw' prostitutes had a pivotal place in her approach to politics and the representation of women. It seems important, then, to at least attempt to see her culture and women's degradation within it in the terms she did. This requires consideration of a number of features of the social context of the 1890s and of the rationale she pursued for women's political representation.

Prostitution was visible in everyday life in the 1890s in ways unimaginable today. The climate in Sydney permitted women and girls involved in the trade to work outdoors on a freelance basis from October to April, many taking clients to parks, fields, vacant lots, laneways and backstreet doorways. Critics at times noted railway stations, public bars, post offices and other public places men went about their business as being 'infested' with sex workers (variously referred to as 'magdalens', 'harlots', 'strumpets', 'ladies of the night', and 'women of ill-repute'). King Street in Sydney, a main shopping thoroughfare, was also a principal place of public soliciting, while the areas around the Sydney Town Hall in George Street, and further along in the Liverpool Street and the Haymarket area were equally noted 'haunts' of prostitutes and men seeking their services.[43]

Not only were prostitutes visible, but men's resort to them was explicitly condoned in many cultural discourses. Prostitutes allegedly offered a necessary service that protected virtuous women and contained men's irrepressible sexual demands. A certain fatalism often accompanied public discussion of prostitution, especially concerning factors that led to women's recruitment. After all, the argument went, it was necessary for *some* women to be recruited for men's sexual demands to be supplied. Despite official moral condemnation of the prostitute (not her client), there was a tacit acceptance that for poor women, prostitution might be a plausible means of self-help, if a breadwinner could not be secured through marriage. Being a prostitute was an option implicitly consonant with being a wife. Both callings turned on the livelihood of women and support of their children being obtained through private, sexual bargaining, preventing the kind of poverty that made women and children a burden on the tax-paying electorate and meagre charitable resources.

If these facts and discourses indicated a condonation of prostitution and of men's use of prostitutes, this could not mitigate a number of adverse consequences for non-prostitute women, particularly wives. In the first place, it enshrined the view of sex as something men did to women, something that implicitly diminished and disadvantaged them and for which generous payment was required to secure consent. The need for men to pay in some way to secure women's willingness proclaimed an expectation of non-mutuality, non-reciprocity in heterosexual relations more generally. This had implications for the ways in which men negotiated sexual relations with their wives, especially those men who hired the services of prostitutes, or even a mistress, on a regular basis. Despite representations of the resort to prostitutes as alternative to marital sexual contact, historical and contemporary evidence suggests that the largest group of clients have been married, currently co-habiting men, and that sexual contact with wives was not excluded by contact with prostitutes.

Historians obviously cannot be certain of the nature of transactions between prostitutes and their clients, especially in the 1890s or earlier. These matters are unlikely to survive in many forms of evidence. Though some historians have assumed that married men used prostitutes for sexual practices they could not or did not wish to engage in with their wives, others believe that the dualism of 'normal coitus' with wives and experimental sexual practices with prostitutes only became prevalent or typical in the interwar period.[44] Yet either way, the purchased sexual mastery entailed in prostitution, where the desires and wishes of the woman did not bear on the interaction because they were disposed of by payment, in all probability inflected contiguous sexual expectations men had of their wives. Where husbands were their wives' sole source of support, they could reason that they had equally 'paid' for their wives' willingness, if not their enthusiasm. For wives of prostitutes' clients in the 1890s, the risks of pregnancy, maternal mortality and venereal diseases could significantly obstruct willingness or enthusiasm, even if they otherwise accepted the view that they 'owed' their husband sexual services, in which their own desires were irrelevant.

The fact that a group of women could be hired, explicitly and entirely visibly, to do exactly as men wished sexually, arguably weakened the industrial position of wives. Whatever their individual commitment to and negotiations of the risks of the sexual aspect of their marriage, the promise of fidelity in the marriage contract was more than a sentimental or romantic convention. Its breach in adultery was the cornerstone of English divorce legislation, constituting recognition that either partner's sexual involvement with third parties challenged the entire basis of the contract. If men's adulteries were in practice more tolerated than those of wives, there can be no doubt of the threat to a wife if her husband's sexual estrangement or dissatisfaction resulted in infidelities with other women.

Most practically, it could result in wife desertion or the loss of a woman's means of livelihood and support for her children. If the husband remained instead in formal co-habitation, but spent large amounts of time and money on other women, the wife could experience poverty or severe deterioration in her own and her children's material circumstances, as well as humiliation within her family and community for her husband's rejection of her. Moreover, if the wife was a mother with several young children to care for, and an 1890s household to maintain, she could be peculiarly dependent on her husband for companionship and everyday social engagement. Loneliness, isolation, depression and low self-esteem might be predictable outcomes of his infidelities.

These problems might be compounded if husbands, empowered by sexual adventures and paid mastery over other sexual partners, made new or continued sexual demands of their wives. In order to 'keep' the home together, wives of unfaithful husbands may have been compelled to 'submit', indeed to evince willingness and enthusiasm, to forestall the threat of complete abandonment. In short, husbands could make them compete with their contracted rivals. If husbands had no such access to other women, wives could feel considerably less coerced in their conjugal relations. They could negotiate terms more convincingly in their own interests.

This is not to say that all negotiation of adultery could have only one direction or orientation. Wives too could both commit adultery and use it to their own advantage. Indeed, Western culture from the 1890s could be characterised as massively preoccupied with the problem, for men, of women's infidelities before and after marriage, especially as represented in visual art, opera, and fiction. Though still a small resort, divorce was petitioned by cuckolded husbands in late-nineteenth-century colonial jurisdictions. Furthermore, historian Penny Russell found much suggestive evidence of women's adultery amongst the middle- and upper-middle-class families of her Victorian study.[45]

Amidst the first ten (and most child-filled) years of marriage, however, it is unlikely that the majority of wives of this period had the same access to alternative sexual partners as did their husbands. Nor had most wives the free time and domestic assistance necessary to allow them to pursue extra-marital sexual encounters, even if they had been so inclined. For women who desired no more children, or fewer than they had, the risk of further pregnancy was not an inconsiderable disincentive. It was, moreover, a risk that required them to continue regular sexual intercourse with their husband, contiguously, if a new pregnancy were not to be a disclosure of adultery. With the faulty prevailing theory of ovulation, such a woman doubled her chances of unwanted pregnancy — a very high price. Some unfaithful wives no doubt dealt with this side-effect by means of an induced miscarriage; if they were lucky enough to suffer no morning sickness and related symptoms of pregnancy, perhaps neither husband nor lover would know of either pregnancy or its termination if all went well. But they could also be unlucky.

Another disincentive for any woman considering adultery was the risk of venereal disease. This prospect was a real consideration if she was in no position to command (or believe in the claimed) fidelity of the lover, especially if her husband was faithful to her. In addition to pregnancy, contracting syphillis or gonorrhoea was a dramatic corporeal disclosure of a wife's adultery against a faithful, even if estranged, husband. It was a risk to take only if a wife was past caring if the marriage would end because of it. Few wives with dependent children and themselves economically dependent on their husbands, would be able to be past caring, unless they had an alternative marriage offer from the lover in the event of the divorce that surely would follow. If such a woman contracted a venereal disease amidst a love affair, she might well take it to be less than an ideal predictor of her future happiness and well-being. So, for reasons such as these, women and men were hardly on the same footing with regard to adultery or extramarital sexual experiences in the 1890s.

Part of the ambivalence late-nineteenth-century women like Scott felt towards prostitutes, then, was that their existence could be used to further disempower the majority of women who were, or would become, wives. Those working for 'the cause of women' tried to alter cultural discourses about women, permitting them to be seen not as mere animals, but as moral, intellectual and spiritual beings with rights to develop to their highest potential, even if this meant restraining the demands of husbands and children.[46] But the visible prostitute publicly proclaimed women's animality. Men, for a price, could know woman as animal and could smirk as 'men of the world' at the claims of Scott and WCTU women on deputations about seduction and vice. Many parliamentarians would comment on the well-intentioned innocence of these ladies. All but confessing their complicity in the use of prostitutes, Scott's disparaging reference to parliamentarians in the drawing room unaware of their own degradation and unfit to touch the hand of women there, had personal force.

Perhaps Scott's less than favourable regard for individual prostitutes can be likened to that of the striking unionist for the 'scab' labourer. Though the case is not identical, the analogy resides in the view of the 'scab' as weakening the bargaining position of the larger proletariat at the very moment of militant industrial action. Breaking the ranks, destroying solidarity, helping the capitalist 'get away with' worker exploitation — these were the effects of the 'scab'. If many of Scott's fellow woman suffrage campaigners would not at all have accepted the comparison of wife and prostitute, Scott often observed that the terms by which many women contracted themselves in marriage amounted to virtual prostitution.

Both callings involved personal sexual service of men in return for keep. The transaction between prostitutes and client dramatically identified the same element in marriage, stripped of the surrounding elements of companionship, parenthood, family life, household management, affection and mutual co-operation.

This identification necessarily generated ambivalent responses. Scott found it on the one hand a source of insight about marriage. On the other hand, the vision supplied by the prostitute was deeply discomforting for and about wives, husbands and sexuality. Gratitude hardly flowed towards prostitutes thereby, nor did Scott embrace them as analytically and therefore politically 'just like' wives and mothers. For, if the problem was the sexual coercion of wives and its consequences, then the solution lay in not accepting sexual contracts between men and women in the guise of either wife or prostitute. Rather 'this constant thrusting forward of the sex relationship'[47] had to be stopped; and for women who were wives, the other elements of marriage needed to be brought to the fore and given heightened legitimacy so that they might displace, or at least effectively compete with, men's sexual demands. If men's access to contract sexual labour in prostitutes weakened the position and negotiating powers of the full-time employees — wives — then, for that majority, prostitutes did indeed seem to be an enemy of the cause of ending women's degradation.

However, this was a vision, a way of seeing women's situation, that would be subject to revision in Scott's writings, utterances and work during the next thirty years. For the moment, the point to note is that Scott's ambivalent view of prostitutes never substituted for her more fundamental address of prostitution as an issue of men's demand for sexual mastery, and its public toleration. Moreover, Scott frequently defended prostitutes' civil liberties and situated them not as 'other' but in connection with most women — wives. Her experiences of work first in the WLS, and thereafter in the WSL, taught her much about the perspectives of wives and mothers on politics, sexuality and power. In the years from 1891 to 1896 Scott formed herself as a committee worker. Despite misgivings she developed about the possibilities of a sisterhood of women, she remained convinced, at least rhetorically, that the vote would be the key to ending vice and women's sexual degradation. She had the resources and time to give this cause her main energies.

FIRST BLOWS

Dora Montefiore originated the scheme to found a woman suffrage society upon learning of Sir Henry Parkes's resolve to draft and enact an Electoral Reform Bill later in 1891. She began with a small drawing-room meeting in her home to which Scott, among others, was invited. They generated suggestions as to those who should be invited to join. A public meeting was set for early June 1891, and from the beginning Scott seems to have under-taken the secretarial job, communicating with all interested parties. On 15 April 1891, J.N. Simpson wrote to Scott:

> I strongly recommend that you add to your list Mrs Lawson who has for years been working in the women's cause and who has pub-lished in her journal *The Dawn* many articles in favour of suffrage. I have assisted . . . with her work and I should not care to join a league unless she had first been invited . . . I have not men-tioned the matter of the League to Mrs Lawson and if you decide to co-operate with her you will of course keep private the fact of my having suggested her name. I should not like a woman who has done so much for women to be left in the rear of one who has done less.

Evidently, Simpson's role in suggesting Lawson did become known. The memoirs of Lawson's daughter, Gertrude O'Connor, report that Simpson assured Scott of co-operation only with the stipulation that 'mother and her following be included in any new movement'. [48]

Louisa Lawson was present at the next planning meeting a week later. Lawson has come down to us, along with Scott, as one of the two famous Sydney-based feminists and suffragists of the period. Why had she not been invited to Montefiore's original meeting? Could she have been unknown to or accidentally overlooked by the WLS members who founded the com-mittee to establish a woman suffrage league? Or had she been deliberately excluded?

Lawson's Dawn Club and monthly newspaper *The Dawn* were both established in 1888, and her pro-suffrage sentiments were well known. The membership of Montefiore's first drawing-room meeting would not have been part of Lawson's circle, but rather, an upper-middle-class group with good connections in government and high culture in Sydney. It is likely that this group saw itself as a small lobby group focussed on this specific issue for a short period. Such leagues had been established in other colonies and the cause seemed well advanced, particularly in South Australia and New Zealand. Initially, though, the impulse in the forma-tion of WSL was not the representation of all workers in the cause of women, nor even necessarily all those working for woman suffrage. The WSL was distinct in its secular stance. This stance concurred with Scott's atheism, and may also have contributed to the foundation of a special Franchise Department of the WCTU of New South Wales. [49] The strategies adopted by the WSL included inviting politicians, academics and other cul-tural figures to be office-holders and members. As such, the original failure to include Lawson is unlikely to have been an accident. Following the first public woman suffrage deputations to him as premier in 1891, Sir Henry Parkes wrote to Scott that the inclusion of Mrs Lawson was unfortunate, for her words were intemperate, bitter and ill-considered. Scott conceded his point in reply: 'we regretted Mrs Lawson's speech, thinking it unwise, but of course that is sure to be the thing the papers seize upon.'[50] Although by 1891 Lawson had become a small-business-woman, this estranged wife and working-class rural advocate of the working woman would not have found the WSL congenial.

Yet, Lawson accepted the belated invitation and joined, donating *The Dawn* office for the League's meetings until 1893. This may suggest that she believed the WSL had a good chance of success. Rather than lead her own independent suffrage league, she joined Scott, Montefiore, Wolstenholme, Windeyer and the others. Gertrude O'Connor claims that from then on her mother 'did not take such an interest in suffrage'. Little correspondence between Lawson and Scott remains, most of what does is businesslike: yes, she would circulate a suffrage petition; could she borrow Scott's copy of an overseas suffrage journal? Occasionally she would express hope that Scott would one day call at her home to see her. She often alluded to her own ill-health. She paid her membership of the WSL for only four years (1891, 1892, 1893 and 1896) of its twelve-year existence. While she held a position on the council of the league from 1891 to 1893, her attendance became increasingly erratic.[51]

Lawson attempted to resign in 1891, and finally did so in December 1893. Scott reported to the executive committee in January 1894 that although she had written to Mrs Lawson urging her to withdraw her resignation, Mrs Lawson had replied that 'she must adhere to her resolve for the present'. Lawson's daughter claims that the 'actual reason of her retirement from that board was that most of the committee consisted of lawyers and barristers and they spent a great deal of valuable [sic] quibbling over points instead of transacting straightforward business'. Lawson's daughter noted in her account of her mother's career that her 'freedom of speech would make enemies naturally and an undercurrent was later at work'. Like Scott, Lawson confronted anxiety, timidity and fear of ridicule in women she tried to organise around the suffrage cause in the Dawn Club. She attributed it to 'many ages of suppression', and responded in blunt, plain challenge: 'whoever heard of a body of men united in a cause abandoning their work for fear of what a woman might say?' Despite a pride in her mother's forthrightness, O'Connor implicitly acknowledges that the suffrage movement's lobbying strategies were best served by speakers like Lady Windeyer, whom she recalled was 'logical, refined and sometimes very eloquent . . . In her soft cultured voice, she would convince where many would fail'.

Lawson's strengths were as a journalist, translator, populariser, publisher and writer of the feminist analyses and preoccupations of her time. The record that is *The Dawn*, her published short stories and her poetry, constitutes a remarkable corpus of work. As Docker argues, she was

among those 'Australian feminists well-versed in international feminist debate and writing' who understood themselves to be participants in
a worldwide movement. For Lawson, as for Scott, Charlotte Perkins
Stetson (later Gilman) was among the most important writers and theorists
of that movement. Gilman's *Women and Economics* was to be particularly
influential upon the way both Lawson and Scott saw the problem of
women's economic dependence and formulated strategies for promoting
'economic self-reliance'. For all the contributions Lawson made, she
was clearly no lobbyist, and found little scope for satisfying action in the
WSL. With her working-class rural background, she was no doubt
uneasy and uncomfortable in the company of many members of the league.
Hence, while for most of their association she and Scott worked in co-
operation with one another, holding very similar feminist values, there
were few occasions for partnership or close collaboration on projects. Scott
worked more intimately in the service of the suffrage cause with many
other women.[52]

The WSL attracted considerable public attention. The premier, Sir Henry
Parkes, was a member and office-bearer. Scott interested him and
received social invitations of various kinds. In general, she declined
them. In October 1892 she did so again, explaining:

> I am not so free as I appear to be. My mother is now 82 and never
> goes anywhere. I never leave her for a night or even a meal nor for
> long even at other times. So I am sure you will pardon my refusal
> for one cannot do wrong to place one's mother, so old and so good
> first.[53]

Some of the public interest was in the radicalism of the proposed enfranchisement of women. The possibility that the proposal might be linked with
other revolutionary sentiments was strengthened with Eliza Ashton's critique of the lifelong marriage contract late in 1891. She proposed a voluntary annual review by spouses. The governor's wife, Lady Jersey,
wrote promptly to Lady Windeyer urging her as president of the WSL to
publicly dissociate the WSL from Ashton's 'atrocious' sentiments, which
she argued had raised the spectre of 'free love' and concubinage in the minds
of the conservative and stood to tar suffragists as a whole. While Jersey was
herself ambivalent about woman suffrage, she wished Windeyer, Scott and
others well and so: 'I trust that you will not consider it undue interference
on my part if I express a sincere desire that you . . . should hasten to dispel the idea that opinions like these are held by any thinking portion of
womankind.'[54]

Scott was to be the agent of this message. She publicly replied to Ashton,
concentrating on the disadvantaged position most wives and mothers could
face were Ashton's proposals instituted. The likely dishonourableness, selfishness and faithlessness of men underlay Scott's stated opposition,

rather than some rosy reassessment of marriage. Louisa Lawson also obliquely criticised proposals for 'free unions' in the name of freeing women. For her the issue was simple: 'women grew old much more quickly than men . . . they would be more at the mercy of fickle men than they have ever been under the legal union'.[55]

Such public controversies, in this case involving her friends, proved stressful for Scott. Despite all her work on persuading parliamentarians, caution and even bad faith could replace support for the suffrage cause. This was especially so with Sir Henry Parkes. Behind a sweetness of manner, Scott's disappointment was unmistakable in her letter to him in November 1892, a month after she had declined his social invitation:

> We see that the Electoral Bill has passed to the Legislative Assembly without the house dividing on the amendment you wrote saying you intended to propose with regard to the enfranchisement of women. Will you kindly tell me why this is and if you have thought perhaps of a better way of bringing about this reform with regard to which you have already shown us so much kindness and sympathy.[56]

Parkes made political excuses and by the end of 1892 the road ahead seemed longer and harder perhaps than Scott had first anticipated. Conflicts concerning strategy and procedure within the WSL did not make matters easier. Commiserating with her, Maybanke Wolstenholme wrote 'we cannot yet hope to have many women without the pettiness that seems inherent in our sex.' South Australian suffragist, Mary Lee, wrote to Mary Windeyer in the same vein, remarking that women are 'weak and mean in the mass, but look at their long subjection to a sex which . . . has not been able to discover any means of arranging a disparity but by blows, moral or physical'. Evidently, Windeyer had complained about Scott to Lee; and in some recent WSL exchange, Scott had become angry with Windeyer in public. In response to a note from Windeyer, 'which brought tears to my eyes', Scott apologised: 'I felt as if I was not fit to be secretary for getting so cross.' The issue was Scott's lecture invitation to the theosophist, Isabel Cooper Oakley. Having secured the consent of the WSL vice president, a member of council, and, she believed, the president (that is, Windeyer) *prior* to the booking of the event, Scott felt she as secretary had been entitled to make the invitation on the WSL's behalf. Her letter to Windeyer on this dispute is a curious mixture of affection, deference, and stubborn assertion of her own position:

> If I do not agree with you in any detail it pains me more than to disagree with any other members. Oh if there was no detail. If only we could work away at the spirit of the thing and not be worried with the wretched organisation part . . . I feel I must be more patient about those details which always worry and hamper me so.[57]

Mary Lee was sorry to hear of the problems in the WSL, especially the wounding chide by newer members that Windeyer was 'conservative'. Lee called these people 'the tug rag' of an important movement. 'Is it any wonder,' she asked, 'that the other sex distrusts us, while in every attempt at organisation amongst women there always arises the shabby jungle and scramble for everyone to be first?' On the issue of her relationship with Scott, Lee advised Windeyer to regard Scott and herself as 'the very core of the movement — for no provocation give up that role'.

Despite this advice, Windeyer did give up 'that role' in an emotional resignation as WSL president in September 1893. Mary Lee later reported that after this 'rupture' she never again 'penned a line to Miss Scott'. The precipitation of this 'rupture' was the proposed amendment of the constitution of the WSL with new rules recognising suburban branches and granting them an extent of autonomy, admitting to league discussion matters other than suffrage, a changed fee structure, and a drop in minimum age of members from 21 to 18. On the rights of branches and the wider brief, Scott was in agreement with the dissidents: Windeyer saw this as betrayal and accused Scott of fostering a conspiracy against her presidency. In response Scott wrote:

> I do not see how we can call ourselves League of New South Wales if we do not knit our branches to us . . . I would ask you for the sake of all the love and unity in the past in our beloved cause that you tell me how I have offended you. I may be able to explain or I may see your point of view. My own heart says I have been true to all my old friends on the council and if I do not agree with them in two points or anything else, I said so straight and have done nothing behind their backs that I would be ashamed for them to know or ask me about.

Scott assured Windeyer that she was not 'forsaking the old tried hand of the pioneers for the new members', and reported that Louisa Lawson too was in great distress about Windeyer construing loyal friends as enemies. Scott and Windeyer chased each other with various letters, which Scott declared unequal to unravelling the 'network of misunderstanding' between them. She complained that she was being misunderstood by both sides in the conflict, while if 'I have failed in my temper twice I had thought that I was forgiven'. She resented the charge that the new constitution was 'concocted' at her house, assuring Windeyer emphatically that she had nothing whatsoever to do with the drafting of a new constitution, 'I . . . hope to understand what vexed you in my actions . . . if in impatience or hastiness or any other way I have failed to respect you as President I beg your forgiveness.'[58]

In the background of these tensions was a changing membership alluded to by Windeyer in her resignation speech and letters, a membership hostile, she believed, to the 'position given me by my hard-working husband'.

The new members, prominent in the suburban branches, were jealous of the position of the original Sydney League or the 'Central Branch' as they called it. To them, the value of her services as president was, in Windeyer's view, infinitesimal.[59] Despite her reassurances, Windeyer believed that Scott's sympathies were with these new members.

Windeyer promptly assumed leadership of a newly established Franchise Department of the Women's Christian Temperance Union. In time her relationship with Scott regained some of its former cordiality. During the 1894 visit of United States WCTU delegates led by Jessie Ackermann, Scott attended Lady Windeyer's garden party for them and wrote about it to Windeyer's daughter, Margaret (who was studying librarianship in the United States). Scott noted that we all 'work in the same cause, it may be in different ways, but that only makes it stronger if we are all united in spirit as I am sure we are'.[60]

Other members of the WSL were unhappy at the resignation of Windeyer and her replacement by the new president, Emma Palmer. During 1894–95, through a new suffrage newspaper of the Surry Hills branch of the WSL, *The Australian Woman*, they launched attacks on Scott and Wolstenholme, claiming they had wronged Lady Windeyer, 'our first President and the next if she desire'. The prospect of defamation litigation was mooted and tension generally surrounded Scott's work in the WSL. Perhaps she was cross or tactless in asserting the seriousness of matters before members. Annie Kelly, who had tried so hard to persuade Scott not to publish the petition in support of the Vice Suppression Bill in 1892, demanded that Scott withdraw an insulting reply to the president, Palmer, otherwise, Kelly said, she would resign, for 'I now look on the WS cause and the WS League as two distinct things'.

Challengers to Scott were emerging, particularly the sisters Annie and Belle Golding. When Scott reported on having rapidly formed a deputation to interview the Labor League on the inclusion of woman suffrage in their platform, she explained that there had been no time to consult the council about it at a full meeting. Annie Golding insisted that this non-consultation amounted to exclusion of council members. She 'sought the opinion of the council with regard to the power of the Hon. Gen. Sec. to exclude any member of council who desired to be present from attending any deputation'.[61]

Scott's work as honorary secretary meant that she was always first to know the state of argument, debate, opinions and manoeuvres relevant to the struggle, and able thereby to spend more time than others in the WSL planning strategy and forming opinions as to how to intervene. This had her poised to control and orchestrate WSL business; but it also stimulated difficulties and understandable resistances to her suggestions among fellow workers with alternative judgements and usually with less information than she. Consequently, sometimes they found her extremely difficult to work with. If we cannot know for certain how Scott conducted herself in meetings, letters from women who mattered to her may be indicative. Maybanke Wolstenholme wrote to her during the 1894 New South Wales election campaign about the effect Scott was having on the new electoral sub-committee of the WSL, which was working to extract commitments from politicians and to maximise publicity:

> I am really sorry to know that you are worrying yourself about what I can only call nothing! What wrong are we doing? Where are the old members who are now slighted? I must confess that I knew of neither. Believe me I would not act in a way that would injure the cause nor would I offend my friends however slight [sic]. We have never in the past had as active and as willing workers as now and your dislike to our work is utterly beyond my comprehension. If you by personal influence (you will get it no other way) get a majority who will make it impossible for the electoral committee to work you will do the cause more harm than you or I can calculate. Not one member on that committee desires to annoy you (I speak plainly) *everyone* has the kindest personal feelings for you, and the deepest interest in the work, and yet, night after night, *you*, who love the cause, raise objections to all they do and so make division and waste energy. It is to me incomprehensible. Do like a good dear soul as you are put aside quibbles and help us to work in harmony. The committee will do anything you suggest if you will only let them work . . .

This was not the first nor would it be the last letter of this character received by Scott as committee member. Of course resignations and disputes, accusations and paranoias commonly beset the history of political organisations, especially those that are voluntary and part-time for most members. It is striking, however, that throughout the suffrage struggle, it was always others who resigned, often amidst aggrieved questions about Scott's role in their difficulties.

Despite Scott's involvement in conflicts and strategic disagreements, evidently she too could be anxious and distressed over 'falling out' with other women workers in the cause. She tried to ameliorate Eliza Ashton after disowning her views in public. Clearly there had been considerable fondness between them and Scott would continue a friendship with her until her untimely death in 1900. Ashton's reply to what was evidently an emotional letter from Scott over their differences is interesting. She addressed not only the current issues between them, but also ventured some opinions on Scott's methods and beliefs:

> Don't be absurd. We could never be enemies unless you begin to think me incapable of respecting opinions I don't quite agree with. In the main our faces are set in the same direction. To squabble over details would indeed be absurd. I love your whole souled earnestness in what you believe to be right. I will stand

> meekly any amount of argument or even severe criticism from
> you because I know you are single hearted and sincere . . .
> You're a goose — excuse the energy of the expression, you're too
> sensitive to criticism. To my mind, the man or woman who sets forth
> in these days determined to live life but from within and not
> from without, to say what he or she believes to be true instead of
> what we are told ought to be true must prepare to be mud bespat-
> tered, abused, cried down, misunderstood, to bear the imputation
> of the vilest motives instead of the simple one of being true.
> There can be no half measures. For my part I have made up my
> mind to disregard the conventional cackle that means so little
> yet does so much mischief . . . Why notice these things? They are
> beneath a woman like you who thinks that life is real and earnest
> and society a sham.[62]

The combined impression left by letters from fellow suffragists is that Scott
was critical and discouraging towards her co-workers, especially those who
attempted to shape the course of the league's business. Her most successful
relationships seem to have been either with followers or those whom she
admired. Relations with her peers were more problematic, and she
seems to have been unwilling to recognise many women as such.

At first sight this seems to contradict her ethic of a sisterhood between
women, though it is unlikely that Scott herself recognised any such
contradiction. The difficulties of her methods of committee work may in
part reflect her lifelong role of big sister, manager, and independent
carer for the old and the young, as adult daughter and mother. But
more tellingly, it may signal Scott's reluctance to delegate work, authority and influence. The 'cause of women' gave her the first fulfilling public work of her life. She held onto its pleasures jealously and tended to
represent herself as uniquely better qualified than others to negotiate and
direct. In fact, her lack of formal education and the nature of her upbringing
may have made her quite insecure concerning her qualifications and authority; and this insecurity may have caused her difficult, often petty and manipulative, behaviour with women co-workers at this early stage in her
public career.

Beyond the issue of Scott's qualities as honorary secretary was the weekly
and monthly grind of her public tasks, and the political lessons they
could teach her. She corresponded fully and regularly with the key parliamentary faction leaders and spokesmen of the early 1890s, as well as extra-
parliamentary political groupings. One lesson learned from this work was
the contradictory nature of these men's projections about women as
citizens. The conservative Bruce Smith explained to her that his main fear
of woman suffrage was that women would usher in socialism and thereby ruin the colonial economy. By contrast, S.A. Rosa, of the Socialist League,
explained that women were naturally conservative and of inferior intel-
lect, so obviously would be ruled by the clergy: thus they were 'natural'

enemies of socialist reforms. J.D. Fitzgerald, future lord mayor of Sydney, stated his principal objection to woman suffrage to be women's obvious intellectual inferiority and their lack of original creative genius. Meanwhile, Labor men such as Arthur Rae and Frank Cotton believed, with Rosa, that women would vote more conservatively than men, but that this was due to their ignorance, inexperience and exclusion from paid labour or responsibility for matters beyond their own households. The way women might vote, however, was for them irrelevant to the question of their *right* to vote. They worked to overcome opposition to woman suffrage within the labour movement, urging that the measure be adopted, as part of the platform of the Political Labor League. This was done in 1895.

A motion proposing the extension of the franchise to women was first debated on 30 July 1891. Future premiers of New South Wales, George Dibbs and George Reid, expressed opposition without hesitation. 'I think it is a highly dangerous proposal in a country like this to introduce politics into the domestic circle', thundered Protectionist Dibbs, while Reid, the Free Trader, claimed that the proposal 'amounts to a revolution of the whole political system'. Other members of parliament conjectured that women would vote either the same way as their male relatives, or worse, the opposite way. The matter was debated among much salacious and misogynist humour, with George Reid dubbing the proposal 'a debating club topic'.

Scott also learned political lessons in the first five years of the WSL campaign from the erratic, opportunistic and cynical factors that organised the adoption of reform Bills by political parties. Politicians wrote frankly about Sir Henry Parkes's cunning and insincerity, and about the constraints party loyalty and policy imposed on reform initiatives. Parkes managed to be absent from the House when the relevant clause of the revised Electoral Bill proposing the enfranchisement of women was debated in 1892, and nobody else was sufficiently briefed or persuasive enough to carry the day.[63] Within a political system developing class-based parties, Scott and other suffragists remained convinced that the franchise must remain a non-party or cross-party issue in order to have any chance of success. In the context of frequently changing governments, the task was to persuade each one to move on the matter. One method Scott used to confront unsympathetic politicians was personal visits and interviews with the premier and various key ministers. She combined this with extensive correspondence with them, more formal deputations from the WSL, and an intensive publicity campaign.

Yet, despite these strategies, progress was slow. If Scott and her allies outside and inside parliament favoured the private member's motion approach to social legislation, to avoid the constraints of 'partyism', the reality was that party programmes organised the allocation of space, time and priorities in parliamentary business. Unless woman suffrage became a public Bill, promoted as government business, it had no prospect of enactment. In 1894, Dowell O'Reilly, a close friend of Scott, presented the motion for debate that 'the time has come for the franchise to be extended to the women of the colony'. The vote was fifty-eight ayes, and thirteen noes. Some interesting correlations emerged. The men most vocal in opposition to raising the age of consent were just as vocal against woman suffrage. Another feature was that several key parliamentarians opposed to the vote for women in 1891 declared themselves converts by 1894. Sir George Dibbs conceded that the ladies of the WSL had persuaded him, while other honourable members believed that the degree of publicity, the meeting and work the ladies had manifestly done since 1891 had elevated and educated 'the sex' as regards politics. Women could be improved.

However, one judges the sincerity of these 'converts' and whatever other factors might have made them judge supporting suffrage for women as 'expedient', the ladies had done their work well. Opponents ridiculed converts for seeking the favours of the three or four worthy ladies really behind the measure, and threatened manly men with the spectre of 'petticoat government'. They quoted British authorities hostile to the measure and deemed it inappropriate that the colonies should precede the Mother Country in this matter. However, O'Reilly and others argued that in this young country there was the possibility and the general support for true democracy. Being 'in advance' of undemocratic Britain would be a source of pride, not anxiety. They denounced as contemptible the separate spheres and masculinist arguments of opponents like Crick. As Mr Wilks, the member for Balmain, observed of Crick:

> The honorable member would have women nothing but mere automata . . . the mere replica, the mere counterpart of man. He would not give her either in the married or single state the liberty of individual opinion. These are the men who fight under the guise of freedom and yet use the weapons of Tories.

George Reid, the next premier, argued that however laudable the proposal, the government had no mandate from the electors of New South Wales and no visible evidence that the women of the state wanted this reform. While supporters rebutted this by arguing that no mandate was secured for much necessary legislation lately enacted — the Lunacy Act, for example — Reid's criticism stuck.[64] For as several members observed, the measure would add 300 000 new electors to the electoral roll, with momentous implications for the demographic shape of the electorates for different parliamentary seats. Furthermore, it would revolutionise the political relation between the sexes. If some opposed the reform as redundant — women would simply vote as their husbands did — more believed women would bring distinct elements, interests and hence voting patterns into political life, which would affect the customs and behaviour of men. Even supporters of woman suffrage had apprehensions. After the success of his motion, Dowell O'Reilly expressed a certain masculine fear in a letter to Scott:

> Do you know that politically speaking — I am a little afraid of you. You are so dreadfully sincere — so persistently on the war path that you make the average male politician feel that he and the world he lives in are very far indeed from what they should be. And you won't just step down for a minute into *our* world and see how very difficult the path is from our point of view and how what seems to you looking down from your serene heights — smooth green fields to walk upon is in reality thick jungle through which we must slowly hew our way.[65]

For Scott, the task ahead appeared to be to persuade as many parliamentarians as possible that women could make a positive, desirable contribution to the political life of New South Wales. Only with such an incentive could the measure become a priority of the legislature. It was time to draw a larger picture, and make wider connections, now that the O'Reilly motion had demonstrated that, in principle, the majority could support the abstract notion of woman suffrage. By 1896, Scott had deepened her understandings and her criticisms of the masculine monopoly of public life and its consequences for women and children. It was these political lessons that she endeavoured to teach women working in the cause. In years to come, this mission took her beyond the suffrage campaign.

Chapter 4

Expanding the Brief
(1897–1902)

Let slaves get their freedom or franchise and before long they protest against the rule of their master . . . In the Womanhood Suffrage League some of us are free traders and some protectionists. For my own part I am above all a woman suffragist.

Rose Scott,
Letter to the Editor, *Daily Telegraph*,
21 October 1901

Saranna Scott died at the age of 85. By 1897 Nene Scott Wallace was 19. His life was centred on amateur theatre and training to be an architect. Scott's old admirer, Arthur Rae, after dealing with WSL business in February 1897 wrote: 'In regard to personal matters, allow me to offer my sincere sympathy with you in the loss of your mother . . . I trust however that you are not lonely and that your life is as busy and as useful as ever'.[1] Scott was now in the fiftieth year of a life intimately bound up with that of her mother, more so than was the experience of her married sisters and friends. Even with the ambivalences that routinely attended mother and daughter relationships, the passing of the mother to whom she felt she owed so much, and who had always been a central part of Scott's calculations and obligations, must have had momentous significance.

Yet, on the other hand, this moment bequeathed a number of contributions towards Scott's political life. Most practically, it expanded the time she could devote to 'the cause of women', especially now that Nene no longer required parenting as a child. Saranna Scott had not approved of this 'cause' and its place in her daughter's life, and this may have hitherto constrained the extent of Scott's involvement in issues and campaigns connected with that of woman suffrage. It was now possible for her to make new links. Moreover, her mother's death more than her father's raised the question of mortality: the finiteness of allotted time. The average age at which Australian women died in 1900 was 55, nearly Scott's own age.[2] Her mother attained a longer life, as would Scott, but all around her, women of her age — especially working-class women — could have no certainty about living much longer. In 1900 her friend, Eliza Ashton, died. Scott's correspondence from this period onwards is dotted with condolences.[3] A late starter on a public career, Scott had entered the phase of the life course in which invalidity and death were expectations.

Paradoxically, she had only just become part of the true 'older' generation of her family, and by extension, of the women's movement. Until then, a large part of her kinship and social definition had been as 'daughter'. It is conceivable that part of the expansion of her brief of activities entailed becoming emotionally an adult, by discarding the identity of daughter. Moreover, in some of the links she made in this period, she may have for the first time practised the psychical identity of mother, beyond that experienced through the role of adoptive aunt, socially mothering Nene in collaboration with her own mother. Three younger women became important friends in this period: from 1899 Vida Goldstein, leader of the Victorian woman suffrage movement; from 1900 Florence Wearne, a prominent public servant; and most significantly, from 1902, the writer Miles Franklin.[4] Scott also developed important links with older Australian women activists, including Catherine Helen Spence in South Australia, Edith Cowan in Western Australia, Alice Henry in Victoria, and numerous other women through her work on the National Council of Women (NCW). It was arguably the relationships with younger women, however, that sustained the quarter of a century of active public life that remained ahead of Scott. Many of the younger women friends with whom she worked, such as Frances Saul and Frances Levy, are difficult to investigate, since their only public intervention appears to have been the organisations and committees on which Scott worked. On many occasions a mother and daughter dynamic characterised these relationships, producing the benefits and costs this can entail. The death of Saranna Scott occasioned a reforging of Scott's *modus operandi*, perhaps leading her to recreate the familiar intimacy of that important relationship, herself occupying the position of 'mother'.

HEAD OF THE FAMILY

In 1894, when Scott was assuming an increasing share of responsibilities and when most of her older men relatives were either deceased or away, her newly bedridden uncle, George Rusden, dubbed her 'the kind head of the family'. This identity enlarged in the years after Saranna's death. Between 1896 and 1902 three more men of the family died: Bowyer Shaw, her brother-in-law, in 1896, Arthur Edward Selwyn, her maternal uncle, in 1899, and Hope Wallace, her brother-in-law, in 1901. With their passing, Lynton expanded to become the home of Millie Shaw, now aged

44, Mollye, her 5-year-old daughter, and Rose Selwyn, aged 75. Scott's correspondents during the early years of the century routinely sent their compliments to Millie Shaw and Rose Selwyn. It is possible that the presence of Millie, widowed mother of a young child, facilitated Scott's expanding public life. Though the Shaws became a responsibility, Scott may have been freed to some extent from otherwise unavoidable domestic demands. There were now other sources of domestic companionship for Hope and Nene.

The larger household also generated new quandaries. The Lynton cottage showed the strain of over-population, and for a time the idea of Scott borrowing money for renovation and extensions was mooted. David Scott Mitchell, whose opinion she sought, advised her against this proposal. Though the details of his advice are not available, Scott's uncle, George Rusden, concurred with it:

> I do not at all wonder at your shrinking from borrowing money for building and am glad that you had so kind an adviser in David to consult. If by any turn of events Millie should have afterwards left you, you would have been loaded with an irksome and useless encumbrance.

Some problem had also arisen in relation to Hope Wallace, about which Rusden wrote, 'As for Hope, I don't know what to think, much less what to say'. It may have been some personal or business scandal, or it may have been the diagnosis of a terminal disease that finally claimed him in 1901. Rusden expressed the hope that Nene may 'be a help to you as time goes on and never forget how much he owes to your thoughtfulness for him'.[5]

Rusden frequently sent Scott bank drafts between the late 1890s and early 1900s, partly to support his niece, Florrie Rusden, resident in Sydney, and partly to help with running expenses at Lynton. The state of Scott's assets and bequests from her parents remains uncertain, but certainly these years were marked by continuing liquidity problems. Perhaps Scott's 'cause of women' was one source of strain. Scott's biographer, May Munro, ventured that it was well for the suffrage cause 'that Rose Scott was left £500 a year, for much of the first expenses came from her purse'.[6] Her uncle, Henry Keylock Rusden, recorder of the Legislative Council of Victoria, wrote to her critically about the suffrage cause, once the issue looked as if it might actually secure a majority parliamentary support:

> I do not think it wise to extend the franchise. Too many have it now. Would it not be better if we could confine it to prudent people? I think we might entrust it to all men and perhaps women when 35 years old. You wrote to me I think a card saying that you object to the Commonwealth Bill because it did not provide for women's suffrage. I voted against it because it did provide one man one vote.[7]

It should not be underestimated how actively conservative Scott's relatives were, on both sides of the family. She later alluded to considerable conflict within her family about her views and political activities. No doubt she was at times a considerable embarrassment to them, and much criticised in conservative social circles frequented by the family in Sydney, Melbourne, Newcastle, Singleton, Brisbane and rural Queensland. Contemporaries of Scott recalled moments of such criticism. One, a journalist writing in 1923, described an occasion on which, at a meeting at Scott's home concerned with legal problems for women and girls — probably in the late 1890s — a society dame entered and sat in the middle of the room. She denounced social reformers generally and Scott in particular, accusing her of inappropriately mixing with the riff-raff and 'scum of society' and taking up their dangerous schemes. An up-and-coming 'press man' rebuked her and she departed shortly after. Without a word, 'Scott crossed the room, clasped his hand, and a lifelong friendship was born'.[8]

Counterbalancing family disapproval, the later 1890s and turn of the century were times of friendship, as well as political alliances, for Scott. She became better acquainted with women she admired, including Dr Mary Booth, Caroline David, Louisa MacDonald, and her companion, Evelyn Dickinson. MacDonald had declined an earlier invitation to stand as a vice president of the WSL. Her reason was that such a public political office was inappropriate while holding appointment as principal of Women's College. This was by no means a rejection of engagement with feminist reform initiatives. She and Evelyn Dickinson were regular guests at Scott's Friday night salon, when their busy professional schedules permitted. On occasion, when MacDonald disagreed with the stance of Scott and women's organisations she represented, she was not afraid to say so. Such an occasion arose in 1897, when the WSL passed a resolution urging the establishment of compulsory domestic training for girls in the schools. MacDonald promptly wrote to Scott, charging that she was striking

> one of the most serious blows to women's freedom and there is something rather tragic in thinking that one of the champions of the franchise could help to strike it. Don't you see, you who would help forward women's work and education and lessen her disabilities, that the one idea of the ladies at your drawing room meetings is to get good servants cheap. And they are certainly going one way to do it by having every woman trained compulsorily to one trade.[9]

Lack of formal education probably prevented Scott from sharing MacDonald's perspective, who held a university higher degree. However, they certainly met to discuss the matter further and Scott always spoke of MacDonald with unalloyed respect. While no repudiation of the compulsory domestic training resolution or formal revision of her concurrence with it was forthcoming from Scott, the influence of friends like MacDonald, as well as public servants such as Florence Wearne, increasingly oriented her in other directions on questions related to women and paid work. From the turn of the century, equal pay and equal access to job and career opportunities became more significant in Scott's rhetoric. The experience of her new young friend, Miles Franklin, ended any sanguine view of domestic service as the chief paid occupation for women.

Scott also became close to another young woman in this period, Frances Saul, with whom she discussed literature and the occult. Saul borrowed from Scott's large book collection and accompanied her to occult events. In 1898 Saul wrote to her 'I don't want any supernatural breathings into me . . . "Flames" is a most interesting book. The occult transformation of souls or rather exchange of souls and all that part of the book I thought utterly unconvincing as you did.' Saul also noted how Scott had enlarged her sympathies towards prostitutes, for 'I had always regarded them as incomprehensible human beings, I could never see life from their standpoint.' This suggests some revision of the harsher views of prostitutes contained in Scott's writings of the 1880s and early to mid-1890s. This young friend had also an affectionate relationship with Scott's nephew, Nene, who sent her photographs.[10]

Scott also became considerably more familiar with the writers Henry and Bertha Lawson in the late 1890s. She made some interesting notes when she visited them in Lavender Bay, Sydney, in April 1899. Of Henry Lawson, she wrote:

> Don't mind him, he's all right. Loving, sensitive, brooding and thoughtful. Loves wife and child. Drinking in Sydney, given it up. Want of excitement, change much obstinacy — generous. Little wife aesthetic hand — loves to draw pencil, trys [sic] to write, think it good.[11]

Lawson wanted to see more of Scott by herself. He discussed with her his difficulties writing and his battles with alcohol. She was very taken with his *The Golden Nineties*, and collected all his published poetry and short stories. She was particularly fond of his 'Joe Tries His Hand at a Sex Problem Story', published in 1898, and marked the following passage:

> Seems to me that a good many men want to make angels out of their wives, without first taking the trouble of making saints of themselves. We want to make women's ways our ways — it would be just as fair to make our ways theirs. Some men want to be considered God in their own homes; you'll generally find that those sort of men are very small potatoes outside; if they weren't, they wouldn't bother so much about being cocky on their own little dunghills.[12]

Scott's interest in Lawson was part of a more general interest she pursued in Australian writers and artists. Dr Creed, New South Wales Legislative Councillor, teased her that she was always trying to discover new geniuses. She believed in fostering Australian cultural production and that this in no way imperilled an increasing commitment to internationalism.

Her circle expanded, but special friends were Dowell O'Reilly, Bertram Stevens, William Lane, J.F. Archibald, Julian Ashton, Ellis Rowan, Nellie Melba, Florence Rodway, Roderic Quinn, John Farrell and Frank Fox. The latter, editor of the *Australasian Art Review*, wrote to her from Quirindi in 1900: 'If you were near I should tell you all maybe for you have taken a great hold of my hero worshipping heart.'[13]

One of the most important friendships Scott made in the period after her mother's death was that with Miles Franklin. It began with a 'fan' letter in early 1902 written by Scott after she read Franklin's *My Brilliant Career*. 'Your book is so life like, I cannot disassociate yourself from the heroine . . . Let me my dear fellow Australian, my dear fellow woman, serve you in any way I can.'[14] From this first letter began a twenty-three-year friendship, the significance of which continued for Franklin for the decades following Scott's death. The initial impetus for Scott's approach to Franklin no doubt was identification with Sybylla, the heroine of *My Brilliant Career*. A country girl of high spirits, Sybylla declines all offers of marriage, including that of the handsome pastoral heir, Harry, because of her conviction that marriage and motherhood will prove incompatible with the project to which she most wants to devote her life — being a writer. At a time when Scott was pained by criticism from old friends about her involvement in public affairs, Franklin's text was a refreshing reminder of the larger life options spinsterhood could make possible. 'Leila' (possibly Leila Darley, the future governor's wife) had evidently criticised Scott, who replied in defence of her activities:

> I respect and honour those who make their homes happy and comfortable, at the same time I think I may take some credit myself for making my own so and I am sure I would never fear to go to any of my servants for a character. And yet I do think it my duty to take an interest in things beyond my home.[15]

Scott obviously enjoyed the chance to 'take up' the young Franklin, introducing her to key literary and other cultural and political figures and keeping her briefed on their comings and goings. The Lawsons were of particular interest, especially since Henry Lawson helped Franklin to secure her novel's London publisher and wrote a foreword to it. Franklin quickly became part of Scott's household and extended family. This included visits to David Scott Mitchell, who Scott assured Franklin, 'would be delighted to do anything for you. He is an invalid as you saw'. Scott wrote to Franklin about the family cat, Tibbie, about Nene's holiday, and the housekeeper Bridget's dental troubles. She also trusted her with her vulnerabilities, fears and weariness. Franklin evoked in Scott a great nostalgia for a rural Australia remembered from childhood, now lost. She lamented at how Sydney was full of interruptions, visitors, suffrage league annual reports to be written, letters to be read and replied to — 'One often longs for a week with silent gum trees and no human being within a mile'; and in another letter later in 1902 she wrote 'I would like to be quiet with books for a bit and have no more meetings or organisations for a while'. She concluded this letter by answering Franklin's question as to what she wore at an important public meeting: 'I wish I could have you with me always . . . Black and white, grey box bonnet with pink rose and within, a distracted sort of heart'.

Scott and Franklin shared a concern about Henry and Bertha Lawson. Scott had always maintained that Bertha had talent as a writer. When Henry was on a drinking binge and earning no money, Bertha wrote articles. After observing sarcastically the publisher and poet A.B. 'Banjo' Paterson's engagement to a rich woman, Scott wrote to Franklin: 'He is nice to wish to be kind to the Lawsons. The poor little wife wrote an article *for her husband* about the asylum for the *Evening News* — for which *he* was well paid, but she wrote! She really might write well, things like that.' Both Scott and Franklin were to be affected by the fortunes and misfortunes of the Lawson family over years to come.

Once the vote was won in 1902, Scott reported to Franklin that 'I am almost a writing machine now'.[16] She was quite exhausted by travelling to regional centres, writing letters, doing newspaper interviews, giving public lectures, and yet more meetings and committees, including a big campaign for drought relief. The 'head of the family' branched out in the six years after her mother's death, making new political links, taking up more issues and tackling further conflicts and difficulties. The *Sun* newspaper dubbed Scott 'a Sydney Institution and a very important one too'.[17] These were the years during which she made that so.

LINKS AND DEPARTURES

Rose Scott threw herself into the heady politics of turn-of-the-century Australia. After the failure of age of consent legislation she confined her attention to the woman suffrage campaign in the years up to 1895. However, a similar failure of the Women's Franchise Bill in 1894, and continued disillusionment in her experience of lobbying politicians during 1895 and 1896, seem to have caused Scott to reconsider her priorities. From 1897 until the vote for women was secured in 1902, she diversified the fronts of her public political work. Issues to attract her attention included prison reform, pacifism, the oppression of women in overseas countries, working women's conditions and women's organisations outside New South Wales. A strong strand of her work continued to be the woman suffrage movement: in this period she established links with other forces — particularly the Victorian, Queensland and Western Australian woman suffrage movements — and she lobbied members of the Federal Convention for the inclusion of woman suffrage in the Federal Constitution. Her experiences here led her to adopt a strong stand against federation.

The federal era occasioned heated debate within the women's movement on foreign policy and international affairs, as well as adoption of organisation, causes, and concerns originating overseas. The NCW, founded by American pacifist May Wright Sewall in 1884, was established in New South Wales in 1896 by Margaret Windeyer upon her return from work in the United States. It co-ordinated the activities of a variety of women's organisations and movements working for various objectives, and Scott promptly affiliated the WSL. This promoted correspondence, journal subscriptions and increased familiarity with the progress of 'the cause of women' in other countries. Links with the United States and Canada were to prove most significant.

The combination of new colonial and international links with women's movements and the federation ferment and its implications led Scott to embark on new campaigns. In tandem with women workers overseas and interstate, she assisted Dr Emily Ryder's campaign against child brides in India through the Little Wives of India Fund. She also began researching and lecturing to meetings of the National Council of Women on peace and international arbitration, and was an outspoken critic of the Boer War and Australia's involvement in it. In her pacifist critique of 'might' dominating the weak on the international stage, she was able to connect national rivalry with the dominance of men over women, illustrated by 'white slavery', prostitution and women's bodily and spiritual degradation. These longstanding preoccupations of Scott's inflected her developing pacifism, marking her apart from her co-workers in a common cause.

A similar critique of the strong unjustly dominating the weak motivated a wider range of involvements. The Political Labor League's inclusion of woman suffrage in their party platform led to closer involvement for Scott in movements concerned with labour questions, especially those affecting working women. She also became involved in the agitations of women 'white collar' workers, especially those working for equal pay in the Public Service. In this Florence Wearne was an important co-worker.

Allies she made in this work were to endure through other campaigns of her public life. She and several of these women established the Women's Club for professional working women during this period. Many of the founding members of the Women's Club had belonged to the WLS. The club's moving spirit was Dr Mary Booth, a distinguished practitioner involved in public health and child welfare policy formulation. Booth sought Scott's support for the establishment of the club, in mid 1901, which she stressed should be for working women 'not fine ladies'. An earlier attempt to found a club had failed, as one colleague explained to Scott, because 'the fees were too heavy to attract many members outside those who have a husband's purse to go to'. Lilian Wise was among those invited to join and consulted as to the club's ideal constituency and constitution, and she told Scott that 'I do think there is a real need for a women's club in Sydney and quite agree that it should not be representative only of the University or of society people'. The rules of the club identify the objective as being to: 'provide a place where women interested in public, professional, scientific, literary or artistic work may spend their leisure moments'. There was an entrance fee of half a guinea and an annual fee of one guinea.

Beyond providing for the leisure moments of members, the founders of the Women's Club were well aware of the important informal role of men's clubs in the formation of political, cultural and other social networks. Women's movement members in other Western countries also sought to form women's clubs so that those working on behalf of women might obtain shared knowledge and support in reform endeavours. Measures relating to women's paid work and position in industry had elsewhere secured particular advantages, including wider advocacy through women's club networks.

It seems that Scott's work on industrial questions had motivations of different provenance from those of her labour movement allies, whose target was the exploiting capitalist. By contrast, Scott's motivation was the enhancement of women's capacities to sustain themselves independent of marriage or prostitution, and through a really viable, attractive choice of careers and livelihoods. A central obstacle to this in the industrial domain was not just exploiting capitalists, but men of the labour movement — women's co-workers and class brothers, who often held more traditional notions of 'women's place' than the crusted conservatives in the Legislative Council, with whom she battled on many occasions. In this sense, her work for young factory women shaded readily into her work in two other areas: for the Girls' Friendly Society and the Society for the Prevention of Cruelty to Children. Common to these diverse campaigns was the element of protection from men's domination and abuse.

It was this same concern about sexual degradation that resulted in an important new addition to Scott's repertoire of activities in this period. The women's committee of the Prisoners' Aid Association addressed the specific problems of prison conditions for women, and the possibility of a separate prison for them. This work had complex effects on Scott's understanding of women's situation, and entailed lobbying politicians and bureaucrats, some the same as those she approached on the suffrage issue. It was work that dramatised, at a crucial point in the suffrage struggle, the need for women to claim citizen rights.

All of the new elements in Scott's turn-of-the-century work were tributaries into her new suffrage speech entitled 'Why Women Need a Vote', presented in March 1901. The shift from 'want' in the 1892 speech to 'need' nearly a decade later is telling. It signals a decisive shift in her discourse, which repays examination. If Scott's own brief of activities expanded and diversified in the new federal era, so did that of other key workers in 'the cause of women'. The increasing solidification of class-based party politics began to inflect the operations of the WSL. Scott's determined 'non-party' position became anathema to many, especially to three powerful suffragists from working-class branches of the league, the Golding sisters, Annie and Belle, and their close friend, Nellie Martel. Though on many questions they and Scott worked collaboratively, friction and contest was more typical of their relations after 1900. A fragmentation of earlier suffrage unities was in train in this period. It was undoubtedly fuelled by frustration at the bitterness and misogyny of the parliamentary struggle in readings of the Women's Franchise Bill in 1900, 1901 and 1902 when, though passed in the Legislative Assembly, the Bill was thrown out by the Legislative Council. The terms of both the support of and opposition to women's enfranchisement prevailing at the time of its enactment marked important constraints on the achievements possible for the citizenry of women envisaged by Scott.

By the end of the 1890s Scott's name and face symbolised the movement for women's rights in New South Wales. The WSL received extensive publicity in the widely circulating popular newspaper, the *Daily Telegraph*, but beyond that, any of the doings of Rose Scott, especially her gracing of the platform at public meetings on a wide range of causes, became newsworthy.[18] When workers in 'the cause' from interstate or overseas wanted to know the state of play in Australia's most populous colony, it was to Scott that they were referred. The period after her mother's death was one of increasing recognition; she gained more and more authority to speak. Links between issues in women's degradation became more obvious to her. Her work for various reforms other than suffrage, and with women reformers outside her immediate circle, extended the range of her analysis. Her speeches, her letters to newspaper editors, her interactions with recalcitrant politicians and officials, became perceptibly more confident, more righteous and authoritative — but as well more maternal, recalling and claiming reforms for women on the basis of their insights and duties as mothers. She began to inspire fear and awe in public men, sometimes of a kind that resembled naughty schoolboys confronted with their disappointed or enraged mother.

The neglect of the Woman Suffrage Bill was the immediate basis of Scott's reproach. She was concerned about the likely eclipsing of social reform brought about by the federation controversy of the period. A number of further factors about federation disquieted her. In 1897 the chief justice and delegate to the Federal Convention, William Cullen, when discussing federation at a monthly meeting of the WSL, was asked about the likelihood of woman suffrage being included in the federal franchise, if enacted by national referendum. His answer evoked a critical response from Scott. The next day he wrote to her:

> I thought you would explain why my reply at last night's meeting seemed so inexplicable to you. The question I was asked was as to the insertion of a provision for female suffrage. I answered no . . . I take the view that the framing of the constitution must not be made the occasion of settling questions not essentially connected with federation. If that is attempted in this instance it will lead to others. Have you conceived what it means for a convention unconnected with parliament embodying new and radical provisions in a measure which is to take away powers from local legislatures?[19]

The federal Bill did indeed reduce powers of existing legislatures. Not only did it seem from Cullen's response that the cause of women would gain little from federation, but also that it would change the scope and meaning of local colonial franchise. As parliamentarians debating woman suffrage argued, the federal Bill, if adopted, would create a major redefinition of colonial politics as the province only of domestic and social legislation, while the larger international and national questions would be the province of federal government. While this was used by some New South Wales parliamentarians as an argument *for* woman suffrage, because women were arguably suited to domestic issues, it was hardly likely to appeal to suffragists of Scott's ilk.[20] She resisted the re-deployment of such a putative public/private split within the public political sphere between the implicitly 'masculine' federal sphere of taxation, foreign policy, defence, trade and economics, and the 'feminine' sphere of education, welfare, law and order, prisons, labour, industry, land and health. At the very moment when women claimed access to what had constituted a representative citizenship, politicians were diluting or reducing the scope of the prize to be won. So it seemed in 1897. With only South Australian women enjoying the franchise, insufficient pressure existed for Scott to see federation as an occasion for advancing the cause of women.

In the context of women's struggle for political representation, the announcement of a referendum upon the federal Bill in which, of course, only men were eligible to vote, reminded suffragists painfully of their disenfranchisement on the basis of sex. Scott spoke bitterly at a meeting of those called the 'anti-billites':

> Unlike the women of S. Australia we have no vote but that is no reason against our speaking, rather the reverse, for though we pay taxes and are even more law abiding citizens than men are, and though we clearly love our homes . . . yet we are utterly powerless to voice our views in the national referendum . . . [T]he sentiment among women in the colony is (as a rule) against the Bill.

She denounced a number of anticipated consequences of federation. One was the great cost of armies, federal government buildings and so on, which would be 'borne by women taxed without representation'. The Commonwealth could only be a 'huge white elephant'. The artificial unity it would impose could be compared to 'an arranged marriage'.[21] Clearly the activities of federal government were to be funded by taxation and, given demographic differences between the colonies, it was the unrepresented women of the most populous colonies like New South Wales who would be most disproportionately exploited, subsidising men's developments in the less populated rural colonies. Scott designed and sent a circular to the Commissioner of Taxation protesting against taxation without political representation and urged other WSL members to do likewise. Shortly after their altercation about the inclusion of women suffrage in the federal Bill, William Cullen wrote to her, again in criticism: 'I am sorry to say the argument as to taxation without representation does not seem to have much weight with me. Is it not possible that you yourself are less patient than formerly with diversity of opinion on this question?'[22] The indications are that Scott was becoming considerably less patient, but the focus on taxation was largely prompted by the threat she detected in federation. Unlike other anti-billites, she was not motivated by simple colonial-rights arguments. It was rather that the entire enterprise was a graphic instance of women again not being consulted on matters vital to their living conditions.

The defeat of the anti-billites was a bitter blow. Actually, by the time federal franchise was being drafted and enacted, Western Australia had also granted women the vote. Indeed, parliamentarians debating the New South Wales Women's Franchise Bill in 1900 conceded that federal adult franchise would probably be adopted, to avoid the anomaly of women in two states having state but not federal suffrage. If so, New South Wales women would be in a most curious position, possessing rights to federal but not state franchise.[23] Vida Goldstein, who assumed leadership of the Victorian suffrage movement from 1899, supported federation precisely because she believed it would speed the issue in Victoria, forcing the government's hand. As it turned out, the Victorian state parliament refused woman suffrage until 1908, compared with its Queensland counterpart, which resisted until 1905, and Tasmania until 1906.[24]

The anti-federation movement was demoralised by the end of 1899. Scott tried to battle on, and wrote reproachfully to pro-federation friends like James Ashton. He defended himself and criticised her continued stance: 'My view was that the difference between what was asked for and what was obtained did not justify continued opposition . . . I find the poorness of your views is largely the result of morbidity of mind if you will permit me to say so.'[25] Though Scott's opposition to federation continued, the political realities it imposed had to be recognised. It produced conditions for greater exchange and contact with suffragists in other colonies. The enactment of woman suffrage in Western Australia in 1899 began to acquaint suffragists in eastern states with their counterparts in the west. Edith Cowan, who was to be Western Australia's first woman member of parliament, wrote to Scott on most personal terms. They shared an opposition to federation and to the areas in which the federal government was seeking to promulgate nationwide legislation. Divorce was of particular concern. Cowan feared that any federal divorce law based on New South Wales or Victorian models would cause even greater hardships for women and children.[26]

Part of recognising the federal era was addressing issues as 'national' and viewing 'national' developments in other countries. Work in woman suffrage enhanced awareness of the history of women's organisations in other countries dating back to the mid-nineteenth-century. The WCTU, founded in the United States in 1874, was one international movement that was imported to different colonies in the 1880s. Another American women's movement initiative was the NCW. It was a federation of a wide range of women's organisations which worked through standing committees of representative delegates on various topics and conferences. In 1893 the various National Councils of Women formed the International Council of Women (ICW). Its objectives included the forging of a truly worldwide parliament of women to intervene in the widest range of issues affecting women. The particular domains of its address included legal and citizen rights, peace and international arbitration, social and economic conditions, and vice and the international traffic in women and girls.[27]

Through ICW networks, activists like the American, Dr Emily Ryder, made contact first with temperance, then with suffrage workers in Australia. She endeavoured to draw world attention to the plight of 'child brides' in India: their subjection to injuries from marital intercourse, their bodily sufferings, and the common premature deaths shortly after marriage, sometimes before reaching adolescence. The Little Wives of India established fund-raising circles in different parts of Australia. Scott and Eliza Pottie of the WCTU were the chief New South Wales organisers and workers. The scope to contribute to such a cause was quite limited. Nonetheless, Scott's interest was consistent with her continuing concern with the age of consent, sexual abuse of young girls, illegitimacy and prostitution. Moreover, it provided a widening in her vision of the continuum of women's sexual degradation by its consideration in an Asian culture. It was also an early instance of women from a wide range of state and federal contexts working together on behalf of women in a different context — women who were apparently powerless to challenge their situation. Ryder's campaign was one of many made by Western women on behalf of Indian women against violent rituals surrounding marriage and widowhood. The rediscovery of such efforts, such as celebrated in Kathleen Mayo's *Mother India* (1927), have embarrassed contemporary feminists as moments of Eurocentric cultural imperialism and racism, and to a considerable extent, justly so. Again, however, it is important to acknowledge that the intellectual and political discourses that permit this critique now did not ordinarily prevail at the turn of the century in Anglophone cultures. White workers in the cause of 'women' as a unified category, as well as socialists and liberals, were 'no better than they ought to have been' on such questions. They were manifestly not ahead of their time — and to understand their vision, their time has to be taken seriously.[28] Understanding is not support or concurrence.

Scott responded enthusiastically to Margaret Windeyer's invitation to join in the founding of the National Council of Women of New South Wales (NCW). During the first years of its operation over 20 organisations affiliated, including the WLS, Sydney University Women's Association, WCTU, WSL, Working and Factory Girls Club and the Queen's Jubilee Fund. However, there appear to have been obstacles to the NCW developing a strong momentum. Louisa MacDonald wrote to Scott in 1901: 'The pity about the National Council is that there is no one devoted to working up the organisation. We each of us have our own business'.[29] Despite this problem, the NCW became a vehicle for Scott's growing interest in pacifism and international arbitration. At a general NCW meeting in May 1898 she delivered a speech entitled 'Arbitration Versus War'. Scott connected these issues with the oppression of women:

> I implore you to consider the position women hold in the world, a position which carries with it very serious responsibility and let us ask ourselves whether we can defend our passivity upon this question — and whether it is not our plain duty to gain step by step more real straight power in the control of national affairs instead of leaving them in the control of men. The poverty and misery engendered by war are wholly unnecessary. The national housekeeping is in danger of bankruptcy; the starving, the oppressed, the sorrowful people and the 'White Slaves' of civilization cry out to us, and we see that like children they need Maternal as well as Paternal Government. Shall we rest content or shall we realise and take action upon those words of Ruskin's 'There is no suffering, no misery, no injustice in the world but the guilt of it lies with women — man can bear the sight of it, but you should not be able to bear it.'

With increasing familiarity with the works of theorists and statesmen on war and peace, she was particularly incensed at Australia's involvement in the Boer War. She denounced British criticisms of undemocratic features of the South African citizenship rights as sheer hypocrisy in the light of that nation's own undemocratic refusal to enfranchise women. The resort to physical force over moral suasion was deplorable, in view of the weakness of the Boer nation compared to Britain. Furthermore, she was scandalised at the British establishment of concentration camps in which Boer women, children and elders were incarcerated, as a strategy to secure the surrender of the Boer army. These sentiments were reinforced when English anti-war activist, Emily Hobhouse, discovered that two-thirds of these prisoners died from starvation-related diseases amidst unsanitary conditions. Scott's anger about the Boer war also extended to its effects on British and Australian women. The 'rich women, the working woman and the white slave woman of English birth continue to pay the taxes by money, work or slavery and remain voteless and unrepresented'. Despite this injustice, the state still robbed these women, in their capacity as mothers:

> And women who have gone through pain and suffering have given those brave and bonnie soldiers to the state have no power to say whether or not, an evil and barbaric war shall mow down their sons upon the hills and plains of a distant land. When the contingent went away, no more pathetic sight could be seen than men, women and little children rushing about to see them off. 'Will they all get killed?' cried a poor little boy to his father. Let us ask, how many Boer fathers, brothers, sons and husbands will they kill? But let those who make quarrels be the only men to fight and let no nation be called worthy . . . who resorts to physical force instead of moral suasion.[30]

Scott's concern about the strong dominating the weak was not confined to the physical coercion and violence of war. Part of the widening of her work from 1897 was her involvement in industrial issues affecting the weakest sector of the paid workforce — women, especially young shopgirls, factory hands and tailoresses. Ever since the Political Labor League had added woman suffrage to their platform, she was in demand as a speaker at various labour movement reform meetings. William Main, president of the Sydney and Suburban Early Closing Association, arranged for a group of shopgirls to call on Scott 'and explain exactly how they are treated'. In many cases they were required to work six days, usually until nine, but sometimes until eleven o'clock at night. Their exploitation at work and the lack of safety in getting home in darkness agitated her. The obstacle to an early closing Bill was the strength of free trade opinion in parliament, opposing any interference in business interests. So, Scott began a campaign of having shopgirls meet her conservative political acquaintances, such as Bruce Smith. While a prior engagement prevented his acceptance of her first invitation of this kind, he wrote in reply:

> As you can guess I do not approve of legislation in the direction of compulsory shop closing. I think that those matters are in the hands of the working-classes themselves. I am not 'cut and dried' on the question and should have opened my mind with pleasure to the shopgirls, especially if they were nice.

Scott became a regular speaker for the Early Closing Association, collecting information to assist the argument for this reform. In July 1898, a medical friend, Dr James Julian, offered her his view that shopwomen should have shorter hours than shopmen because 'custom and usage have given them also the burden of domestic duties to bear'. He was convinced that existing hours led to dyspepsia, neurosis and dangers to the 'progeny' of these women.

The issue of early closing proved controversial, and was vehemently opposed by retailers. Scott tried to involve her friend, factory inspector, Annie Duncan. The New South Wales Department of Labour, Duncan's employer, forbade her proposed attendance at a conference on early closing in 1899. Ultimately, however, a limited Bill was passed. Scott's concern for shopgirls did not end there. She enquired about their rights, under existing industrial legislation, to have the use of seats. Duncan informed her that certainly employers were required to provide seats 'but no girl would risk being seen by the shopwalker sitting down. Of course she would not be dismissed for sitting down, but some other charge would be trumped up against her'. Few girls were in a position to complain and magistrates were reluctant to enforce the law in the event of complaints. Duncan concluded: 'I am perfectly certain that nothing can be done until the girls are sufficiently independent and courageous to insist upon using the seat after they are provided'.[31]

From 1900 to 1902 Scott also involved herself in the meetings of the Sydney Tailoresses Union, with women such as Dora Coghlan Murray, who was working to improve the conditions of women in the civil service, and with E.W. O'Sullivan, Minister for Public Works, on amendments to the Factories Act to ensure the provision of adequate sanitary facilities for women. Timothy Augustus Coghlan, government statistician, also consulted her about various schemes to ameliorate working women, as did socialist, Harry Holland.[32] These activities for working women addressed their safety, the quality of their conditions, and their capacities to bargain for a decent livelihood for themselves. It was work that made Scott more aware than before how little independence working women had, and how work opportunities were denied to them by custom and prejudice. If women were not to bargain themselves away in marriage, or be forced into prostitution, then paid work had to become a viable alternative.

The obstacles to altering paid work for women to allow full independence were enormous. The Labor Party, whose members were crucial in the enactment of woman suffrage, were committed to a traditional sexual division of labour that located man as breadwinner, woman as his helpmeet and dependant. Paid work for women was prescribed as a temporary phase before marriage in unskilled areas defined as 'women's work'. Women were not to work in 'men's work', as Louisa Lawson had found to her cost when employing women compositors. As such, the question of equal pay simply did not arise, with the exception of 'white collar' occupations in the civil service or teaching. Women and men did different work, or so Labor rhetoric had it.[33] If only for strategic reasons, then,

Scott was hardly likely to advocate dismantling the sexual division of labour by urging that women should be coal-miners, electricians or engineers. She maintained the view that little could be done to fully challenge the situation of working women until women were enfranchised. For that, the cause needed Labor support more and more as the party came to hold the balance of power in parliament between the other two parties — the Free Traders and the Protectionists. Maintaining links with Labor was crucial, but also increasingly problematic.

Probably her Labor allies viewed Scott's work with young working women as non-industrial or perhaps philanthropic. Some of her other work could be seen in this way. Her continued work with the Girls' Friendly Society focused on providing accommodation, leisure and recreation for young working women in Sydney. But these activities were integrally linked to her broader vision of the plight of women. The problems of seduction, illegitimacy, intemperance, cruelty to women and children, family breakdown, and prostitution preoccupied her as much if not more than ever.[34]

The options facing young women visiting or residing in Sydney were dramatised through intersecting friendships with Henry and Bertha Lawson and Miles Franklin. Scott and Franklin shared news of the deterioration of relations between Henry and Bertha Lawson, along with discussions about literature, social reform and suffrage. Scott was startled to realise that the only employment open to Franklin if she lived in Sydney would be domestic service or comparable unskilled, poorly-paid female labour. This came to pass when Franklin moved to Sydney's eastern suburbs a year later to investigate the conditions of live-in servants by working as one. But in August 1902 she wrote asking Scott a favour, revealing the rural culture of anxiety about city life for a 20-year-old spinster:

> I am sorry to worry you now when I see by the paper that you must have a lot of business to worry about but could you come to my rescue? Mr A.B. Paterson (this is a secret yet a while) has asked me to collaborate with him in a story and it is awkward as father and mother are not able to come down with me now and I have to see him for a day or two . . . I will go to you but if you could not have me would you mind getting me some inexpensive lodging . . . I hope you will forgive me for troubling you but I am such a silly about the city and mother is in a state for fear that I will come to some harm so I have written to you dear Miss Scott.

In December that year, Scott informed Franklin about their friends, the Lawsons: 'Oh dear Stella, Lawson has been drinking so . . . his poor little wife seems heart broken; when he is so demented he tells such wicked lies about her.'[35] Comfort and ease hardly characterised the lives of these later celebrated Australian cultural figures. The hardships of their lives were readily linked by Scott to those of thousands of others all around. In this period of new and expanding links, Scott addressed public meetings supporting the establishment of an inebriates home, a foundling hospital, a maternity hospital, and the Mothers' Association.[36] By 1902, when women finally were enfranchised, Scott's links were wide and new, interstate and international. Yet they served an analysis of singularity and clarity: the sex 'woman' was degraded and had to be elevated. The work was diverse but the cause particular.

PRISON TALES

Scott received the following (undated) letter probably in mid-1897:

> deer miss,
>
> this is always going on and we are torn to pieces everywhere we are lockup. The Lockup Keeper will say we are nousy and put us in a cell of oursefs he will then do what he likes. even at the centril when the matrons are away for holidays they do it. do help us deer lady for God sake. We are bad enuf dont let us be made worser and we wil bles you for ever
>
> Mary Canes
> Rilly Strett

Scott began systematic prison reform work from July 1897. She had a number of objectives, the most important of which was the appointment of police matrons in all lockups that received women prisoners. The longer-term objective was to have women removed from existing prisons to a women's prison for the minority of women whose crimes left no choice but some form of incarceration. For the majority, however, she contended that prison was an inappropriate treatment, since most women in gaols were charged with offences against good order, primarily associated with prostitution. According to Scott they were victims rather than villains — casualities of vice and degradation.

She tackled the issue of police matrons first, enlisting the support of influential friends, like Louisa MacDonald, to petition the Police Minister on the matter. The inspector-general of police, Edmund Fosbery, proved uncooperative. Scott's next step was to obtain the help of Charlotte See, wife of future premier Sir John See, to bring pressure to bear upon Fosbery. She also sought the advice of her old ally, J.C. Nield, who had tabled the Vice Suppression Bill in 1892. Nield suggested a deputation to the Police Minister, James Brunker, who could then simply advise Fosbery as to the course of action to be pursued. Scott also secured the support of philanthropist, Helen Fell, in October 1898. In November Sir John See wrote advising that Fosbery had finally decided to put the matter before the Premier. Fellow worker Frances Levy was pleased by these developments. She reported:

> Those tipsey women are sometimes stark naked — and in a greater state of animal filth than can be represented. I told Mr Brunker that a woman might go into one of his police stations with some self respect (on the first time of going there) but she left it with *none*. They took it all out of her and sent her home shamed and degraded.

As a result of these initial representations, the police minister conceded the desirability of a separate lockup for women, but agreed that in the meantime, a woman matron was needed to supervise the women at the Central Station. Gertrude Browne was appointed in November 1898.[37]

On a related front, Scott had begun lobbying Captain Frederick Neitenstein, who was appointed comptroller-general of prisons in 1896. At the end of 1898 he granted Scott's request to visit Darlinghurst Gaol. Earlier that year, she and some other women had formed the Ladies Committee of the Prisoners' Aid Association of New South Wales, the presidency of which Scott held until 1918. She visited Darlinghurst and Biloela Gaols, and within months had drafted a report to be presented to Neitenstein. A major element of the visit was the comparative inspection of men's and women's conditions. The report was entitled 'The Amelioration of the Conditions of Women Prisoners', and began by comments on the general adequacy of facilities and conditions available to men prisoners:

> We were very differently impressed with our visit to the quarters of the women in Darlinghurst. First, the class of *warder* appeared to us of a very inferior type to the men warders; and it also appeared to us that the women criminals were more isolated and more in the power of the women placed over them, who appeared also to have but little sympathy with them . . . A *second* important difference we observed in the treatment of the men and women prisoners was that the men had a great variety of occupations; in consequence everything seemed brighter, more wholesome, less depressing . . . [H]ow terrible to our minds was the contrast we found in the women's quarters [where their work] appeared to consist solely of scrubbing, cleaning, washing and needlework of the most hideous and boring description. Colorless flannel skirts 9 to 12, 2 to 4; to bed at 5. Could any better preparation be found than this for scenes of terrible reaction and outbreaks? Naturally in a mixed gaol women could not garden, could not choose books unless they had a library of their own. Everything seemed to indicate how important is the desire of Captain Neitenstein to have a separate gaol for women. That at night women prisoners appeared to be locked up alone or any refractory ones left in the charge of two fellow prisoners seemed to us a factor against all reform or pacification of the unruly [mixed vans, no matrons]. To be degraded before men, to be in company of men who are aware of and see a woman's degradation is the surest way to block that woman's reform forever.

Scott advocated numerous reforms on the basis of this and other visits. Women needed more varied activities, less drab dress, a more cheerful environment with good conduct incentives and educational opportunities. Above all, they needed trained women warders, who were 'motherly'. Neitenstein received the report favourably, thanking Scott for her 'valuable advice' and expressing the hope that a women's prison would be established. He finally observed that there is 'much to discourage one in prison work and it is impossible to avoid a feeling of depression'.

An obstacle to change was the fewness of women prisoners, relative to men, and the triviality of their offences, for which they were generally awarded short sentences. The police and prison bureaucracies saw little value in investing in the creation of special, if admittedly more appropriate, conditions for women prisoners. Yet all agreed that recidivism rates were higher among the small group of women prisoners than among men, and that prison was not helping, and probably was hindering, the women's development. In the 1880s and 1890s, scandals occasionally came to light concerning women prisoners, specifically when those sentenced to two or more years' imprisonment became pregnant late in their sentences. In one instance, the father of the child was the son of a warder: the prisoner was used as a servant in the family quarters, a common practice in prisons all over the Australian colonies. In another, a woman prisoner proceeded against a warder in a paternity case. Whether the sexual transactions entailed in such situations were with the 'consent' of the prisoner or otherwise, as in the incidents reported by Mary Canes, the abuse of custodial power and impropriety of such conduct by warders was, for Scott, indisputable. Thus the spectacular women's riot at Biloela Gaol in 1898 was hardly cause for wonder.[38] That so few sexual scandals reached public disclosure in part could be explained by the brevity of the vast majority of women's sentences. It was only in the case of prisoners incarcerated for longer than nine months that the 'proof' of pregnancy while under sentence could possibly emerge. The odds were against abusive practices becoming visible in this way.

Scott and her friends, Margaret Hodge and Frances Levy, worked on two fronts: first, the short-term supervision and care of women prisoners by carefully selected women staff; and second, the long-term creation of separate institutions to deal with the specific problems of most women prisoners, especially those classified as 'inebriates'. The existing system was the perpetrator of violence, sexual abuse and degradation. The solution was to be the removal of women from sexual danger by protection and reclamation.

Since this analysis, and the policy demands it signalled, presented a significant critique of the existing criminal code, administration of justice, the police and prisons' departments, and by extension the government responsible for them, the strategy adopted by Scott, Hodge and Levy was crucial, since they had to secure co-operation, not defensiveness or hostility. From the time of Elizabeth Fry there had been a long tradition of women's philanthropy for women prisoners. In more recent times it had been a key aspect of WCTU work, given the strong association between prostitution, drink and incarceration. Such philanthropy shaded into 'rescue work' among fallen women. It was familiar, respectable and worthy. The philanthropic model thus gave them access as women visitors to prisons, and the capacity to 'see' conditions for women.[39] If the vision attained was vital, it also stood to be isolated and ineffective, if it remained purely in the philanthropic domain.

In this way, forming themselves as a Ladies Committee of the Prisoners' Aid Society was a means of lending an official status to their activities; and it gave them access to a wider network of contacts. This provided scope for lobbying for policy and institutional reform and legitimised their working beyond the amelioration of individual women prisoners. Scott obtained support for prison reforms by seeking information from her interstate and overseas contacts about policy and conditions for women prisoners. From her correspondence on various topics it is clear that her concern was not only with women prisoners once sentenced, but with their entire experience of the criminal-justice system, from the arresting constable onwards. Scott was horrified to learn that there was only one woman searcher in the employ of the police department. This searcher lived in the suburb of Redfern and obviously could not service all police stations in the event of any woman being detained. Moreover, when those charged with offences were conveyed from lockup to court, and from court to gaol, men and women alike were herded into the same police vans. Scott learned from Brisbane suffragists, Ellen Parsons and Leontine Cooper, that the situation was comparable in Queensland. In 1900 Cooper led a deputation to the Queensland premier demanding police matrons, and was quoted in a newspaper as saying 'The dignity of the whole sex was affected by female prisoners having male attendants to look after them'. In July 1900 Vida Goldstein was able to report a different situation in Victoria:

> In 'progressive' Victoria we are still without Police Matrons, Asylum and Prison Inspectors (women) but I am taking steps to urge the appointment of Police Matrons and would be glad of any up to date information you can give me of their work in NSW. This month there has been a woman sanitary inspector appointed by the Melbourne City Council at £100 per annum and a bicycle! Still, we must be thankful for small mercies. I don't know whether it is generally known that our Female Penitentiary at Coburg (you hate the word expediency; so do I and I also hate the word *female*) is managed entirely by women officers. Mrs Henderson, the governor is I understand, the only woman governor of a gaol in Her Majesty's dominions. She and her subordinates were appointed six years ago when the new Penitentiary was built in the teeth of violent opposition. Many of the authorities stated that the system would not work for a week — women could not possibly manage those desperate prisoners. Not once during the whole six years has it been found necessary to call in the assistance of men.

Strengthened by the Victorian experience, Scott visited other New South Wales gaols in 1900 and 1901, and reported not only to Neitenstein, but also to B.R. Wise, now the government's attorney-general. Wise was most interested in implementing what he called 'American reforms'; and he supported the establishment of a separate women's gaol. Seeing that as the long-term objective, however, he proved less constructive than Scott would have wished about the interim reforms she and her colleagues proposed for the existing system. They were not content with his 'after the revolution' position. Neitenstein was becoming more hopeful by the end of 1901 as a result of his own, Scott's and other reformers' work. He reported that 'I have the best reason for hoping that within a comparatively short time the construction of a new prison for females will be commenced.' Scott promptly donated £10 towards this new public work.

By 1902 her profile in the area of prison reform was such that John Hughes, future Minister for Justice and executive officer of the New South Wales Association for Aiding Discharged Prisoners, nominated Scott as a member of the Association. He asked for her suggestions as to other women who could be brought into the Association's activity. Scott replied that it would be advisable for women to be appointed to the council of the Association, and Hughes nominated her without delay. In June 1902 she sent him a list of women she considered appointable to the Association, as well as a list of those she would not like to see appointed. While his reply does not disclose exactly who Scott disapproved for this work, the Golding sisters and Nellie Martel were mentioned in the context of explosive tensions that had recently developed in the WSL. Hughes assured her that 'there is not the slightest chance of them being named'. He then explained the nature of the work involved, perhaps implicitly suggesting to her the way he would like to see her and her women colleagues operate:

> If I may be allowed to say so, we do not want 'fussy' women, however good their intentions may be, for the work done is of a peculiar nature, in which at first failure will be the rule not the exception. The information obtained also is of so difficult a character that as a rule it is thought advisable at our meetings to simply submit it to the chairman for reference if required and not to circulate it. If we talked about our cases outside we should become distrusted by the very people whose confidence we require if we are to do them any good.[40]

Scott's ladies committee no doubt proved to be very 'fussy', fired by the extensive information on the tragic situations of women they obtained through this work. Longstanding concern about the seduction of young girls was enhanced by the cases of prostitution and of women convicted of infanticide. In 1902 Scott and the others petitioned the Association to demand that parliament raise the age of consent to 17 years, providing would-be seducers with some disincentive. They also protested at the poor conditions of women prisoners when released on licence, due to their poverty, lack of accommodation or friends, almost ensuring their lapse into 'vice' and eventual re-incarceration.[41]

A mark of the degree to which the wider links facilitated by the new federal era of Australian politics had expanded Scott's vision and activism was her involvement in the case of Selina Sangal, a Victorian woman sentenced to death in October 1902. Public agitation was undertaken in several states, but Scott's tactics and arguments caused considerable local controversy. Sangal and her lover had murdered her abusive husband. Her accomplice had already been executed. Sangal was heavily pregnant and debate ensued as to whether she should be executed after the birth of the child. Medical testimony was offered to the effect that at the time of the murder she was suffering from 'nymphnophobia', a side effect of pregnancy. A public meeting in the Sydney Town Hall was called and chaired by Rose Scott. Its purpose was to raise funds for an appeal and to protest against the proposed execution of Sangal.[42] In a letter to the editor of the *Sydney Morning Herald*, Scott wrote:

> The woman is a great sinner. True. So was another woman who the Jews were prevented from legally stoning to death . . . I appeal to the public not that this woman should be saved from gaol, but that she should be saved from the death penalty under laws which her sex had no part in making.

This amounted to a strong public assertion of sex specificity, as well as a spirited re-vamping of the 'no taxation without representation' argument — no execution without representation. In the context of the preceding months of bitter struggle to have the Women's Franchise Bill assented to by the Legislative Council, quasi-egalitarian arguments had been to the fore of public debate and enemies of the Bill had asserted sex specificity as an obstacle to women's rights advocacy. To have Scott now publicly using such specificity arguments in favour of women outraged some readers. The Australian author, Ethel Turner, a member of the Women's Political and Educational League (WPEL), a body that succeeded the WSL from 1902, had questioned the advisability of the league's association with the case. Edward Smithurst replied to Scott's letter in a forceful letter to the editor:

> Miss Rose Scott your correspondent has been teaching the community that men and women should be equal before the law. She now denies the whole principle of her past work by claiming that a notorious criminal should not receive the same punishment as a man because she is a woman, and raises the objection that women should not be executed, further, on the ground that women should not be punished at all because all our laws are man-made. Miss Scott may learn that woman is losing much of the advantage which she formerly enjoyed as woman. The sexes will be — as she has claimed they should be — equal before the law, and in other

> respects also, where in the past woman has held the superior posi-
> tion, which she can do no longer . . . No one wants to see a
> woman hanged, or a man for that matter, but the sickly senti-
> mentality of your correspondent strikes at the root of all justice. As
> to the criminal 'ugly vice hath all unsexed her'.[43]

Had Smithurst completely misunderstood the terms and objectives of Scott's public advocacy of women's rights, or was she really being inconsistent in the Sangal case and others like it? She was informed at the end of 1902 of an unfortunate pregnant hotel maid, Ethel Herringe, who pursued and shot her rural employer, John Lee, after he had 'seduced and abandoned' her.[44] Residents of the area wanted to involve Scott in a campaign for her release which was to take place across the next two years.[45] How did a tension develop between defending women in terms of their specificities, and Scott's and other suffragists' profile as egalitarians? To situate the response of Smithurst and other critics, Scott's turn-of-the-century suffrage arguments should be considered in relation to the course of public political arguments for and against the measure. Although considerable points of unity existed between supporters of woman suffrage, there were also a number of critical areas of difference, pointing by 1902 in the direction of organisational and discursive fragmentation.

UNITIES AND FRAGMENTATIONS

In March 1901 Scott delivered her new suffrage lecture, 'Why Women Need A Vote'. The themes of the lecture indicate the expanded brief of her work in the cause of women. She drew links between the problems of different groups of women with whom she had been working, posing women's enfranchisement as the means to their solution. While she still stressed the importance of representation in some of the terms of her earlier 1892 and 1895 suffrage lectures, the effect of federation was evident in her argument about 'a voice in the National housekeeping'. This challenged the masculine association of the 'National' by designating it a sphere requiring housekeeping — 'women's work'. Her definition of women's degradation was wider than hitherto, drawing on her political experiences:

> During the many years (now 12) I have worked for the enfranchisement of women I have seen more and more wrongs to redress, realized more fully those 'silent tragedies' in women's lives, and the depths to which man's brutality can descend and more and more the utter want of sympathy which even most good men have for the needs of women in a class to which their wives and daughters do not belong . . . I have been through the gaols, I have seen that men there are understood and consequently far better treated than the women. Woman is the worst off and least considered. Walk through the shops, streets or factories, enter the homes. Everywhere, women's life and happiness are at the mercy of the individual man. If ever there was a Being who needed the

protection of a vote, that being is woman, especially the working woman.

What kinds of protection did Scott propose for women using the vote? She described the women of Western Australia, who had deployed pressure, once enfranchised in 1899, to secure within a year a rise in the age of consent from 14 to 16. This was a simple example of how the extension of franchise to any group resulted in greater legal protection for them. In New South Wales, a particular group of women who needed protection were so-called 'imbeciles' who appeared and reappeared in benevolent asylums with babies in their arms. The men responsible suffered neither disincentive nor penalty. Moreover, Scott contended that women had different criteria and priorities in the area of criminal law. If parliamentarians thought the death penalty appropriate for the crime of murder, but condoned a maximum of only five years' imprisonment for a child molester, women, she contended, would reverse these judgements, finding in the latter 'the crime of the Devil in human form'. If enfranchised, women might have some chance of achieving the ownership of their own children. They might also deliberate on policy concerning the care of state children and 'the poor criminal women'. Women would also seek changes in laws governing the drink traffic, taxation, and marriage and divorce. They would also alter industrial conditions, since 'our own limited experience tells us of girls who are paid wages so miserable that they can hardly live upon them and keep body and soul together'.

In the face of the evidence of the criminal and divorce courts, charitable institutions, and the industrial and social statistics of New South Wales, men's claims that they represented and protected women was, Scott declared, nonsense — an arrogant assumption, absurd and ridiculous, since women 'have never been consulted, no one pretends they have!' Men's claims to represent women were undermined by this failure to consult them:

> They have come to look upon a woman as a sort of appendage to themselves, a sort of tail that has only to wag — when man — the dog is pleased. And many men's attitudes on the woman question is that of serious and painful surprise such as might reasonably overcome a respectable dog if he was informed that in future his tail would assert its own individuality. Men and women are very different beings. Hence men cannot represent women any more than she can represent him. One class of men cannot represent another class of men, and yet men of whatever class differ less from each other than man does from women.

Few of Scott's claims in 'Why Women Need A Vote' depended on notions of equality, sameness, or parity between men and women. The same could always be said of parliamentary supporters of woman suffrage. In 1900 the Women's Franchise Bill was adopted as a government measure, in response to Labor Party pressure and lobbying by Scott, the Goldings, and others.[46] Labor members tended to see the vote as justifiable for working women, spinsters, widows — women not directly represented by men. This involved recognition of similarities between the position of these women and men. Against claims that women were intellectually inferior to men, therefore unfit or unable to wisely exercise the vote, Labor members and other pro-suffragists either denied charges of women's inferiority, or else argued that intellectual excellence was not a criteria for enfranchisement, given the universal right of men to vote on the basis not of intelligence, but simply on the basis of their sex. Labor men tended to redefine women as workers unjustifiably excluded from representation.

Many Freetraders and Protectionists also supported the Women's Franchise Bill, but selected arguments distinct from those of Labor members. They laid less stress on the egalitarian aspects of pro-suffragism than on those that hinged on acknowledgement of sex differences and specificities. They argued that the presence of women in political life would purify and ennoble, enhancing justice by drawing upon women's special qualities. They tended to accept Scott's argument that the differences between the sexes were so great that men could not adequately represent women. In general they were divided about the question of women parliamentarians. The WSL had made the strategic decision to ask for suffrage only, reasoning that to ask for the right to be elected would be more controversial and reduce support for the vote. Parliamentary supporters, however, tended to think candidature for women would be only a matter of time, though some saw women's domestic duties as an insuperable obstacle.

Opponents of woman suffrage also believed that women parliamentarians would surely follow women's enfranchisement, and contemptuously described the imagined future: the Speaker of the House holding the wailing baby while the new woman member made the 'maiden' speech. As well as this objection, opponents pursued a number of common themes. One major claim was that, federation notwithstanding, the women of New South Wales did not want the vote. Its advocacy was confined to a few Sydney women. These women were described by opponents, within the hearing of Scott and others sitting in the visitors' gallery, as estimable ladies, earnest and sincere, but blinded by prejudices on this question. Others, in a more disparaging vein, called suffragists undesirable types, social failures, women who failed to secure or keep a husband. In general, it was alleged with some irritation and hostility, that amidst suffragists there were 'aunt Tabathas', 'gushing Girton girls', sometimes 'very much married ladies', but usually spinsters, unmarried women who lurked around the Parliament House late at night, 'buttonholing' honorable members.

Invariably, debate on the Bill from 1900 to 1902 was conducted after dinner, and the emotive speeches of opponents extended proceedings into the early hours of the morning, so that the divisions and votes on second and third readings took place after 2 o'clock, 3 o'clock, and on one occasion 5 o'clock in the morning. Issues of propriety confronted Scott and other suffragists, since unchaperoned, unmarried women were not regarded as behaving properly if disporting themselves in public places at night. One issue was their safety, another was respectability. When opposing the vote on the grounds that it would lead to women members of parliament, one honorable member predicted untold trouble arising from the custom of late-night sittings. The lady MP would have to be seen home by one of her gentleman colleagues. What would the neighbours say? What would her husband (if she had one) or his wife say? What if they exchanged a goodnight kiss and it was reported in the newspapers? For reasons like this it would be inexpedient, not to say calamitous, to allow women into politics.

If opponents saw the prospect of women in politics in such sexualised terms, and considered such sexual dimensions sufficient grounds to repel the threat, the presence of Scott as witness to the proceedings provoked discomfort and hostility among members who felt invaded by 'the sex'. Ridicule and pointed reminders of 'her place' ensued. A legislative councillor denounced the invasion of the House by unmarried women. He told the House the amusing story of how, the night before, a certain lady visitor to the house had sent him her card after 10 o'clock. Affecting to have misunderstood, and presuming — as any man of the world would — as to the character of a lady who would do such a thing, he explained that he had not wanted to tell the lady that he was 'very much' a married man with nine children. When further enquiries revealed she was there in connection with what his clerk termed 'that female woman bill', he sent her away with the message that he was 'tee-totally opposed' to it — a close swipe at the temperance association with the woman suffrage movement.

This 'lady' witness was not entirely anonymous. Members of the three parties named Scott directly in different ways. The only other woman named as often was Miss Golding. A Labor member attacked Scott for giving little attention to the Labor Party men once she had secured their co-operation, instead devoting herself to flattering and cajoling members indifferent or hostile to woman suffrage. She had wrongly attacked labour organisations in violent terms for failing to do all she wanted; and he speculated that, beyond this issue, she had little sympathy with Labor. John Norton, editor of the salacious weekly newspaper, *Truth*, concurred, stating boldly, 'she is a tory on all other questions'. Scott personified woman suffrage in parliament, and the strongest line of opposition was the claim that she, the spinster, was unrepresentative of the wives and mothers of the State, especially those from rural areas.

Another 'sexualised' objection to woman suffrage was to women entering the polling booths. Members claimed that unscrupulous men would round up the army of women of 'ill repute' from Woolloomooloo and elsewhere to infest the area around the polling booths as voters. Would any decent man want his womenfolk coming into contact with the likes of these? Would any decent women want to vote under such circumstances?

Other themes recurred in the speeches of the minority opposing woman suffrage. Parliamentarians argued that there was no visible evidence that women suffered any legal disadvantage from remaining unenfranchised; that South Australia, Western Australia and New Zealand had accrued no visible benefits from enfranchising women; that enfranchising women would advantage city over country, unfairly disadvantaging rural women, whose other duties would prevent them from travelling many miles to vote; and that the political relationship between man and woman would thereby be revolutionised with disastrous consequences. This latter theme received lengthy elaboration. Women's special attributes fitted them for the private sphere, while the sterner sex, with 'nine times the responsibilities of women' as breadwinners, taxpayers, conquerors, explorers, builders, cultivators, police and defenders of the land, were the only appropriate voters. Treating the sexes as politically separate would be a body blow to family life, causing strife. Parents would lose control of daughters bent on ambitious political careers. Such women would decline the trouble and cares of childbearing and the already dangerous decrease in birthrates and family sizes would accelerate. Men would be afraid to marry women who talked about politics instead of domestic matters.

Several supporters of woman suffrage noted that young and single members of parliament were the most vocal opponents of citizen rights and political involvement for women. Young parliamentarians warned that women voters would be ruled by clergy or their emotions, and that they were intellectually inferior to men. Older speakers attributed this youthful misogyny to their inexperience of women. When they had known the love and support of a wise wife, they would realise the great contribution women could make to politics in the new federal era. An incensed bachelor replied that 'lookers-on see most of the game'. These young, unmarried men invariably were the ones who dismissed suffragists like Scott as 'the same old faces' year after year, and who commented adversely on their spinsterhood.[47]

As well as her work in Sydney, and not only for suffrage, Scott travelled to country towns and other cities to speak on the suffrage question, sometimes at the invitation of local members. If her family disapproved, others who had known her as she was growing up could have other views. Some time in the later 1890s, she was invited to address the Bill before parliament in Newcastle, from the upstairs balcony of a hotel in the open air. She confided her feelings about this occasion to her friend Dowell O'Reilly in a way that gives some insight into the satisfactions Scott obtained from life as a public figure:

> I almost felt as if I could not speak — for I hate drink so — and then
> when I saw the sea of earnest faces and heard them saying 'we want
> the lady', 'Is that Miss Scott?', I felt as if I could do anything and when
> it was over I had what was dearer to me than all — the men and boys
> I used to know in the hospital and teach in the Sunday school grown
> out of all recognition and coming to me and shaking hands and hold-
> ing my hand in theirs as if they would never let go — at any rate
> that part of it was perfect.

Scott was in high spirits about the prospects for the Bill by the 1900
session of parliament. Louisa MacDonald had invited her to address the
students at the Women's College, whose strong support for the franchise
resulted in a telegram to the Premier 'from the Principal tutor and fifteen
students'. Scott's letter to the editor of the *Sydney Morning Herald* was, in
MacDonald's view, 'splendid — such admirable reasoning and good temper.
In itself as compared to the twaddle spoken and written by our opponents,
it was a very strong argument in favour of at least one woman in politics.'

A depressing blow for Scott and the WSL came in late 1900, when the
attorney-general, B.R. Wise, played a role in the Legislative Council's rejection of the Bill, after it had passed an all-night sitting in the Legislative
Assembly. He opened by confirming the claim made in the Assembly that
he had never been a supporter of the vote for women, and that only prag-
matic factors like federation might make the measure expedient. This speech
was made on 28 November 1900, five months after his wife, Lilian Wise,
wrote to Scott:

> I am anxious to join the women's suffrage league and I enclose 2/-
> subscription. I am taking the Attorney General as far as Melbourne
> to give his brains some fresh air before settling down to his duties
> in that unventilated assembly. One cannot expect men to legislate
> in such an atmosphere. Some of them look grey after prolonged
> debate.

In fact, at an earlier deputation to the premier by the Labor Party, seeking
adult suffrage, Wise had claimed that women 'did not want it'.

Scott cannot have been entirely surprised by Wise's sabotage of the Bill
in the November Legislative Council debate. Of course, she must have hoped
that Lilian Wise's membership of the WSL from June would influence him,
at best towards support, or at least towards muting his opposition. A letter she received from Wise in August declined the WSL's invitation to attend
a large public meeting: 'I won't attend your meeting. I can't humbug (con-
sciously) in public and I really don't believe in Woman's Suffrage . . . tho'
it is one of many questions that . . . would allow one to support without
believing in it.' Though this letter could have been read as fair warning of
what was to come, Scott (and others she told of it) may have accepted without question his final undertaking: 'I am not and shall not oppose it in
Cabinet or Parliament.'

Lack of support from the attorney-general damaged the credibility of the Bill as a government measure. Scott, Martel and others were furious, blaming Wise directly not only for the defeat of the Bill by three votes, but also for the misogynist utterances of members, especially those of the Honorable J.H. Want, widely reported in the press. Vida Goldstein wrote to Scott in considerable indignation and regret that the members of parliament supporting the Bill did not demand the retraction of the slander against women, *as a sex*, that characterised the Women's Franchise Bill debate; 'and yet we are told that after we get the vote we shall lose the chivalrous regard of men. Isn't it all sickening!' Of B.R. Wise, Scott's friend Mrs E. Woolley, observed: 'You could not expect anything better of him — he is notoriously unreliable — so much so, that they dare not risk including him in the first federal Cabinet.' Though Woolley thought the Victorian parliament would shortly enact woman suffrage, and that there would then be speedy action in New South Wales, 'since they cannot afford to be behind her in voting power', Goldstein was more pessimistic: 'I greatly fear that the defeat on your council will militate against our chances of success.'[48]

Scott, Martel and seven others on the WSL council wanted to have a censure of Wise included in Scott's 1900 Annual Report of WSL, but nine other members voted against this course of action. The casting vote of the president resolved the motion in the negative.[49] Such division formed part of the more general situation of strategic and organisational disputes that characterised league business from 1900 to 1902. The suffrage movement faced charges of being unrepresentative of all groups of women, of being anti-Labor, and of being over-centralised in Sydney. From 1900, when success in parliament became a real possibility, the Anti-Female Franchise Society, led by P.J. Gandon, secretary of the Licensed Victuallers Association, was founded. Soon he printed letters to the editors of newspapers reporting that 'the little coterie represented by Miss Scott is hopelessly at variance even to the point of publicly repudiating each other'.[50] How true was this report? The Golding sisters and Martel promoted closer ties between the WSL and the labour movement. They sought to maximise the participation of 'working women' and to build up their Sydney working-class branches — Glebe, Camperdown, Annandale, Redfern, Newtown and Lilyfield. Under the original league rules such branches were to pay an annual capitation fee to the Central Sydney headquarters of WSL. For some activities, the branches could send delegates, but they were not entitled to elect council members, nor to attend and vote at council meetings of the Sydney league, the so-called 'central branch'.

The suburban branches increasingly sought autonomy and resented the centrality of the Sydney group. They began to protest against the capitation fee and to demand rights of audience, debate and voting at all central league levels, moves Scott resisted and that led to a legal and constitutional impasse. Conflict erupted in 1901 when it emerged that branches involving the Goldings and Martel had organised a deputation to the premier without the knowledge or authorisation of the central branch. Hasty motions of censure, half-hearted apologies and eventual standoffs resulted, with unwelcome rebel delegates attending and refusing to retire from council meetings or to retract public repudiations of the honorary secretary and her work. Scott's annual reports marked the storms of the WSL operations in this period of frustration and organised anti-suffragism. Mr W.E. Gundry, of the Australian Society for Social Ethics, was a member of the WSL who frequently corresponded with Scott about her difficult relations with the Goldings and Martel. After a particularly stormy meeting in July 1900, when their attempt to censure Scott failed, he wrote criticising the cruelty of their attack, having learned that Scott was ill:

> the culminating point of your enemies' efforts having been reached and over reached and the reaction will witness their descent into harmless obscurity and your own victory in the triumphal tenderness that suffers all and forgives all.

In August, following another such meeting, he wrote that he had 'always seen eye to eye' with her with regard to Mrs Martel, adding that the Goldings would have been better friends and more loyal supporters if not for her. For his efforts to support Scott, he reported he was 'now in the worst possible bad odour' with Belle Golding, 'united with the party of lying and conspiring and we are guilty of all sorts of nameless and dreadful things'. The conflicts between her and the Goldings and Martel led Scott's old friend Frank Cotton to write in support:

> I can fully sympathise with you over your troubles with the refractory and unconvincible members of the WS League for I have gone through the same experience myself in reform movements. To be a pioneer in reform work is indeed a thankless task but don't lose heart.

Another WSL colleague, May Tomkins, commenting also on Belle Golding's conduct towards Scott at this time, ventured: 'Poor Miss B.G. thought she had unearthed perfidy. I am inclined to think her health and nerves are in a very poor state.' Finally, Belle Golding announced in the press on behalf of the Glebe, Annandale, Camperdown, Redfern and Newtown branches (which she called 'United Branches' of the Womanhood Suffrage League), that they declined to tender the capitation fee. On 26 August 1902, Scott successfully moved a censure on the 'United Branches' for using the WSL name, referring to them as the 'former branches'.[51] However, by this point the Goldings and Martel, joined by Louisa Lawson, had already founded a new organisation, the Women's Progressive Association (WPA). P.J. Gandon took great delight in capitalising on the divisions in the suffrage movement. In a manner reminiscent of

Henry James's character, Basil Ransome, in *The Bostonians*, he wrote to Scott in October 1901 of his attendance at a WPA meeting:

> the most conspicuous thing about the meeting was your absence . . . [T]hese 'progressivists' are trying to steal your thunder. Seriously, I would like to publicly testify . . . that if the granting of the suffrage depended on mesdames Martel, Golding and Co. I could have unaided snuffed it out long ago. There was but one factor I had to reckon with during my long campaign, and that was yourself.[52]

Relations between Scott and the Goldings and Martel had deteriorated badly, but although mentioned during the 1901 debate, it was not widely enough known to prevent Sir William Lyne being surprised in 1902 when congratulations and celebrations over the final passing of the Women's Franchise Bill were being organised. Of course, closer friends knew. Dowell O'Reilly, who had moved the 1895 motion, wrote delighted at the success in 1902, complimenting Scott on the way she had handled the campaign: 'you seem to me to belong rather to the men's side of reform — that thinks always and tries never to "shreik". My how it is a pleasure to me to think that Belle Golding may now depart in peace! But will she?' In a similar tenor, Frances Saul noted there would be for Scott no more 'horrid annual reports followed by the criticism of small, envious minds. I felt so mad with those Misses Golding'.[53]

Scott's relations with Louisa Lawson underwent difficulties as well. By resigning from the WSL in 1893 and concentrating her energies on *The Dawn*, Louisa Lawson had ceased being part of woman suffrage lobbying and committee work. Once the success of the Women's Franchise Bill was known, Lawson began asserting her own pioneering role through the pages of her journal. At the public meeting celebrating enfranchisement, Lawson was called onto the stage and introduced by Scott as 'The Mother of Womanhood Suffrage in New South Wales'. Lawson published in *The Dawn* a letter Scott sent her afterwards:

> I hope I shall always feel as I do now and have done all my life that the chief honour is always due to the pioneer and that those who come after simply had the honour of carrying on the work begun. I feel nothing but joy that you should have been seen, and that the audience clapped and mentioned your name, as you walked up and took your proper place on the platform. But I can feel nothing but contempt for the people whose one object in life seems to be to glorify themselves at the expense of truth!

The fact that Lawson had to be called up on the stage at all suggests that it was conceivable by 1902 to organise such a celebratory meeting without her being in the official party. Clearly she had not been invited or honoured in the planning of the event. Evidently, neither Scott and her co-executive members of the WSL, nor politicians involved in the parliamentary passage of the Franchise Bill, regarded Lawson as sufficiently central to the successful campaign to secure her presence.

Gertrude O'Connor's account of this meeting and her mother's experience is interesting. She states that 'Mother was ignored', the later workers 'taking all the credit'. Lawson was in the hall as part of the audience.

> Mother was quietly leaving the hall to go home and stopped for a few moments to chat to Mrs Windeyer at the door when the audience called for her. She took stage fright and was going to bolt but Miss Windeyer had the presence of mind to deprive her of her bag and cloak and persuaded her to face the music. She was cheered from door to stage and cheered again as she was introduced to different members of Parliament gathered there as the Mother of Womanhood Suffrage in NSW. After fourteen years of labour in the cause of suffrage Mother was declared pioneer of the glorious cause of womanhood by the voices of the people and the press of NSW.

Quoting from the same letter from Scott to Lawson printed in *The Dawn,* O'Connor comments on its 'historical value' since 'it places beyond doubt that Mother was pioneer of the franchise in NSW'. In this comment she accords significant authority to adjudicate any such claim to Scott. Perhaps she saw Scott as a competing claimant whose co-operation was needed if her mother's place in history was to be secured. Yet her account of Scott's work for suffrage betrays no hostility or sense of Scott as a rival for Lawson's claim, concluding with 'God bless this sister of the people and reward her in thy time'.[54]

Lawson, understandably enough, may have felt unfairly eclipsed by Scott, and insufficiently acknowledged for her 'pioneering' role. Perhaps Lawson's feelings lay behind Scott's letter to her. Scott may have been aware that the speech she gave at the celebration meeting — 'A Short Account of the Woman Suffrage Movement in New South Wales' — offered Lawson somewhat less than the generous acknowledgement sought. She named Dora Montefiore as the pioneer in the formation of the league, as well as eight people Montefiore invited to the first meeting. Lawson was not among them. Nor was Lawson mentioned at the second meeting. Only in the account of the first *public* meeting was Lawson referred to:

> Our pioneer woman suffragist Mrs Lawson, the mother of Henry Lawson, spoke also and has been a constant and consistent worker in the cause, lending her office at one time for our meetings although our first meetings were held in a room placed at our disposal by that gallant gentleman, Quong Tart!

The nuances of this sentence both acknowledge, yet qualify, Lawson's claims. Scott did this in the context of a more general irritation about people who claimed to be 'first'. Mary Sanger Evans had written to her claiming to be the first Australian woman suffragist, dating back twenty-eight years. As if to rebuke this kind of claim, as had Mary Lee in letters earlier in the 1890s, Scott asked of the celebrating audience:

> Are we to rush around like so many puny children crying out, one 'it is mine, I saw it first', another 'it is mine, I touched it first? Oh foolish and blind! A thousand unseen influences have gone to sustain those hidden roots. Let the 'I' fade from our lips . . . [W]e stand in the presence of freedom . . . Make no mistake! Accept no petty, local, short-sighted interpretation of this double victory for women.[55]

Lawson at this time was seriously weakened after falling from a tram in 1901. She had ceased production of *The Dawn* while injured and convalescing, the work undertaken instead by Gertrude O'Connor. As well, these years were preoccupied with litigation between Lawson and the Sydney General Post Office over a patent mailbag fastener she had invented. In all communications, she evinced a sense of feeling 'got at'. She ceased publishing *The Dawn* in 1905 after a few of years of trying to continue in the post-suffrage context.[56]

For a while Lawson enjoyed a new sense of peer support in Annie Golding and Nellie Martel, founders of the WPA. Perhaps aware of Lawson's tension about those aspects of Scott's prominence Lawson may have believed were rightfully her own, these dissenters from Scott's WSL made a natural connection with her. Lawson joined the WPA, and reported upon its activities in extremely favourable terms. All Mrs Martel's activities were given the kind of attention in *The Dawn* that Scott received in other newspapers, and often at the expense of representations of Scott's work. In 1904, Martel left for England and thereafter the decline in Lawson's engagement with her newspaper was palpable. She retired to a house in south-west Sydney and tried to write.[57]

Scott's lessening contact with Lawson was, in part, a legacy of suffrage struggle divisions. These divisions were to persist into the post-suffrage period, the first era of 'the woman citizen' as it was called. If woman suffrage had been a unifying objective for workers in the cause of women in the 1890s, the events of the turn-of-the-century period drew sharply the different fragments that constituted that political unity. Conflicts of emphasis and incommensurable objectives could be expected in any such political grouping, so that unities forged would necessarily be contingent and unstable. They were the more so because of the solidification of party politics along class lines, and the redefinition after federation of colonial politics as 'state' politics.

In addition, however, Scott's firm non-party stance, and her opposition to federation, placed her 'against the tide' at the point of women's enfranchisement. Norton's description of her as 'a tory' may be under-standable from the perspective of a Labor populist and editor of *Truth*, but it is neither illuminating nor convincing from a wider perspective. In her vision, party politics and federation were seducers, powerful forces that would appropriate the energies and resources of women, and erase or ignore their specific needs and interests as a sex, distinct from the other sex. She urged that the only way in which women could effectively use their vote in the interests of their sex was if they remained united, above party pol-itics, as a powerful lobby group that politicians would have to serve and be answerable to, or risk defeat. The expansion of her brief of causes and interests in the years from 1897 to 1902 appears consistent with her earl-ier concerns with marriage, sexual commerce, and independence for women. At the turn of the century, Scott increased her understanding of key organisations and functions of government, bureaucracy and culture. Arguably she made deft uses of places that became open to her intervention and of links with people and projects consonant with her sexual politics objectives. She had also made potentially fruitful working connections with women in rural centres such as Grenfell, Orange, Casino and Albury.

Now that women had the vote, the way forward was to galvanise its use in the interests of fundamental and radical changes in the sexual sta-tus quo. Would women know how to do this? After all, it had taken Scott some time to learn how the political and legal systems worked. Upon news of her enfranchisement, a woman from Orange suggested: 'I think you will have to give us poor, ignorant women instruction classes in politics. I myself know nothing.'[58] So Scott founded the Women's Political and Educational League (WPEL) at the end of 1902 and set about establishing statewide branches. This would be the framework and platform for Scott's work in the cause of women for the next eight years. Many friends tried to urge her to take a break or, conversely, to consider a political career by standing for Commonwealth parliamentary office. Meanwhile, the grand old lady of social reform in South Australia, Catherine Helen Spence, advised her to go to the United States to see the work of the women's movement there: 'Think it over, don't say it can't be done. You would come back ten years younger as I did.'[59]

Scott did not go then, or as it turned out, ever. Instead, she was powerfully moved by a sense that the work had only just begun. Now pos-sessed of the means to make a real difference as a new and, she believed, unified political constituency, it was the task of the WPEL to deliver to women the vision of ending women's degradation that Scott had been developing since the 1880s.

Chapter 5

The Woman Citizen (1903–10)

Woman to Man

You have loved my soft body for ages
And my heart has been dear to your soul
But my spirit you have not discovered
And its spectrum has never been told.

Like Radium long hidden for ages
It has burnt out its fires unseen
and blank are all history's pages
on all that its wonders may mean.

Oh Radium, a wise woman found thee
And we must our own spirit discover
Or they will lie perdue for ages
If we must to the husband or lover.

We have shone with a light that was borrowed
Been creatures men wished us to be
And see how the great world has sorrowed
Steeped in misery as deep as the sea.

The strength of all spirit has been ours
for weakness belongs to the man
Let us rise up to conquer the morrow
and be the great force that we can.

Rose Scott, 1903
Scott Family Papers, Mitchell Library

While New South Wales suffragists awaited the final promulgation of the Women's Franchise Act, Scott's friend the educationalist, Margaret Hodge, wrote from London:

> I think we ought to form a society for educating women to use their votes. It will be so very serious if the enfranchised women show themselves to be crassly ignorant of politics, as people will say 'Women are manifestly unworthy of the privilege.' We must give the enemy no cause to blaspheme.[1]

Scott founded the WPEL in October 1902 with a sense of strong support from former suffragists. By its first quarterly meeting in February 1903 branches had been founded in the New South Wales towns and suburbs of Glen Innes, Maitland, Newcastle, Hamilton, Wallsend, Parramatta, Gordon, Homebush, Lithgow and Marrickville. More branches followed shortly in rural and suburban areas.[2] The WPEL was to represent the women of the state to all political parties alike. For most of the first decade of federation, when Scott spoke in public, it was as the WPEL president.

The activities she embraced at the turn of the century continued, and expanded further after the enfranchisement of women. Scott was spectacularly busy, especially in 1903 and 1904. A central task was establishing and extending the scope of the WPEL, specifically in country areas. In order to do this Scott travelled constantly, promoting her vision of women citizens and of the demands that should be made of their elected representatives. This work entailed considerable research, speech-writing, correspondence, interviews, deputations and negotiations within a rapidly changing political climate. In 1903 and 1904 the campaign for the release of Ethel Herringe, convicted of the manslaughter of John Lee, and the promotion of the Crimes (Girls' Protection) Amendment Bill, absorbed Scott's energies. These campaigns convinced her of the urgency of women voting *as women* for legislation and policies to protect their sex. She was in frequent contact with women reformers confronting similar problems interstate and overseas, partly through the National Council of Women. Her interests in pacifism and internationalism deepened.

Yet while Scott's efforts to secure legislative change with regard to sexual abuses intensified between 1905 and 1910, it is possible that the effectiveness of these efforts diminished. If the liberal state governments of this period favoured reform, it was oriented towards the regulation, rather than the prevention, of social problems. The age of consent measure was opposed and repeatedly shelved, while prostitutes were subjected to new forms of surveillance and regulation. Moves to extend women's rights were singularly less successful than those regulating the position of children. Everywhere the strong seemed to dominate the weak, and in 1907 Scott turned her attention to establishing a peace society with the aim of preventing war.

Scott's focus on pacifism and international issues began to displace that on immediate, local and state reforms by 1910. Scott increasingly revised her earlier vision that representation by means of the vote would forge a citizenry of women who would work, as a sex, for their sex. Instead, she came to see the solidarity of women as being fissured by party politics. The non-party stance of the WPEL became more contentious and incomprehensible. Old rivalries from WSL days imperilled unified action on various reform measures and, finally, the WPEL lost momentum. So, by the end of the decade who did she really represent? Scott found herself sharply at variance with women co-workers in the range of other projects and associations with which she was involved. By 1910, the vision of women's political representation had failed to deliver its promise. The task of revision of feminist strategies began, for the same problems remained despite the gaining of citizenship and the achievement of at least some of the legal reforms Scott and her co-workers had sought.

PUBLIC WOMAN

If the suffrage victory and post-suffrage feminist politics meant anything for Scott, it was travel. Never was she so in demand as a public speaker. She quite simply could not keep pace with all the engagements expected of her. A major feature of this hectic period was the undermining of her health. Bronchitis and rheumatism taxed her. She wrote to friends of her dread of winter, which severely aggravated both conditions to the point where she was often bedridden. In August 1904 she wrote to Miles Franklin:

> And 11 meetings in 6 days — Carcoar, Cowra, Lydhurst, Narrandera, Grenfell and so cold. Got home Friday morning, collapsed — writing in bed. *Could not vote alas*! The irony of fate — congestion of lung and bronchitis. Must stay in *bed* for a week at least.

So, after the long struggle for the vote, at the first opportunity she had to exercise it, this foremost woman citizen was unable to do so.

In October 1903 Scott had been on the road, this time in support of Queensland suffragists and women's movement activists. Through her exhausting schedule of towns and lectures, she spent some time with her sister, Alice Hamilton. To reach Queensland, she endured a rough coach trip from Sydney and a steamer trip from Ballina on the New South Wales north coast. She sent her young friend, Frances Saul, an account of her travel adventures:

> we had a quick passage in spite of a head wind. I was very ill and wretched. The cockroaches swarmed and used to come creeping out at night from their various nooks and crannies. The steward was I fear too kind to them — he certainly was not kind to us. Oh I was glad to get home and have a warm bath. I used to dream I had had one then woke to wonder what cockroaches wanted, why they were ever created.[3]

The large Scott household and its extended family of 1903 was set to change again across the next few years. Scott's uncle, George Rusden, died in 1903, which ended his benign, long-distance support. Terrick Hamilton, now estranged from Scott's sister, Alice, died in 1907. Significantly, also in 1907, David Scott Mitchell died at the age of 71. Scott received condolences from many people, but there is little, written in her own words, about the impact his death had upon her.

The death of another woman relative had a much more obvious effect on those who remained after her. Aunt Rose Selwyn had lived with Scott since Arthur Selwyn's death in 1899, there joining her niece, Millie, and Millie's daughter, Mollye Shaw, who had resided with Scott since the death of Bowyer Shaw in 1896. As well, Scott's niece from Brisbane, Rosie Scott, the 20-year-old daughter of Scott's deceased brother Helenus and his wife Emily, lived at Lynton during this turn-of-the-century period. Rose Selwyn died in 1905 and a bitter dispute between her nieces ensued.

Shortly before Rose Selwyn's death, Millie Shaw took her to the lawyer to have her will altered. No longer were Scott and Alice Hamilton beneficiaries: instead, all Rose Selwyn's money, jewellery and property were bequeathed to Millie, with a provision also for Scott's brother Robert's widow, Aimée Scott.

Alice Hamilton was outraged. Her life on the land with seven children and a problematic husband (from whom it seems she separated in this period) permitted her little time for family correspondence. Thus, this letter of the youngest of Scott's siblings is a rare glimpse of her picture of the family history. She wrote from the Brisbane suburb of Toowong, hundreds of miles from her husband's Tambo station, in reply to Scott's letter of a couple of days before setting out the full details of the new will:

> I am speechless with indignation. When you wrote to me some time ago I replied that I could not believe Millie would act in so dishonest a manner and I thought you were over wrought by many worries . . . I agree with every word you wrote. Who has been more petted and pampered by us all than Millie . . . why she would be in her grave now but for you . . . [T]he bulk should be certainly yours in all fairness . . . I don't see that Aimée comes into it (as you say) . . . she is only niece in law . . . But Rosie Scott by her devotion was certainly entitled to be remembered substantially. . . . I feel quite upset by such duplicity and greedy grabbing . . . Goodbye dear old woman. You must be having a sad time just now.

Alice Hamilton noted the comfort to Scott that the extended stay of their niece Rosie Scott must be, which may suggest that the atmosphere was otherwise rather tense at Lynton.[4] Millie and Mollye moved out, presumably into an independent household. Some of this bequest from Rose Selwyn was from Grace Rusden who had made Millie beneficiary of her estate in the event of her sister Rose Selwyn's death.

Part of the sadness for Rose Scott at this time was the maturing of Nene Scott Wallace's clear commitment to a life on the stage. With a lucky break as understudy in a major production, he was on tour by early 1905, with an extended season in Adelaide. This threw Scott into great uncertainty about her life direction and future. She confided some of her fears to Miles Franklin.

She had always loved to advise Franklin and give her accounts of her busy political life. A farmer's wife from Spicer's Creek who wrote a hate letter in 1903 specifically attacked Scott's spinsterhood, representing an old maid as one in no position to comment on either women or men. Scott replied to the woman, and informed Franklin that 'Mrs Anon from Spicer's Creek wrote me an awful letter in reply to mine. I cd not answer it, it made me shiver.' In dealing with this and other taxing work, she assured Franklin that when the young woman drafted any letters, she should always 'send them to me at once — they are a tonic — I need them — they start me on fresh tracks. I might get morbid in political work'.

This emotional dependence on Franklin sometimes produced jealous responses from Scott to her involvement with other friends, contacts and projects. It left her ill-prepared to cope with Franklin's news of March 1905 that she was going to the United States to live, work and write. Rather desperately Scott wrote to her in an attempt to dissuade:

> As it is I have felt lately as if you were miles and miles away from me and I know nothing of your plans and motives. Why this long journey? Why, why, why? What has my clever little girl's mind and heart been occupied with?

She continued the letter with a mixture of anxiety, manipulation and despair, certain to evoke a sympathetic response from Franklin:

> all last year I was full of worry and troubles many and that unsettled feeling that I did not know what my life in future would be — where I would live or where go — even now I am unsettled but if not too expensive I will stay on here. It is such an expense to keep on a place like this all for oneself and the things in it. What could I do with the old things and furniture. Then Nene being away. My life is all changed and if it were not for outside work and books, I do not know what I would do or feel.

Franklin did respond kindly, trying to help Scott, over the next few months, to deal with her difficulties. Rose Selwyn died, the will furore erupted, and Scott was publicly humiliated by a New South Wales Labor Party conference voting to refuse to hear her speak on feminist reforms, because of her well-known, non-party stance. These events drove Scott into a partial withdrawal from usual activities. In the space of three years, she changed from being frantically busy, to feeling an emptiness. Franklin offered a diagnosis which Scott accepted:

> I am, as you say, very lonely; it seems as if one by one all had gone.
> There is much to do and I am very busy — so that is the best cure
> for loneliness. Nene writes always once a week and often postcards
> in between and I hope that in a month or so he may be back in
> Sydney. He is now in Adelaide and then on to the west. I am very
> uncertain as to what I shall do eventually. To keep up this home
> just for me would be absurd and too expensive but at present there
> is too much to see to think too far ahead.[5]

Veteran social reformer, Catherine Helen Spence, wrote of seeing Nene
in Adelaide in the same period, and observed that Scott must be very lonely now.[6] A life so fully committed to the needs of others residing with her,
to be suddenly transformed into one with few such demands, was
recognised by others around her as a genuine life-crisis for Scott. It
both coincided with difficulties in her public life and, perhaps, contributed to those difficulties.

An increasing remoteness from usual emotional commitments, and
a fragility in her sense of identity and confidence, may have left Scott more
vulnerable than otherwise to some forms of external acquaintance. A journalist and chronicler of Aboriginal and Maori massacres, Arthur Vogan,
wrote Scott an extraordinary series of letters from 1903 to 1906. Under other
circumstances, Scott might have found the vigour of his sentiments at least
uncongenial, and certainly inappropriate, for a continuing correspondence.
Yet she not only responded to his communications, but invited him to dinner, to her political meetings, and to other activities. She did this despite
intense and fully articulated political and philosophical differences
between them.

Vogan was unemployed at the time. By his account, this was because
he was 'impractical enough to attempt to fight the great system of native
slaughter' that has been going on in Australia since colonisation took place.
Thereby he became 'disliked', dubbed an 'anti-Australian', and was fired
from 'the Australian Press'. Vogan wrote the book *Black Police* and various
syndicated articles. Scott often recalled the many Aboriginal people she had
known and played with in the beloved bush of her childhood. Her sister,
Alice, and her niece, Annie Rose Scott Cowen, lived close to the Aboriginal
people of the Queensland Barcoo River area, befriending and employing
them on the Tambo Station. Such contact with Aboriginal people, and her
stance of opposition to their mistreatment by whites, was a repudiation of
Scott's Uncle Robert and father Helenus's racist pursuit of regional genocide. It was a stance that also brought Scott into collision with Labor and
socialist men of her acquaintance. Thus, Vogan had ethical credentials that
evoked her sympathy and identification. He had suffered for a cause, opposed
by those around him. So had she.

'Only those of independent means can afford to be truthful and
just', he wrote to her.[7] Probably because he touched her sense of public

obligation, and her aspirations to both truth and justice, and because she was aware of his relative misfortune, Scott was set to give Vogan space and fair hearing. Since he was an ardent opponent of woman suffrage, this was no slight endeavour on her part. He was also a militarist, critical of her publicly expressed opposition to the Boer War, and worried that modern men were becoming effeminate. Meanwhile for modern women, the emancipation so favoured by Scott amounted to nothing more than the avoidance of their part in the work of the world — 'motherdom'. While Scott saw women as the spiritual sex and deplored men's animalism, Vogan claimed, on the contrary, that women were closer to the animal, while manly animalism, necessary for the best evolution of the human race, was diminishing with women's emancipation. He wrote:

> What has encouraged the growth of all these fads: so called democracy, women's rights, theosophy, spiritualism etc. is the decline of that animalism that you and your schools much decry. It is animalism that keeps the race going. Before entering into any of the arguments that you put forward, this one must logically be first decided: should the human race be preserved? Is it worth preserving? Let us say you answer by all means. Then how do you mean to preserve it? Through the co-operation of the overstrung females and undersized (alleged) males that form the main body of your command?

Their encounters and correspondence were marked by intense dispute and conflict. As was Scott's custom when a communication irked or irritated her, she annotated Vogan's letters with sarcastic questions or one-line quips. Perhaps she used these annotations in the writing of her letters of reply. For instance, when Vogan wrote in 1904, deploring Scott's spinsterhood, she annotated his pronouncements as follows:

> I have sincere admiration for you as a beautiful and clever woman of undeveloped affections and strong energies, hampered and crippled for some reason — I would be loathe to say what might hurt your feelings . . . [but woman] must lean on something [RS or something must lean on her! Ha! Ha!]

To his claim that every married woman spends a large part of her husband's earnings on abortion-related doctor's bills, 'a sad fact that you know is a fact', Scott wrote 'Do I?' He declared Scott's 'school of thought' to have, logically, no future. The modern woman he confessed he held in 'absolute horror', owing to her 'loose ideas', which caused a decline in chastity. Scott added sarcastically 'The men are so very chaste'; and to Vogan's rhetorical question 'What has the present generation to offer in exchange for the women of the past generation?', she responded 'Why not marry a woman with a past!'.

Despite all these differences, Scott and Vogan exchanged photographs and poetry each had written. They also discussed new eugenic ideas then being popularised, without any apparent recognition of how such discourses buttressed racism. They also discussed political figures such as William Lane. Scott probably did not share Vogan's assessment of Lane as ethically dubious, a quality which 'gave him his power over women'.[8] A photograph of Scott and Lane outside her home had recently been published.

Vogan's significance for Scott at this time was probably that he actively, negatively, and even jealously engaged with her life, her opinions and her doings, in a period of revision and reorientation of her public goals and private aspirations. Part of her difficulty was the discrepancy she experienced between the process of her creation as a public identity, a person whose seasonal illnesses could be reported in daily newspapers on the basis of work on behalf of her sex on the one hand, and a sense of disillusionment and loneliness on the other. The death of relatives was part of it, and something she shared with friends. Dowell O'Reilly, whose letter of condolence had so saddened her at the time of her mother's death in 1896, lost his own mother in 1905. His response to a letter from Scott captured some of her own feelings exactly:

> After a certain point in life (and it is a very strange thing to realise) our friends begin to grow fewer — my mother was always my closest and best friend and her absence leaves a big gap in a little band. May you long keep your place amongst them, long after I shall have said goodbye.[9]

But Scott was also revising her analysis of the causes of women's degradation and its redress, her beloved cause. She had written to Miles Franklin of an incident involving a group of working-class, inner-city women and herself late one night in King Street, Sydney. King Street was a place where prostitutes congregated to solicit clients. Scott was on the way home from a political meeting, waiting for the tram. Scott described three young women who

> abused each other with flaming cheeks and sparkling eyes on the footpath and *men* sniggered and laughed 'Ye dare to hit me, try it, ye dare!' and the other 'You're a liar you are', 'I don't walk the streets! And I laid my hand on one's arm and said 'Oh *don't, don't*, the men are laughing, come away' and the third woman told me to 'mind me own business' and not interfere — so I got my tram and came home and pondered and wondered why I cd never mind me [sic] own business.[10]

Little by little her experiences of *seeing* the lives city women lived, learning of the working conditions of domestic servants from young friends like Franklin, and witnessing the complexities of how marriages like those of the Lawsons and the Hamiltons deteriorated, exposed weak points in the analysis of women's situation advanced in her suffrage speeches and private writings of the 1890s. Their weakness, as revealed in the political work of these first years of women's citizenship, was too simple a notion of women as a single, political constituency in which common interests readily and visibly surmounted differences between constitutive groups. Scott had always been pained by the facts of women's different forms of collusion with and accommodation of oppressive and degrading circumstances; but almost as a matter of principle, she had refrained from integrating these facts into her feminist advocacies. These years would disclose the costs for Scott of this principle and refusal.

A sign of her shifting analysis and the range of influences upon her was her response to Henry Lawson's 1904 poem about prostitutes, 'The Women of the Town', published in *The Worker*. Despite the tragic impasse between Bertha and Henry, Scott held a sincere admiration for the poet, upon whom the impact of the feminist agenda of his mother and other friends could be seen. Scott clipped and kept this poem:

The Women of the Town

It is up from out the alleys, from the alleys dark and vile
It is up from out the alleys I have struggled for a while
Just to break of Heaven ere my devil drags me down
And to sing a song of Pity for the Women of the Town.

Jonnies in the private bar room, weak and silly, vain and blind
Even they would shrink and shudder if they knew the hell behind
And the meanest wouldn't grumble, when he's bilked of half a
    crown
If he knew as much as I do of the Women of the Town.

For I see the end too plainly of the golden headed star
Who is smiling like an angel in the gilded private bar
Drifting to the third rate houses, drifting, sinking lower down
Till she raves in some low parlour with the Women of the Town.

To the dingy, beer stained parlour, all day long the outcasts come
Draggled, dirty, beered, repulsive, shameless, aye bootless come
    some
They have sold their bodies and would sell their souls for drink to
    drown
Memories of wrong that haunt them, the Women of the Town.

Some have known too well, God help them! to what depths a man
    can sink
Sacrificing wife and children, name and fame and all for drink
Deeper, deeper sink the women, for the veriest drunken clown
Has his feet upon the shoulders of the Women of the Town.

There's a heavy cloud that's hanging on my spirit like a pall
Tis the horror and injustice and the hopelessness of all
There's the love of one, God help her that no sea of sin can
    drown
And she always loves a bully does the Woman of the Town.

Oh my sisters, oh my sisters, I am powerless to aid
'Tis a world of prostitution — it is business, it is trade
And they profit, from the landlord to the wealthy brewer down
To the bully and the bludger on the Women of the Town.

But the heart of one great poet cries to heaven in a line
Crying Mary, pity women, you have whiter souls than mine
And if in the grand hereafter there is one shall wear a crown
For the hell that men made for her — 'tis the woman of the
    Town.

Even with Lawson's insight and his 'great gift', as Scott called it, the client or his demand for prostitution remained substantially unscrutinised by the poet. Scott's problem as a feminist reformer remained how to translate such a scrutiny into public policies regulating prostitution.

The speech most in demand on her 1903 northern New South Wales and Queensland tour was called 'On the Social Evil' (sometimes 'The Social Problem'), the accepted public reference to prostitution. It was published by the Women's Christian Temperance Union of Queensland, and widely circulated. In it, she devoted less attention to prostitutes than hitherto, and considerably more to criticism of naturalistic, fatalistic assertions of men's need for a supply of women for sexual use. Fiercely upsetting such essentialism as nonsense, she outlined the harm that these representations of men's sexuality inflicted upon all women and the vast social costs of the consequences.

Scott, the public woman, was subject to unprecedented publicity in this period of reassessment and uncertainty. Her woman suffrage work of the 1890s was the source of the interest, the claim on public attention. It seemed that all her co-workers of that period were gone: retired and ill, like Mary Windeyer, or like Eliza Ashton, dead. Louisa Lawson closed *The Dawn* in 1905 and all but retired from public life. Maybanke Wolstenholme and Scott were estranged, while the issue of party politics claimed other friendships. Louisa Lawson's poem *Life's Battles* was clipped from a magazine among Scott's papers of the period:

Some battles we are called to fight
With Comrades cheering on
With Certain victory in sights
But some, we fight alone;
And though the one we cannot share
Is oft the hardest fight
A martyr's courage makes us dare
When fighting for the right. [11]

When preparing for various interviews in these years, including one of 1907 arranged by J.F. Archibald for his new journal, *The Lone Hand*, Scott listed her various reform campaigns in the following order: woman suffrage, age of consent, police matrons, women's college, early closing, tailoresses union, women's hospital, hospital Saturday fund, restaurant keepers and hotel employees, National Council of Women, Little Wives of India secretary, Women's Club, Women's Literary Society, cooking in schools, against federation, kindergarten committee, Boy's Brigade, Factory Club, and the Orphans and Widows Fund.[12] This list is neither alphabetical nor strictly chronological, but instead suggests some sense of those activities uppermost in Scott's estimation. This process of accounting her career, part of being Rose Scott, Sydney celebrity, also involved her in providing details of her daily life and routines. In 1909 the *Sydney Morning Herald* asked about her leisure activities. She replied:

> I think I must be a bit of a crank. All sorts of cranks come to me with their ideas and theories. I have always a great deal of letter writing to do. I am reading the mail now. *But* I love my garden and am in it as much as possible. I study social reforms, the occult and mystic sciences and biographies of every sort. Pictures, old bookplates I am specially fond of, but music saddens me and unfits me for work.

The reporter concluded with a description of Scott — her sweet, gentle manner, her blue dreamy eyes of mystic expression, her grey hair 'as if a sudden frost had touched it'.[13]

THE FIRST YEAR

The Women's Political and Educational League (WPEL) was, unlike the WSL, composed only of women. Branches were to be formed by electorate, and were to comprise at least twenty members. At the beginning of 1903 there were seventy-six financial members. It is difficult to know how this modest number compared with the first memberships of other women's organisations affiliated with party politics — notably the Women's Progressive Association (WPA) and the Women's Liberal League (WLL). The WPEL had a structure of quarterly and monthly (executive and branch) meetings attended by a guest speaker (usually a politician), and an annual conference, opened by a presidential address. After the first year of work, Scott's address discussed a wide range of issues. These included an explanation of the WPEL's non-party ideal, the progress of Bills before parliament, especially the 'Girls' Protection Bill', the principles of peace and arbitration, the need for police matrons, and the efforts being made to secure the release of Ethel Herringe. It was the report of the New South Wales government's Royal Commission into the Decline in the Birthrate that evoked the most polemical sections of the address. Here Scott found a link with many of her earlier concerns. But as an enfranchised citizen, now speaking to her fellow women citizens, tact was less of a consideration than it had previously been. The Royal Commission report, according to Scott, was:

> A whirlwind of talk and superficial comment. A commission
> composed of men only, a report in which the only evidence
> printed was such as these men approved of, a commission which
> like Adam of old wound up very contentedly with assuring the pub-
> lic that everything was the fault 'of the woman thou gavest to be
> with me'. My friends so long as men keep up the demand for a sup-
> ply of thousands and thousands of women in every city who are
> to lead degraded lives apart from the sphere of wife and mother,
> so long they can take the blame to themselves of a terrible evil which
> influences the birthrate not only directly but indirectly in three
> different ways — disease, selfishness and immorality. Women,
> whether as wives or outcasts, are being sacrificed physically and
> morally . . . quality should be placed before quantity.[14]

This passage combined her critique of hydraulic notions of male sexuality, the condonation of men's enforcement of their so-called 'conjugal rights',
and their use of prostitutes. She also drew clear connection between the
lot of wives and of prostitutes. Rhetorically, at a moment of public criticism
of women's 'selfishness', Scott diverted attention back onto men, in her
stress on the consequences for fertility of *their* selfishness. She saw pronatalism as an insidious enemy of her efforts to secure the notion of voluntary
motherhood and women's right to forego at will sexual intercourse with
their husbands. Her stress then, on quality over quantity, was an attempt
to undermine unqualified pronatalism. In support, she condemned
numerous features of the environment into which children were born, concluding that 'we think more of our plants, our flowers, our animals than
we do of our children'.[15]

Her attack on pronatalism was simultaneously an attack upon the misogynist view that citizenship for women led to their neglect of maternity.
The attempts to probe the extent of wives' resort to abortion, and to restrict
their access to abortion facilities, were consequences of this moment of public pronatalism. Scott did not publicly address the issue of abortion. It is
unlikely that the topic was unknown to her. Married women's average completed family sizes by 1910 had declined to four children, even in the context of a faulty theory of ovulation and numerous obstacles to effective use
of barrier methods of artificial contraception.[16] That women resorted to abortion in order to manage difficult living conditions was testament to their
problems in negotiating forms of marital sexuality without hazardous consequences. Presumably Scott wanted no part of the pronatalist cacopho-
ny condemning 'selfish' married women. By her analysis, however,
abortion was no solution to the problem of men's animalism and women's
degradation. Rather, unwanted pregnancies — whether delivered or
aborted — were symptoms of that very 'animalism' and 'degradation'.
Abortion could in principle mitigate, as an outcome, but like philanthropy
applied to poverty, it meant that the heads were only chopped off the weeds:
the roots remained intact.

The dominance of women by men in marriage was the subject of one of Scott's earliest WPEL speeches, directed to the economic position of married women. This speech was widely reported in the Sydney newspapers. It is significant that Scott integrated into it current forms of eugenic arguments about the deterioration of the race. The *Sydney Morning Herald* gave the following account:

> Her contention was that wives should not be called upon to render unpaid household services and to be as dependent as little children for their very subsistence upon the capricious doles of their husbands. [S]uch a state of things sapped the spirit and independence of womanhood and retarded her development and through her, that of the race. Many women submitted to the most degrading and tyrannical conditions, because they and their children were economically dependent upon their husbands, being compelled thereby to sacrifice very much of their self-respect, and being in many instances cut off in the eyes of their children from that dignity which always surrounded the woman who is not economically subservient, and who gives love and administers comfort with the spontaneous impulse of wifehood and motherhood. Miss Scott's emphatic conclusion was that every wife should have a right to a sure and regular portion of her husband's income.[17]

This challenge to the notion of breadwinner as the marriage partner with the sole right to determine the economic allocation of household resources remains unsecured in Australian law to this day. The servility of Scott's married women colleagues on questions confronting men's behaviour, as shown in the campaign in support of the 1892 Vice Suppression Bill, was, in her view, a consequence of this dependence. Scott's analysis here did not presume that simply by legally guaranteeing women half the family income, servility would cease. Matters were more complex. What she did believe, however, was that the cultural interconnections drawn between men's economic ascendency and their right to rule the household — a woman and her children — influenced the social, psychological and sexual character of relations between men and women. She hoped that a legally guaranteed income for wives, as well as acknowledging the importance of their work through direct payment, might work to weaken the male monopoly on power conferred by breadwinner status. Women's domestic work would be recognised and redefined as equally breadwinning. This could reduce the tendency to servility, enabling wives and mothers to intervene in public life as fully responsible citizens.

If economic dependence for wives led to their submission to degrading conditions, they sometimes attempted to resist, by leaving and suing husbands for maintenance. Bertha Lawson, although pregnant, left Henry Lawson in 1903 and obtained financial support from Scott while she sought lodgings and a maintenance order. The limits of existing provisions emerged clearly in subsequent events. Even though an order was granted, Lawson refused to comply with it. He arrived drunk at Scott's home, demanding his wife's new address, so that he could make her return home. Bertha Lawson had to commence non-compliance proceedings, but amidst all the stress she went into premature labour and 'had a wee dead babe'.[18] Too ill to earn a living to adequately care for the children and manage a household alone, she returned to her husband, remaining until 1909. Then, with the children somewhat older, she applied for a job with the State Children's Relief Board, for which Scott supplied a glowing personal reference.[19]

The fact that dependence and vulnerability were not confined to wives was demonstrated dramatically in the period of the Birthrate Commission. A young domestic servant, 'seduced' by a married man, subsequently unemployed and with a sick baby son whom no institution would take unless accompanied by her, strangled her baby in 1903. Her conviction aroused the sorrow and sympathy of Scott and her friends. The tragic story of Ethel Herringe also unfolded during 1903. 'Seduced and abandoned' by her employer, she had pursued and confronted him, and finally shot him with his own gun in a hotel room. Local residents were active in an appeal campaign. The electorate was represented by William Arthur Holman, future Labor attorney-general and premier of New South Wales. Ada Holman, a journalist, wrote to inform Scott about the case, as did Anna Hazelton, a Grenfell activist who enlisted Scott's help in negotiating with the attorney-general, B.R. Wise, in the matter. Herringe gave birth to twins in Darlinghurst Gaol. They were immediately taken from her and made wards of the state. Hazelton reported that other families in the local area had daughters 'shamed' by the same man, John Lee, one of whom had also borne twins.

Scott and others involved were unsuccessful in persuading Wise to be merciful. He simply stated that it was too soon to consider releasing Herringe.[20] In all his interactions with Scott on this matter he staunchly resisted her argument that Herringe's act had to be understood as a woman's defence of her honour in response to the provocation of abandonment. Whereas criminal law might acknowledge notions of unreasonable provocation in the case of a man slaying his wife or her lover (or both) upon finding them in the marital bed, there was no such acknowledgement of different kinds of provocation experienced by women at the hands of men, ones that could justifiably mitigate the severity of criminal-justice responses to their criminal acts. For Wise, Herringe was just another 'fallen woman' and a common criminal — immoral and dangerous. For the Holmans, Hazelton and many others she was a poor victim of vulnerability and coercion; but Scott also saw her imprisonment in political terms. Herringe was a political prisoner, emblematic of women's degradation.[21]

Wise's obstinacy incensed her. He was not so merciless in release appeals affecting men in this period. Moreover, the effects of party politics could be detected. Herringe's release could only enhance the popularity of the local member, Holman, a Labor man. The Liberal Party had nought to gain here. There were, however, ways in which Wise's response on the Herringe appeal was over-determined. As Scott's co-worker, Florence Wearne, noted, the 'Girls' Protection Bill' was to be debated the next day and Wise continued his trenchant opposition to raising the age of consent above 14 as he had in the 1887 debate on the Seduction Punishment Bill and the 1892 Vice Suppression Bill. If Scott was obsessed with the exploitation and degradation of women too young to understand the significance or deal with the consequences of sexual intercourse, Wise was just as obsessed with the liberty of men and the threat of false charges and blackmail from promiscuous, precocious 'harlots'. Once again, in the 1903 debate, he succeeded in galvanising opposition to the Bill drafted by Charles MacKellar, in collaboration with Scott. Wise's opposition to the Bill was widely known and in July 1903 MacKellar confided in Scott:

> You know that Mr Wise is very strong against the bill and he thinks and I am told says that the women are by no means unanimous in its favour — in fact that a large number are against it — for that reason you had better communicate with the various leagues in order that petitions in its favour may be signed as numerously as possible and sent to various members of the Legislative Council. I think that a petition should be sent from each league of women separately and that a petition should be sent from women who don't belong to any league also. However if you wish the bill to pass you had better work the matter up,
>
> Yours truly,
C.K. MacKellar
>
> Private
>
> I hear that Mr Wise, Dr Creed and Mr Hawken are all collecting material to be used against me.[22]

Certainly these three members of the Legislative Council were decisive in the defeat of the 'Girls' Protection Bill'. The argument was advanced that in sub-tropical Australian conditions girls ripened into women by the age of fourteen. The same climatic arguments were used as those that had appeared in the earlier Bills, as well as the arguments that population needed to increase. Moreover, a higher age would open men to the risk of blackmail. They constantly represented the measure as unduly empowering malicious women to act against men.

Perhaps this reading of the significance of the measure was a simple inference drawn from the fact that its chief supporters were the politically active former suffragists working in the cause of women. In criticising the Bill, the Honourable Mr Hawken expressed grave concern at the role of women outside parliament applying pressure for it, and urged the men around him to resist 'petticoat' government.[23] All three had also opposed woman suffrage. It seems that these oppositions were interconnected in ways difficult to appreciate fully nearly a century later, especially in Wise's case.

His responses to both issues involved the assertion of a particular kind of 'manliness' within prevailing political discourses. Scott had political negotiations with him, as well as social ones. Wise had often attended her 'salon' and good social relations with him would have been essential during his tenure as attorney-general. Despite her anger and disappointment at his responses to the reforms most important to her, she offered him considerable support in his enthusiasm for child welfare and prison reform. But relations between Scott and Wise must have been tense and rather complicated in 1903 and 1904, despite her later warm memories of him as a brilliant, witty, charming man and a favourite guest.[24] Miles Franklin made a number of observations about Wise after she met him at Scott's home late in 1904, when he was no longer attorney-general.

> B.R. Wise was dressed correctly and did not sin against the usages of etiquette, [he] had the advantages of education, a career of being talented and in a position . . . [g]raceful Mrs Wise . . . is so well seasoned that what she says is a mask to what she might have originally thought and suffered . . . As for Mr Wise, dearest you must not for a moment worry because he was ill at ease. It was merely that he found me an ignorant, inane, unattractive little creature — his palate is so used to spiced dishes . . . the epicure's taste sated and exacting cannot always be satisfied. He shut me into myself by his first words because he hoisted the sex placard like a 'keep off the grass' notice in the gardens.[25]

If Wise's public utterances on woman suffrage and the age of consent were marked with sex antagonism and a distrust of women as hysterical and wicked, it would not be remarkable to find that these qualities were detectable in his social intercourse with women, particularly a young woman like Franklin. His administrative responses to interventions on behalf of Herringe or the 'Girls' Protection Bill' disclosed the unresolved tension between egalitarianism and assertions of sex differences in liberal discourse. On the one hand, Wise resisted arguments that hinged on the recognition of special problems, interests or disadvantages suffered by women requiring specific legal reforms. Herringe, for Wise, was a criminal like any other. Girls needed no special protection and adolescents of both sexes should be covered by the same provisions and regulations. In this framework, men did not go about seducing young girls and, if sexual contact took place, it was a consequence of the mutual gratification of natural instincts. Women were as carnal as men. The vote for women was not needed to ensure special provisions for their sex because they would vote the same way as men.

Such contentions amounted to a position of gender neutrality. Wise wanted public life and public policy to be de-gendered, applying alike to individuals, without regard to sex.

On the other hand, however, his arguments against sex-specific measures and administration entailed descriptions of women's characteristics and conduct in private life that implied anything but gender neutrality. For Wise, private life seemed to be almost a sex war. Men had to keep up their guard against conniving, seductive women, especially since men could not help submitting to their 'nature'. Women's worst leanings had to be kept under control and as far out of public life as possible. With such beliefs about imperilled 'manliness' it is little wonder that Franklin found him hoisting 'the sex placard' in ordinary conversation with women.

Yet, despite limitations of his character and career achievement, Wise's legal arguments and social philosophy continued to influence parliamentary debate throughout the decade. He insisted on amendments to the 'Girls' Protection Bill' that considerably modified its effectiveness, or more precisely, narrowed the group of men ever likely to be vulnerable to prosecution for carnal knowledge. He told MacKellar he would accept a revised Bill only if exemptions were provided for men who believed the girl was a prostitute or otherwise already 'immoral', and for men who had honestly believed by the demeanour and appearance of the girl that she was over 16.[26]

Why was the issue of the age of consent such a flashpoint in sexual politics at this time? Why did a liberal like Wise find this central demand of the much reviled newly enfranchised woman in general, and Scott in particular, such anathema? Fundamentally, liberalism was manifest in concerns for individual liberty, consent, freedom from coercion and surveillance in private matters, and the belief that conventional social arrangements and relationships were the outcome of social contracts freely negotiated between individuals. Scott's analysis of women's sexual position in relation to men disputed these liberal principles, contradicting the validity of liberal assumptions. In the same letter about Wise discussed above, Franklin thanked Scott for a previous letter on prostitution and the preventative possibilities of raising the age of consent, saying it was 'balm' to her. Scott had written in impassioned terms about some prostitutes she had visited:

> when we women see that is the use of our vote, to work for women, our deeply degraded sex and save the children from being every such as these. Prevention is better than cure, — most girls fall under 18. No my dear Stella, I ask you to find no balance on this question — there is none — on one side plenty, on the other disgrace, shame, misery, moral enslavement for women — and man the murderer of their souls . . . long ago I learned that to most men women are *women*, not human beings — women for their use and pleasure — variety is charming. Some virtuous — their own relatives — the rest the other thing.[27]

This kind of analysis made nonsense of any political creed radically separating public and private life and speaking in terms of sexless individuals with rights and freedoms. Instead, it implicitly specified and sexualised those whose rights liberalism defended, and challenged the actuality and validity of 'free choice' or 'consent' for women. Scott held that in many key instances women actually had no real meaningful choice at all — whether to marry or not, or whether to bear children or not — because of the coercive conditions accompanying the marriage contract and customary relations between the sexes.

In the case of the seduction of a 14-year-old girl, with the harm done to her and the next generation if she faced options like poverty or prostitution, the validity of focusing on her technical 'consent' was for Scott entirely questionable. The more important issue, surely, was the advisability and desirability of men having sexual intercourse with young, dependent daughters. What could consent mean when the man was her employer, parent's boarder, relative, neighbour, or music teacher? Scott urged the importance of 'impressing upon men, especially men of ripe years, who are too often to blame, the selfish wickedness of tampering with and the great necessity of protecting young girls.'[28] To Wise's arguments about blackmail, and his urging that immoral girls be exempted from protection, Scott replied:

> The dread of blackmail exists only as a bogey in the eyes of men who even if innocent themselves have too much sympathy with the vice of others. There is but little difficulty in proving a girl's bad character but the fact is that men should be taught to protect even silly bad girls at so tender an age from evil in themselves. That would be true chivalry.[29]

Scott simply would not accept Wise's Hobbesian account of the sexual 'state of nature'.

In letters to the newspapers and in speeches delivered on her tours in both states, she observed that all Australian states except New South Wales and Queensland had raised the age of consent to 16 or 17. In October 1903, she visited Brisbane, Gympie, Bundaberg, Ipswich, Toowoomba, Warwick, Armidale, Glen Innes, Tenterfield and Newcastle.[30] In Queensland she addressed the need for woman suffrage there, particularly so that women could exert effective pressure to make the state government repeal the Contagious Diseases Acts, in force since 1867, despite their repeal in Britain in 1884.[31] Her lecture on this topic was entitled 'The Social Problem'. In it she criticised the double standard to which fallen women were subjected, and official indifference to the existence and extent of prostitution, much of it originating in men's carnal knowledge of young girls:

> It is *men* and *men* alone who have divided women into two classes
> — the virtuous and the fallen, and they have done it for centuries
> for selfish reasons. The prostitute they require and extend a

hideous protection to, on the mere selfish plea that she is necessary for their health. This class of women must live in secret and
apart, she is not openly acknowledged, lest any of the dust which
cleaves to her raiment should in the public eye soil that of her pro-
tector or protectors. She is known as immoral, and alas often feels
hopelessly so and has long since abandoned all self respect. The man
on the other hand does not even know that he is immoral, his self
respect is unimpaired, and he has nothing to regret, except perhaps
some money. *Men* occupy the pulpits and preach righteousness to
the people, and yet how seldom do they allude to this serfdom of
women . . . In London there are 80 000 women on the streets,
27 000 little children treated for disease . . . In Sydney there are
already 1000 women on the streets alone . . . There is a close connection between vice and crime, criminals thrive and live on
the proceeds of vice.

Scott criticised the Contagious Diseases Acts for degrading women 'in order
to give license to man'; men, she argued, would suffer no injury whatever
from periods of celibacy. The destruction of women through prostitution
was not only unnecessary and evil, but also destructive of 'the race'. She
often asked what use was the much praised civilisation of her day if its man
acts the same as 'the savage'. Her ideal was 'the gradual elimination of the
animal in man'.[32]

   This preoccupation with animality was linked with a view of evolution current early in the twentieth century, which posited the diminution
of the physical relative to the intellectual and moral faculties of human societies. Such evolutionary arguments were congenial to those who sought
to elevate the position of women, but also to pacifists. In a speech Scott delivered in 1904 to a meeting of the NCW on 'Peace and Arbitration', she
observed the interconnections between the peace question and the
woman question, since 'both contained a strong ethical element firmly
bound up with the most pressing social and economic needs; both constitute
a struggle against the right of might and for the might of right'.[33]

   What were the matters most 'right' for the attention of the woman
citizen? E.W. O'Sullivan, a friend of Scott's and a member of parliament active in support of woman suffrage, asked her in March 1904 what
the state's women wanted in the way of remediable legislation. She
scrawled the following list on his letter:

   own their own children, family maintenance, Infants' Protection
   Bill, Equal Pay for equal work, sanitary arrangements in the city
   as in Melbourne and in the offices; offices of dignity and power in
   the State; juries, judges; Police matrons, economic independence
   for married women; prisoners position of women. Prostitution prosecuted. Procurement. Barrister. Senate University. Railways,
   trams night.

In reply he conceded that much that she sought 'may not be "in sight" for
some time yet'.[34]

REGULATION, PREVENTION AND PROTECTION

Between 1903 and 1910 Scott was involved in campaigns around a number of key reforms pressuring the See, the Carruthers, then the Wade Liberal governments. These included: the Juvenile Smoking Suppression Act (1903); the State Children's Amendment Act (1903); the Infants' Protection Act (1904); Neglected Children and Juvenile Offenders Act (1905); the Police Offences Amendment Act and the Prisoners' Detention Act (both 1908); and the Crimes (Girls' Protection) Amendment Act (1910). Her work with the NCW and the ICW became increasingly associated with the legal position of women and children during this period. She regularly met and corresponded with workers in other states, keeping abreast of legal developments. The general character of the legislation with which she was most concerned was protective. Even in those reforms ostensibly concerned with equal rights, such as guardianship, she actually argued in terms of the capacities of mothers to protect their children in various ways.

While the Liberal state governments of this period were willing, even enthusiastic, about measures regulating and normalising childhood and the conditions of children, they were unwilling to see the 'Girls' Protection Bill' in this light. Nor were they so ready to enact measures which, though possibly beneficial to children, primarily extended rights to their mothers. The Testators' Family Maintenance Bill, debated several times in the period, proposed preventing men willing away their goods and assets to others before providing for their wives and any dependent children. This was opposed by many parliamentarians as a shocking interference in the liberty of breadwinners and property owners. A good and deserving wife would of course be provided for by her spouse. The state had no business interfering in the privacy of family life. Similar reservations attended the suggestion that women might have equal legal guardianship of their children. Authority on this matter should rest with the head of the family.[35]

Why did Scott devote so much energy to matters concerned with children of both sexes, when her main concern was with women and girls? In view of the predilections of the three attorneys-general of the period, B.R. Wise, T.H. Waddell and C.G. Wade — all of whom had been anti-suffrage, but who all shared an interest in child-welfare legislation — Scott's co-operation with their agenda was, at least, expedient. Moreover, she reasoned that any measure that enshrined a special, protected status for childhood stood to elevate the status of nurturance and hence motherhood as a side effect. Since the majority of women were mothers, anything that improved their claims on public resources and their general civil standing was progress. If women could be authorised to speak publicly as mothers, the gamut of urgently needed reforms had some chance of success.

Women interstate and overseas took up similar measures, especially work establishing children's courts. Alice Henry sent information from the United States on this measure, while Catherine Helen Spence in South Australia and Vida Goldstein in Victoria did the same.[36] In New South Wales this was a particular enthusiasm of Wise's. The measure was congenial because it removed children from the adult system of criminal justice, but it also constituted juveniles as a distinct class of persons with attributes, interests and needs that required specific provisions. Since Scott wanted precisely this kind of recognition for women as a group brought into the ambit of the criminal-justice system, support for the 1905 Neglected Children and Juvenile Offenders Act was hardly a detour.

Similarly, despite its pronatalist associations, the Infants' Protection Act of 1904 earned her support because of its implications for women. It established that an illegitimate child's father had a financial responsibility to support that child until the age of 14 or 16. In order to maximise the chances of infants surviving, the mother could now sue the putative father for expenses incidental to childbirth, and for support for herself, for six months after the birth. While such a measure hardly solved all the problems of unmarried mothers, whose most difficult struggle might be to satisfy a magistrate as to paternity, it was a clear improvement. Men who failed to comply with maintenance orders could be proceeded against in police courts, like deserting husbands. Scott utilised currently fashionable anthropological theories of matriarchy to help support the case for the rights of mothers through child-welfare legislation. With the assertion of the difficulty and futility of attempting to separate the interests of the mother from those of the child, she reported that:

> the original organisation of the family was through the mother not through the father and the most ancient system in which the idea of blood relationship embodied was a system of kinship through females only . . . The mother and wife became more and more a mere creature of sex and less and less of a human being.[37]

In 1904, Scott addressed a new speech to the WPEL called 'Legislation Affecting Women and Children', reviewing the progress of law reform since women's enfranchisement. It included some of the themes of earlier speeches, such as one delivered to the NCW in 1903 in which she defined the basis of political action as 'our common womanhood and that great foundation stone of our very being . . . the evolution of our maternity'. The twentieth century had become the historical moment for the heralding forth of 'the motherhood of women encompassing the world'.[38] From this claim for the recognition of the dignity and centrality of motherhood, Scott contended that mothers should possess 'equal ownership with fathers over their legitimate children'. Unmarried mothers had sole and uncontested guardian rights, while wives had none, even in the event of widowhood. Under English law, reformed in 1886, widows automatically became their children's guardians (though they still had no other legal recognition as

guardians). In New South Wales, however, widows obtained guardianship only if the husband had not made other arrangements, such as
nominating a guardian of his choice in his will. Dora Montefiore recalled
that learning of this aspect of her legal position upon the death of her husband enraged her and converted her instantly to the cause of women, particularly the struggle for woman suffrage.[39]

The wives and mothers of New South Wales did not obtain equal legal
guardianship of their children until 1934, nine years after Scott's death.[40]
Her negotiations with the Liberal government of Carruthers were singularly
unsuccessful on this issue. Carruthers evidently saw equal guardianship in the same light as the Testators' Family Maintenance Bill — an unwarranted interference in the authority and prerogatives of male household
heads, husbands and fathers. As premier, he was far from accepting
Scott's representations on civil motherhood. On behalf of the WPEL, she
advocated *equal* rights on the basis of women's specificities or particularities,
pre-eminently as the mothers most of them were. He would not allow her
notion of a public motherhood that authorised them to 'enter Parliament,
if the electors so desire, or rise to any position of power or dignity in the
state . . . have an equal chance with men . . . be allowed to enter the legal
or any other profession'.[41] Scott increasingly recognised the importance
of these 'equal' rights, the more so since woman suffrage proved not to be
the golden road to reform that she had hoped. The problems that had concerned Scott for many years remained — unmarried mothers, seduction
of young girls, prostitution, men's 'animalism', and the 'ill-use' and
degradation of wives. In various measures of protection and prevention she continued to challenge these practices and institutions.

The pronatalist climate of the period inspired marked and punitive publicity about infanticide and unmarried mothers. Scott tried to cultivate a
sympathetic view of these scapegoated women by connecting their plight
back to men's exploitation in seduction. In a speech on poverty and
wealth she asked her audience:

> Can you see the poor starved children whom no woman loves; the
> murdered babies in fields, in drains, in gutters, for whose treatment
> you sometimes punish wicked and sometimes desperate women
> whose instinct would be to love and cherish? Such as these con-
> tinue to live and die in vain. Do you ever see the faces of the women
> who walk the street, do you ever hear them laugh? . . . Let them
> not live and suffer in vain.[42]

In view of the problems of unmarried mothers dramatised during the decade,
Scott publicly advocated the establishment of a foundling hospital for abandoned babies.[43] She also supported various child-welfare measures aimed
at securing adequate care for children in deprived circumstances. The socialist activist, Bertha MacNamara, was worried, however, that Scott seemed
unaware of the coercive potential of the proposed Bill, which became the

Neglected Children and Juvenile Offenders' Act (1905). MacNamara believed that an unscrupulous government would use the measure to remove the children of the poor and institutionalise them, on the pretext of removing them from 'immoral' living conditions. She felt that the mere condition of being illegitimate might itself be used as proof of immorality:

> but what is still worse, it gives profligate men the opportunity to ruin as many girls as they can get hold of. If there is any issue to touch their consciences on relations with such girls and women, it will not sit too heavily on most of these fellows' consciences and if they are a little cunning it will not touch their pockets for the state will take the children for the very reason that the mother and the father cannot be found. I should be so glad if I could have a talk with you about it.[44]

It is unclear whether they met and discussed the matter further, though later, friendly letters from MacNamara suggest some resolution was found. This problem of seduction and its consequences preoccupied politically active women, philanthropists, journalists and other members of the general public moved to write to Scott. As a Mr Taylor observed, poor girls like Ethel Herringe, wronged by men, were driven by misery to murder, owing to the inadequacies of the laws affecting women.[45] Despite her representations through both the WPEL and NCW, Carruthers refused to bring on the Girls' Protection Bill after it had failed to pass second readings in 1903 and 1905. In October 1906 he replied to her repeated requests stating that other measures were more urgent. She protested this decision, and his replies were cool and firm.[46] During 1906, through both the WPEL and the NCW, Scott and her co-workers tried to lobby parliamentarians on the issue of the age of consent as part of making the case for the urgency of the measure. This was the same strategy used by the WSL in the 1890s in support of woman suffrage. A majority of those who replied declared support. Labor members were more hostile than Liberals, since they believed that the amendment, if enacted, would victimise working-class boys. Zara Aronson distributed circulars in September 1909 on behalf of the NCW and received the following reply from Arthur Griffith, Labor member for The Darling:

> I have a little lad at home with light in his eyes and *red* blood in his veins. Suppose when he is 16 he is seduced by some pretty little girl of his own age (for in the case of boys and girls the seduction is usually mutual). You ask if under circumstances such as these I will help to pass a law that will brand the lad a criminal, my reply is No! and a much more emphatic no than I can use in addressing a lady.[47]

Scott's women correspondents took a very different view of the matter. A country minister's wife wrote that an age of consent of 14 was a disgrace to civilisation, proof that 'men legislate for themselves. It is time women should use their vote in favour of their own sex, especially for the protection of ignorant children.'

If time could not be found in parliament for the age of consent measure, Scott and her colleagues were appalled to see in 1907 and 1908 time made by their male representatives for Bills to secure the regulation of prostitution. The Police Offences Amendment Bill proposed the prohibition of soliciting, among other things, by prostitutes, while the Contagious Diseases Bill proposed the further incarceration until cured of any woman prisoner found to have a venereal disease, regardless of the brevity of the original sentence. Reasoning that these Bills, if enacted, would establish English-style Contagious Diseases Acts by means of two acts instead of one, political women registered their vehement opposition.[48]

C.G. Wade, premier in 1908, re-drafted the second Bill to cover both men and women, and retitled it the Prisoners' Detention Bill. These changes and other developments rendered Scott's position more complicated than in earlier years. On the one hand, she was implacably opposed to 'regulation' that condoned the masculine right to commercial access to sexual mastery over women's bodies, which was manifestly entailed in prostitution. On the other hand, concerns in her WPEL and prison reform work focused on the lack of adequate treatment facilities for women suffering from venereal diseases, and the need for a separate women's prison.[49] By 1908 the State Reformatory for Women was about to open at Long Bay, Sydney, and a locked hospital for infected women was to be established there. Scott continued to receive letters about the abuse of women when imprisoned under the supervision of men, the original context of opposition to the Contagious Diseases Acts incarcerations. In late 1907 a correspondent who signed as 'An Admirer of your work' reported:

> I heard of a case at Newtown some time ago where a constable named Mitchell used to insult women in the cells in the most cowardly and disgusting language especially if only one woman was in the cell. It is shocking that the government do not provide matrons throughout the State instead of leaving women at the mercy of such ruffians. I am travelling out west and I see a good deal of the police tactics in towns and country. A constable named Regan used to punch great blue blotches on women's arms.[50]

Scott hardly favoured measures that would put women into men's hands as prisoners. Yet the popularisation of eugenics, a 'progressive' social theory, convinced her that something had to be done to check the effects of increasing rates of venereal disease. The premier organised for her to visit the venereal diseases wards of hospitals to see children born with deformities and abnormalities. He assured her that the Prisoners' Detention Bill, if enacted, would apply to both sexes. As such it would be nothing like the loathsome English legislation (1864–84), which was, at the time, still in force in Queensland and Tasmania.

Considerable division ensued. The Women's Liberal League (WLL) gave clear public support to their premier's Bill. Conversely, Vida Goldstein wrote in both indignation and gloom about Wade's 'CD Act' — what difference did woman suffrage make, for which she still struggled after eight long years, if New South Wales governments felt safe to introduce such measures?[51] A WPEL co-worker, Alice Wilson, wrote to Scott early in August 1908, disturbed at a rumour about Scott's allegiances:

> I have heard today with what amount of truth I know not that you are in favour of this Bill brought forward last night by Mr Wade ... I am sure that if the rumor I heard is true it must be that you have not yet had an opportunity of seeing the bill. I know how strongly you feel against regulation. Will the authorities do you suppose take a man before the magistrate for some small offence for which he is consigned to gaol, examine him, keep him at the cost of the state for two years, whilst his wife and family are left to be looked after by the state or private charity? ... It will never be applied to men and is just the thin end of the wedge which we women must oppose with all our might.[52]

Scott's friend, public servant, Florence Wearne, sent her several copies of the proposed Bill a few days later. Wearne insisted that the legislation was nothing like the 'CD Act', and urged that the WPEL support the Bill. Premier Wade wrote Scott a personal letter asking her to 'please explain to your sex' the provisions and purposes of the Bill.[53] It seems Scott decided to discontinue opposition to the legislation, convinced that, applied to both sexes, men would be those most likely to be incarcerated under its provisions. Her complicated responses to prostitutes may partly account for this outcome, but another consideration may have been her lobbying prospects with the new premier regarding the Girls' Protection Bill. Perhaps her tacit support for his Prisoners' Detention Bill was a trade-off or an attempt to enlist Wade's commitment to moving on the age of consent. As it turned out, men did indeed constitute the vast majority of detainees under its provisions.

The Girls' Protection Bill was again debated in 1909, but amended so that the age would become 16, not 17, to the regret of Goldstein and other commentators. A common argument was that if women could not marry, make contracts, dispose of land and so forth until they were 21, that should be the age of consent. Goldstein, the Golding sisters, and many of Scott's co-workers took this view. Once again, the late-twentieth-century reader risks anachronism if too readily judging this proposed age to be evidence of wowserish puritanism. The context should be recalled. Most women in the period married in their early to mid-twenties. There was no contraceptive pill, no penicillin, and as yet only little sexological literature enjoining mutual, equal or multiple orgasm. There was a rampant double standard of sexual morality confronting unmarried women who were either visibly promiscuous or even monogamously sexually active. There was little notion that women would engage in sexual intercourse just for the pleasure of it; rather, their motive would have to be material gain. In this way, the 'voluntary' sexual activity of young unmarried women was readily associated with prostitution, whether or not this was reasonable. In such a context then, advocates hardly saw the measure as depriving young women of a valuable and happiness-enhancing option.

Political crises in the Liberal Party in New South Wales resulted in further delay. However, with a promise from W.A. Holman (shadow Labor attorney-general) that a McGowen Labor government would enact the amended Girls' Protection Bill, the Wade government finally gave way. The Crimes (Girls' Protection) Amendment Bill was enacted in 1910.[54] The Liberals were defeated in the subsequent election, and succeeded by the first Labor government in New South Wales history.

Yet the moment of this final success of the measure that symbolised so much of Scott's motivations and aspirations in her public life in the cause of women was curiously anti-climactic. No joyous meetings are recorded, nor does an avalanche of congratulatory correspondence remain to mark the occasion, compared to, say, the moment of the Women's Franchise Act in 1902. For in the background of the drama involved in work such as the Ethel Herringe case and lobbying for legislation affecting women and children, another serious drama had been taking place. In part it was a familiar story — that of Scott, other women, and organisational power. It was also the story of the defeat of Scott's pivotal requirement for an effective citizenry of women — their independence of class-based polit-ical parties. This part of the story involved a degree of disillusionment and turning away from her fellow women. However, it also entailed the deep-ening of Scott's revised interrogation of masculine dominance and women's options, resulting in a perceptible shift in her strategies and pri-orities. By 1910, at the age of 63, Scott's public recognition was at a premium, but her political effectiveness at state government level was, arguably, at an all time low.

A ONE-WOMAN LEAGUE?

Mindful of the parliamentary criticism of the woman suffrage movement as being centred in Sydney and unrepresentative of rural women, Scott put great effort into extending branches of the WPEL into suburban and country electorates. Notwithstanding this, the WPEL, from its foun-dation in late 1902, was criticised for having a Sydney bias. Rival women's political organisations proliferated, exhorting women not to 'follow blindly in the wake of the original leaders of the movement'.[55] While the non-party ideal of the WSL was proclaimed by many of these organisations, party commitments soon became apparent, particularly when these organisations established branches in the same electorates and were competing for available women members. For Scott the bitterest rivals were the WLL and the WPA. The latter was led by the Goldings and their married sister, Kate Dwyer, and its members were often also members of the Women's Central Organising Committee of the Political Labor League. A propaganda war took place between the WPEL, the WLL and the WPA between 1903 and 1906. The WPEL minutes of 8 September 1903 recorded that Miss Scott 'also wishes to deny a statement recently made in the press to the effect that the league was a "one woman league"'.[56] Was it?

In 1904, WPEL country branches operated at Casino, Lithgow, Katoomba, Albury, Armidale, Deniliquin, Glen Innes, Penrith, Maitland, Newcastle, Hamilton, Wallsend, Lawson and Grenfell, while its suburban branches were in Parramatta, Gordon, Homebush, Marrickville, Chatswood, North Sydney, Rockdale, St George and Waverley. The league minutes and correspondence disclose the difficulties of sustaining the momentum of a women's voluntary, non-party, regionally-dispersed organisation in the context of state politics dominated by men and class-based parties centred in Sydney. Country branch secretaries would write pleading for Scott to come and lecture to win back adherents from the party leagues sweeping through their electorates. Ethel Hamilton of the Casino branch wrote alleging that a party league branch 'was formed with the deliberate purpose of crushing our league'. In Glen Innes, Rebecca Swan reported that the local newspaper's editor constantly misrepresented the WPEL as identical to a party political league in order to sabotage its viability.[57] Although Scott travelled and lectured a great deal in response to branch requests, the struggle between leagues also demanded enormous attention in the Sydney branches.[58]

Scott's friend, J.D. Fitzgerald, future Labor lord mayor of Sydney, informed her of 'many pitfalls for the unwary in connection with women's organisations'. Clara Molyneux Parkes, leader of the WLL, had mentioned Scott's name and Fitzgerald had agreed to lecture her league, unaware of its affiliation with Carruthers' Liberal Party. Meanwhile, Carruthers himself publicly attacked non-party leagues and their leaders. Scott confronted him, eliciting the following reply:

> I thought I made it clear to you personally that my remarks at Paddington did not refer to you or your league. I think you ought to know me better than to think I would speak slightingly of you or afterwards tell you an untruth. You must know that during the last year or two of battling for the Woman Franchise I have listened to quite a multitude of speeches on the subject and on questions affecting women and their children . . . Few women have spoken as you have done, so earnestly and so well . . . Believe me that there are few men who regard you more highly and admiringly than I do.

Scott kept Victorian suffrage leader Vida Goldstein well informed about local developments. On Carruthers, Goldstein asked 'Isn't he rather impossible and didn't he vote against woman suffrage?' Indeed he was an anti-suffragist, and for Scott and Goldstein it was profoundly dispiriting to see women 'laying their political allegiance at the feet of a man like Carruthers'. Despite Victorian women remaining voteless until 1908, party leagues were organising women's branches there just as in New South Wales. Goldstein considered that the outcome of this was division. It was antithetical to the kind of cross-party lobbying needed to secure the suffrage. She gave Scott a grim account of this in 1903:

> None of our women's organisations has a clearly defined political platform. The consequence is that we have conservative, liberal and labor women all hopelessly entangled and when we wish to take any decided political action we are torn in all directions by the conflicting elements.[59]

The situation Goldstein observed in New South Wales must have dampened her enthusiasm for the effects the vote could have on non-party social reforms affecting women and children. Rewarding former anti-suffragist politicians with women's support was bad enough, but the conflict between the WPEL and the WPA — arguably a replay of old conflicts between Scott and the Goldings — caused Goldstein and other observers considerable distress, particularly when they were compelled to declare an allegiance.

It is clear that the WPEL and the WPA were in competition from the beginning. Both claimed to be non-party, both sought a similar range of reforms such as the Infants' Protection Bill and the Girls' Protection Bill, and often attended the same deputations and meetings in their support. Interactions must have been tense if a government minister like John Fegan had to write to Scott in 1903 defending himself against the charge that the Goldings were being allowed undue deputation time.[60] Yet the Goldings, as Labor women, worked against the government that enfranchised women, purely on party grounds, which led Goldstein to remark to Scott that 'the ingratitude of some women passes all understanding'. Like Scott, she believed women's votes would make no difference if they simply added to existing parties and factions. Women had to insist on good men and good measures, regardless of party or faction, if political life was to change in the interests of women and children.

This non-party stance tended to be seen by members of the labour movement as anti-Labor, especially when non-Labor politicians like B.R. Wise could congratulate the WPEL on its stance. Conflict over the relations between the WSL and the labour movement had been one of the sour points in Scott's interactions with the Goldings at the turn of the century. It persisted into 1903, and crossed the southern border into Victoria. Goldstein was editor of a national newspaper, the *Australian Women's Sphere*, and sought comprehensive reports on all women's organisations, including the WPA, not dreaming that Scott 'could possibly be hurt by that'. In response to Scott's affront, Goldstein informed her that she had decided to give the two leagues' reports first place in alternate months, published separately. This did not satisfy Scott, who promptly informed Goldstein of 'lies', 'false claims' and 'misinformation' in the WPA report just published in *Australian Women's Sphere*. Goldstein replied: 'I am almost in despair about the WPA business; the only thing I can suggest is that when mistatements or downright falsehoods are made, that you or someone else should write and give the facts. I will publish any letter sent to me'. Evidently Scott had suggested that Goldstein should have one person to collect and co-ordinate reports, but Goldstein replied that she could not afford to pay someone to do this, as she was running the newspaper 'at a dead loss'. She then observed that Scott's 'independent means enable you to be the leader in New South Wales but I have to work hard for the barest living'.

Perhaps this representation of Scott as 'the leader' was at the heart of the dispute between her and the Goldings. Shortly after, Goldstein informed Scott that she had received a furious letter from Miss Golding 'complaining about me regarding Miss Scott as the head and front of the suffrage movement in New South Wales and stating that "the Sphere" is run as an advertisement for Miss Scott'.[61] The WPA declined therefore to send a report of its activities.

Relations between Scott and the Goldings worsened thereafter. *The Dawn* had been the main vehicle for promoting WPA activities, with Louisa Lawson enthusiastically reporting its members activities, especially those of Mrs Martel, in contrast to slighting references to Scott. Martel's departure with her ailing husband for England in 1904 was deeply regretted by Lawson, who wound up *The Dawn* only a few months later. Upon arriving in England, Martel promptly joined Emmeline and Christabel Pankhurst, Dora Montefiore, Flora Drummond, and other suffragettes of the Women's Social and Political Union. Soon news was heard of Dora Montefiore's 'no taxation without representation' siege in her Hammersmith home, the bailiffs poised to seize her goods and chattels in view of her outstanding taxes.[62] Without *The Dawn*, the alliance between Scott and Goldstein became more threatening to the WPA leaders. Some hostile correspondence Scott received in 1904 suggests some dimensions of this. One letter was from a former Victorian suffragist, Augusta Von Heinbeuld:

> About two months ago, some members of a former Society over which you ruled informed me that when I first came to Sydney, now five years ago, and called upon you, as the representative woman and leader in the franchise movement, you were willing enough to accept the little help I was then able to offer and also listen to the story of my work in Victoria, but discrediting, so my informants tell me, the accounts I gave you, you placed yourself in communication with Miss Vida Goldstein and I was discountenanced. Of course, I should not trouble myself about this affair in which you had perfect liberty to decide as your liking swayed you,

> were it not that the letter received from Miss Goldstein was read
> by you at a meeting of your committee . . . For a long time I felt very
> keenly . . . the attitude you adopted towards me, never dreaming
> you had gone for my credentials to so unreliable a source as Vida
> Goldstein, for in my time, when the Franchise Movement in
> Victoria was in real life, Miss Goldstein and her mother were
> outside members altogether, she was simply known to us as a mem-
> ber of a little club . . . When we did meet, I disliked the two sisters
> very much.[63]

This letter may indicate the degree of ferment within post-suffrage women's
organisations over leadership and recognition. Goldstein took the unprecedented step of standing as a candidate for the federal Senate elections in 1903,
making her the first woman in the British Commonwealth ever to stand for
parliament.[64] Scott warmly supported her, but other women's league
members did not consider such a course appropriate. Though unsuccessful,
Goldstein's step established her nationally as ambitious, competent and hard-
working. Other women, even other unmarried women, could react with
ambivalence; certainly they could detect hostility in others towards
Goldstein. Miles Franklin was recommended to Vida Goldstein by Scott, and
invited to stay in Melbourne with her and her sister Aileen over the sum-
mer of 1904. Franklin later wrote to Scott in 1904 of a gentleman she met
who had heard Goldstein in Sydney and said ' "she was absolutely repellant
— metallic and repulsive". I do wish she would melt more, don't you?'[65] Scott
replied quite unequivocally: 'I have been quite demoralised lately. I am sorry,
I do not consider Vida repellant, repulsive — She is too bright, smart and taking, clever also — there is nothing to melt. There is no reserve force of love
and self sacrifice as one sees in some people.'[66] It is not clear that Scott meant
the last remark as a criticism of Goldstein. Despite their differences on some
issues, Scott and Goldstein offered one another considerable support and
respect. Scott needed to draw on both later in 1905.

The Political Labor League annual conference often had guest speakers. In 1905 Scott attended to address the need for various laws affecting
women and children. The Goldings and other WPA members present
moved that Scott not be heard, on the grounds of there being evidence of
her speaking at a meeting in support of a candidate contesting a Labor candidate. They had the numbers and Scott was dismissed. The incident dismayed many of Scott's old friends, especially those associated with
socialism or the labour movement. Arthur Rae was 'deeply grieved and
shamed to hear you defamed by your own sex'.[67] The Prime Minister, J.C.
Watson, wrote too, regretting the incident and expressing his appreciation
of what she had accomplished in New South Wales. But, he ventured:

> I know you won't be offended if I say that your political innocence
> evidently led you into an appearance of partiality. Probably a
> few might be able to distinguish between speaking at a candidate's

> meeting and speaking *for* a candidate, but the great majority would conclude that Miss Scott spoke for Mr Hawthorne. What was complained of I understand was that the best men were all outside the Labor party, which was our bad luck I suppose. Seriously though, if your league is to continue non-party it must religiously refrain from speaking for party candidates or even speaking at their meetings. In the abstract I agree that party is a poor thing, but without it I doubt whether we should have political progress.

The socialist, Bertha MacNamara, disagreed with Watson's view of the matter, since 'I think I am right in stating that thousands of women as well as myself in favour and connected with labour work would not endorse the opinions of the few women antagonistic to you for reasons of their own'. Anna Hazelton too reported that she had many companions in her grief over the affair of 'the Golding Sisterhood', but concluded on the optimistic note that as 'the Labor party have come out as Socialists there will be a cleansing out of such miserable bigots as we know these women to be'. She concluded her letter of comfort to Scott with an effusive assertion of Scott's centrality: 'Dear Miss Scott, your name will shine on the Roll of Honour when they are gone from the memory of all — Christ must suffer and you are no exception.'[68]

The centrepiece of the speech Scott was to have delivered concerned the raising of the age of consent. A correspondent to *The Worker*, dismissive of the proposal as a labour question and of the significance of the whole affair, earned Scott's ire in a letter in reply:

> Never have I ceased to work for what I consider the first of all reforms where women and children are concerned. In fact the work in the Women's Suffrage League, which came after was chiefly inspired by the feeling that this sort of Bill could not become law until women had the vote . . . If the Labour League refused to hear me on the ground that I do not belong to the Labor Party and never will do so or any other party either, they had a perfect right to refuse and I am proud that such women as Mrs Hickman and Miss Hall who have known me for years could speak as they did . . . As to the question of whether I said certain words or not or what I did say I leave it to the people of Australia who know me perfectly well and testified over and over again their trust in me and dependence on my word and consistent action.[69]

Despite the support forthcoming from friends, the 1905 incident dramatised the extent to which the non-party tenet of Scott's work in the cause of women had become Utopian and increasingly incomprehensible in the new federal era. She had become a public figure, one increasingly called upon to comment and advise on the situation of her sex — rather like an unappointed, unpaid minister on the status of women — and yet she was becoming increasingly 'alone of her sex' in urging women to stand against the tide of party politics. As such, her public profile could excite irritated, even lunatic, responses such as a letter signed 'another angry letter you busy body', written by a farmer's wife of Spicer's Creek.

> May I ask who made you dictator to the women of the colony? You appear to have plenty of assurance in issuing your manifestos. I can assure you we require none of your advice and you show gross ignorance in giving your orders that we must not vote for party government. You are an ass. You seem to want to run the country it is a fine coming about when old maids wants [sic] to rule the roost . . . you prate about clean living men I wonder where they are to be found a pack of psalm singers who are nothing but a parcel of hypocrites . . . You are a lot of blow hards. You [sic] officious articles wanting to make yourself conspicuous. You are all gas why don't you act instead of troubling yourself with having your orders to women printed. dont [sic] you interfere with our husbands and their business. You must be a bit of a favourite with the editors to have all your claptrap printed. it [sic] is not your good looks according to your photo in a paper I saw.[70]

By the end of 1905, and decidedly by 1906, the WPEL had failed. Branch after branch reported trouble retaining members and motivating action, then the resignation of executive members, then the formal lapse of the branch. Country branches fell first, but the more outlying suburban branches followed. Two Sydney branches remained viable longer — Chatswood and North Sydney — presumably because of their solidly middle-class membership, and proximity to the city centre ensuring no difficulty in attracting members, speakers, and a sense of involvement in legislative debate. Scott did not publicly acknowledge the failure of her league; she continued to use its nominal existence as a basis or platform from which to speak, and to affiliate with the NCW.

Faced with the slow but unmistakable defeat of the non-party principle in post-suffrage women's politics, Scott increasingly re-allocated her efforts. The NCW began to supercede the WPEL as her banner, the 'we' for whom she spoke. However, her work in other committees and women's organisations was not unscathed by the fallout of the WPEL experience. As vice president of the Women's Club, she encountered difficulties. In 1908 the secretary of the club, Elimina Sutherland (also formerly a member of the Chatswood Branch of the WPEL), rebuked Scott for allegedly insulting the deceased former president, Lady Beaumont. Sutherland evidently had expressed discomfort with the name the Women's Club, perhaps on philosophical and political grounds. Scott understood her to have suggested naming the club after Lady Beaumont, the first president and the woman of highest conventional social rank among the club's members. This irritated Scott, some of whose criticisms offended Sutherland. Instead of approaching Scott directly, Sutherland immediately wrote to the club's president demanding that she secure a retraction and apology from Scott. The president put the matter before Scott and the result was

strained correspondence between Scott and Sutherland and an acrimo-
nious meeting of the club committee. These interactions between Scott and
Sutherland display how Scott had become a figure to challenge and call
to account by a younger generation, quite beyond any question of personality clash or individual friction:

> To say I disparaged Lady Beaumont's work for the Club is to
> state an utterly false and mistaken view of what I said. My remark
> had no reference whatever to her or her work for the Club which
> no one appreciated more than I did. If the proposal had been to call
> the Club The Booth Club after its founder and I had said the
> same proposition was ridiculous I would not mean that I thought
> Dr Mary Booth ridiculous. Miss Fry took another view and
> thought I had called *her* snobbish!

In reply, Sutherland denied that she was advocating a change of name for
the club. She defended writing to the president on the grounds that
Scott's insulting words were uttered in front of the whole committee, without challenge from anyone present, despite Sutherland's own indig-
nant silence. Sutherland would no longer work on such a committee, unless
the offending words were retracted. To Scott's denial of any insult,
Sutherland asserted:

> The words you uttered were 'What has Lady Beaumont done for
> the Club? She did nothing. All this talk of Lady Beaumont in the
> Club is just snobbery' and more words to the same effect. These are
> your exact words. I have not forgotten them — I could not.
> These words I ask you to withdraw . . . You say you are an older
> woman and imply a want of respect in me and if it were against
> myself alone you might be right but I hold it everyone's duty to
> defend the absent when unjustly accused and I certainly think the
> dead should be sacred.

Sutherland's effective and uncompromising adherence to her position
secured a remarkable outcome — Scott's retraction, albeit qualified.
Two days later, she wrote to Scott that she was 'glad you repudiate the words
which you certainly did say', observing also that 'we always seem to be running counter just now'; but then it seems she pushed Scott beyond the line
of the tolerable. By her retraction, Sutherland maintained Scott had
removed the grounds for 'words being said at the annual general meeting which would be certain to raise a storm'. The incident was now, she
declared, closed.
    Scott exploded:

> Your last letter is impertinent. I endeavoured patiently to bear with
> your rude letters and took the trouble to explain the few words I
> said simply because the president asked me to do so. In each
> letter you add to the summary of the things you say I said and which
> I did not say . . . Who are you that you should presume to judge my

words and add to them and then give me the lie direct. I do not regard 'the incident' as you are pleased to call it, closed.

Rose Scott

Scott had the president call a special meeting of the club committee to air the entire incident. She reported to the meeting that when the president phoned her with Sutherland's complaint, she 'could not make out all that was said on the telephone', a reference to her increasing and isolating deafness. Whether Scott's objective had been simply to tell her own side of the story, thereby defending her impugned integrity, or to divide the committee in the quest for Sutherland's resignation, is difficult to determine in the absence of detailed club minutes.

The outcome was Scott's, not Sutherland's, resignation. No one forced Scott out of secretaryship of the WSL, and Sutherland embraced her office as secretary of the Women's Club with the same resolve that Scott exhibited across the 1890s as secretary of the WSL. As part of the new generation of young, university-educated professional women who eventually founded the Feminist Club, Sutherland understandably regarded Scott with something less than the reverence the older woman expected. Had the matter come to a vote of confidence in the secretary, Sutherland probably had the numbers, though no evidence located indicates the putting of such a motion. [71]

This committee resignation was the first of several over the next few years, some on the basis of her ill-health, others after the familiar pattern of Scott's conflict with the secretary or other office-bearers. Decades before, a phrenologist had predicted Scott's need to lead, her greed for power, and her difficulty being a follower or among those led. The collapse of the WPEL threatened to place her in exactly this position. Rather than accept this, especially at the hands of younger women, she adopted the strategy of withdrawal. This had the costly consequence of isolating her from wider influences and reduced her capacity to keep pace with the rapidly changing discourses and moves in the pre-war period relevant to her beloved cause.

Scott became embroiled in more trouble in another organisation — the New South Wales Ladies' Amateur Swimming Association, of which she was president. The dispute concerned constitutional, staffing and policy matters, and resulted in a split. A particular matter of contention concerned the admission of men as spectators, Scott opposing the suggestion. [72] This same matter would re-surface again in a few years.

With all this strife emerging from her work with her fellow women, many pressing problems seemed to remain despite the vote. Until 1908 Victorian women were voteless, and as Goldstein remarked to Scott, 'we have had to be low for a very long time because of incurring the hostility of both the Labor and conservative parties', fighting only for suffrage by itself. Once the vote was finally obtained there, Goldstein informed Scott how precarious it remained as an international commitment when she learned of a plot to have suffrage excluded from the demands of the ICW at its 1909 Toronto Conference. She asked Scott to ensure that the delegates to the forthcoming conference from the New South Wales NCW were specifically instructed to vote against any attempt to exclude the word 'suffrage' from the name of the relevant sub-committee, as she had so arranged in the briefing of the Victorian delegates. Goldstein was still fresh from the successful 1908 campaign for state suffrage, fiercely denouncing the 'anti-suffrage and flabby suffrage members of the councils who are frightened of frightening possible friends from joining'. Noting that, internationally, woman suffrage was becoming 'one of the leading questions of the day', she asserted the special responsibility of 'we women who have won the great right of voting' to resist any attempt to haul down 'the suffrage flag' from the ICW.

Goldstein may have been unaware how jaded and disillusioned Scott had become about the value the vote conferred upon women. Her disappointment about women's absorption into party politics, and their failure to use their vote on behalf of their sex, dampened her general enthusiasm about suffrage battles elsewhere. Hence, when confronted with the press stories of suffragette militancy in England, she was unable to offer the enthusiasm or sympathy of one who believed that the end justified the means.

It was the controversy surrounding the suffragettes of the Pankhursts' Women's Social and Political Union that influenced Goldstein's judgement of the internationally leading status of the suffrage question. Australian women went to aid their English sisters on the streets and wrote home about it. Canadian NCW correspondents of Scott's also commented on the stir being made by United States suffragettes. The woman colleague with whom Scott worked closely in pacifist work during the next decade, Marian Harwood, wrote a relatively sympathetic account of the troubles of the suffragettes, not realising Scott's already publicly stated opposition to militant methods: 'for physical force is the weapon of the Barbarian' as she telegraphed the international woman suffrage conference in Amsterdam in 1908. In 1910, Harwood wrote from London:

> The poor suffragettes are again in trouble and I must confess that some of them do not restrain themselves as they ought . . . but it is hard to be calm and patient when tried and treated as they have been for nearly 50 years and when feeling runs high . . . [T]he government have been much to blame in the stupid and . . . cruel orders they gave the police to worry and weary the women out before arresting them. The whole affair is a miserable one . . . I am almost glad I have not a vote here, for in my present mood I should not feel inclined to give it to either Asquith or Lloyd George owing to the mean way they have treated the women.

By 1910 Scott was entirely unreceptive to pleas for sympathy for the suffragettes. After a spate of window breakings and arrests at the end of 1908, she had penned a letter to the editor of the *Daily Telegraph* condemning the adoption of physical force as a means to persuade, convince or coerce. The conservatism of English society required greater patience and self control of its suffrage workers. Asserting the political reality that enfranchisement was a concession granted, a right won only through the support of men in parliament, she claimed that 'if we had gone about breaking windows, defying laws and inciting the mob to do so, we would . . . have been as voteless today as we would well have deserved to be'. As a final note of condemnation, and one that was hard for younger co-workers like Goldstein to abide, Scott wrote: 'I consider the militant suffragettes of England are disgracing not only the cause but the womanhood of England'.[73]

Underlying Scott's stance on suffragette militancy, which was to harden after 1910, was a sadness at the hollowness of Australia's suffrage victories. Her hopes that citizenship would accord her sex dignity and erode the servility of wives, for instance, were dashed by letters she continually received from wives once she became known as a public representative of her sex. One rural woman wrote to her that:

> I am daily meeting and hearing of men who say that as their wives swore to obey them at the altar, they must vote as they direct. One man varies this a little by promising to break his wife's legs if she attempts to vote — this is probably figurative language employed by him to typify the extent of the love and protection he swore to bestow on her on the altar.[74]

Other letters simply told of women's abuse by husbands. Florence Roberts described her husband's violence, constant drunkenness, desertion and non-support, and the bias of magistrates towards him when she tried to obtain help. Another women, Florence Aspley, described the miseries of abused wives accelerating in old age, concluding that there 'should indeed be two houses of parliament — a woman's house and a man's'.

At a more general level, it was obvious that the vote had not proved the key to women's elevation from sex degradation. In fact, Scott used these terms less and less. The absence of plausible political alternatives to existing class-based party politics gave women citizens few spaces to make the differences Scott dreamed of, even if 'the sex' had united: which of course, it had not. Part of the revision of Scott's original feminist vision was underway, as she reluctantly came to terms with the minimal impact of enfranchisement. Though this re-thinking did not obstruct her continued support for the still-voteless women of Australia's second-most-populous state, Victoria, it limited her patience with extreme claims for the revolutionary promise of woman suffrage and extreme methods in its pursuit. The militant suffragettes, then, aroused in her irritation and distaste. She even went so far as pronouncing that they would delay further the long overdue enfranchisement of British women.

Miles Franklin initially may have shared some aspects of Scott's views of suffragette militancy. She believed, however, that English sisters were 'forced' to militancy. In 1909 she wrote a fascinating novel about the impact of woman suffrage in rural New South Wales, called *Some Everyday Folk and Dawn*. Written in the United States' mid-west, Franklin's fulsome and sentimental dedication of her novel struck a pointed note:

> To the English *men* who believe in votes for women. This story is Affectionately Inscribed, Because the Women Herein Characterized Were Never Forced to be "SUFFRAGETTES", Their Countrymen Having Granted Them Their Rights As SUFFRAGISTS In the Year of Our Lord 1902.
>
> M.F.[75]

Scott's growing sense of disillusionment with previous strategies had several outcomes. One may have been an insecurity about her own value and position, manifest in tactless assertions of her own centrality, as if others around her needed persuading. She penned the greetings and goodwill message for the worldwide struggle for woman suffrage from the NCW to the ICW Conference in 1908, beginning with: 'as the chief worker in N.S.Wales from first to last I beseech all women to work for this reform'.[76] An undated note from Anna Gale, daughter of Susannah Gale, a WCTU suffragist, reads: 'Don't be unjust to your friends dear pioneer.'[77] Perhaps such utterances were provoked by Louisa Lawson's renewed demands for recognition, four years after closing *The Dawn*. In the context of disquiet about present progress, a degree of reminiscence and re-constructing of the history of the woman suffrage movement seemed to be taking place more generally. In part this also may have been inspired by the international controversy over the English militant suffragettes. If the despised Nellie Martel was making a splash at the centre of this movement, the timing of Scott's self-assertions may be explained. Similarly, since Martel was her friend, Lawson's moves may be as logical. Conflict emerged at the end of 1908 when Lawson accused Scott's friend, W.E. Gundry, or Scott herself of misappropriating some minutes of WSL meetings, which she now wanted back for a history of the movement she was writing:

> I cannot understand Mrs Lawson's statement that I took some minutes of meetings she held, saying I would take them to you. I don't think I was ever on sufficiently friendly terms with Mrs Lawson to ever feel free to even proffer such a request for, much less make an appropriation of records which in her eyes at least would be sure to be regarded as specially valuable . . . Mrs Lawson as far as I can remember was not particularly identified with or at all active in support of WSL work, however she claims credit as a WS pioneer.[78]

Lawson and Scott met during these weeks, partly over the missing book and partly over some original letters of the poet, Henry Kendall, which Lawson hoped Scott could sell for her for a sizeable sum. She wrote to her: 'I had much that I would like to have said but will wait an opportunity for another chat.' Scott responded further over the minute book and in the light of Gundry's letter to her, eliciting this reply from Lawson:

> Don't trouble yourself anymore about the minute book. I have a friend who is a government detective who secured several valuable books for me after my tram accident — said he will I know do his best to recover . . . it. I will also offer a reward through the press for anyone having seen it; I was so sure that it was safe in your keeping all the time or I would have taken steps to recover it long ago. It was understood that it was to go to you or it certainly never would have been out of my keeping.[79]

The outcome of this incident is unclear, but it no doubt caused Scott unease or disquiet.

A further result of Scott's disillusionment with a conflict-ridden political scene was the turning of her attention to national and international issues. In 1907 the famous Australian pacifist and religious leader, Charles Strong, a friend of Goldstein's, wrote asking Scott to found a New South Wales branch of the London Peace Society. This she did, enlisting the involvement of two WPEL workers who were at this time central in her affections, Florence Wearne and Marian Harwood. The Peace Society opposed military training and compulsory military service, and sought to educate the community in the principles of pacifism and international arbitration. For the next decade this society assumed a privileged place in Scott's activities. So concerned did she become about accelerating militarism that she conducted a correspondence with the Prime Minister, Alfred Deakin, in 1908. As a leading spiritualist, his support for military training was, in her view, incomprehensible: 'I fear these preparations will sow a crop of dragons teeth . . . suspicion breeds suspicion. I dread the military spirit and the rule of the military force . . . they are merciless and have no thought except for their own red tape and discipline.' Unfortunately, his replies to her have not survived, but he clearly attempted to justify his government's policies, especially compulsory military training, in some detail. Replying to his various points, Scott urged that a better use of the vast public monies involved would be the promotion of industrial peace and the payment of a living wage to sweated and overworked government officials. She begged him to reconsider this terrible evil he may bring to Australia. Scott asserted further that the military, opposed utterly to the spirit of liberty, were without any redeeming ideals. Confident that Deakin would 'be good enough to forgive my plain speaking', she urged in a further letter, 'let us not attempt the portals of the future with the past's blood rusted key'.

Scott failed to move him from his resolve and she ventured that the division and unease produced by militarism posed a greater threat to Australia than any invader: 'I think our imaginations are creating our enemies and invaders — and we are dying a thousand deaths instead of only one.'[80]

Nevertheless, Scott's colleagues and many figures she admired predicted war. The futile squabbles of her political life since the 1890s had worn her down. She was now ill as often as she was well. Her cousin David Scott Mitchell was dead; her generation was passing. Co-pacifist, S.D.K. Aitkin, wrote to her in 1909 as if the whole world was imperilled:

> All the world is in a tremor. Beneath the surface may be felt the travail that shall bring forth a universal harvest of death. Day and night, the arsenals roar and the anvils ring as gun is added to gun and sword to sword and bayonet to bayonet. And men say "It is all for peace", but in their hearts they feel that it is not so, but the premonition of the coming storm . . . Everything points to a war of nations such as has never been seen before.[81]

As a key feminist in one of the first Western countries to confer citizenship upon women, it was logical that Scott, of all people, would have high hopes for the difference women could make through the use of their vote. Insofar as her brief of causes expanded, prior to the 1902 enfranchisement of women, she was identifying and foreshadowing priority areas for feminist advocacy and reform. To these areas, once enfranchised, the citizenry of women might turn its attention. That was her vision. Her expectations about women citizens were shared by both friends and foes of women's citizenship.

Scott's rationale for the reforms on behalf of women and children that would be undertaken by the woman citizen was a feminist analysis of women's systemic degradation by men, and their subjection and subordination in all social and cultural spheres of life. The timidity and fear of men's disapproval displayed by women co-workers in the 1890s could be represented as but another symptom of this very degradation, which must cease. To the same cause, Scott could attribute the misogyny, insecurity, pettiness and ambivalence about leadership evident in women's political organisations and their efforts to work together in common cause. Such attribution bears a resemblance to twentieth century Marxist explanations of the failure of the proletariat to unite in socialist revolution as manifestations of 'false consciousness' within its ranks.

Like 'false consciousness', this blanket explanation of 'women's degradation' undertook no investigation of how, from the viewpoint of many or most women, investment in the sexual status quo made sense and paid dividends. Most women were not, and in Scott's lifetime never would be, feminists. Even some of those who were her close colleagues in 'the cause' of woman suffrage displayed little or no adherence to the full analysis of systemic sexual degradation and disadvantage offered by feminists like Scott,

Goldstein or Lawson. Were Scott's vision of ending women's degradation ever to be realised, women would need to 'see' matters in that light. At the very least, Scott needed a better recognition and understanding of the forces which obstructed her vision from becoming more widely shared.

Unfortunately, she over-privileged the significance of woman suffrage in both her analysis of the problem and her strategies for solution. Often she elided incommensurate levels of claims for it. Not possessing the vote was, on the one hand, a symptom of women's degradation. This left the inference that the moment enfranchisement was granted, a major and inescapable alleviation of that degradation would occur. On the other hand, she contended that the serious and recalcitrant manifestations of women's degradation, such as the almost compulsory institutions of women's economic dependence and loss of bodily self-determination in marriage, the condonation of prostitution, men's seduction of teenage girls, illegitimacy, unequal pay and paid-work opportunities for women, unequal and discriminatory laws around marriage, divorce and child custody, could only be substantially challenged by women obtaining and deploying the vote, as a unified block.

Scott spent the first years of her own citizenship caught between these inconsistent expectations about what the fact of enfranchisement signified within the polity, and what it was henceforth possible and likely that women as a sexed group would do with their vote. At first, continued resistance to enfranchising women in Queensland, Tasmania and Victoria, despite the possession of the vote at Commonwealth level, worked to maintain a focus on the vote as the critical prize, magnified by the continuing refusal of Britain, most of the United States, South America, Europe, Canada and South Africa to budge before suffragist and, increasingly, *suffragette* pressure. The interstate and international publicity, publications, initiatives and correspondence that overwhelmed Scott in these years heightened, if anything, the discursive significance of the vote itself. Such input would have counted against the revision of her original vision, which so prized the sexual politics significance of enfranchisement.

Yet the course of Scott's post-suffrage experiences had planted doubts that were the prelude to revision. Only the small group of feminists who had gained the vote by the early years of the twentieth century were in a position to evaluate the unfolding significance of that achievement, the difference it did or did not make to the position of women, and where possible, to adjust existing objectives and devise new ones in the light of such evaluations. This proved to be a difficult but unavoidable task throughout Scott's second decade of citizenship.

Chapter 6

Against the Brotherhood (1911–19)

What is our 'native land'? It is a cherished and fading illusion
. . . Excessive patriotism . . . is a narrowment . . . of the mind and
the arrogance of the white race, especially that of the British
Empire, w'd be comical if it were not so sad.

Rose Scott to Dowell O'Reilly,
'Sunday' [n.d.],
O'Reilly Family Papers, Mitchell Library

In 1912 Scott resigned her presidency of the New South Wales Ladies'
Amateur Swimming Association in a storm of publicity. She had lost the
debate about the admission of men as spectators to women's carnivals.
Olympic hopeful, Fanny Durack, succeeded in having the bar on both male
spectators and members competing in mixed-sex international professional
competitions revoked, thus securing her own eligibility for the forthcoming
Stockholm Olympics. The conflict between 20-year-old Durack and 65-
year-old Scott was bitter, charged with accusations of bad faith and
duplicity.[1] In a newspaper interview Scott maintained:

> I think it is disgusting that men should be allowed to attend. We
> cannot have too much modesty, refinement and delicacy in rela-
> tions between men and women. There is too much boldness
> and rudeness now and I am afraid that this new decision will have
> a very vulgar effect on the girls . . . I also object to mixed bathing
> on the beaches. I was brought up in a school that considered it an
> insult on the part of a man to stare at a girl . . . It is not a compliment
> to be stared at by a man. Familiarity breeds contempt and I am afraid
> that the rescission of the rule will lead to a loss of respect for the girls
> and the increasing boldness of the men. It would be alright perhaps,
> if the men would behave themselves properly, but a lot of bad men
> would be attracted who would make all sorts of nasty remarks and
> who would go rather for the spectacle than for the skill.[2]

Responses to her position show that she could no longer assume that it was intelligibile to others. W.W. Hill, secretary of the New South Wales Amateur Swimming Association, criticised Scott for asserting that it was a poor mother who would like her daughters to swim in the presence of men:

> Why the daughters of the leading people at Manly, Bondi and Coogee engage in Continental bathing daily and without the presence of their mothers, and of the young ladies taking part in your carnivals, Misses Durack, Tate, Meades and others are in the constant habit of indulging in mixed bathing, so this clearly shows that your best swimmers do not object to swimming in the presence of men — the carnivals will never be a success until gentlemen are permitted to witness the swimming by the girls and manage the carnivals.[3]

While some women colleagues, such as Alice Bentley, supported Scott, urging her not to resign 'as the public would think you were beaten', the unequivocal verdict of most commentators was that Scott was 'old fashioned', or behind the times, on this matter, since among women swimmers polled, 'more than half were in favour of the men'.[4]

This seemingly trivial issue might be taken to provide a classic case study of the collision between, on the one hand, an older women's movement bent on protecting women and enabling them by asserting their sex differences and specificity; and on the other, the new feminism, preoccupied with the assertion of women's equality, sameness and common humanity with men. Within this framework of analysis, the last years Scott devoted to public life might be represented as her struggle to come to terms with the increasing irrelevance of her own position in a new feminist context. Scott had become a relic from a dim past, a prophet of doom attempting to obstruct the initiatives of progressive, enlightened, and above all *feminist,* younger women. Such a reading of these difficult years for Scott has an alluring clarity and singularity. It is one important interpretative tradition that histories of feminism need to consider seriously.

How did Scott's activities, preoccupations and writings in this period contribute to and intersect with the development of feminism? Was the course of Australian feminism during the First World War comparable with that of other Western countries? Or might the earlier antipodean achievement of woman suffrage, which was still a central focus in Europe and North America into the inter-war period, have inflected different conditions, chronologies and possibilities for Australian and New Zealand feminism?[5] For women like Scott, a measure such as raising the age of consent was the pivotal reform, envisaged from the beginning of her public life in the 1880s. Despite disillusionment, she could still write in 1919 that it was the woman's vote which would prevent the supply of girls for seduction and prostitution, and all of the evils that resulted for all women's relations with men, for their life options, and for their position in the world.[6]

Portrait of Rose Scott, 1903. (Mitchell Library, State Library of NSW)

Rose Scott's bedroom at Lynton. (Mitchell Library, State Library of NSW)

Miles Franklin (1879–1954), writer, feminist, labour activist and friend of Rose Scott. (Mitchell Library, State Library of NSW)

Bertram Stevens (1872–1922), literary and art critic and friend of Rose Scott. (Mitchell Library, State Library of NSW)

Lady Mary Windeyer (1836–1912), leader of the woman
suffrage movement in New South Wales. (Mitchell Library,
State Library of NSW)

Rose Scott and William Lane, *circa* 1903. Lane (1861–1917) was a journalist, trade unionist,
Utopian and ally of Scott. (Mitchell Library, State Library of NSW)

Louisa Lawson (1848-1920), journalist, feminist and
radical, was active in the Womanhood Suffrage League
with Rose Scott. (Mitchell Library, State Library of NSW)

Women surf bathers at Coogee Beach, Sydney, in the early 1900s.
(Mitchell Library, State Library of NSW)

Louisa MacDonald (1858-1949), first principal of Women's
College, University of Sydney, with the first cohort of
students, 1892. (Mitchell Library, State Library of NSW)

Rose Scott (seated) and her housekeeper, Bridget Conneally.
(Mitchell Library, State Library of NSW)

Rose Scott (centre, seated) and the Women's Political and Educational League, 1903. (Mitchell Library, State Library of NSW)

Bernhard Ringrose Wise
(1858-1916), New South
Wales Attorney-General
at the turn of the century.
(Mitchell Library, State
Library of NSW)

Maybanke Wolstenholme,
later Anderson (1845-
1927), feminist and educa-
tionist. (Mitchell Library,
State Library of NSW)

Portrait of Rose Scott by Sir John Longstaff, 1922. (Mitchell Library, State Library of NSW)

While such objectives were shared by women's rights advocates in other Western countries, their struggle for the means, the vote, was, from the Australian and New Zealand perspective, *protracted* into the inter-war period.[7] In the Australian and New Zealand context, it was not the vote itself that constituted the ultimate success of the 'cause of women', but the use of it, in securing reforms relevant to sexual relations, such as raising the age of consent and challenging men's use of prostitutes and their assertions of conjugal rights. Arguably, the logical timing for Scott to assess the progress of her feminist vision would have been in the period surrounding and succeeding the enactment of the Girls' Protection Act in 1910.

What did occupy Scott in these years? She explained in a speech to the NCW in 1914 that the WPEL, the non-party league, had disbanded in 1910 following the passage of the Crimes (Girls' Protection) Amendment Bill — the league's chief objective.[8] By 1911 the NCW had acquired sufficient autonomous shape and constituency to allow Scott to accelerate her participation without any longer purporting to lead a representative women's organisation. Her work in the Peace Society became a new and primary source of affiliation with the NCW, as well as a source of increased contact with women workers overseas.[9] Work for peace became intensely embattled in the countdown to the outbreak of hostilities in 1914. To many of her contemporaries, Scott's pacifism was as incomprehensible as her non-party stance. This was compounded when her hostility to animalism and militarism formed the basis of her public denunciation of the militant suffragettes of the Women's Social and Political Union (WSPU). Other Australian feminists, including Vida Goldstein, Miles Franklin and Bessie Rischbieth, warmly supported the British suffragettes, placing Scott once again against the tide.

In the darkening years before and during the war, Scott continued to work through the NCW for legal reforms affecting women and children. In campaigns for laws preventing men from disinheriting their families, extending guardianship rights to mothers, removing the disqualification of women from access to public office and the legal profession, and for *in camera* hearings for women first offenders, she encountered difficulties in negotiating with the state's first Labor governments. The fact that her long-time friend, William Arthur Holman, was attorney-general, then premier, during the period, proved to be of little assistance to feminist law reform campaigns. Yet if the Labor women of the WPA, in principle, had better access and influence than Scott and her colleagues, the results they achieved were hardly spectacular during the first decade of Labor rule. Of course, with her critique of party politics, Scott was hardly surprised by the slow progress of reform.

She was, however, dispirited by it. As with the age of consent measure, every reform that stood to advantage women vis-à-vis men not only met opposition and procrastination from the legislating brotherhood of

Labor, but also erratic, masculinist complicity from their Liberal opposition. In Scott's view women had ceased to operate as an identifiable interest group affecting the legislature. The outbreak of the war heightened her gloom about the prospects for change. The regime that war imposed at home and abroad was masculinist, nowhere more clearly than in legislative priorities of governments. However, the horrors of war for women and girls imprinted themselves on Scott's understanding through contact with women friends living in Europe. Rape in war, and its consequences, confirmed her longstanding concern about men's sexual behaviour and attributes. Her fears were compounded when her beloved Nene volunteered for military service against her wishes.

Scott continued, stubbornly, to oppose. With Nene at the front, she lived a very personal anxiety about the war. Nonetheless, she opposed conscription and continued pacificist and internationalist work, which brought her to the attention of the Commonwealth Censor and the Ministry for Defence.[10] She defended the anti-phallic sex reformer, William James Chidley, against persecution by the masculinist Labor government, which incarcerated him under the Lunacy Act in Callan Park Mental Asylum, where he died suddenly in 1916.[11] She continued to criticise party politics, to the irritation of politicians and women political workers. Moreover she chided women in public and private life for their lack of solidarity with their sex and their submission to the interests of the other sex. Her efforts against the brotherhood of public life require characterisation. They also should be set in the context of the efforts of a woman in her sixties to prepare for the end of her life.

UNFINISHED BUSINESS

Scott's public involvements contracted in range and scale during the 1910s, partly the result of changed configurations and partly her own ill-health. Nene reappeared for stays intermittently when in Sydney. His acting career took him for long periods to New Zealand and all Australian states. Miles Franklin wrote admiringly of his success in 1913, asking when he would play in the United States. She recalled how, when she was a young visitor to Scott's home, Nene, when reading the lines of Gilbert and Sullivan to her, had 'very tastefully omitted all those horrible jeers at elderly unmarried women which disfigure libertarian humour'.[12]

Nene's success and his many theatrical friends supplied new circles of guests to Scott's now antique Friday night salon. J.D. Fitzgerald, who had been 'a regular' since the later 1890s, wrote to her about it in 1912:

> How can you find so many interesting animals for your collection? Where do you dig us all up? Pardon my vanity but I always feel so flattered at being in the company of so many interesting people at your salon. Yours is the last of the salons of the world. I believe they have quite died out in the northern hemisphere. More's the pity.[13]

One of the salon guests, the young artist, Florence Rodway, persuaded Scott to sit for a portrait, as part of the artist's 1911 exhibition. Rodway enjoyed the sponsorship and support of J.F. Archibald, editor of the *Bulletin*, and his cultural set. She was received warmly by Scott. Archibald believed that the result was a fine oil painting, but a failure as a portrait. He expressed his disappointment, blaming the medium in part. Oils, he contended, portrayed a Rose Scott too sombre and cold, not 'smiling and gracious as she is, kindness to the world at large, but a certain chilled and formal Miss Scott, devoid of her tasteful plumage'. In pastel, Rodway's best medium, Archibald was sure the mistake would be repaired, and urged Scott to agree to a second sitting. Moreover, he wondered if she 'might be induced to help' in getting Dame Nellie Melba, the famous Australian soprano, to sit for Rodway.[14] It is not clear how Scott responded to this suggestion, and no evidence located reveals the existence of a further portrait.

Immortalising the self for posterity by means of a portrait was, at Scott's stage of life, preparation for old age and death. Other signs of her preoccupation with the end of her life were her involvement in two organisations of this period: the Twilight League and the Cremation Society of New South Wales. Founded in 1912 by Florence Clarke, the lady mayoress, the Twilight League's object was to provide 'a comfortable home at a moderate charge for educated women who are unable to follow their calling any longer and whose means are limited'. Clarke believed that the League would appeal to wage-earning women needing to provide for their later years. Scott was asked to address its first meeting.[15]

The Cremation Society had as its object the establishment of a crematorium and the creation of legislation to permit citizens to choose cremation over burial. Scott and her colleagues favoured cremation on grounds connected with public hygiene and sanitation. It was the method of disposal of the dead favoured by theosophists, spiritualists and freethinkers of Scott's period. The fatalities of the First World War and the influenza pandemic of 1919 provided an occasion for re-examination of methods for disposing of the dead. The Cremation Society made considerable progress, lobbying for legislation eventually enacted early in the interwar period. Scott's support was no doubt helpful to the cause.[16]

The theme of death continued among Scott's family and friends. Relations with her sister, Millie Shaw, were sufficiently restored, after the will dispute of 1905, for Scott to care for her at Lynton in the weeks prior to her death in 1913, at the age of 64. Then, in 1916, Scott's only remaining brother, the police magistrate, George Scott, died. His death appears to have affected her badly, and friends' letters offer great sympathy at her sadness, her 'trouble' and bereavement.[17] Apart from Glendon Scott, the son of her brother, Robert, there were no more Scotts. She and Glendon were the last bearers of the name; and she and Alice Hamilton, at the ages of 66 and 62 respectively, were the only remaining family members of her generation.

Annie Rose Scott Cowen reports that the death of George Scott initiated what became a bitter impasse between 'the Scotts' and his widow. As the last remaining son, Saranna and other relatives had bequeathed to George much of the silverware and *objets d'art* brought by the Scott and Rusden families from England. Instead of in turn bequeathing these family heirlooms to Glendon Scott, her nephew by marriage, George's widow, Marianne Scott (née Boydell), left them to her own relatives.[18] If the Scott family was, as Cowen reports, bitter and angry, then the key players must have been her mother, Alice Hamilton, her aunt Rose Scott, and possibly her Brisbane cousin, Rosie Scott.

This threesome were the mainstay of the family in the 1910s and 1920s. Scott's correspondents frequently sent their regards to Mrs Hamilton in this period. She probably lived permanently at Lynton as Scott's widowed sister. Her six children had, by this stage, married and embarked on careers of their own, some in Sydney, the rest in Queensland. With her Queensland upbringing, Rosie Windon (née Scott) knew the Hamiltons well, especially the cousin closest in age, Annie Rose Scott Cowen. These cousins shared their aunt's Christian name and came to maturity in a cultural world in which Scott was increasingly honoured. '[T]he gracious . . . lady with the complexion of milk and roses and the adorable bonnet . . . that the public knows and loves so well,' as J.F. Archibald put it.[19]

As young women they may not have precisely understood the source or significance of their aunt's public standing. Certainly, nothing suggests that their parents had offered Scott strong emotional or other support for her political and social reform work of the 1890s. Rosie Windon's father, Helenus Scott, was a bank manager, a vocation more noted for conservative world views than not. Since he died unexpectedly in 1881, he would not have been part of the family opposition to the cause of woman suffrage that Scott increasingly recalled in newspaper interviews of the 1910s; but had he lived, there is certainly some chance that his views of his sister's conduct would have accorded with those of the rest of the family. In Scott's voluminous correspondence, no routine comments, let alone supportive ones, remain concerning Scott's suffrage work from Helenus's widow, Emily. She certainly visited Lynton and stayed there during Rosie's childhood in the first years of the century, the same period during which Millie and Mollye Shaw lived there. Miles Franklin later recalled her own fondness for Scott's beautiful young nieces staying at Lynton during her earliest visits there in 1902 and 1903.[20]

Similarly, while Alice Hamilton met and accompanied Scott for some of her 1903 Queensland lecture tour, this was more a matter of family ties than political support.[21] Probably active work on behalf of woman suffrage would have been extraordinarily difficult for this mother of six living in the isolation of Tambo, even had she been so inclined. However, there is little evidence that she had any real understanding of the arguments and issues that so occupied her sister, nor any impulse to see radical change in the position and relations of the sexes. Her daughter's various forays into written reminiscences and family history mention Scott's feminist work, but nothing in this connection about Alice Hamilton.[22] Nor is it likely that Annie Rose Scott Cowen's father, Terrick Hamilton, was a champion of rights for women. He was very much the man on the land at Tambo Station and the authority in the household, family and larger employee community there. He was known as 'Boss' or 'Old Boss', even signing his letters to his daughter in this way.[23]

Scott's relatives, then, no doubt experienced pride in her celebrity status, but little connection with its rationale. In the increasing disillusionment of her last years they could offer little practical comfort. Perhaps this lies somewhere behind her greater willingness to report her family's disapproval of her involvement in 'the cause of women' and to characterise them as 'conservative' in newspaper interviews.

The war years reduced Scott's tact and public niceties, in a framework of desperation about world events. She was one of the personalities asked by the *Sun* newspaper in 1915 'Who would I like to be?'. Scott answered 'I'd be the Kaiser. I should withdraw from Belgium, acknowledge I'd done a wrong thing and have done with the war immediately.'[24] Her pacifist work lost its *raison d'être* by later in 1914. She could see no place to intervene effectively in either feminist politics or state, national or international politics.

Increasingly, Scott adopted the position of an anxious spectator watching a world going wrong. One sign of this is the proliferation of her newscutting collections in the years from 1916. Australian history was a particular topic of interest to her, judging from clippings on heritage, Sir Joseph Banks, museums, the Royal Australian Historical Society, early explorers, Caroline Chisholm and local history. This interest in Australia was framed against an equally clear interest in the history and politics of other nations, especially Japan and Russia. The more she learned of Asian and other cultures, the more trenchant became her critique of imperialism and war. Her letters to friends in the war years convey unmistakably her sense of a world lost and rolling away. In 1918 she reported to Dowell O'Reilly the constant influx of visiting nieces, nephews and their children.

> What troubles and worries I have had since I saw you last. A raid of white ants which upset two rooms in the house and eventually cost me over £30 and still boxes and baskets of papers have to be looked over and destroyed. I was wearying of turning up letters which seemed to speak of another world from that we live in now . . . However, what are all our local troubles to this terrible war and its sacrifice of life and money. Everything seems futile. War Loans. Peace Conferences. New devilish machines. Perhaps the only hope lies in the prayers of the women whose loved ones are in the fighting line.

At this stage in her life Scott was a vegetarian, her newscutting collection full of meatless recipes, especially those using eggs. She had been a long-standing financial contributor to animal welfare associations and evidently saw needless human dominance over animals as having some connection with imperialism and men's degradation of women. The deaths of ninety cattle left for four days without water in an open train truck in northern Victoria aroused her to protest.[25]

Yet despite an active mind and an earnest ongoing interest in the world, ageing and increasing infirmity left her daily more and more alone and lonely. She awaited Nene's comings and goings. Once he volunteered, she worried about whether he was dead or wounded. In these years, her attempts to reassess and revise her earlier feminist vision took form.

'LAWS WOMEN NEED'
In 1912, the same year as the male swimming spectators' controversy, Scott wrote and presented a new speech for the NCW. It was to be the basis of the New South Wales council's report to the ICW standing committee on the legal and economic position of women, Scott's major continuing area of NCW work. If the content of this speech is compared with that of her suffrage speeches of twenty years before, the impact of international contacts and the practical grind of working with class-based party politics, at state and federal level, can be traced. In 'Laws Women Need' Scott addressed a cluster of issues: the economic position of married women, access to the legal profession and public office, equal pay for equal work, women prisoners, divorce, guardianship, protection of imbeciles, deserted wives, habitually drunk husbands, public administration and party politics. The global appeal of her speech was her call for an enhanced position for women in public and private life. As well, she called women to account for their failure to use their vote to remedy the injustices suffered by their sex.

How did she see these injustices by 1912? The need for the economic independence of married women, so prominent in her WSL speeches of the 1890s and her WPEL presidential addresses of the federal period, was restated fiercely. 'In what partnership on earth' she asked 'does one partner give all and receive no legal right in return?' Wives' legal right to a part of the breadwinner's income should be established:

> How amusing it is to hear men talk of the exalted position of the wife and mother! and yet she is frequently the most ill-treated creature on earth — a servant without wages, a partner without a say, worse still, even her children do not belong to her, but can be torn from her arms and sent off if the father wills, to the care of strangers in far distant lands, and even when her husband dies, he can leave her penniless.[26]

The category 'the state' is a major referent in 'Laws Women Need', but not in Scott's earlier speeches. In her criticism of the arguments against equal pay — namely that women are apt to get married — Scott replied that such women thereby shift from unequal pay to none, for 'they . . . continue their service to the state without payment by bringing children into the world'. This was a departure from her earlier representations of childbearing and rearing. Motherhood hitherto was a private activity that provided a just claim of women to expertise, bravery (equivalent to military service) and distinct political interests, all of which formed a sound basis for participation in democratic citizenship. In 'Laws Women Need' Scott represented motherhood unambiguously in public and industrial terms — it was work from which the state benefited, and for which the state should pay or ensure payment.

As well as payment for bearing children, she also insisted that mothers were entitled to equal guardianship of their children, noting that this was now the legal position in thirteen American states. A testator's family maintenance measure was needed so that men could be prevented from disinheriting their wives and children, since if 'when living a man must support his wife and children, why then at death should he be allowed to leave them to charity?' Furthermore, despite her earlier opposition to easy divorce, Scott now urged that lunacy should surely become a valid ground for divorce. The position of deserted wives whose husbands escaped obligation by moving interstate had to be remedied, as did the position of wives of prisoners or habitual drunks left destitute. Noting a Dutch law which provided through magistrates' order that all the money and property become legally the wife's until the husband reformed, she wished 'we had that law here: it might act as both prevention and cure'.

Scott argued that the poor position of wives and mothers, the majority of women, was maintained through the exclusion of women from the practice of law, and from positions of authority and dignity in the state. Women practised law in Victoria, Tasmania, South Australia, Canada, France, the United States, 'and even in British India', but not in New South Wales. Women needed to be eligible to be magistrates, justices of the peace, jurors, judges, members of parliament and local councils.

Scott's woman suffrage speeches of the 1890s and 1900s had had a polemical target which organised the descriptive sections. Generally that had been men's animalism and sexual exploitation of women. In 1912 'Laws Women Need' had a polemical target too: but it was, primarily, women. For instance, after a long account of married women's legal disabilities, she asked:

> Why have we not won all these rights for our fellow women? *We* with our vote we have had for ten years . . . Here again comes the eternal sex question and it shows that the majority of women have chosen rather to serve men at election time than work to ameliorate the wrongs endured by their own sex.

This theme recurred throughout the speech.

> Australian women have the vote — but the vote is only a tool, and
> the question is how has this tool been used in the past and how will
> it be used in the future? Let us hope it will not be used as it has been
> too frequently, merely to add to the strife of nations, and the build-
> ing up of class hatred, but to help those women and children whose
> misery and suffering is our continual reproach.

Finally she commented:

> We see Government programme after Government programme —
> men's needs, interests or fads always first — women's nowhere.
> Before the Woman Suffrage Cause was won, these reforms I
> have indicated were most of them advocated as *reasons* for the
> woman's vote. And even now if women would only combine and
> work for these reforms and stand apart from Parties and faction,
> there is nothing that they would not be able to accomplish for their
> fellow women and the children . . . Greater far greater is justice than
> charity — for justice spells emancipation, liberty and freedom.[27]

What account had Scott for this failure of nerve or commitment of her fellow women? Previously, of course, she had had to deal with the problem
of workers in 'the cause' being subservient to men — such as the incident
of the petition for the 1892 Vice Suppression Bill, when notable women
would not sign for fear of masculine wrath. Now, twenty years later,
surely the position had changed?

Scott and other older women tried to make sense of what *had*
changed. Florence Aspley wrote to her in 1912 that women were reacting
against their past servile condition, refusing to go into domestic service, to
waste their youth in drudgery, reasoning that it would only continue in
marriage 'with the additional burden of childrearing thrown in'. Aspley
believed this resistance constituted a revolt among women, one which was
generating 'a sort of panic' in men (which served them right), however,

> I don't think women will ever stand solidly enough together to claim
> any permanent benefit. They don't realize their own power and
> don't know how to use it. And men so love their own sense of power
> that they have engaged all through the ages that they will fight bit-
> terly before they give way one inch. Their chief power now as always
> is centred in their control of all things domestic — the children, occu-
> pation, education, and above all the money . . . Women suffer so
> much more than men from the lack of money.[28]

Of course, Aspley's identification of these sites of men's power were for Scott
all the more reason why women should strive for independence. In this context of legal, economic and cultural control by men, the women swimmers'
move to admit men appeared as one more ceding to men of another site for
control over women. Scott was wearying of conflicts of this kind; and she
was frequently ill. Evidently she was also conveying her disappointment
in her sex widely among her friends. Louisa MacDonald wrote early in 1913:

I can't have you saying — even to yourself — that you are sick of
women! And if you say it to any of us who are your friends we can
only laugh because if there were no one else you would be the living contradiction yourself. It isn't easy to get rid of chains when habit
and lack of training and tradition have made of slavery a virtue.

MacDonald then rebuked her in the gentlest way for not recognising how
much things had changed and how many younger women were working
for feminist transformation:

though I am old enough to realise the greatness of the pioneers of
women's freedom who, like yourself saw the earliest dawn of it,
and worked to wake the dreamers, I know too that for a handful
of the courageous and farsighted who came forward thirty years
ago, there are hundreds of thousands now who are awake and stir-
ring. And I hope that before we die you and I, we may see the whole
world awake in the broad noonday.[29]

In these years that were the eve of the First World War, Scott finally admitted the failure of her vision of women's political representation and its benign
cultural consequences. She externalised her disappointment. She blamed
party politics (men) and feminine servility (women) — 'the eternal sex question again'. From friends like Miles Franklin, she received lively sympathy.
Scott's complaints fitted into Franklin's version of expatriatism, especially in the heady years from 1912 to 1915, when she met prominent
American feminist theorists, especially Charlotte Perkins Gilman.

I am so glad she took a fancy to me . . . I told her of you and how
you were the first to put *In This Our World* into my hands when my
young heart was breaking with the immorality of a man-
worshipping society and I could see no way out . . . She is a great
admirer of Miss Spence and plans to go to Australia the year
after next, when she hopes to see you.

Franklin completed the letter with an amusing account of how Gilman's husband and her beautiful young secretary won the best-looking couple prize
at a fundraising ball: 'I told Mrs Gilman I was brimming over with satisfaction
because the husband of the boss cocky feminist could take a beauty prize.'
    The analysis of women's enforced economic parasitism upon men pro-
vided by Gilman made sense of the servility of which Scott was complaining. Franklin was content to attribute the cause as somehow residing
in 'Australian-ness', as if the same problems did not beset American or British
or New Zealand or French or Canadian sex relations. In June 1913, in
response to Scott's complaints, she wrote a glowing account of Gilman's significance and originality, compared with the more famous Jane Addams:

she is incomparably the greatest American woman alive . . . I refer
to a vivific force who promulgates new thought, who changes the
ideas of her generation . . . Jane Addams has a wider fame but I don't

> think of her in the same street with Mrs. Gilman . . . Jane Addams
> uses other people's minds . . . and is very cautious . . . whereas Mrs.
> Gilman is as bold as a lioness and never hesitates.

As if by contrast:

> I am very discouraged by what you tell me of the man serving
> propensities of Australian women and I know it's true as Miss Henry
> and I discover it in the newspapers' tone. It is terrible altogether that
> women are such fools. I have come to the conclusion that they are
> not worth worrying about. They are happier serving men and slob-
> bering over their feet than the rest of us are in our hot demand for
> freedom and a system of society that will nurture self-respect. [M]ost
> of people are fit for nothing but to breed weaklings to feed the dive
> and the sweatshop — tenement scrap heap vermin — let them rip.
> Do you suppose we are ahead of our time; are we deluded fools or
> merely conceited?[30]

At this stage, Franklin had an 'us/them' dualism: she and Scott and
their kind, the enlightened workers for women's emancipation, against
the rest — fools. By 1919 her quips concerning women's position in
Australia had sedimented into truism. She wrote to Scott: 'England
perhaps once in the dim ages was a pioneer with baths, and has made
herself ridiculous by imagining thereby she is still a bathing nation. I
expect Australasia is going to do the same sort of thing about women's
emancipation.'[31]

Dora Montefiore, who hosted the first meeting of the WSL and
joined the WSPU in 1903, expressed similar sentiments about Australian
women in 1911 at a Women's College lunch held in her honour. Unlike
their British sisters, who really had to fight for the vote, and thereby become
strong and able public political women, Australian women were handed
the vote and had done little with it. She recalled this 1911 speech in her
memoir of 1927:

> I considered from my observation that in many respects Australian
> women were backward in organising themselves either politically
> or industrially . . . I pointed out that though still unenfranchised,
> the long, hard fight which had been the lot of us English women
> in the winning of citizenship had, to a great extent, emancipated
> us more thoroughly and given us more self reliance than if we had
> obtained the vote before we were prepared for it, as happened some-
> times elsewhere.[32]

In short, she argued, the vote was wasted on Australian women.

This was a forerunner of the 'doormats of the Western world'[33] representation of Australian women, and it is important to note the extent to
which it is a reversal of the earlier portrayal of the vigorous womanhood
of a young, progressive country undertaking legislative experiments
that made it 'the social laboratory of the world'.[34] It was as if, by already

having the vote before the war, Australasian women were unable to join in the one great international moment of women's history, the militant suffragette struggle and its aftermath. According to many historical accounts British and American women were rewarded with citizenship rights after their magnificent contributions to the war effort.[35] Being out of the suffragette struggle and out of the war effort meant being out of history. Most historians have ignored the different timing and different conditions in Australasia, and the specificity of purported generalisations remain unacknowledged.

Scott perhaps contributed to this negative assessment of woman suffrage and Australian women. Yet the comparison was being made between groups of women whose political and legal status and struggles were incommensurate at that point — a phase apart, as it were. Moreover, she was exceedingly negative about the two developments of pivotal significance in shaping the perceptions and comparisons of contemporary commentators and later historians — the campaigns of the militant suffragettes and the First World War of 1914–18. Her stances on these developments warrant further examination.

A PHASE APART

In 1912 Emily Leaf, press secretary of the English National Union of Women's Suffrage Societies wrote to Scott asking for her help. She sought condemnation of the militant tactics of the suffragettes from countries where women had already gained the vote through peaceful means. In 1913 she supplied Scott with a copy of the union's resolution: 'That the NU of WSS reiterates its protest against the militant methods . . . made by the National Union in 1908, 1909, 1911 and 1912. The Union remains convinced that the use of violence in political propaganda is wrong itself and injurious to the cause of women's suffrage'.[36]

Scott sent offers of assistance, despite the fact that many of her friends supported the WSPU. Earlier, in 1910, co-pacifist Marian Harwood had written from England about the notorious Conciliation Bill, and about police harassment and brutality towards the women. She warned Scott that the press offered exaggerated and sensational accounts of everything and that the government have been 'very much to blame'. She concluded that 'we may thank our stars that we had not such an incorrigible government to deal with'.[37]

Some months later, Harwood wrote to Scott from Paris about an article she had written for a suffragette newspaper qualifying what she called Vida Goldstein's claim to be 'the leader of the Women's Movement in Australia'. In Harwood's view 'the militant suffragettes were possessed with the idea that Miss G. was the only person who had taken a lead in Australia'.[38] Considering the past anxieties over recognition of expertise and leadership in the Australian movements, Scott was probably displeased at this news of Goldstein's work with the WSPU. Later, Goldstein could be seen in the streets of Melbourne selling the WSPU newspaper, *Votes for Women*, and fundraising for the suffragettes in many different contexts.[39] Franklin, who had irritated Scott in 1908 by describing Goldstein as needing to 'melt', felt safe to comment on her again rather slightingly in 1913: 'Yes, isn't it a pity that Vida has to grab all the money for herself. She is really true and clean and yet there is that survival of the fittest strain in her'. However, despite Scott's publicly stated difference with Goldstein over suffragette militancy, she continued to give newspaper interviews confirming 'I am with her in everything else'.[40]

Nellie Alma Martel sent an appeal to Australasia in 1912 detailing the torture and violence being inflicted on suffragettes in England.[41] Louisa MacDonald protested against such treatment and the derogatory representation of suffragettes in public discussion in a letter to the editor of the *Sydney Morning Herald*:

> Whether I approve of their action or not I think it unseemly that I or any woman who values the right to vote on which these and others are risking life and liberty to gain should sit quietly by and hear them called futile, hysterical, fanatic, without uttering a word of protest.[42]

In the face of the involvement of New South Wales suffrage pioneer, Dora Montefiore, as well as the support of important co-workers, Scott's consistent, vehement and unrepentant opposition to suffragette militancy needs examination. Why did she so eagerly respond to Emily Leaf and the National Union of Women's Suffrage Societies' call to publish articles criticising the WSPU for unwomanliness, aggression, militarism accusing them of aping men and retarding the progress of the British woman suffrage cause?

Several factors were probably in play. Scott, as a veteran leader, seems to have identified strongly with Millicent Fawcett, who was being underestimated by an impatient younger generation. Fawcett's association with John Stuart Mill, and the origins of the first official movement for woman suffrage in the Commonwealth, dating from 1866, made her a candidate for Scott's respect, while Fawcett's letters of encouragement and congratulation on her achievements in New South Wales were undoubtedly gratifying.[43] Hence, she would have been heartened to learn that her supportive letter had been forwarded to Mrs Fawcett 'who was much interested in it'. Another friend of Fawcett's replied to a letter from Scott in these terms:

> I hope we may look upon you as our correspondent; at any rate you can put us in touch with others as you kindly mention you may be able to do . . . The militants have damaged us in more ways than by jeopardising the grant of the vote, I fear, as you say. It is most distressing. We have a great desire to get some organized influential opinion sent from Australia . . . [44]

Such recognition was undoubtedly flattering to Scott in 1912, amidst local losses and impasses. Her loyalty to Fawcett was such that she refused to consider alternative viewpoints, untroubled by the fact that she had no first-hand knowledge of the English situation. This loyalty and sense of connection had no doubt been strengthened when the former Australian prime minister, Edmund Barton, sent to Scott the framed address of congratulations to the women of Australia upon their enfranchisement from the leaders of the English suffrage movement. It had been presented to him in London on an official visit in 1902. In retirement he lacked space for many such valued objects and so after 'your great services to the cause of Adult Suffrage in Australia who is so fit as you to keep, if you chance to hold it in regard, a memento of those who have championed the women's cause in England?' This reinforced her conviction of entitlement to comment on the WSPU controversy.

Other feminists were infuriated by Scott's armchair judgements, based on National Union of Women's Suffrage Societies propaganda and the distortions of the newspaper press.[45] A young activist, Agnes Murphy, who had gone to London and joined the suffragettes, returned to Australia in 1912 to secure support for them. Regarding the militant movement as 'the greatest spiritual movement in the world today', Murphy was 'absolutely astounded' at Scott's position. Her response to Scott's praise of Fawcett was blunt:

> Mrs Fawcett is a most estimable woman . . . but . . . [she has a] complete lack of political foresight. Her nervous attitude has made it possible for the politicians to play fast and loose with the women's movement and to juggle with such questions as the White Slave Traffic. But for Mrs Fawcett, the women of the UK would now be enfranchised. She has no policy. One day she alienates Lloyd George by her criticism of the 'destructive celt'; another day she fawns on him who is pledged to destruction of the very measure she is working for.[46]

This criticism of Fawcett signals another dimension of Scott's identification with her: Scott's lobbying of hostile politicians had also been denounced in the 1890s, generally by women not themselves placed to undertake such a venture. In part, then, this tension may revolve around implicit charges of class privilege. It was also a charge of social complicity with those denying women their rights and the belief that such complicity undermined feminist political strategies involving confrontation. The notion that the kind of confrontation prosecuted by the militant suffragettes could be an ennobling or empowering experience for women was unimaginable for Scott, despite Murphy's claim that this was the case.

The year 1913 was a key one for another young Australian woman of Scott's acquaintance who was visiting London: Bessie Rischbieth, future leader of the major Western Australian non-party women's organisation. She sent a series of moving letters to her sister, Olive Evans, chronicling the activities of the Pankhursts and her own process of conversion to the suffragette cause. As a young married woman accompanying her husband, a wool merchant on a business trip, she had clearly not planned a suffragette adventure. Moreover, in the early letters to her sister she was adamant about opposition to militant methods. In her analysis of woman's degradation she shared much common ground with Scott. Yet in the space of two months she became a convert, denouncing the government and the press, attending the funeral of Emily Wilding Davidson, the suffragette who threw herself in front of the King's horse at Ascot, and waiting in a vigil outside the house in which Emmeline Pankhurst lay critically ill from hunger striking in prison. How did this happen? It is worth the slight detour of examining Rischbieth's account, because it helps illuminate the process of formation of such a gulf between Scott and women such as Rischbieth (who were otherwise in accord) on the suffragettes.

For Rischbieth, it all began in May 1913. Some Perth women with whom she worked in various charities recommended that she go to hear Mrs Perkins Gilman, currently on a lecture tour in England. She explained in the first letter to her sister that Gilman argued that 'we have erred in emphasising *sex* as we have made women economically dependent on man'. She found this argument very persuasive. Going to hear Gilman was an unforgettable experience in itself:

> When I got to this great theatre I found it pretty well crammed and I also discovered that she was speaking from the platform of the WSPU . . . So I thought oh this is alright! First of all, the doors outside were swarmed with police . . . After lunch I went to the annual meeting of the British Committee against State Regulation . . . A girl spoke there to the Resolution raising the age of consent and equal moral standard. Oh, how these women speak so logically, with such zeal and knowledge. They call her the 2nd Mrs Josephine Butler . . . So, I am having a glorious time as you can see.

The adventure continued. A week later she reported to her sister a range of suffrage meetings and addresses she attended. The process was a crash course in politics — sexual and party. A principal element of the drama was the operation of the notorious 'Cat and Mouse' Act. Refusing the suffragettes' claim to the status of political prisoners, the government responded to the resultant wave of hunger striking by releasing the imprisoned suffragettes to medical care, then re-arresting them to serve out their sentence once recovered. This horrified Rischbieth in principle, but the impact deepened upon engaging with particulars:

> Mrs Pankhurst was arrested on leaving the hospital and . . . again . . . Committed to Holloway. She is very, very ill and there is hardly any hope. If she dies in prison, the responsibility rests with the Government but I think it likely that she will be taken out just to save their skins as they did in the case of her sister. Of course one

feels, they have broken the law and must abide by it, but why don't they apply the law to all alike irrespective of sex. The cat and mouse is considered by all thinking folk to be the most scurrilous bill or quite an arbitrary one. They let a man out last week after only having served four months out of nine of his time. He was imprisoned for assaulting three little girls under fourteen and is out because his health is suffering. Under the Cat and Mouse Bill as applied to the suffragettes he would have to go out to Hospital and get well and then go back but no.

One month more of participation in this context rendered Rischbieth no longer an observer or commentator, but, instead, a participant. The torture of force feeding, public violence, death, sacrifice, martyrdom and betrayed principles marked this moment in the struggle. After describing the thousands attending Emily Davidson's funeral, the arrest of Emmeline Pankhurst for attending, and her renewed hunger strike and re-release critically ill, Rischbieth marvelled that she was still alive, and noted that it was difficult 'to explain the situation, but it all comes back to the damned government'. She and a Mrs Cameron (a new suffragette friend) 'drove around the street where Mrs Pankhurst is lodged at present and saw the detective who guards the door. She is very ill and likely to die at any time, and then there will be great trouble here'. Rischbieth went to the Ethical Church to hear a doctor speak of the women hunger strikers he had treated in and outside prison. She concluded the letter to her sister with: 'Oh well you will think I am dotty now.'

Yet even earlier (before her 'conversion'), in a letter to a Perth friend, Mrs Donnelly, Rischbieth gave a stark account of the consequences of the suffragette controversy:

> Of course, the militants are going strong and will be going stronger. I really think there will be murder before things get much further. Let me warn you to believe *nothing* of the Press. It is the topic of the day wherever you go. Men don't know whether or whether you are not a disguised suffragette or what women will do next. These women are all fearless speakers and although I do not believe in militant methods, I think the lives are too strenuous and too full of deeper meaning for one society of women suffragists to be critic of another.

Why was Scott incapable of the same generosity? Surely Rischbieth was just as invested as she in ensuring that Australian achievements were acknowledged? Indeed, Rischbieth concluded that English women were in an infinitely worse position than Australian women, specifically with regard to industrial, sexual and legal exploitation: 'Some of our laws . . . are far in advance of the laws here, and I can see the influence of the woman's vote in Australia. But we ought to do much more and could do it by educating ourselves on economic lines and doing away with the God of Party Politics.'[47] Scott would have wholeheartedly agreed. Yet she seemed unable to concede that local reasons made the battle for the vote much tougher in Britain, even though she had seen the longer, harder struggle of the woman suffrage movement in Victoria led by Goldstein. That experience undoubtedly contributed to Goldstein's sympathy with the frustrations of her British counterparts.

Perhaps insularity and inexperience of the British context is sufficient to explain Scott's stance. Even if she had wished it, she was by 1913 too ill and, in the view of most, too old, to undertake the voyage to that cold, damp country of which her friend, Marian Harwood, said 'I am never warm except when in bed and not always then'.[48] Another facet of the situation, however, may have been the publication of a book by Nellie Martel in 1913 entitled *The Women's Vote in Australia*. The text offered only token recognition of Scott's efforts, contained factual errors about achievements in New South Wales, and gave credit to others that Scott would have seen as her due.[49] Furthermore, Martel was prominent in the inner circle of the WSPU, often photographed with Emmeline and Christabel Pankhurst, Annie Kenney and Flora Drummond.[50] Might some of Scott's unwillingness to consider the suffragettes favourably have been the outcome of unresolved conflict and rivalry with Martel dating from WSL days at the turn of the century? Did she experience the much-publicised tactics of the WSPU as undertaken in criticism of workers like herself and Fawcett? Though Fawcett had not succeeded, she had. Perhaps the defence of Fawcett was a displacement, a replay of the earlier struggle to defend herself against Martel. The world needed to be told that she, not Martel, had succeeded in New South Wales. Likewise, Fawcett, not Martel, deserved recognition and support in England.

Neither Scott nor her contemporaries addressed this possible dimension to her opposition to the suffragettes and the WSPU organisation. Adela Pankhurst had intended to pay her respects to Scott upon arriving in Australia until learning of Scott's anti-suffragette pronouncements. Like others, she found them incomprehensible. She sent Scott an angry, but very sincere letter, urging her to consider the differences between the Australian and English contexts of the woman suffrage question:

> The conditions are entirely different here. There are not the strong vested interests against the enfranchisement of women . . . I mean the liquor interest which is stronger than you can imagine; those who are interested in immorality; the sweating employers; and the many commercial concerns that depend on women's labour. We have also great opposition from politicians who fear the effect of the woman's vote. These forces have been united against us for 50 years and the press has constantly helped them. Now things have changed and in spite of abuse and ridicule and cruel brutality, the militants have cleared the way . . . [W]e are making it easy for women to be suffragists and Mrs Fawcett herself would have to admit that her own society has gained new life and thousands

of adherents since militancy began. In place of a society there are now upwards of 60, many of them men's . . . I am so sorry that in such a crisis a woman whose name is justly honoured should be quoted as condemning those fighting for justice, without saying anything in condemnation of those who are denying justice and using methods of the greatest brutality to crush the women's spirit.[51]

Despite her forceful letter, Pankhurst's arguments about the special difficulties in England displayed an outlook as parochial as Scott's. Her arguments would have had little impact on Scott, who encountered exactly the same obstacles to suffrage in the 1890s and after. The powerful vested interests were hardly confined to England, and so failed to explain or justify, for Scott, the departure entailed in suffragette tactics. More cogent and unsettling for Scott were the arguments of her friend, Marian Harwood, who lived for periods in England and Europe. Compared to Scott and other women workers in the cause, Marian Harwood, Master of Arts, was highly educated. The suffragette issue brought her and Scott into open dispute, with Harwood telling Scott that 'you have to have lived there' to understand the issues, and that she, Harwood, knew 'something more than you'.

That 'something more' was English demography. Harwood contended that women suffered in England from their demographic preponderance and, with the outbreak of war in 1914, she wrote to Scott that the inevitable slaughter of men would increase that majority. As a labour force and a social force women 'are too cheap in the old country and no one who has never been there can quite understand how much that means'. The abuse of women in England long before the militancy began was deplorable, and the non-militants like Fawcett had been treated 'just as badly' as the 'Pankhurst set'. Hence, just as the preponderance of women was a basis for their ill-treatment and abuse, it was equally a basis for the fears of politicians. Harwood dined with politicians who 'frankly admitted that Mr Asquith was simply afraid of our sex because of its overwhelming majority'[52] — a case of the spinster and her enemies.

If Scott was at all persuaded by the specificities of the situation faced by the suffragettes, and revised her opinion of their actions, she did not publicise any such revisions. Her own experience of the past decade taught her that *how* the vote was marshalled as a tool for women's emancipation was the critical question. The militant suffragette controversy emphasised the gaining of the tool. Why would the British movement be any less imperilled by the divide and rule effect of adherence to party politics — the interests and causes of men — than the Australian and New Zealand movements had proven to be? However, before any further resolution of revision about the suffragettes was canvassed between Scott and her contemporaries, a further development altered the position entirely — the First World War.

Upon the announcement of hostilities, the suffragettes ceased campaigning against the government and instructed all their members to throw themselves behind the national war effort. While this directive dismayed socialists like Sylvia Pankhurst and Dora Montefiore, it confirmed the line of Scott's judgements. Militancy and militarism were the methods of men, doomed to wreak barbarism and domination. Suffragettes were being brought into the service of the party in government. The limited franchise for British women over 30 in 1918 was pitiful recompense for such complicity. Scott reported in a newspaper interview that Millicent Fawcett 'very much resents the fact that a woman in England must be 30 before she can exercise the vote'.[53] Meanwhile, the militants were now domesticated and the politicians need not fear.

Scott's judgement here was inextricably intertwined with her more general disillusionment about women's absorption into the war effort. The peace society had failed to prevent war, just as it had failed to prevent the institution of compulsory military training for school boys, or to have a version of peace studies introduced into the school curriculum, or even to secure the removal of jingoistic text books.[54] If party politics always placed men's interests first, how much more so in war? What war offered women in public life was the renovated identities of helpmeets and philanthropists. Australia–France friendship societies, conscription propaganda, and work for the Universal Service League, became the work of women, enticing more and more young men to Gallipoli and other places of doom. Censorship and danger to civilian shipping disrupted lines of communication with workers overseas. Life consisted of waiting, working, watching, dreading, subject to unique compulsion. Yet Scott remained convinced that women were not merely the victims of war — they were accomplices who could change the situation. She wrote to Alice Salomons, president of the ICW, in 1914, 'What a catastrophe this war is ... Oh if only women would wake up surely there would not be any more war?' A few days later Scott wrote to the eminent Anna Howard Shaw, president of the National American Women's Suffrage Associations: 'Hope rests alone with the mothers of men', in response to Shaw's general appeal to women of the world to demand peace.[55]

All the small tyrannies of war pressed upon Scott. Meredith Atkinson, a prominent Sydney University academic, was prohibited from 'the propagation of anti-militarist doctrines in Australia', while her co-pacifist, Flora Timms, reported in 1915 that the 'authorities got on my track and my last article ... was censored and no more are to be allowed'. Scott resisted patriotic pressures by promptly joining the newly founded International Council of Women for Permanent Peace, and corresponding with Emily Hobhouse (earlier active in work against the Boer War), Jane Addams, Chrystal Macmillan and Aletta Jacobs.[56] The occasional letter that got through from Miles Franklin must have struck a cheery note amidst the gloom.

Nursing the wounded, as young women did, took Franklin to Macedonia and into concentrated contact with men. She wrote some reflections on men to Scott in May 1915:

> The male mind is an astonishing invention. The Titanic couldn't be sunk. It sank . . . Many men are still prating that the only way to ensure peace is to prepare for war . . . Why should there be any meaning? Myself, I am a violent neutral. I am disgusted with all belligerents . . . The male mind, I repeat is an astonishing invention. I see that in contemplation of the curious gymnastics of which it is capable I shall have entertainment for my declining years. I had a narrow escape from matrimony last year but this war has emboldened me to make up my mind on the negative side. Fancy running the risk of reproducing such a species![57]

If, in general, Scott preferred to consider the problems of war, peace, patriotism and masculinity as transnational or international problems, the reality of the arrangement of the world into specific warring nations could not be denied. Propaganda flooded Scott's cultural environment and she asked friends living in Europe about the reliability of German atrocity stories circulating in Sydney. From Paris, Madge Donohoe, a veteran WSL and NCW co-worker, replied to some of Scott's questions about life in occupied Europe at the end of 1915. Yes, it was true 'that little children have been mutilated by these butchers'. She told of another Australian woman who offered to adopt an orphaned Belgian child, a 10-year-old girl, and was still in shock from first seeing the child's horrible mutilations. Donohoe also told Scott the story of a 19-year-old French girl, Stephanie Clausse, who remained on the family farm near Nancy while her mother left to seek the release of her father, taken hostage by the Germans. One day:

> when she was in the house alone a patrol of Germans, 7 or 8 in number, came. She does not know how many violated her for she lost consciousness and her two little brothers found her in that condition . . . She told me that at first when she knew this child was coming she felt very bitter and felt that she would hate it. Now she has learnt to love it . . . What an experience for this poor young girl! And she is only one among thousands. And the poor, poor babies, think of them, the little *unwanted* things . . . How unthinkably sad it all is![58]

With only censored information and allied propaganda on which to base opinions, it was difficult to maintain a genuinely internationalist viewpoint in wartime Australia. Madge Donohoe reported on the 'dreadful tensions' that erupted between French and German delegates to ICW conferences, while at home Louisa MacDonald wrote to Scott advising against her proposed nomination of Lady McCallum for president of the NCW in New South Wales because of her 'German blood'.[59] The failure of pacifism and internationalism, at least for the duration of the war, caused Scott to re-orient her efforts at reforms to state level. Was she correct in her prediction that wartimes were bad times for law reforms relevant to women and children? What progress was made during the war years on the agenda of law reforms required that she announced in 1912?

HUSBANDS, FATHERS, SONS . . . BROTHERS

On 29 May 1919 Scott read a new paper on the legal position of women and children in New South Wales. It was published by the NCW and sent to the ICW as the law report for the year. She offered various reminiscences about her motivations for involvement in the cause of women and children. Recalling the 1892 debate on the Vice Suppression Bill, an unnamed barrister had said that raising the age of consent would stop the supply of women for certain purposes, and 'this to him and other men was an incredible position. Upon hearing this my heart and soul blazed with rage and I thought . . . we women must get the vote.' Later in the paper she explained that in those days the woman's vote 'became part of one's religion'. Her shopping list of what remained to be done, however, had changed somewhat since 1912.

In 1913, a Deserted Wives' Bill was tabled in the New South Wales Legislative Assembly, though not debated. Its main purpose was to facilitate the interstate extradition of defaulting husbands. Meanwhile, in 1916, a Testators' Family Maintenance and Guardianship of Infants' Bill was enacted, preventing the disinheritance of widows and their children and making widows automatic guardians of their children. Equal guardianship remained outside the scope of reforms that Liberal, Nationalist or Labor governments were prepared to embrace. Nor had anything happened to secure the economic independence of married women — and Scott certainly did not consider the token of the £5 Commonwealth Maternity Bonus a measure in this direction.[60] Meanwhile, equal pay legislation or an amendment punishing men who sexually took advantage of imbecile women were nowhere to be seen.

However, two measures Scott had supported were enacted — the Women's Legal Status Act in 1918, and the First Offenders' (Women) Act in 1919. Women could now practise law, stand for local or state government, and be magistrates and justices of the peace, though still not jurors. And if a woman was charged on a first criminal offence, the case could be heard *in camera* without publicity. Parliamentarians who supported equal citizen rights for women justified this largely in terms of the British experience of women's loyalty and unexpected competence during the war effort. Nothing specific about Australian or New South Wales women was introduced into this discussion. The entire matter of women's eligibility to enter public office was treated as the correction of an anomaly. The same session and the same legislators proclaiming women's equality and potential sameness to men, also supported the assertion of women's special, specific attributes in passing the women first offenders' Bill.

The New South Wales attorney-general, David Hall, noted when introducing the Women's Legal Status Bill that women had been eligible to stand as federal members since 1902 and that Vida Goldstein had been a candidate several times. Notwithstanding this, he reassured the doubting among his brother politicians that not many women had contested federal elections, primarily because they had not succeeded in obtaining pre-selection in either party; thus the measure was unlikely to have 'a very revolutionary character'. Hall's elision of British and Australian experience was evident:

> We have seen in the last four years hundreds of thousands of women taken from domestic occupations and called upon to work in industries, in transport, in banking, and in commerce; women working in every direction, in unexpected quarters, and with unexpected successes. We have seen the suffragist movement which created so much trouble for authorities prior to the war, directed to assist the authorities in every way that no one could have anticipated. A woman such as Mrs Pankhurst, when the declaration of war found her recovering from a hunger strike, went up and down England telling the women that to do nothing when the nation needed help was a crime. We saw her daughter return from France where she had fled to escape arrest, to give up the suffragist propaganda in order to undertake the work of feeding the starving children of England while industrial readjustments rendered necessary by the outbreak of the war were being made. Therefore, as a tribute to what has been done in the last four years, and because of the inherent justice of the proposal contained in this measure I commend it to the house.[61]

Scott's feelings about the 'warmongering' Pankhurst's being represented as the exemplary instance, proving Australian women's fitness for full citizen rights, are not recorded, nor are those of Annie and Belle Golding and others working since 1904 for women's admission to the legal profession and public office. Another Golding sister, the labour activist, Kate Dwyer, became the first woman appointed to the Senate of the University of Sydney at the end of 1918.[62] However, Scott's voluminous papers and correspondence contain no joyous, celebratory speeches and letters. In her published speech of 1919 on laws in New South Wales, she recognised that finally having the right to offices of dignity in the state would by no means ensure women's appointment to them, for 'we see how averse men are' to this, and 'if there is a high salary in question, they simply could not bear it to be wasted upon a woman!'[63]

If relatively little of the revised reform agenda of women like Scott had been achieved by the end of the war, other areas of Labor legislation certainly had implications for women and their children. Panic and scandal about drunkenness among soldiers stationed in Sydney, and the alarming prevalence of venereal diseases, led to the introduction of six o'clock closing of hotels in 1916 and a select committee into what was called 'the red plague'. Some women advocated prohibition in wartime. The early closing measure was supposed to provide some check against excessive evening drinking. Its effects on women and children are difficult to evaluate. The notorious 'six o'clock swill' — whereby a man would buy several large glasses of beer at once upon closing time — came into existence, and no doubt led to the rapid inebriation of many a breadwinner, bound homeward for the family evening meal. The much vaunted connection between excessive masculine drinking and domestic battery was hardly seriously challenged by six o'clock closing, and women interested in temperance for men could have been forgiven for disappointment. Six o'clock closing may have been a compromise delivering the worst of the other alternatives, as well as providing the conditions for the emergence of a lucrative sly grog trade and illicit after-hours drinking venues, increasingly managed by organised criminal interests.

Since prostitutes had always solicited among hotel patrons, transactions may have become more indoors and surreptitious. Dr Ralph Worrall, a specialist testifying at the Venereal Diseases Select Committee in 1915, alleged that protected brothels operated through a system of police bribery and corruption, facts conducive to the spread of disease. Police and other medical testimony was that professionals were clean and safe — it was 'the amateurs': that is, less experienced promiscuous young women having sexual relations with soldiers for pleasure rather than payment, who were the dangerous sources of infection.[64] If public discourses such as these stressed the equal, if not greater, carnality of women, politically active older women, such as Florence Aspley, wrote to Scott expressing concern about men's sexual practices in wartime. In particular, Aspley alluded to the prevalence of married men posing as bachelors, seducing, embezzling from, then abandoning pregnant young women: 'I am hoping that out of this appalling war a new manhood and womanhood will be raised.'[65]

During this period, the problem of venereal disease was discursively relocated as no longer in the moral and implicitly criminal domain, but rather as a modern, civilian and medical matter. One third of the first Australian Infantry Forces returned from active service in Egypt infected. The nations heroes could not, it was argued, be treated as criminals, nor could their morality be questioned. A Venereal Diseases Bill was enacted in 1918 (in the same week as the Women's Legal Status Bill), establishing free public treatment through Venereal Diseases Clinics. In his speech on this Bill, Dr Nash, member of the Legislative Council, who had returned from five-and-a-half months in charge of the army venereal hospital at Abassia in Egypt, contended that:

> our soldiers fell in with the worst varieties of the disease that we have in this country. For the last fifty years there has been no place in the world worse than Sydney . . . The soldiers who went from

this country to Egypt brought just as much of these diseases into the city of Cairo as they got there and the virulence of the diseases was as great.[66]

In 'man-of-the-world' speeches on venereal diseases, men's resort to prostitution and other non-marital and extra-marital sexual encounters were normalised and condoned by their elected representatives. The spectre of 'the amateur', the 'animal' woman as willing as the man, was pitted effectively against the 'passionless' woman, seduced and victimised, of feminist representations. The famous and popularised sexologists, who offered scientific validity to new accounts of women's sexuality, achieved their currency in the 1920s and 1930s.[67] Nonetheless, these wartime discussions of venereal diseases and sexuality certainly foreshadowed the context in which inter-war sexology was written, read and found plausible.

Women in 1919 were not getting the laws they needed, they were getting the laws men needed, and thereby, in Scott's view, were being represented in law in a manner inimical to their interests. She reiterated: 'I deeply regret that the majority of women (flattered by the obsequious deference of their one time tyrants) . . . neglected every warning and threw themselves and their votes into the evils of party politics.'[68]

The telling feature of modern, fraternal democracy was that the more solidly divided the legislating brotherhood by class, party and faction, the more striking was their unity on questions of sex — on men and women's place, on sexuality and morality — especially in the new era following the war. Had Scott's war against this brotherhood failed? Who were 'the modern women' into whose hands the baton of reform would pass in the last years of Scott's life and after? As the war erupted in 1914, another significant development occurred — the founding of the Feminist Club in Sydney. Younger, university-educated, professional women, civil servants and artists would comprise its membership, and many would be active in politics in the inter-war period. The club lasted until 1929, when disputes over communism spelt its demise. It had as members key feminists of the twentieth century, including Jessie Street. This club was of longer duration than any of the many organisations in which Scott held office or gave support, except the NCW. Scott's coming to terms with transformations within feminism was, to a great extent, a coming to terms with the feminists of the younger generations, represented in the Feminist Club and organisations like it.[69] The task for Scott was to battle with her own disillusionment, her tendency to blame others for the failure of her feminist vision, and to grasp the implications of its failure. Only then could she define a satisfactory revision of the rationale for feminist analysis and advocacy. To do this, she had to yield; and she had to heed more of her own advice to women since the 1890s: she had to see.

Chapter 7

The Modern Woman
(1920–25)

Wise and useful work may be done in framing laws for a country, but all that is greatest in history is contained in the word 'emancipation'.

Rose Scott,
Letter to the Editor, *Sydney Morning Herald*, n.d.

Scott's final years were the first half of the 1920s. She used them for a number of purposes. If her active role in politics and public life had effectively declined during the 1910s, this fact was now formally marked. With considerable ceremony she retired from public life, giving herself space to reflect upon developments in her beloved 'cause of women'. Her decision to retire was not easy: it was only with great reluctance that she relinquished the pursuit of her earlier vision of reforms to end women's degradation.

Despite formal retirement, Scott made various forays into public life on behalf of her sex. Yet her earlier vision did give way to a gradual recognition of new forces in the women's movement of the 1920s. The elaboration of equality-oriented perspectives within feminism seriously challenged many aspects of Scott's former positions. The way in which a new generation of feminist leaders proceeded, however, did not involve entire abandonment of the concerns of earlier leaders like Scott. The work of the Western Australian feminist and founder of the Australian Federation of Women Voters, Bessie Rischbieth, provided an important example of transition, but also connection, between two divergent strands in early-twentieth-century feminism. Contact with Rischbieth allowed Scott to reconcile herself with new directions. By the time of her death she had at least partially revised her previous negative judgements of 'the modern woman'.

In the last five years of Scott's life, Australian feminism became more diverse, complex and international. The war and its aftermath had altered irrevocably the way in which public feminist advocacy would take place. The advent of Soviet socialism arguably eclipsed earlier debates over non-party feminism, changing the terms of the relationship between feminist and other politics. Some of the programme and concerns of feminists of Scott's generation endured throughout the inter-war period and the crisis of the Great Depression of the 1930s. In several key areas, however, changed cultural conditions led to revision of earlier analyses and strategies, particularly with regard to sexual issues. Scott came to understand these revisions and looked forward to women's emancipation.

This gradual acceptance of changes in feminism took place amidst a more general acceptance of her own mortality. Scott was diagnosed as having cancer and while battling with its effects on her body and sense of identity, she worked at putting her affairs in order. She arranged to see old friends, and had concerns over family configurations: such matters occupied her increasingly painful waking hours. Rose Scott had a difficult death.

RETIREMENT WITH RESISTANCE

'Be passionately in earnest and loyal to your womanhood and to your sex and in the end you will certainly win.'[1] With these words, Scott concluded her speech upon retirement from public life in April 1921 at the age of 73. Her intention to retire was announced in 1920 and occasioned by an interview she gave to the *Sydney Morning Herald*.[2] This was the first of several newspaper interviews published prior to her death. Reporters were interested in two topics: her reminiscences of the past, especially of politics and famous people she knew, and in her views on 'the modern woman'. Analysis of these interviews, together with her public speeches and correspondence of the period, display Scott as being torn between the past and the future. Illness and disability brought on retirement and a necessary acceptance of the inevitability of her own passing; and yet she resisted the limitations of ageing and illness by continuing in limited public roles and commenting, at times adversely, on directions taken in feminist politics.

Scott's illness probably disrupted the regularity of her Friday evening salon during the years of the war. Another major constraint on her activities was her rapidly deteriorating hearing, which reduced her ability to interact and made her prone to giving monologues or speaking uninformedly, even tactlessly. Signs of a hearing problem were obvious as early as 1903. While on her tour of Queensland as president of the WPEL Scott sent Nene a postcard: 'Train brought on deafness in one ear again — throat better, nice and warm — cool air, Love RS.'[3]

In 1908, during her conflict with Elimina Sutherland over the naming of the Women's Club, the issue of her hearing difficulties was familiar enough for her to mention it in her public account of the misunderstanding — she had been unable to hear on the telephone.[4] In 1920 Scott had a fall and was seriously incapacitated; the announcement of her retirement followed shortly after. Probably, by this point, she had become exceedingly difficult for others to work with. Only a few weeks before the accident, the honorary secretary of the NCW had resigned, unable any longer to endure the tensions between herself and the international secretary, Scott. The NCW had become Scott's principal remaining affiliation, but she found it difficult to accept how it was changing. Instead of organising membership solely by delegates from affiliated societies, the NCW increasingly recruited associate members on the basis of the expertise they could bring to the council. Professional women were prominent among associates and they were in demand to provide expert advice, public lectures, and consultation, on behalf of the council to official inquiries and bodies. The secretary seems to have been the recipient of Scott's ire about changes in the style and recruitment of NCW members:

> Miss Scott makes attacks upon my administration of the affairs of the council . . . these attacks being accompanied by remarks which have become more personal at each successive meeting . . . [A]ny proposal put forward by me to increase the efficiency and facilitate the working of the council is vehemently and insistently opposed by her . . . it is useless to attempt to carry out the duties of the Hon.Sec. . . . under these conditions. Miss Scott seems quite satisfied with the present status and reputation of the council with its 38 affiliated societies and its 128 financial associates — frankly I am not.[5]

Scott appears to have been embroiled in ongoing strife with NCW members — one of whom wrote 'I am sorry that you are so worried about the NCW . . . I think you rather overstate the position if I may take the liberty of saying so'.[6] There are many signs that she was not dealing well with change, tending to interpret events and motives in the light of her past experience, rather than understanding new contexts and new struggles. Her deafness isolated her from direct contact and undermined her interactions with people. These factors probably diminished her capacity to relate to or make common cause with the younger generations of women. Evidently she wrote to Louisa MacDonald upon her retirement, critical of her successor as principal of Women's College, Miss Williams, unaware how tactless this might seem to MacDonald, who had played a significant part in her selection. MacDonald replied:

> You really are naughty about my successor and you don't give us much credit for doing our best for the future of the college . . . You know my dear I am not the college, I am only a student like another who has had happiness for 27 years of working . . . my desire is that my successor may be as happy in her work and her friends as I have been. And as that cannot be unless her heart is in it, that means the college will be equally happy with her. You will change your mind about Miss Williams I know.[7]

MacDonald had often been the recipient of Scott's confidences, her complaints, and sometimes her most emotional outbursts. She seems always to have offered Scott guidance, balance, calm and carefully phrased criticism, as the situation warranted. Scott was probably fearful about losing her friend, in the context of the loss of others close to her. The war, the 1919 influenza epidemic, and the usual course of the life cycle meant loss of siblings, nieces, nephews, and friends, while success or political changes kept abroad friends who mattered — Vida Goldstein, Miles Franklin, Lilian Wise, Margaret Windeyer and many others.

Amid such loss and isolation, Scott pronounced in various ways on the significance of her own public career. In the *Sydney Morning Herald* interview in 1920, when asked about the great and most rewarding moments of her work, Scott quoted from Millicent Fawcett's letter of congratulation on the Women's Franchise Act: 'Your name is very well known and much honoured here and I often make quotations from your letters and speeches.'[8] Scott also said: 'People think I am opposed to men but I am not really. I think women are much more subtle; men are more easily summed up. I look upon men as children of a larger growth.' This was a favourite Scott representation of men.

She continued to remark on her family in such interviews: 'It is not always a happy thing to be in advance of your time. It has always been my fate to differ from my dearly beloved relatives, but I seem to have been destined to blaze a trail.' A later interview extended this point: 'I came from a very conservative family. None of them cared at all for suffrage. But I simply had to take it up and shock them and vex them — although I loved them very much.'[9] A committee was established under the presidency of Sir Charles Mackellar to raise funds for a memorial to Scott's thirty years of public service. The committee consisted of Maybanke Anderson, the photographer, Nina Murdoch, Hugh Dixson, Judge Docker, May Matthews, Dr Mary Booth, Bertram Stevens, Florence Wearne, Judge Rolin, Mrs McCallum and Lady McMillen. The *Daily Telegraph* reported in March 1921 that the committee resolved to take up a subscription to have Scott's portrait painted by the celebrated artist, Sir John Longstaff, perhaps most acclaimed for his 1902 portrait of Henry Lawson.

Scott's retirement was sufficiently newsworthy for the *Sydney Morning Herald* to publish a story on the forthcoming occasion a week beforehand. It would be a luncheon in her honour sponsored by the Feminist Club, presided over by the parliamentary hopeful, Millicent Preston Stanley, at Farmers' department store auditorium. There would be 110 guests. The *Herald* observed how fitting it was that the Feminist Club should host the event: 'that body of women which owes its very existence to the pioneer work done by her [Scott] for woman suffrage.' The menu was suitably splendid: '*Sardines et olives, Crème de Tomates, Filet de Squire, Sauce Colbert, Cotelette d' Agneau aux Primeures, Crème Venecienne, Café Noir.*'[10]

On the day, Scott was presented with a sum of money and the announcement of the commissioning of her portrait. Rather than accepting the money for herself, she declared that she would bequeath it to the University of Sydney Faculty of Law to establish the Rose Scott Prize in International Law. It would be worth £50 and would be open to women undergraduates.[11] She gave a much-remembered retirement speech. Recounting the tale of the 7-year-old Rose Scott pacing the garden enraged at *The Taming of the Shrew*, she attempted to explain how she had become interested in 'the cause of women and children'. Then she re-stated her agenda of still-to-be-secured laws in the interests of women. This was pointed in the context. Scott was irritated by Preston Stanley's decision, as the first woman political candidate in New South Wales history, to stand not as a feminist independent, but as a candidate for the National Party. There was so much to do, Scott declared, yet women, with their citizenship, had done so little:

> We have not yet elected women to Parliament or Municipal Councils. The economic independence of married women is a dead letter. Education with its horrible system of home lessons and mental overwork still exists. Cremation, so important and so necessary, exists in almost all countries but New South Wales. Western Australia is the only *state* where women can go into the Upper House . . . [I]f I might presume to offer any advice, it would be best you avoid classes and Party politics and the factions and squabbles of men. These things limit our outlook and power for good . . . In public work, never descend to personal abuse of the opposite side. To study the arguments of our opponents is a means of power. Be sure of your facts and do not forget that every cause demands patience, self-sacrifice and eternal vigilance. Be passionately in earnest and loyal to your womanhood and to your sex and in the end you will certainly win.[12]

On this occasion Scott still had not fully recovered from her fall, while her chronic respiratory illnesses recurred and worsened in winter. Her friend William Cooper regretted her inability to visit 'the more particularly on account of the disability. I hope it will not be long before you are over your present trouble and able to get out again; not that anyone expects you to take your old place in the public life of the city, but at least to encourage others for another few years.'[13] By September 1921 she had recovered sufficiently for the portrait painting to begin, and a celebration was held to mark the event. But even this could not be fully enjoyed by Scott, as she explained to Florence Wearne, who replied: 'I was so pained that you did not hear everything that was said . . . I am sorry to put you to so much trouble and that the men mishandled the talking.'[14] In November Louisa MacDonald wrote from abroad, having heard belatedly about Scott's accident, and sympathising: 'that sort of thing, even if the bad effects apparently pass, is so apt to leave unpleasant reminders of itself in rheumatic pains.'[15]

Meanwhile, Scott's deafness was accelerating, and she complained bitterly about its effects. In May 1921, a friend, Charles Hoening, offered her advice on ways she might cope:

> After your 30 years of incessant work the cessation thereof must cause you to feel a void; the more so if increasing deafness causes your friends first to shorten their visits, then to call less often. Now you might readily fill your time by taking up press work in the line of building out your achievements. You have made yourself a name that will induce either newspaper editors to publish and pay for columns or the book trade to publish books from your hand and this, even if you should become stone deaf would give you as much zest as your committee work and your parleys with ministers hitherto did.[16]

Scott did not take his advice. Perhaps the photographs of her wearing spectacles at this stage indicate that her eyes would not have permitted extensive writing work. It is also possible that a lifelong defensiveness about higher education rendered her less able to write and publish with confidence in an inter-war context in which most of the younger generations of politically active women were university educated.

Despite physical deterioration, and difficulties of adjustment, Scott was thrilled about the portrait. She greatly enjoyed her meetings with Longstaff in the process, later recalling that when she first visited his studio in spring 1921 she had been very ill:

> Then came summer, with its glorious sunshine, bluebirds and dragonflies, and I most aggravatingly became ten years younger! At any rate he painted a Rose Scott that cannot make speeches or argue upon every subject in Heaven or earth — silence being an excellent gift in a woman — and *this* Rose Scott, being a restless being, found it very hard to sit still — and so she moved the only thing she could move, and that was her tongue.[17]

Longstaff also came to Lynton for sittings. Annie Rose Scott Cowen recalled that she was staying there on three occasions when Longstaff had lunch with the household while painting her aunt's portrait:

> I remember that he appreciated most warmly the excellent meals he has [sic] at Lynton and compared them ruefully with the chop and milk pudding that Dame Nellie Melba whose picture he was also painting gave him. My cousin Rose Windon and I went to his studio once to see Auntie's picture, and I was disappointed in it; when I said so he explained that he wanted to paint her as she must have looked in her middle age when she was in the midst of her activism.[18]

The portrait, of a white-haired woman in elegant black dress, attracted considerable publicity when in progress, as well as upon its completion. It dramatised the visual collision between former ideals of femininity and the much discussed 'modern woman'. Women activists of the early 1920s frequently commented on the so-called vices of the flapper — especially the spectacle of women in short skirts, plunging necklines and shingled hair, dancing, drinking and smoking in public. At that moment of publicity for Longstaff's in-progress portrait of the woman famous for her antique objections to mixed-sex bathing, Scott was an obvious interviewee on 'the modern woman'. The newspapers delighted in her views, such as those reported in the *Evening News* in November 1921:

> If girls and women here had always worn the present day garments we would not feel so shocked. Now the old forget to grow old gracefully and the young grow bold and paint and powder too frequently transform lovely complexions . . . into the lowest grade of amateur theatricals.[19]

Scott's friend, Mrs Vickery, wrote from London assuring her that women's fashions were as bad there, in fact 'positively indecent'. At her hotel she saw a woman with 'simply a band around the waist only just hiding the nipples of her breast, her back absolutely bare, her short dress slit up to show her bejewelled garters'.[20] Scott concurred with this condemnation in the midst of publicity for her portrait. She deplored bobbed hair and smoking, while girls 'who go in for surfing are the limit'. The suggestion that women might play football was appalling. Sunbathing was as repulsive: 'Red necks, blistered noses and brown arms are very ugly and unattractive.' It seemed that the modern woman was in relentless pursuit of the attention of the other sex: 'some of our girls dress like nightmares. They stalk down the street like gaily bedecked barber poles.'[21] What did Scott advocate as an alternative 'look' for the modern woman? Primarily, 'woman' had to engender respect, especially from men, not assume the identity of a vulgar, gaudy, empty-headed plaything. A plain, elegant frock, a simple rope of pearls as adornment, and the hair drawn back arranged in a knot to grace the neck — this was womanly beauty. It was gone — gone with the ashes of the First World War.

Clothes are far from a trivial matter and Scott's alarm should be placed in the context of the history of dress and its cultural meaning. Women's hair had been long for 500 years, while in European fashion the knees, even the ankles, had never been publicly visible. Thus the changes of the 1920s were alarming, even revolutionary, their meaning unclear and subject to intense debate even to the present. As fundamental markers of gender and, for women, of conjugal status and sexual morality, throughout Scott's life, dress codes were important. The 'flapper' look in dress has been described as 'democratic', dissolving boundaries between types of women in most unsettling ways. It has been conventional to see 1920s dress as 'emancipated', 'fast' and, in the display of more of the limbs, as sexually alluring. This interpretation may be flawed by an uncritical deployment of modern libertarian criteria. An important part of outrage about the flapper dress was its obscuring of womanly attractions. The flattening of the breasts, dropped waists, straight lines and short hair suggested androgyny, a rejection of the conventional spectacle of femininity and the sexual allure hitherto highlighted in small, tight waists, which emphasised breasts and hips. The flapper image could be seen as a refusal to be marked as maternal — a rejection of sexual difference and an assertion of egalitarianism.

Since feminists like Scott had struggled so hard against the argument that citizenship would 'unsex' women, a strong reaction against the flapper image is at least understandable. The complexities and confusions as to what was at issue in Scott's reactions are clear in another newspaper interview from the period entitled 'Divine Discontent — Rationalism in Clothing'. The interviewer related a cheeky exchange in which he put it to Scott that, with her radical views on women and her support for equal rights, she should support what he dubbed the 'rationalism' of the flapper's attire. He accused her of being old-fashioned and inconsistent. Her response was that the flapper look was extremely exaggerated rationalism, holding women up for ridicule and disrespect. Her interviewer, and most men of the early 1920s, did not necessarily see flapper dress as 'sexy', though it did lead to the eroticisation of the legs — the 'birth of the leg man' as United States historian Kenneth Yellis puts it.[22] Yet, Scott clearly saw the move to admit male spectators to mixed-sex surf-bathing, and the flapper, her mores and mode of life, as all of a piece. Instead of her fellow women of younger generations seeking to curb the animal in man they sought to heighten it and, as well, the animal in woman. This was the flapper's version of equality. It was antithetical to her sense of the political rationale for feminism. For her, the androgynous egalitarian, animal woman, was not radical and emancipating: rather, she aided women's degradation.

In early 1922, Scott regained sufficient mobility to visit Longstaff for portrait sittings and to resume certain public roles, including newspaper interviews. In February 1922, Sir Benjamin Fuller wrote asking her to speak at a forthcoming election campaign meeting since 'you have been the foremost fighter for women in this state . . . you must feel very disappointed at their present status'. His appeal was astute, touching exactly her need for recognition, her continuing preoccupations with the wrongs suffered by women and the failure of younger women to redress them. No doubt in considerable physical discomfort, she mounted the platform in March 1922 and endorsed this candidate, insofar as he advocated a better deal for women.

Scott raised the issue of men's carnal knowledge of mentally-handicapped women: 'There is a great deal said about motherhood but nothing about right motherhood — and the protection of those poor imbecile girls who are mothers over and over again.' Finally, this was remedied in the Crimes (Amendment) Act of 1924, which provided penalties of up to five years' imprisonment for men who had carnal knowledge of 'idiots', though as Emily Barnett of the Women's League of New South Wales wrote in Bessie Rischbieth's Perth newspaper, *The Dawn*, the act 'is full of flaws and loopholes whereby a man can evade punishment'. In the speech, Scott also commended Fuller's support for women's right to sit on juries, as they did in England, the United States and other countries, as well as his advocacy of equal pay for equal work. 'This is important, for women are human beings first and creatures of sex afterwards. Why should their sex interfere with justice? It is an absurd fiction that men only have others dependent upon them and so need more money.' Since her rationale for speaking at all was Fuller's standing as an independent candidate, Scott did not let the occasion pass without reference to the folly of party politics: 'I have often seen men going into Parliament with good intentions and enthusiasm and the Spider of Party Politics winds them round and round with his web till they become like a fly, mere mummies and are without conscience of individuality.'[23]

The fact that Scott gave this speech may signal an inability to let go of public life, as well as a more longstanding distrust of her fellow women. Perhaps there was nobody she could send in her place in March 1922, because nobody shared views that had become increasingly singular. Historically, she had not delegated, but by 1922, perhaps she could not. Giving the speech for Fuller may equally well have been part of her resistance to isolation and alienation.

Longstaff's portrait of Scott was unveiled at the Soldiers' Club on 22 September 1922. Lady Foster, the Governor's wife, presided, and Scott gave a brief speech. She noted humorously that: 'My nephew, my chum since babyhood, regrets as much as I do his absence in Melbourne, but writes with his usual humour that he hopes I will make a tactful speech and begs people not to think I am really as bad as I am painted.' She spoke of how the last few years 'have brought many ruins. But my own case . . . the beautiful ivy of friendship covers many ruins.' She concluded with comments on the importance of friendship in all areas of life. Some of these comments signalled her loneliness and isolation. She attempted to resist. In a letter in October 1922 to Dowell OReilly, the friend who had been such a vocal supporter of woman suffrage in the 1890s, she wrote:

> I saw such a nice glimpse of you and Mrs O'Reilly at the picture presentation. I had to go out of the room and sit by myself for I was so hoarse, having a touch of bronchitis that I knew I would not be able to speak at all if I did not keep quiet. I wonder if you and Mrs O'Reilly would come next Friday evening? I fear to ask for it — such a long way — but if it was fine. How I would like to see you both. Mr Longstaff will be here, you may like to meet him — and Judge and Mrs Rolin — who are coming. I am 75 today so you see I cannot look forward to many such happy reunions with dear friends.[24]

Scott's resistance to misfortune was not confined to her social life. When her father's fortunes had faltered, he had embraced a new career and became a magistrate. Whether in response to Scott's own lobbying, or at the suggestion of others, she allowed herself to be nominated to the position of honorary magistrate by H.V. Jacques, MLA, in October 1922. This would have been an ironic second public career for her, in view of its paternal association, and was embraced after only eighteen months of formal retirement. Her acceptance may mark her desperation at being cut off from the world, but it also reveals a disavowal of the disability her deafness would be in such a post.

It was not to be. The New South Wales chief secretary informed Jacques (Scott's nominator) that she was ineligible:

> I desire to say that the age of nominee (75 years) precludes her appointment. It has been laid down that nominees who have entered upon their 60th year shall be ineligible for the position of Honorary Magistrate . . . it cannot but be regretted that it should stand in the way of the appointment of one of Miss Scott's unqualified standing in the community.[25]

Scott's papers contain no direct references to her reaction to this outcome. It seems that she became seriously ill, however, around or soon after this rebuff. Her letters in this period were written in pencil from her bed. On 28 December 1922 she wrote to a friend, Dr Crossle:

> I have been ill with a bad foot for 4 weeks but it is getting on well now and I am able to get out of bed and go into the drawing room and today I am actually writing at a table with ink. Pencils are all so blunt now so much I had to manage to write with them lying in bed . . . I ought to be and am very grateful to be out of danger and getting on so well. I still have a nurse and Dr C. Bowker comes now only every second day. I supposed agonies of pain but that is gone now. I had a great longing at one time that the crematorium should be in working order.

Scott then offered Crossle her reminiscences of a meeting she had had some years before with Norman Lindsay, the Australian artist whose Rabelaisian watercolour paintings of erotically-posed nude women made him famous. On his subject matter, Scott ventured:

> I thought he was then not a bit conceited and very interesting . . . with all his genius . . . He has seemed to me to be on that path ever since, and to be morbid and repeating himself as if he were a sex maniac. His women have no souls, only bodies . . . I feel sad whenever I think of him, for he certainly was lovable — but even in his writings, which have not the genius of his art, he is lamentably decadent, as well as positive he is right . . . To me his women are degrading. Sex dominates his pictures . . . I think AF would be rather shocked at Norman Lindsay's mania, for constant repetition becomes a mania. I pray you do not be deceived by his genius or

his nice personality. I am a woman, with a lot of the 6th sense and I think I can judge fairly.[26]

Scott's letter writing and general desire to intervene was not confined to her friends. In 1922 a memorial for the late Henry Lawson was launched and one of its supporters, in a letter to the *Sydney Morning Herald*, made a slighting reference to Lawson's wife's less than full support for her genius husband. Scott sent him a fierce reply:

> Married at 17, a young woman, sick and ill with two children to support will have to do all she can for these children. Some women go under — others like Mrs Lawson set to work and worked and slaved to support two children who love her most dearly. From these children I know that they were always taught to love their father, to love his work, to pity his weakness . . . Are you aware what happened when H. Lawson was ill at the Coast Hospital? I could tell you many things if I saw you and Mrs Lockley. I like to prove all things. I knew the poet, his mother also and I could tell you much more — Do you remember that Lawson had a pension — what became of it?

A newspaper report on Scott in 1921 mentioned that Jim and Bertha Lawson, the poet's children, still visited Scott; and their mother's book of 1949 makes favourable reference to Scott, the woman who supported them through the hard years of Lawson's alcoholism.

It must have been an eerie and rather macabre confrontation with death for Scott, Franklin and others who had been friends with the Lawsons and familiar with their sufferings, to live to see memorial statues and pomp and ceremony in his honour. As Franklin wrote to Scott in 1924 in her matter-of-fact manner, upon returning to Australia for a visit:

> Poor old Lawson, he had great gifts and in a less efficient community might not have drunk himself into years of imbecility and a premature grave . . . Do you ever see Mrs Hy Lawson now? I shd so much like to see her again if she is anywhere at hand. It seems a gruesome thing to stick up a hideous effigy of Lawson now that he is dead.[27]

Scott's retirement, then, to a significant degree, was forced upon her, rather than being a stage in the life cycle she desired or embraced with enthusiasm. She found it difficult to refrain from public debate and comment, even though her capacity and rationale for doing so had demonstrably diminished. Whereas the cause of women and her name were once inextricably linked, her avid daily reading and clipping of the newspapers made perfectly clear that the significant and diversifying inter-war women's movement was proceeding without her. A major task of her retirement years was learning to deal with this intelligently and constructively.

'LOYAL ALWAYS TO YOUR . . . SEX'

Scott's worst reading of developments in the women's movement was that it had been 'hijacked' or detoured by the values and agendas of 'the modern woman', of whom she was so publicly critical. Despite the generous newspaper claim that she adored young people and sympathised widely with their aspirations, she found it difficult to accord with the university-educated young flappers of the Feminist Club. Scott hovered inconsistently between a portrayal of them on the one hand as reckless, scandalous, immoral libertarians, who sexualised womanhood and thereby 'sold out' their feminist heritage, allowing men to degrade women even further; and on the other, a depiction of them as desexualising woman or repudiating the feminine, denying all difference between the sexes, and thus, it seemed to Scott, any basis for feminist politics.

The inconsistencies and tensions in Scott's depictions of modern feminists of the 1920s have been central to feminist theory throughout its history. The tension between equality and difference, de-gendering and sexual specificity, within feminist philosophy and rhetoric has received sustained and insightful analysis by contemporary feminist scholars. Many have attempted to devise strategies whereby feminist theory might overcome the tendency towards unhelpful 'either/or' dualisms in grappling with these tensions. Recognition that both ends of the spectrum — de-gendering and sexual specificity — constitute recognisable feminism, leads current work to propose the use of a notion of 'continuum' and related metaphors to represent the dilemmas facing feminism.[28]

Such analytical literature was not available to Scott in her last years. So she struggled with her incomprehension of and tendency to judge adversely the new generation of feminists. One new feminist friendship facilitated this process. Scott took an increasing interest in developments in Western Australia, and especially in Bessie Rischbieth. On Rischbieth's return from the ICW conference in Europe in 1922, she met with Scott in Sydney before returning to Perth. Shortly after, Scott wrote warmly to her:

> I hope you had a happy return to Perth and all your labours. I have often thought of you, and was so very, very glad to meet you and have even that brief chat. But you did not seem like a stranger to me, so much had we in common. With most cordial greetings and remembrance.[29]

The instant trust and identification she felt for Rischbieth is interesting in the light of the development of Australian feminism in the 1920s. A passing of Scott's baton took place, and thereafter she really did retire from the women's movement.

Scott's alienation from other feminists in the early 1920s had personal and physical, as well as political, causes. Events had caused her to revise her own feminist vision, while younger feminists themselves revised the programmes of the early-twentieth-century women's organisations created by Scott and her contemporaries. From 1910 new associations of women proliferated and specialised. By the 1920s they held the political space. In New South Wales, Scott's earlier programme had begun to reveal the co-existence of struggles around equality and women's specificity. The tensions between these objectives and the different women they could serve had been symbolised by the emergence of the Feminist Club in 1914, comprised of university-educated and professional women, on the one hand, and the Housewives' Association, on the other, dedicated to the needs of the majority of adult women who were or would be wives and mothers. These two organisations were indications of the direction women's politics would take in the inter-war period.

Despite the diversity and specificity of inter-war organisations, the principal study of them, undertaken by Meredith Foley, demonstrates that they had remarkable commonalities of goals and perspectives. They shared a discursive space and negotiated common cultural conditions of possibility. Reactions to the Russian Revolution and policies on communism (often formed on the basis of the extreme propaganda that saturated official agencies), unionism, strikes, the Depression, and unemployment loomed prominently on the agendas of inter-war women's (and all other political) organisations. Foley maintains that class has been the principal axis of analysis in the work of most historians of the inter-war women's movement. The notion that feminism in Australia died after the war, or after the vote was gained in Britain and the United States, can only persist in the absence of serious analysis of inter-war feminism — politics organised to challenge existing power relations based on sex.

Amid the labyrinthine organisational history of the inter-war women's movement, Foley identifies some core preoccupations underlying feminist activities. One major concern was preventing the recruitment of young working women into prostitution, as well as challenging the belief that men could not help their demand for prostitutes. Another major concern was working women. Rather than the former focus on legal constraint, interwar women's organisations undertook welfare work among young working women, especially those under the age of consent. This involved supervision of their leisure activities, accommodation and skills training, to help these women cope with workplace tedium and low rates of pay. From Scott's campaign for an age of consent raised to 16, inter-war feminists sought a raised school-leaving age of 16, aimed at much the same problem. The labour movement opposed this, seeing it as a threat to the living wage formula of support for wife and two children under 14, by placing the burden of two more years of dependency of sons and daughters on the breadwinner. Feminists also sought factory and shopfloor supervision and education in sex hygiene in schools, especially to deter young men from seducing girls.

A further area of concern was the economic independence of wives and the recognition of the work and services women contributed to the community as wives and mothers. The working conditions of wives and mothers urgently needed reform. This cluster of concerns led to work on many fronts in the changed circumstances of inter-war Australia. There were also other demands, including wages for housework or a legally guaranteed portion of the husband's wage for the wife, child endowment, maternity hospitals, a university chair in obstetrics, domestic science, and legal reforms to discriminations against married women as paid workers and as legal guardians of their children. At a cultural level, the women's movement sought to have the wife and mother recognised as an expert, a professional and scientific manager, not a secluded, unskilled drudge; and on the basis of her skills and professional contribution, the wife and mother had to be a recognised force in politics and public policy — through women candidates representing their interests.

Accordingly, the non-party ideal, so important to Scott, remained a central belief of large sections of the inter-war women's movement, despite the significant re-casting of its wider political framework. Some organisations did have party affiliations or associations, but the official and avowed stance of most was non-party. Paradoxically, the non-party stance became more viable in the inter-war era than it had been in the years immediately after federation, despite Scott's gloom. The novelty of the party system was eroding, and the eclipsing of feminist issues by the mainstream electoral parties was well demonstrated to many women's movement leaders. In the engagement between feminism and other politics, the contest had moved onto a level both more global and more abstract — that between capitalism, on the one hand, and communism, on the other. Yet such contest meant little in the struggle for things such as more funded maternity hospital beds. When the issues required the lobbying of state governments, the non-party stance proved most practical.

The non-party stance continued to be represented as anti-Labor, as it had been in Scott's day, and the umbrella nature of organisations such as the NCW lent itself to members, and often officeholders, from wealthy and privileged backgrounds. Foley observes, however, that this did not prevent labour-movement friends of Scott, such as May Matthews, from holding office and serving the NCW for several decades. Though it is clear that by the 1930s non-party feminist organisations in New South Wales were plunged into various crises, most of these resulted from causes extrinsic to their feminism and the problem of the position of women relative to that of men.

Adherents of inter-war feminism confronted a range of difficult choices in responding to challenges of the era. Just as the 1914–18 war constituted an emergency that readily eclipsed feminist advocacy, so the 1930s Depression threatened to upstage feminist demands. It was all very well for women to experiment with new activities, even paid work, in good times; but in a situation of mass unemployment, it was claimed that the needs of men must come first. Women were accused of taking men's jobs despite the reality of a profoundly sex-segmented organisation of labour and industry in Australia. The feminist rhetoric then deployed around the campaign for equal pay for equal work betrayed a certain defensiveness in response to the unfounded allegation that women were the cause of men's unemployment. Some of the divisions within the women's movement were, understandably enough, divisions concerning the best response to such allegations. While some women abandoned feminist agendas for the duration of the emergency, others stood firm, resenting the scapegoating of women and the masculinism entailed in the mass exhortation of Australian women to stand by their men in an unaltered sexual status quo.[30]

Significant challenges to feminist thought and rhetoric were also presented at the level of cultural politics. The inter-war debates and popularisation of scientific and secular approaches to sexuality presented particular problems for earlier negative feminist views of male sexuality and the subsuming of women's sexuality to maternity and other more spiritual forms of relationship. Meanwhile, discussion of psychoanalytic concepts such as repression, hysteria and neurosis emerged with the problem of shell-shocked, psychologically disturbed veterans of the war.[31] Often the full ramifications of veterans' problems did not become clear until their marriage, parenthood or marital estrangement in the later 1920s. The view that the repression or distortion of 'sexual urges' could be psychologically dangerous received wide publicity with the advent of terms like 'sex maniac', 'sex pervert' and 'psychopath', used to classify new forms of sex crimes and serial slayings of women during these years. Despite the lack of evidence that women resorted to such criminal acts, they were held to be in as much danger as men if they failed to develop healthy, happy sexual lives. Indeed, they were said to face a lurking menace equivalent to the problem of impotence in men — frigidity.

Through the work of numerous sexologists addressing the specific problems of frigidity and the unhappy marital sex relations attested to by rising divorce figures, a number of findings with implications for sexual ethics were canvassed. One was that women's fear of pregnancy when they were not yet ready for children, or when they already had enough children, was a major cause of this 'frigidity' condition. If earlier feminists had advocated voluntary motherhood in the form of conjugal continence — men's self-restraint — sexologists sought a solution that did not risk the repression of supposedly innate sexual urges. The currency of sexology, then, became historically synonymous with an increasingly official endorsement of artificial forms of birth control.

To a considerable degree many inter-war feminists took such changes 'in their stride' and were as persuaded of their wisdom as were other participants in political culture. Historian, Sheila Jeffreys, contends that psychoanalytically based sexology of the 1920s undermined feminist attempts to transform sexual practices by corroding their rationale and their plausibility. In the longer term this is likely. The first sexologists' representations of irrepressible sexual urges, augmented by supporting work of Kinsey in the post-war period, certainly weakened the purchase of feminist claims that men's demand for prostitution and other sexual services was cultural, contingent and capable of being discouraged or reformed. At one extreme, some legacies of pioneer sexological arguments were cultural discourses in which prostitutes were represented as happy nymphomaniacs who chose this work because they derived sexual pleasure from it; and girls of 11, 12, 13, and 14 depicted as suffering from sexual repression by the antiquated notion of an age of consent.[32]

In the short term, however, the effects of these changed cultural conditions were less even and logically reconciled. Prominent feminists of the 1920s and 1930s simultaneously endorsed birth control in the interests of happier marital sexual relations, and yet condemned men's continuing demand for prostitution and carnal knowledge of schoolgirls, apparently without perceiving a contradiction. The woman whom Scott almost endorsed as her successor was such a feminist and it is tempting to think that had Scott lived on, she may have accommodated her arguments to these changes, just as she had to the changes that confronted her in earlier decades.

Bessie Rischbieth emerged as one of the most important Australian feminists of the inter-war period. She immersed herself in the key campaigns of the women's movement, most classifiable as egalitarian in character. These included campaigns for equal pay for equal work, equal guardianship rights for mothers, equal rights for wives in domicile and related citizen rights. She supported women's full participation in public life, especially in politics, since life 'rests on a two sex basis, and politics should not be kept on a one sex basis'. From 1920, she edited a feminist newspaper, *The Dawn*, its title an effective tribute to that edited by Louisa Lawson in Sydney and last published in 1904. Increasingly, Rischbieth attempted to ensure its national distribution.

The Dawn contained international as well as interstate news of women's movement activities and achievements. The election of Lady Astor to the English House of Commons was hailed as the infusion of 'Mother Spirit' into politics. The admission of Australia's first woman barrister, Ada Emily Evans, to the full court of New South Wales, was applauded in August 1921, as was the appointment of the first Australian woman gynaecologist, Dr Mildred George, to a Perth public hospital in 1921. Rischbieth took advantage of the Women's Legal Status Act and became one of the first cohorts of women justices of the peace. The Women Justices' Association of New South Wales was founded in 1923; its counterparts in other states were also founded during the 1920s.

Reports were included in *The Dawn* on the controversy over venereal diseases legislation, the continuing struggle for the suffrage cause in South Africa, the World Conference on the Traffic in Women and Children, the campaign for women's admission to the clergy, family endowment, widows' pensions, the unveiling of a statue in honour of Emmeline Pankhurst, and the music composed and played by Dame Ethel Smyth. Congratulations were offered to Dame Millicent Fawcett in the New Year's Honour conferred on her in 1923, as well as protest at the return of long skirts in the late 1920s. Divorce law reform, the intrepid air-woman Amy Johnson, Vida Goldstein's criticisms of Australian women's insularity upon her return in 1936, incomes for wives, discrimination against married women workers in the Great Depression, high maternity mortality rates in Australia, sex education, women jurors, censorship, women on radio, contraception, eugenics, international feminism, and women's conferences of the League of Nations were all topics discussed in *The Dawn*.

One of Rischbieth's fundamental objectives was to achieve a unified, federated organisation for Australian feminist activity. Her favourite way of putting this, recalled by Irene Greenwood, was her call for 'An all Australian outlook and international understanding'. In much of her writing for *The Dawn* she stressed the solidarity of women and the internationalism of feminism. An article of 1921, called 'Women's Political Attitude — The Value of a Non-Party Basis of Action', would have soothed the disappointment of the retiring Scott:

> We firmly believe that women in Parliament will mean that a new value and meaning will be given to the science of economics . . . woman places commerce second and human happiness and human health and efficiency — the only real wealth first . . . It is this very human basis of citizenship that is uniting women the world over. They are fast learning to realise that their common interests as women matter more than their differences, that what unites them goes deeper than what separates. They are pioneers in helping to establish a new conception of real values and to do this it is imperative that they leave behind them the worn out party shibboleths and seek to create new channels whereby human welfare shall play the first and great part in our social system . . . The principal measures which have received attention from these women members of parliament are all questions affecting home life such as housing, health, education, unemployment and food supplies . . . Australian women . . . have been too long separated by political differences and have been drawn hither and thither by changing opinions and party prejudices.[33]

Contact with Rischbieth's work, and the tendency in inter-war feminism that she represented, greatly reassured Scott. All was not lost. She could recognise an adaptation of her own values and strategies in this work. Probably less obvious to her was the way that familiarity with the work of Rischbieth and other feminists of the time was gradually changing Scott's own feminist understandings to ones more in accord with changed conditions. In coming to terms with inter-war feminism, Scott came to a kind of resolution about the significance of her own feminist career. One effect of changed directions and her increased marginality was that Scott could now move on from her long and rather unproductive focus on the failure of her original vision of the difference the inclusion of women should and could make to the body politic. Scott's questions and the anguish they had caused her were not the pressing questions of inter-war feminism. Ironically, this set her free. It was possible to begin a new kind of understanding of feminism and its changing context; and this coming to terms with feminism corresponded with a more general coming to terms with the end of her life.

COMING TO TERMS

Scott made her final will on 6 June 1922. Her total estate was then estimated at £7157 18s 11d, and her nominated trustees were her nephew, Nene Scott Wallace of Paddington, her niece, Rose Windon of Petersham, and Richard Yeomans, a solicitor. Her will is a remarkable document, setting out a detailed web of relationships between valued objects and valued friends and relatives. To her nephew's wife, Edna, 'my large gold and white vase'. To her niece, the gold chain with the pearl cross, the opal ring belonging to her brother, George, 'also my painting 'Desert Pea' by Miss Crieth'. Other nieces, nephews and sisters-in-law received personalised bequests of jewellery, ornaments, watercolour paintings and furnishings, as did her godchildren in Crookwell and Brisbane. Among many friends mentioned, to Miles Franklin 'my opal and diamond ring', to May Matthews 'my large silver Irish brooch with shamrocks', to Violet Wynne 'the spray of silver shamrocks', to Lydia Rolin 'a gold amethyst brooch with her mother's hair in it' and a painting of 'Wild Violets' by Mrs Halligan, and to Lydia Marks 'my gold and greenstone brooch'. To Twilight House, the Boys' Fire Brigade, Crown Street Women's Hospital and the Peace Society of New South Wales she left £10 each. To her long-time housekeeper, Bridget Conneally, she left £50, and to her housemaid, Gladys Jones, £20. Her final wish was this: 'I wish my body to be cremated and the ashes thrown into the sea or scattered in the bush for I desire no monument and no grave.'

Twice before she died Scott changed her will. In a codicil dated 8 May 1923 she revoked the bequest to her housekeeper and maid and directed £10 each to be left to Jim and Bertha Lawson, 'the poet's children'. The reasons for these changes remain unclear, but in another codicil of March 1925, just before her death, she reinstated the £50 for Bridget Conneally, and also left £50 to Dr Cedric Bowker, family friend and the signatory to her death certificate, who treated her in her last days.[34] Franklin noted in her 1938 memoir of Scott that her 'last days made demands upon her courage that medical science was powerless to avert and which the loving care of her nephew H.H.S. Wallace and her niece Rose Scott Windon and many faithful friends could do little to soften'.[35]

Scott's friend, Dowell O'Reilly, died in November 1923 and to his wife, Marie, Scott wrote, 'I was indeed grieved to see that you had lost dear Dowell — I did not know he was ill — I have been ill nearly the whole year myself. Please accept the love and sympathy of your sincere friend, Rose Scott.' Marie O'Reilly wrote back an account of Dowell's death and her grief. Scott replied with great kindness and in terms that reflect her own state of mind:

> It was good of you to write and tell me about it — yes I was shocked but my chief feeling was for you and his children . . . Yes dear friend it must indeed be a blank in your life, but thank God he had you for a time . . . One asks why should so talented and dear a soul be taken and others left who may really want to depart. There is so much mystery.

A year later, in December 1924, she wrote again to Marie O'Reilly to thank her for sending a photograph of Dowell:

> I have been thinking about you and Dowell . . . but alas I am not always able to sit at the table and write and the evenings I could do so people came and then I was too tired . . . I never had a photograph of him, and it is a great pleasure to have that . . . I have been ill and am an invalid, for I've never been outside the gate for nearly all the year — I am a bit better but there is, alas no summer.

By February 1925 Scott was no longer able to sit up and write letters — a pencilled note thanked Marie O'Reilly for a recent letter: 'I am sorry I am very ill and have a nurse now so forgive a scrawl, much love and good wishes'.[36] As Scott had always been a prolific letter writer, this must have been one of the worst aspects of the process of dying for her, but she tried to make the best of it. A scrawled pencil note of 23 March 1925 to Dr Crossle reported that 'Books are my tonics. I am very lucky that I have so many and have still eyes that do not wear out . . . I have been so very ill for some time — but am a bit better now though weak.'[37] Three days later Sir John Longstaff wrote her his last letter:

> Assured by the doctors that recovery from your illness is impossible you yet face the situation calmly and bravely and so far forget yourself as to write me a letter full of general interest with only the smallest reference to your condition. Dearest friend, if I am not to have speech with you again, know that I am thinking of you and that the memory of you will always be with me. I am glad you have got Mrs Rolin and Mrs Aberden with you, both dear women, with much love . . . [38]

Scott died at 8.45 p.m. on 20 April 1925 at her home. The death certificate records the cause of death as 'cancer of the body of the uterus'. Nene
Scott Wallace responded to a prompt condolence from Bertha Lawson with
the report that: 'Her end was quite peaceful I am happy to say but why she
should have had to endure so much suffering in the last 6 months
Heaven alone knows. I can scarcely realise yet that she is really gone.'[39]
Scott's body was cremated at the Rookwood crematorium on 26 August
1925 and was the eighteenth cremation ever carried out in New South
Wales. The ashes are recorded as having been returned to her nephew Mr
Wallace at her home on 11 November 1932, though Franklin wrote
that they 'went back to her beloved bush'. Memorial tree no. 252 was
planted in the grounds of Rookwood and under it sits a simple gold plaque
mounted on stone 'In Remembrance of Rose Scott, Died 20 April 1925'.[40]

Upon the news of Scott's death , Rischbieth published an obituary
which concluded: 'she touched her generation as few have ever done and
left upon it a deathless impression.' Although Scott had not concurred
with Rischbieth's enthusiasm for the English suffragettes, and Emmeline
Pankhurst in particular, it is difficult to see anything but continuity
between the feminist programmes of Scott, born in 1847, and Rischbieth,
who died, still active in public life, in 1967. Like Scott, Rischbieth saw feminism in international terms, from the 1920s arguing that international issues
'have become the leading issues' and that the women's movement had a
vital place in 'social evolution'. In 1935, Rischbieth received the Order of
the British Empire, *The Dawn* observing that this was the first time such an
honour had been conferred for political and social work of a non-party character. Women generally received recognition only for strictly charitable work.
Rischbieth was then appointed alternative delegate to the League of
Nations and reported that she was 'delighted that the women's movement
had been officially recognised and that feminism once so despised and
ridiculed was now so highly honoured'.[41] Of course Rischbieth and Scott
confronted the different and distinct political and cultural dilemmas of their
eras, but the defining features of modern feminism — in particular the necessary tensions between equality and difference, individual and collective
sexed identity — were manifest in the preoccupations and work of both.
Yet the evidence has revealed that their precisely *feminist* agendas were both
pre-suffrage and post-suffrage. In Australia, feminism existed as a strand
of what Cott calls 'the nineteenth century woman movement', as well as
of the women's movement of the 1910s, 1920s and 1930s.

In Scott's final five years of life she confronted many things. Some were
personal versions of the general stages of ageing, disability and dying.
Formerly an almost compulsive communicator, she had to deal with the
increasing inability to write and speak with others. Deafness made her last
years literally silent. The progress of terminal illness made her invalid,
immobile. Scott's mid-1920s were still and quiet.

Yet she stressed that she still could see. Vision had always been the sense she most celebrated. Around her she could see 'the modern woman', the changing appearance of inter-war femininity, and changing codes of sexual conduct and sexual meanings. If she was quick to condemn initially, she certainly recognised them; and in the work of feminists whom she recognised in positive terms, like Bessie Rischbieth, she saw both continuities and changes in feminist issues and strategies. Though she had spent the decade of the war with disillusionment and the sense of the failure of her particular vision of how the world was to be changed in women's favour, retirement in the 1920s allowed her to see a continuing women's movement. She learned that she was not indispensable, but equally she could be confident that women of her generation had succeeded in some measure. A movement of women, bigger than they and their circles, continued, proliferated and innovated. For Scott this was a most significant revision. Perhaps her best achievement in retirement was that in some part she came to terms, however painfully, with difference and differences, and their salience for feminist politics. This meant giving up her own claims to represent 'women', her sex, singular.

Chapter 8

....

Rose Scott and Australian Feminism

She is a delightful chaletaine and in her day was a beautiful woman, whose black silk gowns and lace caps invest her with an old world charm. She adores young people and has wide sympathy with their aspirations; and while she has led the van in movements which are supposed to eliminate femininity of thought and feeling, she is the gentlest and most womanly of her sex.

The Freeman's Journal,
21 February 1921

I am a passionate Australian but at the same time a convinced internationalist.

Rose Scott,
Sydney Morning Herald,
28 December 1920

Miles Franklin, upon returning some documents to Nene Scott Wallace in 1937, remarked that they belonged with him, since it was to him that future biographers would come.[1] Despite her expectation, no book-length biography of Scott has yet been published in the more than half century since her death. This cannot be due to lack of data. Compared with her most significant feminist contemporaries, including Louisa Lawson, Mary Windeyer, Maybanke Anderson, Louisa MacDonald and Annie Golding, sources for a biography of Scott might be represented as rich indeed. At first sight then, the lack of serious biographers is puzzling.

A clue to the puzzle may reside in some of the representations of Scott that have prevailed since her death. For, while her work and its meaning have been little studied, she has been much mentioned and pervasively represented in various sources that still remain influential. Possibly the cumulative effect of these representations has been to deter the most likely biographers — feminists interested in the history of feminism.

The way Scott has come to be represented is a problem addressed here. But in addition, an evaluation of Scott's career illuminates the history of Australian feminism, and feminism in Anglophone countries more generally. Insofar as the character of representations of Scott may be an obstruction to serious evaluation, they warrant analysis, especially in terms of how, when and by whom they have been established. In this connection, Miles Franklin's involvement in the process of commemorating Scott in dialogue with Scott's relatives and friends, attains some significance. Franklin was required to bear witness in episodes of enquiry into Scott's life in the 1930s and 1950s. Yet for the reader of her letters and accounts, Franklin was also bearing witness to her own life, reflecting on changes of the inter-war and post-war periods, and expressing a degree of disillusionment and regret about the limited achievements of feminism. Such regret was reminiscent of Scott's later years. Franklin's posthumous angle on Scott's life is in itself a fascinating insight into the course of twentieth-century feminism in a period as yet too little documented.

Some revisions will be required to representations of Scott in particular, and understandings of the history of feminism of her period more generally, before feminists like Scott are likely to become subjects of serious biographical studies. A summary of the principal stages in the unfolding of her feminist career acts as a reminder of transnational developments in the history of feminist politics and culture. That career is a pertinent case study, against which a range of currently competing interpretations and readings can be judged.

REPRESENTING ROSE SCOTT

If representations of Rose Scott in printed media increased in the post-suffrage period, they escalated in the 1920s and after her death. These representations have taken several forms. The first were newspaper articles 'about Scott', including those with some element of interview with her, published during her lifetime.[2] A second form was the obituary, many published in 1925 and others at various anniversaries of her death.[3] A further significant form of representing Scott were biographical sketches and studies of feminist issues and campaigns involving discussion of her work or career, especially book chapters and manuscripts. Radio talks on her career by Miles Franklin and Stanford Thomas also belong in this category.[4] A fourth form was the exhibition commemorating Scott's career at the Dixson Library, Sydney, in 1985, sixty years after her death.[5] Finally, there were various family history and genealogical forays produced by Scott's relatives and other contemporaries.[6]

There is a surprising uniformity to many of these forms of representing Rose Scott, notwithstanding vast differences of interest and standpoint between their producers. Three elements deserve particular comment. First, they focus intensely on Scott's individual attributes, displaying a notable preoccupation with her marital status, her genteel class position, and her liberal political philosophy. Second, they tend to provide long and miscellaneous listings of the causes in which she worked. Third, great stress is placed on the people she knew.

The Dixson Gallery of the State Library of New South Wales opened an eight-month exhibition on the sixtieth anniversary of Scott's death in 1985 entitled 'Rose Scott: Remarkable Woman, Remarkable Friends'. The catalogue to the exhibition itself constitutes an assimilation of, and intervention into, representations of Rose Scott. It contained seventeen pages, and six subsections; yet Scott herself received only one page, feminist issues four pages, and her friends eight pages. The exhibition used photographs, paintings, relics, cartoons, newspaper articles and manuscripts from the collections used in the research for this book. With this allocation of topics and material, the issues and work of Scott's public career received half the attention that was devoted to material on famous friends. The issues selected for address were: woman suffrage, the WPEL, the NCW, 'The Age of Consent Bill', the Tailoresses' Union, children's courts, guardianship rights for mothers, Wattle Day, old age pensions, cremation and animal protection, early closing, women's swimming, women's education, and pacifism. Her public career was represented as having 'bloomed late', beginning with the struggle for womanhood suffrage. Scott then simply went on to espouse 'cause after cause'.[7] 'Tremendous vitality was evident', the catalogue informed the viewers, in the sheer range and diversity of her involvement in social reforms. These occasioned much of the interaction with many of her friends, the central focus of the exhibition. Of the friends mentioned, eleven were men and eight women.

Taken as a whole this is a problematic and misleading representation of Scott's life, and its significance for the history of feminism and for changing historical options for Australian women. The exhibition viewer's attention is not drawn to Scott's voluminous private writing, speeches and letters on sexual relations and sexual power. Instead, it could be inferred that the motivation for her work was philanthropic public-spiritedness, and the efforts of a lonely, ageing upper-middle-class spinster to occupy an empty life. Her feminism is allowed no discursive and little visual space. In effect it is displaced by the worthy *salonière*.

All of this is not to suggest some monstrous failing on the part of the State Library. The event of the exhibition was important — Scott was indeed well known early in the century and was an entirely fitting subject for the project. Nevertheless, my point in analysing the representation of Scott is a more general one: that Scott's preoccupations and motivations make sense of her public life and yet they are increasingly unintelligible to late-twentieth-century viewers and readers. To exhibit them has become irreconcilable with the case to be made for respecting her worthiness and historical importance. More precisely, publicising them risks opening the grand old lady of social reform to ridicule and abuse — a 'wowser', a 'puritan', a 'tory', a 'frigid, repressed spinster', a 'fanatic', a 'zealot', an earnest and crushing bore, a monomaniac, immune to the sexual and cultural changes of her era. The authors of the exhibition no more exposed her to such readings than I did in my earlier work on Scott.

The incomprehensible features of her sexual thought for post-Kinsey, post-Freudian cultural discourses alone would have retarded serious, later analysis of Scott, but her class position has also contributed to this outcome. The influence of socialist theory and politics from the 1960s has led to degrees of dismissal of activists like Scott as agents of bourgeois hegemony. She is chided for her neglect of class analysis, her elitism, her enjoyment of priv-ilege and the irrelevance of her work to proletarian women. Miriam Dixson portrayed Scott's women's movement as ultra-moderate, evidenced by its support in high places.[8] The 'Rose Scott and her famous friends' rep-resentation has been so paramount among Australian historians that, for instance, the editor of the anthology *Rebels and Radicals* (1984) commis-sioned a chapter on Louisa Lawson, Catherine Helen Spence and Brettyna Smyth, but not on Rose Scott. Indeed there is a striking tendency to compare Scott and Louisa Lawson to Scott's disfavour.[9] In the absence of serious consideration of her feminism, individual aspects of Scott's work, such as her pacificism, receive ready and apparently plausible characterisation as 'liberal'. After all, Scott spoke frequently in praise of John Stuart Mill's later works, including *On Liberty*. Nonetheless, as this account of her campaigns for suffrage, the protection of girls, the sexual autonomy of wives and much more has signalled, Scott was in clear collision with the lib-erals of her day, because she could not share their phallocentrism. Her struggles demonstrated quite precisely the ways in which the specifying of sex disintegrated the central claims and ethical grounding of liberalism, a position that could only function as sex neutral. This insight has been identified and elaborated more fully by modern feminist political theor-ists. Scott's experience offers a historical case study of this encounter. Her position was rebellious and it was radical. Hence the frequent portrayal of Scott as a 'liberal' is seriously misleading and probably has deterred feminist scholars or biographers. Meanwhile, her opposition to militant suffragette methods makes Scott the exemplar of what is now called 'conservative feminism' by Australian feminist historians.[10]

If the stress upon her famous friends, her reputed liberalism, and her class position in prevailing representations might have combined to deflect feminist historians and biographers from studying Scott, the con-centration upon her beauty, her suitors, her charm and diplomacy might only have exacerbated the situation. Many commentators upon Scott wrote during the inter-war and post-war years, when spinsterhood and the sexual ethics advocated by Scott were increasingly problematic in the context of new sexological discourses. As if to save her from unfair disparagement, her heterosexual credentials are pushed to the fore. In the various family history versions, the message is sometimes set within an amusing family anecdote. Annie Rose Scott Cowen relates the story of the visit of the famous German explorer, Ludwig Leichhardt, to Glendon, supposedly as recalled by her mother, Alice Hamilton. The household sat down to lunch. During the meal, Scott

> was asked by her father why she was so silent, she replied 'I have a bad headache' which gave a chance to one of her many suitors who was one of the party to say with a languishing glance at her 'And I have a heartache' whereupon Leichhardt belched and said 'And I have a stomach ache'.[11]

In Cowen's more extended typescript memoir, written in the 1960s, she attempts to give some explanation of why Scott never married. The version she offers is that David Scott Mitchell fell in love with her, but that she would not have him because they were first cousins, and because so many members of her family depended on her to care for them, she 'felt that she had no right to marry'.[12] Yet Scott had explicitly advised Miles Franklin in 1905 that there was absolutely nothing illegal nor objectionable about first cousins marrying. Cowen's claim here certainly seems inconsistent with the content of Scott Mitchell's letters to his loving cousin in 1875.[13] Although Scott declined all marriage proposals, Cowen remarks that she did this 'so charmingly that as I grew up and met quite a number of her and my mother's contemporaries, I found they could still speak tenderly and nostalgically of how much they had wanted to marry her'.[14]

Nothing of Scott's trenchant criticism of marriage and typical forms of married life is allowed to cloud this representation. If marriage could only be full of pleasure, companionship and fulfilment, Scott's foregoing it to care for others becomes part of the image of the self-sacrificing, public-spirited bourgeois worthy. Scott's resistance to marrying in a context in which it was usual, available, expected and respectable to do so, was one of the more significant choices of her life. It both cost and permitted her much. It could be seen as a kind of moratorium in her life course, as outlined in feminist literary theorist and critic Carolyn G. Heilbrun's authoritative examination of women's biographies.[15] But these prevailing representations of Scott do not allow this to be seen or understood.

So Scott — portrayed as bourgeois (despite the fascinating case study she and her family make of colonial downward social mobility), 'ultra-moderate' not militant, charming not assertive, liberal not socialist, spinster but neither libertarian nor lesbian, eclectic (or catholic) not separatist — has attracted little serious feminist scholarly attention. By now it should be clear how these binary categories ill-fit or distort the case. They produce characterisations of Scott that are simultaneously inaccurate and yet understandable in terms of certain late-twentieth-century political criteria. It is ironic that Scott's beloved Miles Franklin should have contributed unintentionally and significantly to this outcome.

A POSTHUMOUS ANGLE

In a chapter written by Miles Franklin, Scott was included as one of the studies in Flora Eldershaw's *The Peaceful Army*, a tribute to Australia's pioneer women published in 1938. This essay has remained influential in shaping a public representation of Scott. Its legacy warrants some assessment.

The essay offered a celebratory and anecdotal description of Scott's activities and achievements, with considerable emphasis upon the Friday night salon and the famous people who were her guests. Much of its concerned the period of Scott's life before Franklin knew her, and was heavily dependent upon Scott's own reminiscences to her, and subsequent correspondence between them. After listing Scott's achievements, Franklin ventured:

> Had she been humorless and inconsequential of person her work could have reared itself like a monolith, worthy but unexciting, but elaborated and extended as it was, by her genius for making a delight of association, a festival of friendship, her personality divided the honours with her achievements in political reform.[16]

Franklin noted the contribution that the experience of motherhood — in rearing Nene Scott Wallace — made to Scott's career. Nene was an agreeable and humorous companion who kept Scott's perspective balanced.

In researching the chapter, Franklin had contacted Wallace once again, her last communication having been a letter from him in 1925 thanking her for her sympathy upon Scott's death. He had replied: 'Yes I know you will miss her greatly too. Life seems very blank to me and I can't take much interest in anything.' He had worked for eight weeks just sorting the letters and papers at Lynton, since the house had 'been a repository for many members of the family'.[17] He had married an actress after the war and Scott's friends gradually lost touch with him. Upon resuming contact in 1937 (by which time he had a daughter), Franklin sought his approval for the approach she had decided to take in representing Scott: 'Do you agree that it would be best to tell briefly of the solid achievements and lighten them with matter to indicate the dear loveliness of the subject and her unique position as a lovely and entirely Australian great lady?'[18]

Since she was working on Scott's suffrage-related papers at the Mitchell Library, she invited Wallace to meet her there, when they could 'like Adam and Eve, walk in the garden hard by while you advise me'.[19] They met then, and on another occasion at his apartment, and she wrote 'I wish I could see more of you'.[20] Once the article was published in 1938, Wallace congratulated her, describing it as 'simply splendid' and including 'everything of importance'.[21] In 1948, a decade after publication of the chapter, she wrote to Vida Goldstein's sister, Aileen, of a recent visit to Nene Scott Wallace. A week before, she had learned from journalist, Ada Holman, that he was now partly paralysed, presumably due to a stroke:

> I had lost touch with him for years because we have nothing in common. He hasn't a book in his comfortable, expensive flat, but many expensive bridge pencils and that explains it. How a man reared in Miss Scott's home could escape any taint of sociological, literary, political and other human interests I don't know.[22]

This was a decidedly negative assessment of Wallace, offered in a more general context of critical reflection on her part. Now, at the age of 66, Franklin seemed moved to some anxiety in recognising that a public figure of Scott's importance could, within two decades of death, leave no trace. Things had not advanced for women. Instead, nowadays:

> Sex is running rampant . . . I am looked upon as an unbending puritan by my associates today and self style myself the champion wowser but if one is endowed with the necessary mental equipment one cannot help observing things . . . We haven't advanced any in really freeing women since Miss Scott and Vida were on the job. Women are more free to ape men's vices and amours but not to let out the devils or angels which may be confined in them as men are free to strut and bellow on the motive power of their ego, whatever its quality or character.

And in a postscript to this letter to Aileen Goldstein reflecting on the limited progress of inter-war and post-war feminism, Franklin wrote a message to her sister, Vida Goldstein: 'Tell Vida that perhaps her work is not without fruit . . . I remember Vida drawing my attention to a woman who was considered fast because her *trottoir* skirt was only to the ankle bone. The world has progressed but not in the way we hoped.'[23]

Franklin was registering changes in sexual mores in which women were enjoined to 'the animal'. It was the period of the first publication of the long-awaited Kinsey reports on human sexuality — reports which, by some later scholarly readings, re-asserted in unprecedentedly scientific guise the naturalness and irrepressibility of a hydraulic sexual drive, complete with age-related norms for rates of coitus. Of course, libertarian sexual politics had longer origins, some from the European Enlightenment, manifest across the nineteenth century in Australia (as elsewhere in Utopian socialist communities), in bohemian and political dissent movements, and in urban intellectual subcultures. The First World War was arguably a watershed for libertarian sexual politics, which gained wider advocacy thereafter. Some of the symptoms of its strengthening had been visible to Scott in her last years: the secularising and medicalising of venereal disease policy; the pathologisation and dishonouring of 'the spinster'; the sexual objectification of women in visual media, fashion and cultural practices (such as the increasingly popular beauty contest), and the more general vindication of the rights of the (non-reciprocal) male gaze.

Franklin had not necessarily shared Scott's precise concern about these manifestations, for she was of a sufficiently younger generation to participate in some changing features of sexual culture. However in middle and old age, her letters to the Goldstein sisters endorsed some of Scott's concerns about the co-option of women and the neutralisation of any difference they could have made to masculine political and cultural agendas. In 1946 Vida Goldstein had some impatience with this view, seeing in it a covert misogyny. She wrote: 'Men have governed the world since time began — see what they have made of it yet he [sic] blames woman for not making a brave new world in 30 years'.[24] A year later, however, she substantially concurred with Franklin's position. In a discussion of the worrying trend of world affairs, she wrote to Franklin:

> But what about the women also? I feel they too have failed humanity in two world wars. They have proved their ability to help their country in a time of national crisis but have done nothing to prevent crises recurring. Where are the women's demands and organisations for a practical humanitarian programme?[25]

This was a sad final vision of sexual politics for this Victorian campaigner. Vida Goldstein died in 1949.

The Australian Broadcasting Commission invited Franklin to give a nine-minute radio talk on Rose Scott in 1951, offering a payment of four guineas. The account of Scott was again celebratory, as might be expected, asserting Scott's importance to an audience presumed ignorant and unenlightened: 'Governments came and went; Rose Scott like the personification of the Woman's State, remained to influence them. Her Friday evenings at Edgecliffe were the focus of intellectual life in Sydney.' Here was affectionate, probably unconscious, overstatement. Franklin knew, perhaps better than anyone, Scott's frustrations, the great limits to her influence on governments, her difficulties after women gained the vote. She knew very well the enemies Scott had and the problems that arose in her dealings with other women. Her statement in this talk that Scott 'had opponents but no real enemies because she was hospitable to new ideas and sincere and fair in opposition' is a generous representation. In large part, the motive for Franklin's 1951 'Rose Scott' may have been a defence of 'the spinster' against her post-war psychologistic and sexological detractors, and an attempt to rescue Scott from undeserved obscurity: 'Rose Scott was always normal, humorous, tolerant; she is adored in memory by those who knew her in the flesh, and flows as a legend among great Australians. . . . Fifty years ago she was one of the most distinguished and widely known women in Australia.'[26]

Franklin did not address directly the reasons for Scott's current obscurity. In the 1938 essay, however, she contrasted Scott's era favourably with that of the late 1930s. Scott's methods and manner, for instance, were 'leisurely and gracious, those of the well bred before speed and noise and mechanised entertainment abolished repose'. Personalities like Scott's could develop in her time, taking hold 'like a tree', but could no longer, because nowadays 'smothered in the successive crops of notorieties forced into prominence by hot air, and withering like grass as soon as the artificial sustenance is withdrawn'.[27] For Franklin too the world had gone bad and, as Scott had done in the last years of her life, Franklin in 1951 was also looking backwards.

At this time she undertook a correspondence with Scott's niece, Millie Shaw's daughter, who had married a London economist and now signed herself 'Mollye Menken'. Their letters offer an illuminating account of domestic hardship faced by women in the early post-war period, especially with lack of services (such as shopping deliveries, shortages of food and skilled tradesmen), and power strikes and blackouts. Having told Menken about her forthcoming radio talk on 'Aunt Rose', Franklin was forced to report that owing to power strikes, she did not herself actually hear the programme. A week later 'I was all set to hear the one on my dear Vida Goldstein but off went the electricity again'. The purpose of this letter was to tell Menken that 'poor old Nene died'.[28]

Shortly before his death, Nene's wife, Edna Wallace, had read the published version of Franklin's radio talk on Scott. She wrote to Franklin about the forthcoming marriage of their daughter, Rose, also named after Scott. Rose Scott Wallace would be wearing one of the brooches left by Scott to her mother 'as something old'. Obviously unaware that Franklin was its author, Edna Wallace asked if she had read the piece on Scott in *The Peaceful Army*. Franklin swiftly enlightened her and then outlined her qualifications to speak of Scott:

> Your aunt was one of the enthusiasms of my life. I used to stay with her a lot when I was a girl and I still keep in touch with another niece in London, though I have not heard of Nene for some time. I saw the account of the wedding at St. James. I have a dress ring which Miss Scott left me in her will which I treasure.[29]

A couple of months later, Franklin wrote to Menken expressing something like guilt about Nene Scott Wallace. She had not seen him for a year or two and 'should have made more effort to see him' for old times' sake since his wife had said he 'clung to the memory of me'. If only she had known; but then, he had no interest in anything but bridge and the past. His thoughts 'went back to the days when I was with his aunt and all the world was calling on us and you were a long, leggy girl running in and out with your playmates'.[30]

The question of her relationship with and feelings about Wallace remained on Franklin's mind. Presumably unintentionally, she wrote an almost identical letter about him a year later, partly in response to Menken's statement 'I was always scared of him when I was young. Whom did he marry?' Menken was enquiring more generally about her remaining Australian cousins. Franklin's enquiries on her behalf brought some shocks about ageing and death:

> I too was scared of Nene's critical capacity when young, and so saw very little of him in late years, which I regretted, as his wife told me that he clung to me. I have forgotten who his wife was. She was an actress and I remember Dr Booth and others wondering what his Aunt Rose would have thought of a character of her interests.[31]

Edna Wallace had told Franklin that she had no interest in keeping the vast array of Scott's family heirlooms and treasures and wanted them passed on to Glendon Scott. In response to Menken's questions about her cousins, Franklin tried to track down Rosie Windon and Glendon Scott. Upon phoning Windon, she was referred to her daughter, a Mrs Holden of Strathfield, Sydney, the wife of a judge, only to learn that it was the fourth anniversary of Rosie Windon's death:

> It made me sick. I had never seen much of her. She used to come to Lynton Cottage sometimes when I was there and I the little girl from the bush thought her marvellous . . . Her going seems one of the last links with those days of my girlhood when your aunt was so lovely to me and you'd come streaking in and out again and your mother would be there.[32]

Scott and her immediate family had an emotional significance for Franklin that her straightened circumstances in the post-war period apparently heightened. 'I am weary of being poor',[33] she wrote to Aileen Goldstein in 1950. Somehow she took a kind of authority and even solace in the role of defender of Scott's name and guardian of the truth. In a combination of despair and self-importance she told Menken that a brilliant and well-informed young woman came to ask her who Scott was — a woman she knew she should know about but could find no one to inform her. 'So soon are the worthwhile forgotten.'[34] Meanwhile, she described herself as 'plagued by old-timers who persist in asserting that your Aunt Rose was secretly married.' Menken responded quickly that Scott 'was once engaged for a week, but she always said she never had the courage to marry. She had lots of suitors I know but she remained unconquered.'[35]

Evidently Franklin engaged in quite a number of exchanges with these unnamed persons who claimed that Scott had been married. On the face of it, her anger about these claims might seem excessive: but she linked the ease with which such claims were made — thereby eradicating the meaning of Scott's life and choices — with more general changes in sexual mores and behaviour, which she found oppressive to women like herself. With some exasperation she declared to Menken:

> I can't make out why they are so anxious to marry her. Of course in the changes of behaviour, if they could only make out that she was secretly a great wanton with an archbishop — no with a groom even better — they wd know she'd been a really beautiful and remarkable woman.[36]

This 1950s spinster was declaring that Scott had no cultural space and was lodging her protest by criticising other representations of Scott. The psychologisation of sexual identities and universalising of psychiatric notions of normal sexual practices irritated Franklin intensely. She confessed to Aileen Goldstein that 'I really like kicking up my heels in face of psychiatrists and psychoanalysts — they know about as much as palmists. Once it used to be the toxin of fatigue, then it became complexion, now it is schizophrenia.'[37]

In this way she challenged the expanding authority and legitimacy of these experts in the post-war world. There also are signs that, like Scott, Franklin became disillusioned with her experience of other women — specifically their lack of sisterhood and solidarity. She encountered other women as a spinster, an increasingly anomalous cultural identity. Tensions accompanying this may account for this outburst to Goldstein: 'I have a contempt of women who disparage or dislike their own sex. It is a sign of a nasty or cowardly nature I think.'[38]

Despite Franklin's contention that Scott was not just one more worthy, her 1938 essay and her 1951 radio talk arguably contributed inadvertently to just that representation. Franklin's account influenced subsequent commentators. Nene Scott Wallace donated Scott's unsorted papers to the Mitchell Library in 1950, but they remained unsorted until 1979. Franklin remained a principal source on Scott for Stanford-Thomas's 1966 ABC radio talks on Louisa Lawson, Vida Goldstein and Rose Scott, for Anne Summers's *Damned Whores and God's Police* in 1975, Miriam Dixson's *The Real Matilda* in 1976, and to a lesser degree Ann Mari Jordens's 'Rose Scott: Making a Beginning' in 1984. The main published references to Scott since 1938 stress 'the salon' and the important people she knew. This had been Franklin's strategy to make her contemporaries notice the significance of Scott's achievements. Ironically, the legacy of this strategy is that the important people she knew become her most important achievement, while Scott herself is remembered not as a feminist but as a philanthropist.

Thus, in 1971, upon the death of Annie Rose Scott Cowen the *Newcastle Morning Herald* identified Cowen's significance as being the descendant of 'Helenus Scott's daughter Rose . . . one of the most famous women in Australian history for work similar to that of Mrs Chisholm'.[39] That such a poor comparison could be made by 1971 is testament to the near complete erasure of Scott's central concerns by these various representations, produced late in her life and posthumously. What is lost as a result is her radical, if controversial, critique of sexual relations of her era, and all the other features of her public work that merit scrutiny by contemporary feminists.

SOME REVISIONS

> It is as if every man had a serpent twined around him — the Serpent of Passion — and when men and women love, this Serpent coils round the woman drawing her heart to the man. She longs for the man's own arms to draw her to his heart. She hates the Serpent and would tear it away if she could and trample on it and kill it. But everyman loves his Serpent. He thinks it is a part of himself, it has *become* part of himself. But, oh God, how woman gets to **hate** it . . . it comes between the man and the woman, the husband and the wife . . . the woman cries but seldom aloud. She knows he cannot bear to hear this creature abused, she knows he thinks 'love me, love my serpent' and she speaks with bated breath or not at all. Was there ever a man yet that tore the serpent away instead of hugging it to his heart, with his own strong arms, loving her for love's sake? Some men stretch out one arm. The serpent does the rest, and the woman is clasped tightly and more tightly still in its coils — till she gets to think 'it is no use — if I love him and stay by him I must put up with the Serpent' but her heart faints within her, for she *hates*, it, *hates* it, *hates* it. Oh God, what love women have, to bear with the Serpent for the love of man! And sometimes it seems as if it was all serpent, and the young girl who held her arms out to the man she loved knew of no Serpent, now feels its coils round her at first and then she wakes to what? No wonder marriage is a failure. No wonder divorce, indifference, misery are rampant, and love stands weeping by.
>
> 'Ah' she murmurs 'There is no Serpent here' and she turns to another man. 'There let me rest, be loved even as I love' but no it cannot be, there is no love in man apart from the Serpent Passion, none, none — jealousy, indifference, selfishness, mad anger, these are all the products of the sounds softly hissed into the man's ear by his Serpent. When shall we teach him to love for love's sake. Oh woman, *when*, when?

> Rose Scott, *Journal*, (n.d.)[40]

Despite Rose Scott's own account of becoming a feminist at the age of 7, it was more likely to have occurred in her late twenties. This 'becoming feminist' was not singular or unique to Scott. It was generational and it was transnational. The feminism that emerged in Western countries from the 1870s had a number of common central preoccupations and characteristics. Scott provides an Australian case study of this international political and philosophical development. Her case offers unusual depth and detail on the conditions of possibility surrounding late-nineteenth and early-twentieth-century Western feminism.

Many of the details of Scott's feminism were located in the Australian context, especially the feminist struggles for legal reform through governments in the decades of transition from colonies to federation of states. Furthermore, the comparatively small scale of the educated, professional and literary sectors of the middle classes in late-nineteenth-century Australian cities like Sydney was reflected in the size of the groups of feminist women. Perhaps, in the context, the work of particular women like Scott, Lawson, Montefiore, Windeyer or Wolstenholme assumed greater significance than would have been the case in the larger feminist political cultures of London, New York, Boston, Stockholm, Berlin or Toronto. Nevertheless, the ready intelligibility of that work to their feminist counterparts in these overseas cities and regions — evident in many kinds of exchange between them — suggests that Australian feminists like Scott were more representative of feminism of the period than the converse.

The founding vision informing Scott's late-nineteenth-century feminism was that cultural discourses and arrangements represented women as 'creatures of sex' first and foremost. This cultural fact constrained the options of women *as a sex* in ways that could never be the experience of men *as a sex*. Individuals might escape or minimise the worst outcomes of the common meanings given to being a woman (or a man) through negotiations and fortuitous resources, but not on a scale that appreciably altered the likely sexual patternings of late-nineteenth-century Western cultures. In Australia, rather more than elsewhere, being female meant being 'destined to be wives', to borrow from Barbara Caine. This perceived (if not prescribed) destiny secured different and usually less prestigious forms of education, leisure and work for daughters compared with sons across all classes of white Australian society. Consequently, girls and boys, women and men occupied substantially different worlds marked by distinct 'sexed' or sexual cultures, each with the powerful 'homosocial' bonds identified by historian Carroll Smith-Rosenberg. Heterosocial courtship then was frequently conducted across profound cultural chasms, fraught with misunderstandings. Moments in the relations between Scott and David Scott Mitchell certainly fitted this description.

Once married, Scott observed that women too often submitted to tyranny, especially with regard to sexual relations. Men were selfish, brutal and inconsiderate, proceeding when desire was non-reciprocal. They endangered their wives' health and lives, causing frequent and closely spaced pregnancies. Through adultery, promiscuity and regular use of prostitutes, they infected blameless wives and their offspring with venereal diseases, while the emotional aspect of their marriage was soured by bitterness, humiliation and despair. Wives typically had no income of their own and no secure right to a reasonable portion of their husband's earnings, property and assets, even in widowhood. Men, it seemed, either would not or could not meet their women's needs for adequate love and for real friendship in so intimate a relationship. Indeed, in marriage the sexes resembled 'intimate strangers'.

For Scott, as for other feminists of the period, the major conditions of possibility for women's degradation as creatures of sex included: the hydraulic and essentialist construction of men's sexuality; the double standard of sexual morality that those constructions of men's sexuality permitted; and women's economic and psychological dependency on marriage — an iniquitous sexual contract — for a respectable social identity. These in turn provided perfect conditions for the 'seduction' of young women on the marriage market (a major cause of illegitimacy and unmarried motherhood), and for the proliferation and condonation of prostitution. Despite her own ambivalence about prostitutes and their effects on the sexual bargaining position of wives, Scott usually refused the political division of women into the virtuous and the bad. All women were diminished by the degradation of any.

The endeavour to challenge this degradation of women was the mission of Scott's public career. The vote was symbolically important in this endeavour. For a time the suffrage campaign was Scott's central work. However, struggles around sexuality predated it. Thwarted objectives in these struggles, such as a raised age of consent, substantially motivated her suffrage work. Since the gaining of suffrage was considerably more protracted in English Canada, Great Britain, the United States, South America, and various European societies such as Switzerland, France and Quebec, than in Australasia and Scandinavia, the former activists experienced some constraints in campaigning around sexual abuses of women and girls. Understandably, some leaders feared that association between suffragists and campaigns concerned with prostitution, seduction, incest and illegitimacy threatened to bring suffragism into disrepute. Arousing men's anxieties could retard progress on the vote. This happened in New South Wales in 1892 around the Vice Suppression Bill. Since international feminist work on sexuality was constrained by the instrumental priority given to the elusive ballot, the post-suffrage history of feminist work around sexuality in countries like Australia, New Zealand and Finland is significant for the broader historical analysis of Western feminism: for in these countries, women were enfranchised decades before those in most Western societies.

The era of women's citizenship disappointed Scott, since even with the franchise from 1902, the legal reforms aimed at men's sexual exploitation of women continued to be as elusive as the ballot was for her overseas counterparts. With exceptions like Vida Goldstein, too few women were sufficiently economically and socially independent to either participate in public politics and office as representatives of *women* citizens, or to create viable alternative forms of women's politics. The woman voter then faced the same political culture as the man voter. If historical voting patterns remain undemonstrable, the fact that no vast political swings followed the enfranchisement of women offers no mystery. None of the competing parties focused on 'women's issues' in order to attract an entirely new electorate. That women's votes distributed comparably with those of men of their class, ethnicity, region and age group is probable.

Scott made much of women's betrayal of the interests of their own sex by becoming embroiled in party political organisations, thereby making the demands distinct to women contained and invisible. In fact, she probably made too much of this, or at least attributed more weight to it than it could reasonably bear in explaining the failure of her founding vision of a feminist transformation of sexual politics and culture. Few adult Australian women were able to be formally involved in any kind of public politics. To blame the relatively small number of women who became involved in the early-twentieth-century federal and state political parties for the endurance of women's degradation was implausible and undue. Yet, until the end of her life, Scott adhered to this condemnation of her fellow women, even though it sat increasingly uneasily beside the gradual shift and revisions in her feminism and that of her contemporaries.

By the 1920s Australian feminism displayed marked revision of earlier tenets, strategies and objectives. As in other Western countries, 'feminism' entered public discussion as a shorthand description of a complex range of analyses, ethics, activities and identities. An obvious comparison can be made here with the 1970s, when 'feminism' again emerged, to replace the more specific and more cumbersome Women's Liberation Movement. The term 'feminist' had replaced the earlier ways in which Scott, Lawson and Goldstein had described themselves — such as 'workers in the cause of women' — by the years of the First World War. Vida Goldstein wrote to Scott in 1919, reporting anti-German sentiments among ICW delegates, which she was sure Scott would agree were inconsistent with the 'spirit of feminism'.

The relative contiguity of early-twentieth-century feminist developments across Western countries is striking despite uneven successes with regard to particular feminist measures and reforms. The period of the First World War was marked by increasing identification and characterisation of feminism as a movement, a strand of thought, a lifestyle and cultural influence. Public commentary and criticism of feminism took place transnationally, irrespective of the state of actual feminist achievements in the countries concerned. There can be little doubt that the publicity occasioned by English suffragette militancy was a dramatic impetus for commentary of this kind. Rather than a singular uproar, however, the contention over 'feminism' constituted the latest phase of a longer debate over the 'new woman' and the woman question, dating at least from the 1880s.

The naming of 'feminism' was the naming of an increasingly tangible political and cultural movement. The moment of its naming during the decade of the First World War was a moment of decided diversification as key feminists became involved with a range of different, non-feminist politics and intellectual developments — party politics, eugenics, socialism, sexology, libertarianism, theosophy and various modernist artistic and cultural movements. Such engagements necessarily produced revisions of earlier feminist analyses, manifest in debates, divisions, and new emphases in feminist politics and strategies. Egalitarianism was focused on in feminist rhetoric, often placed uneasily beside demands and convictions anchored in discourses of sex specificity and difference. Although often enough historians have seen the latter tendency as decisively eclipsed by the 1920s, the Australian evidence of a historical continuum of concerns from Rose Scott to Bessie Rischbieth, Muriel Heagney and Jessie Street belies the identification of such clear transition from one feminist priority to another.

What is clearer is that early-twentieth-century Australian feminism, like its international counterparts, responded to and actively negotiated with changing discourses implicating women, men and sexuality. The participation of younger women, many university-educated and professional workers, brought new and different agendas to the movement. The foundation of the Feminist Club by such women in 1914 marked the existence of different generations, bringing diversity, change and, inevitably, conflict.

Though Scott was prevented by ageing and chronic ill-health from full participation in the work and interests of the younger generation of feminists, enough accord existed for her place and contribution to be honoured both at the time of her retirement and after. For a period in New South Wales politics, she had functioned as an unofficial minister for women's affairs, long before the office was created by 1970s Labor governments. Her qualifications and influence had always been informal. In the federal era, with a women's movement demanding direct, formal representation and office, her mode of operation, and both its ethics and etiquette, came to seem antique. Eventually she supported the demands of the interwar women's movement. Though more difficult for her, she came also to be a spectator rather than a protagonist. If she did not fully understand why the context for women was changing, she did recognise finally that feminist transformation required something more than the strategies of elevation contained in her original vision.

The challenges of change, vision, strategy, revision, diversity and age that faced Scott also face feminists today, and many of the dilemmas of her feminist career remain relevant. That so much of Scott's thought and preoccupations are unacceptable to contemporary feminists discloses the rich historicity of feminism itself. It is important to avow and acknowledge *all* of the genealogy of feminism, not just the foremothers to whom current theoretical and political insights accord approval.

Feminist interventions can only benefit from a more situated understanding of present visions and priorities, and of why others called feminists in other times and places have not necessarily shared the same vision and priorities. In her failure, for instance, to separately theorise the position of Aboriginal women within her feminist work and in her involvement in causes such as the Little Wives of India Fund, Scott would, on the face of it, deserve the judgement current in Western feminist discourses of 'racism', 'ethnocentrism', 'race-blindness' and 'cultural imperialism'. She was manifestly unaware of her own race-bound epistemological and political standpoint, as an Anglo-Celtic descendant of the pastoral entrepreneurs who undertook frontier genocide of Aboriginal women, children and men. For failing to specify her own 'whiteness', her ethnic and cultural assumptions, the modern, enlightened feminist reader can dismiss Scott's feminism as fatally flawed. This dismissal can be embraced with rigour and righteousness, especially viewed beside Scott's sexual discourses, her at times negative pronouncements upon prostitutes, and even her employment of domestic servants and her flirtation, like most intellectuals of her day, with eugenics.

Yet there is a powerful case for resisting, or at the very least deferring, if we can, the easy and prevailing tendency to judge feminists of the past in the light of the current feminist ethics. Such judgements can flatten out the complexities of the case and impoverish our understanding. For correct as the representation of Scott as racist or ethnocentric might be, it does not sit well beside other evidence. Her protracted arguments with socialists and labour activists on behalf of Aborigines' and Chinese people's rights, about Kanakas and other indentured labour, would need to be reconciled. So would her friendship with Arthur Vogan, who pursued Aboriginal ethnography and tirelessly worked for white recognition of Aboriginal and New Zealand Maori culture. Scott's papers contain a large scrapbook of newscuttings on Australian Aborigines. She attended New Zealand Maori dance and theatre on tour in Sydney; and asked her erudite cousin David Scott Mitchell about what was then known of different Aboriginal groups in various Australian regions. Several sources claim that Aboriginal children were her playmates in the periods of her childhood spent 'in the bush', and a small purse made for her by an Aboriginal friend was among the relics that Scott treasured, ultimately left to the Mitchell Library.

None of this alters the justice of modern feminist dismissals concerning the absence of race in Scott's feminism, but neither is it likely that a racist would pursue such interests. Scott was interested in the Aboriginal people of Australia, but also in the history and culture of many non-Anglo-

Celtic peoples. This interest intensified in tandem with her pacifism, the prosecution of the First World War and, more mundanely, with the debilitating decline in her health that substantially confined her activities to reading and thinking. She has left large subject-file newscutting collections on Japanese, Chinese, Pacific Island and Indian sub-continent cultures. Moreover, she was always particularly critical of Chamberlain, Rhodes and other famous imperialists of her era, foremost in the conquest and exploitation of Africa.

Faced with unpalatable features of the thoughts and actions of earlier feminists like Scott, modern feminist scholars, as previously shown, have tended to refuse them the title 'feminist', or else to qualify its application so as to create vast distances between cohorts; a 'them' and 'us' effect. The inclination of activists like Scott or Lawson in Australia, and their counterparts elsewhere, to speak of 'women' singular evokes particular unease. With a recent history of heated debates as to differences between women forged by race, aboriginality, ethnicity, class, region, age, sexual identity, disability, and other cultural features, modern feminists increasingly dismiss would-be peers who speak of women as a single group as simplistic, insensitive and polemical.

One effect of this strategy can be to overlook crucial continuities between feminists and, as its corollary, to grasp imperfectly the significance of the discontinuities between them. A much more challenging series of questions confronts the modern feminist analyst of Scott, and other feminists of her era, than that of how they rate according to present criteria. If they insistently observed women as a single group despite, as Scott's case shows, considerable familiarity with the situation of many different groups of women and conscientious engagement with the prevailing discourses concerning Aborigines, imperialism, Asian peoples, socialism and the labour movement, it is important to attempt to understand both why and how this was so.

Moreover, if the modern feminist critic is inclined to resist earlier feminist adherence to women as a unified category, she or he does so from the frequently expressed conviction that serious consideration of differences between women, including those based on aboriginality, race, ethnicity, class and sexual preference, would have fundamentally altered the analysis and work of the protagonist in question — in this case, Scott. To make this conviction persuasive, however, the critic is arguably obliged to demonstrate how the key features of Scott's feminist analysis would have been altered and in what direction. Perhaps as important, a clear-eyed evaluation from such an exercise of the purchase of any differences produced should be forthcoming. Would Scott's principal understandings of men and masculine sexual power, for instance, have been jettisoned by giving analytic centrality to differences between women? Would her understandings in this area instead be qualified or more highly specified or more detailed and comprehensive in the empirical sense, but their basic orientation remain? Or would her conviction of sex-based degradation of women as a group have been so undermined and fractured by consideration of differences between women that she would have had to abandon the woman suffrage struggle and the age of consent campaign? If Scott had abandoned her faith in the category 'women', and committed no sins against current postmodernist, post-colonial and anti-humanist feminist sensibilities, would she, in the context of 'first-wave' feminism, have done or said anything recognisably feminist at all? Would she have been dubbed a 'fighter in the cause of women'? Probably not.

The relevance of differences between women notwithstanding, the self-evident salience of the category 'women' unleashed Scott's feminism and that of her feminist contemporaries. Despite the revisions of the inter-war and post-war feminism, feminists continued to be motivated by a concern about the sex women, relative to the sex men. That concern remains with us today in the myriad forms that constitute contemporary feminism.

Notes

Prologue and Acknowledgements

1   J.A. Allen, Aspects of the Public Career of Rose Scott: Feminist, Social Reformer and Pacifist 1890–1925, unpublished BA (Hons) dissertation, University of Sydney, 1977.

Introduction

1   M. Franklin, 'Rose Scott', Australian Broadcasting Commission, Radio Scripts, Miles Franklin Papers (MFP), Mitchell Library (ML) Manuscripts (MS), 445/36/10, pp. 251–4; and J.A. Allen, 'Scott, Rose (1847–1925)', in G. Serle (ed.), *Australian Dictionary of Biography, Vol. 11: 1891–1939, Nes–Smi,* (hereafter *ADB*) Melbourne University Press, Melbourne, 1988, pp. 547–9.
2   For analysis of reasons why this attains importance see L. Newman, 'Critical Theory and the History of Women: What's at Stake in Deconstructing Women's History?', *Journal of Women's History*, vol. 2, no. 3, 1991, p. 66.
3   C. Mouffe, 'Feminism, Citizenship and Radical Democratic Politics', in J. Butler and J.W. Scott (eds), *Feminists Theorize the Political*, Routledge, New York, 1992, p. 374.
4   For a fascinating discussion of contemporary historians' framings of 'lesbian' and 'gay' difference is J. Terry's 'Theorizing Deviant Historiography', *differences*, vol. 3, no. 2, 1991, pp. 55–74.
5   For a succinct rendering of some of the elements of this preoccupation, see W. Brown, 'Feminist Hesitations, Postmodern Exposures', *differences*, vol. 3, no. 1, 1991, pp. 63–84.
6   For unabashed judgement of earlier feminists through contemporary early 1970s feminist criteria, see A. Summers, *Damned Whores and God's Police*, Penguin, Ringwood, 1975, pp. 469–70; and S. Firestone, *The Dialectic of Sex*, Paladin, London, 1972, pp. 26–31.
7   See for instance S. Rowbotham, *Woman, Resistance and Revolution*, Penguin, Harmondsworth, 1974, pp. 245–7; and for discussion of the dilemmas involved in analysis of race and earlier feminists see A. Burton, 'The Feminist Quest for Identity: British Imperial Suffragism and Global Sisterhood 1900–1915', *Journal of Women's History*, vol. 3, no. 2, 1991, pp. 47–71; and M. Valverde, '"When the Mother of the Race is Free": Race, Reproduction and Sexuality in First-Wave Feminism', in F. Iacovetta and M. Valverde (eds), *Gender Conflicts*, University of Toronto Press, Toronto, 1992, pp. 3–26.
8   L. Gordon, 'What's New in Women's History?', in T. DeLauretis (ed.), *Feminist Studies/Critical Studies*, Indiana University Press, Bloomington, 1986, p. 29.
9   See for instance M. Frye, *The Politics of Reality*, The Crossing Press, Trumansburg, 1983, pp. 1–16.
10   T. DeLauretis, 'Eccentric Subjects: Feminist Theory and Historical Consciousness', *Feminist Studies*, vol. 16, no. 1, 1990, pp. 115–69.

11 L. Newman, 'Critical Theory and the History of Women', p. 62.
12 For instances of this see L. Gordon and E.C. Dubois, '"Seeking Ecstasy on the Battlefield": Danger and Pleasure in Nineteenth Century Feminist Sexual Thought', *Feminist Studies*, vol. 9, no. 1, 1983, pp. 7–26; and J.R. Walkowitz, *City of Dreadful Delight*, University of Chicago Press, Chicago, 1992, pp. 6–7.
13 Most useful are: D. Scott, 'Woman Suffrage: The Movement in Australia', *Journal of the Royal Australian Historical Society*, vol. 53, no. 4, 1967, pp. 299–322; P. Grimshaw, *Women's Suffrage in New Zealand*, University of Auckland Press, Auckland, 1973; C.L. Bacchi, *Liberation Deferred?*, University of Toronto Press, Toronto, 1983; and B. Caine, *Victorian Feminists*, Oxford University Press, London, 1992.
14 For discussion of earlier stages, see J.A. Allen, 'Contextualizing Late Nineteenth Century Feminism: Problems and Comparisons', *Journal of the Canadian Historical Association*, vol. 1, 1990, pp. 17–36.
15 See for instance E.C. Dubois, 'Outgrowing the Compact of the Fathers: Equal Rights, Woman Suffrage and the United States Constitution 1820–1878', *Journal of American History*, vol. 74, no. 3, 1987, p. 846; O. Banks, *Faces of Feminism*, Martin Robertson, Oxford, 1981, pp. 6–9; and M. Lake, 'The Politics of Respectability: Identifying the Masculinist Context', *Historical Studies*, vol. 22, no. 86, 1986, pp. 116–31.
16 J.A. Allen, 'Contextualizing Late Nineteenth Century Feminism', pp. 30–1.
17 R. Delmar, 'What Is Feminism?', in J. Mitchell and A. Oakley (eds), *What Is Feminism?*, Harvester Press, Brighton, 1986, pp. 8–9.
18 ibid., pp. 8–9.
19 N.F. Cott, 'What's In A Name? The Limits of "Social Feminism" or Expanding the Vocabulary of Women's History', *Journal of American History*, vol. 76, no. 3, 1989, pp. 809–29.
20 N.F. Cott, *The Grounding of Modern Feminism*, Yale University Press, New Haven, 1987, p. 20.
21 N.F. Cott, 'Feminist Theory and Feminist Movements: The Past Before Us', in J. Mitchell and A. Oakley (eds), *What Is Feminism?*, p. 49.
22 B. Caine, *Victorian Feminists*, pp. 6–7.
23 For discussion of this characterisation see G.C. Brandt and N. Black, '"Il En Faut Peu": Farm Women and Feminism', *Journal of the Canadian Historical Association*, vol. 1, 1990, p. 76. See also R. Rosenberg, *Beyond Separate Spheres*, Yale University Press, New Haven, 1982; and S.S. Holton, *Feminism and Democracy*, Cambridge University Press, Cambridge, 1987. In addition, A. Kraditor, *The Ideas of the Woman Suffrage Movement 1890–1920*, Columbia University Press, New York, 1965, p. 196, provides a good example of this framework, despite the fact, as Nancy Cott observes, that Kraditor did not designate the suffragists 'feminist'. Dubois argues that in the transformation of suffragist rhetoric to a focus upon women's specificities, 'the women's rights movement moved away from its egalitarian origins; the movement would ultimately become more compatible with conservative ideas about social hierarchy' (E.C. Dubois, 'Outgrowing the Compact of the Fathers', p. 850). I would also include my early essay on Australian feminism in this tendency: J.A. Allen, 'Breaking into the Public Sphere: The Struggle for Women's Citizenship in New South Wales 1890–1920', in J. Mackinolty and H. Radi (eds), *In Pursuit of Justice*, Hale & Iremonger, Sydney, 1979, pp. 107–17.

24 See K. Offen, 'Defining Feminism: A Comparative Historical Approach', *Signs*, vol. 14, no. 1, 1988, pp. 119–57.

25 See for instance G. Lloyd, *The Man of Reason*, Methuen, London, 1984; N. Jay, 'Gender and Dichotomy', *Feminist Studies*, vol. 7, no. 1, 1981, pp. 38–56; E. Grosz, 'Feminist Theory and the Challenge to Knowledges', *Women's Studies International Forum*, vol. 10, no. 5, 1987, pp. 475–80; and M. Gatens, *Feminism and Philosophy*, Polity Press, Cambridge, 1991, pp. 92–5.

26 J.K. Conway, *The Female Experience in 18th and 19th Century America*, Princeton University Press, Princeton, 1982, p. 199.

27 See M. Valverde, *The Age of Light and Soap and Water*, McClelland Stewart, Toronto, 1991, pp. 58–76, for a discussion of the racialist and anti-working-class elements of this 'maternalist' and 'mother of the race' claim of some feminist groupings.

28 N. Black, *Social Feminism*, Cornell University Press, Ithaca, 1989. Cott's critique of the designation 'social feminism', because also published in 1989, could not address Black's formulation, addressing instead earlier uses of the term to distinguish among feminists advanced by Stanley Lemons and William O'Neill. See N.F. Cott, 'What's In A Name?', pp. 815–21.

29 E.C. Dubois, *Feminism and Suffrage*, Cornell University Press, Ithaca, 1978, p. 47.

30 See for instance S. Jeffreys, *The Spinster and Her Enemies*, Pandora Press, London, 1985; C. Smith-Rosenberg, 'The Female World of Love and Ritual: Relationships Between Women in Nineteenth Century America', in C. Smith-Rosenberg, *Disorderly Conduct*, Oxford University Press, New York, 1985, pp. 53–76; L. Gordon, 'Why Late Nineteenth Century Feminists Did Not Support "Birth Control" and Why Twentieth Century Feminists Do: Feminism, Reproduction and the Family', in B. Thorne and M. Yalom (eds), *Rethinking the Family*, Longman, New York, 1982, pp. 40–53; W. Leach, *True Love and Perfect Union*, Basic Books, New York, 1980; and L. Bland, 'The Married Woman, the "New Woman" and the Feminist: Sexual Politics of the 1890s', in J. Rendall (ed.), *Equal or Different?*, Basil Blackwell, Oxford, 1987, pp. 141–64.

31 S.K. Kent, *Sex and Suffrage in Britain, 1860–1914*, Princeton University Press, Princeton, 1987, p. 33.

32 B. Caine, *Victorian Feminists*, p. 247.

33 J.W. Scott, 'Deconstructing Equality Versus Difference or the Uses of Poststructuralist Theory for Feminism', in M. Hirsch and E. Fox-Keller (eds), *Conflicts in Feminism*, Routledge, New York, 1990, p. 144.

34 N.F. Cott, 'Feminist Theory and Feminist Movements', p. 49.

35 E.C. Dubois, *Feminism and Suffrage*, p. 20.

36 N.F. Cott, 'What's In A Name?', p. 814.

37 See for instance R. Evans, 'A Gun in the Oven: Masculinism and Gendered Violence', in K. Saunders and R. Evans (eds), *Gender Relations in Australia*, Harcourt Brace Jovanovich, Sydney, 1992, p. 210.

38 N.F. Cott, *The Grounding of Modern Feminism*, pp. 4–5.

39 ibid., p. 5.

40 ibid., p. 34–7.

41 N.F. Cott, 'What's In A Name?', pp. 820–1, 827.

42 K. Offen, 'Defining Feminism', p. 136. After publication of this article, Offen addressed the French origins of the word 'feminism' and its

meanings in the late nineteenth century. See K. Offen, 'On the French Origin of the Words Feminism and Feminist', *Feminist Issues*, vol. 8, no. 2, 1988, pp. 45–52. Genevieve Fraisse confronts some of the same issues when she asks: 'if we know that the word "feminism" appeared at the end of the Second Empire, how do we define the phenomenon itself before the existence of the term?'. See G. Fraisse, 'Feminist Singularity: A Critical Historiography of the History of Feminism in France', in M. Perrot (ed.), *Writing Women's History*, Basil Blackwell, Oxford, 1992, p. 150.

43 K. Offen, 'A Reply to Dubois', *Signs*, vol. 15, no. 1, 1989, p. 21.
44 N.F. Cott, 'Comment on Karen Offen's "Defining Feminism: A Comparative Historical Approach"', *Signs*, vol. 15, no. 1, 1989, p. 209.
45 E.C. Dubois, 'Comment on Karen Offen's "Defining Feminism: A Comparative Historical Approach"', *Signs*, vol. 15, no. 1, 1989, p. 197.
46 B. Caine, *Victorian Feminists*, pp. 6–7.
47 ibid., p. 6.
48 ibid., p. 8.
49 S.K. Kent, *Sex and Suffrage*, p. 22.
50 N.F. Cott, 'What's In A Name?', pp. 826–7.
51 B. Caine, *Victorian Feminists*, p. 7.
52 N.F. Cott, 'What's In A Name?', p. 820.
53 E.C. Dubois, 'Comment on Karen Offen . . . ', p. 195.
54 See G. Fraisse, 'Feminist Singularity: A Critical Historiography of the History of Feminism in France', pp. 148–9. For a discussion of the development of the term 'first-wave feminism' and significances attached to it, see E. Sarah, 'Towards a reassessment of feminist history', *Women's Studies International Forum*, vol. 5, no. 6, pp. 520–3. See also C. L. Bacchi, 'First Wave Feminism: History's Judgment', in N. Grieve and P. Grimshaw (eds), *Australian Women*, Oxford University Press, Melbourne, 1981, pp. 156–67.
55 J.A. Allen, 'Contextualizing Late Nineteenth Century Feminism', pp. 20–1.
56 The scale of this work obstructs comprehensive listing. Some examples are: D. Kirkby, *Alice Henry*, Cambridge University Press, Melbourne, 1991; K. Spearritt, 'New Dawns: First Wave Feminism 1880–1914', in K. Saunders & R. Evans (eds), *Gender Relations in Australia*, pp. 325–49; S. M. Magarey, *Unbridling the Tongues of Women*, Hale & Iremonger, Sydney, 1985; J. Mulraney, 'When Lovely Woman Stoops to Lobby', *Australian Feminist Studies*, nos 7/8, 1988, pp. 95–114; P. Young, *Proud to Be a Rebel*, University of Queensland Press, St Lucia, 1991; R. Dalziel, 'The Colonial Helpmeet: Women's Role and the Vote in Nineteenth Century New Zealand', and J. Malone, 'What's Wrong with Emma? The Feminist Debate in Colonial Auckland', in B. Brookes *et.al* (eds), *Women in History*, University of Victoria Press, Wellington, 1986, pp. 55–86; D. Gorham, 'Flora McDonald Denison: Canadian Feminist', in L. Kealey (ed.), *A Not Unreasonable Claim*, Canadian Women's Educational Press, Toronto, 1979, pp. 47–70; V. Strong-Boag, '"Ever A Crusader": Nellie McClung, First Wave Feminist', in V. Strong-Boag & A. Fellman (eds), *Rethinking Canada: The Promise of Women's History*, Copp Clark Pittman, Toronto, 1986, pp. 178–90; J. R. Walkowitz, *Prostitution and Victorian Society*, Cambridge University Press, Cambridge, 1980; S. Jeffreys, '"Free From All Uninvited Touch of Man": Women's Campaigns Around Sexuality 1880–1914', *Women's Studies International Forum*, vol. 5, no. 6, 1982,

pp. 629–45; P. Levine, *Feminist Lives in Victorian England*, Basil Blackwell, Oxford, 1990; E.C. Dubois, 'The Radicalism of the Woman Suffrage Movement: Notes Toward the Reconstruction of Nineteenth Century Feminism', *Feminist Studies*, vol. 3, nos 1/2, 1975, pp. 63–71; K. Barry, *Susan B. Anthony*, Ballantine Books, New York, 1990; A.J. Lane, *To Herland and Beyond*, Meridian Books, New York, 1991; and N.F. Cott, *A Woman Making History*, Yale University Press, New Haven, 1991.

57 See for instance N.F. Cott, *The Bonds of Womanhood*, Yale University Press, New Haven, 1978, and 'Passionlessness: An Interpretation of Victorian Sexual Ideology 1790–1850', *Signs*, vol. 4, no. 1, 1978, pp. 219–36; M.P. Ryan, 'The Power of Women's Networks', in J.L. Newton *et.al.* (eds), *Sex and Class in Women's History*, Routledge, London, 1983, pp. 167–86; K. Rogers, *Feminism in Eighteenth Century England*, University of Illinois Press, Urbana, 1980; A. Browne, *The Eighteenth Century Feminist Mind*, Harvester Press, Brighton, 1987; and M.P. Ryan, *Women in Public*, Johns Hopkins University Press, Baltimore, 1990.

58 See for instance S. Jeffreys, 'Sex Reform and Anti–feminism in the 1920s', in London Feminist History Group (eds), *The Sexual Dynamics of History*, Pluto Press, London, pp. 177–202; and L. Bland, 'Marriage Laid Bare: Middle Class Women and Marital Sex c. 1880–1914', in J. Lewis (ed.), *Labour of Love*, Basil Blackwell, Oxford, 1986, pp. 123–46. Here I would also have to include some earlier work published on Rose Scott: J.A. Allen, 'Rose Scott's Vision: Feminism and Masculinity 1890–1925', in B. Caine *et.al.* (eds), *Crossing Boundaries*, Allen & Unwin, Sydney, 1988, pp. 157–65, and '"Our Deeply Degraded Sex" and "The Animal in Man": Rose Scott, Feminism and Sexuality 1890–1925', *Australian Feminist Studies*, nos 7/8, 1988, pp. 65–94.

59 N.F. Cott, 'What's In A Name?', p. 814.

60 D. Spender, *There's Always Been a Women's Movement This Century*, Pandora Press, London, 1983; M. Lake, 'Jessie Street and Feminist Chauvinism', in H. Radi (ed.), *Jessie Street: Essays and Documents*, Women's Redress Press, Sydney, 1990, pp. 20–5; F. Gordon, *After Winning*, Rutgers University Press, New Brunswick, 1986; A. Prentice *et.al.* (eds), *Canadian Women*, Harcourt Brace Jovanovich, Toronto, 1988; and L. Kealey and J. Sangster (eds), *Beyond the Vote*, University of Toronto Press, Toronto, 1989.

61 See M. Warner, 'Introduction', in C. de Pisan, *The Book of the City of Ladies*, Picador, London, 1983, pp. xxvi–xxx; J. Kelly, *Women, History and Theory*, University of Chicago Press, Chicago, 1984, pp. 65–109; and E. Fox-Genovese, 'Culture and Consciousness in the Intellectual History of European Women', *Signs*, vol. 12, no. 3, 1981, pp. 537–8.

62 See L. Faderman, *Surpassing the Love of Men*, Holt, Rinehart & Winston, New York, 1981.

63 E.C. Dubois *et.al.*, 'Politics and Culture in Women's History: A Symposium', *Feminist Studies*, vol. 6, no. 1, 1980, pp. 26–64.

64 A. Echols, 'The New Feminism of Ying and Yang', in A. Snitow *et.al.* (eds), *Powers of Desire*, Monthly Review Press, New York, 1983, pp. 442–54.

65 On this tendency see J.R. Walkowitz, 'Male Vice and Female Virtue: Feminism and the Politics of Prostitution in Nineteenth Century Britain', in A. Snitow *et.al* (eds), *Powers of Desire*, pp. 433–4; and L. Gordon & E.C. Dubois, 'Seeking Ecstasy on the Battlefield', p. 15; and L. Bland, 'Feminist Vigilantes of Late Victorian England' in C. Smart (ed.), *Regulating Womanhood*, Routledge, London, 1992, pp. 33–52.

66 L. Singer, 'Feminism and Postmodernism', in J. Butler and J.W. Scott (eds), *Feminists Theorize the Political*, p. 472; and M. Morris, *The Pirate's Fiancee*, Verso, London, 1988, p. 55.

67 See M. Barrett, *Women's Oppression Today*, Verso, London, 1980, p. 8.

68 C. Mouffe, 'Feminism, Citizenship and Radical Democratic Politics', p. 373.

69 See for instance P. Adams and E. Cowie, 'The Last Issue Between Us', *m/f*, nos 11/12, 1986, p. 1; N. Wood, 'Prostitution and Feminism in Nineteenth Century Britain', *m/f*, no. 7, 1982, pp. 61–77; P. Adams and J. Minson, 'The "Subject" of Feminism', *m/f*, no. 2, 1978; and D. Dumaresq, 'Rape — Sexuality in the Law', *m/f*, nos 5/6, 1981, pp. 50–2.

70 See A. Yeatman, 'A Feminist Theory of Social Differentiation', in L. Nicholson (ed.), *Feminism/Postmodernism*, Routledge, New York, 1990, pp. 293–5; and J. Flax, 'The End of Innocence', in J. Butler and J.W. Scott (eds), *Feminists Theorize the Political*, p. 447.

71 D. Haraway, 'Ecce Homo, Ain't (Ar'n't) I a Woman, and Inappropriate/d Others: The Human in a Post-Humanist Landscape', in J. Butler and J.W. Scott (eds), *Feminists Theorize the Political*, p. 95.

72 J.W. Scott, 'A Reply to the *differences* Questions', in B. Christian *et.al.*, 'Conference Call', *differences*, vol. 1, no. 3, 1990, p. 87.

73 D. Riley, *'Am I That Name?'*, University of Minnesota Press, Minneapolis, 1988, p. 3.

74 ibid., p. 69.

75 J.W. Scott, 'A Reply to the *difference* Questions', pp. 85–6.

76 J.W. Scott, 'Experience', in J. Butler and J.W. Scott (eds), *Feminists Theorize the Political*, pp. 24–5.

77 E.C. Dubois, 'Eleanor Flexnor and the History of American Feminism', *Gender and History*, vol. 3, no. 1, 1991, p. 89.

78 J.M. Bennett, 'Feminism and History', *Gender and History*, vol. 1, no. 3, 1989, p. 257.

79 J. Butler, 'Contingent Foundations: Feminism and the Question of Post-Modernism', in J. Butler and J.W. Scott (eds), *Feminists Theorize the Political*, p. 16.

80 K. Barry, 'The New Historical Synthesis: Women's Biography', *Journal of Women's History*, vol. 1, no. 3, 1990, p. 99.

81 E. Fox-Genovese, 'Socialist-Feminist American Women's History', *Journal of Women's History*, vol. 1, no. 3, 1990, p. 201.

82 L. Gordon, '[Review] Joan Wallach Scott, *Gender and the Politics of History'*, *American Historical Review*, vol. 95, no. 4, 1990, p. 1156.

83 G. Lerner, 'Reconceptualizing Differences Among Women', *Journal of Women's History*, vol. 1, no. 3, 1990, p. 107.

84 L. Singer, 'Feminism and Postmodernism', p. 466.

85 K. Barry, 'The New Historical Synthesis', p. 97.

86 L. Newman, 'Critical Theory and the History of Women', p. 66.

87 See K. Barry, 'Tootsie Syndrome, or "We Have Met the Enemy and They Are Us"', *Women's Studies International Forum*, vol. 12, no. 5, 1989, pp. 487–93; L. Stanley, 'Recovering *Women* in History from Feminist Deconstruction', *Women's Studies International Forum*, vol. 13, nos 1/2, 1990, pp. 151–7; C. Hall, 'Politics, Poststructuralism and Feminist History', *Gender and History*, vol. 3, no. 2, 1991, pp. 204–10; J. Hoff, 'Introduction: An Overview of Women's History in the United States', in G.V. Fischer *et.al.* (eds), *Journal of Women's History*, Indiana University Press, Bloomington, 1992, pp. 25–9; and S. Brodribb, *Nothing Mat(t)ers*, Spinifex Press, North Melbourne, 1992.

88 L. Newman, 'Critical Theory and the History of Women', pp. 67–8.
89 For discussion of this problem in feminist theory, see E. Grosz, 'Notes Towards a Corporeal Feminism', *Australian Feminist Studies*, no. 5, 1987, pp. 1–16; and M. Gatens, 'A Critique of the Sex/Gender Distinction', in J.A. Allen and P. Patton (eds), *Beyond Marxism? Interventions After Marx*, Intervention Publications, Sydney, 1983, pp. 143–61. See also C. Fouquet, 'The Unavoidable Detour: Must a History of Women Begin With the History of Their Bodies?', in M. Perrot (ed.), *Writing Women's History*, pp. 51–60.
90 L. Vogel, 'Telling Tales: Historians of Our Own Lives', *Journal of Women's History*, vol. 2, no. 3, 1991, p. 93.
91 J.L. Newton, 'A Feminist Scholarship You Can Bring Home to Dad', *Journal of Women's History*, vol. 2, no. 3, 1991, p. 105.
92 J.A. Allen, 'Marxism and the Man Question: Some Implications of the Patriarchy Debate', in J.A. Allen and P. Patton (eds), *Beyond Marxism?*, p. 98.
93 See for instance M. Anderson, '"A Helpmeet for Man": Women in Mid-Nineteenth Century Western Australia', in P. Crawford (ed.), *Exploring Women's Past*, Sisters, Carlton, 1983, pp. 87–127; J.A. Allen, 'From Women's History to a History of the Sexes', in J.A. Walter (ed.), *Australian Studies*, Oxford University Press, Melbourne, 1989, pp. 220–41; and P. Grimshaw, 'Man's Own Country: Women in Colonial Australia', in N. Grieve and A. Burns (eds), *Australian Women*, Oxford University Press, 1986, pp. 182–209.
94 G. Riley, *Inventing the American Woman*, Harlan Davidson Inc., Arlington, Ill., 1987, pp. 81–5.
95 See L. Newman, 'Critical Theory and the History of Women', pp. 67–8; and J. Scott, 'Experience', pp. 25–6.
96 See B. Caine, *Destined to be Wives*, Oxford University Press, London, 1986; and L. Gordon, *Heroes of Their Own Lives*, Viking, New York, 1988; C. Stansell, *City of Women*, University of Illinois Press, Urbana, 1987; B. Epstein, *The Politics of Domesticity*, Wesleyan University Press, Middletown, 1981; K. Kish-Sklar, *Catherine Beecher*, Yale University Press, New Haven, 1973; and J.W. Scott, *Gender and the Politics of History*, Columbia University Press, New York, 1988.
97 See for instance L. Davidoff, 'Class and Gender in Victorian England', in J. Newton *et.al.* (eds), *Sex and Class in Women's History*, pp. 17–71; J. R. Walkowitz, *City of Dreadful Delight*, pp. 121–34; M. Lake, 'Female Desires: The Meaning of World War II', *Australian Historical Studies*, vol. 24, no. 95, 1990, pp. 267–84; and R. R. Pierson, 'Experience, Difference, Dominance and Voice in the Writing of Canadian Women's History', in K. Offen *et. al.* (eds), *Writing Women's History*, Indiana University Press, Bloomington, 1991, pp. 79–106.
98 J.W. Scott, 'Experience', p. 37.
99 R. Delmar, 'What is Feminism?', p. 28.
100 P. Levine, *Victorian Feminism*, Hutchinson, London, 1987, p. 15; R.W. Connell and T.H. Irving, *Class Structure in Australian History*, Longman Cheshire, Melbourne, 1980, pp. 203–4; E.C. Dubois, *Feminism and Suffrage*, pp. 60–75; and N.F. Cott, 'Women's Rights: Unspeakable Issues in the Constitution', *Yale Review*, vol. 77, no. 3, 1988, pp. 387–93.
101 United States historian, Paula Baker, advances the fascinating argument that this equation of masculinity and suffrage gradually weakened across

the late-nineteenth and early-twentieth centuries with changes in forms of politics, including the decline in voter turnout and the shift of substantive policy-making power to non-elected bureaucrats, especially in urban, industrialised areas. The weakening of this equation produced a climate facilitating woman suffrage. See P. Baker, 'The Domestication of Politics: Women and American Political Society 1780–1920', *American Historical Review*, vol. 89, no. 4, 1984, pp. 620–47.

102 For discussion of the contemporary Australian case see J. Huggins and T. Blake, 'Protection or Persecution? Gender Relations in the Era of Racial Segregation', in K. Saunders and R. Evans (eds), *Gender Relations in Australia*, pp. 53–6.

103 P. Levine, *Victorian Feminists*, p. 16.

104 For a useful discussion of this problem see E.C. Dubois, 'Working Women, Class Relations and Suffrage Militance: Harriet Stanton Blatch and the New York Woman Suffrage Movement, 1894–1909', *Journal of American History*, vol. 74, no. 1, 1987, pp. 34–58. And see for instance S. Ware, *Beyond Suffrage*, Harvard University Press, Cambridge, 1981.

105 This is most strongly delineated in N.F. Cott, 'Historical Perspectives: The Equal Rights Amendment Conflict in the 1920s', in M. Hirsch and E. Fox-Keller (eds), *Conflicts in Feminism*, pp. 44–59.

106 M. Franklin, 'Miss Rose Scott: Some Aspects of Her Personality and Work', in F.B.S. Eldershaw (ed.), *The Peaceful Army*, [1938], Republished Penguin, Ringwood, 1988, pp. 92–113; A.R. Scott Cowen, 'Across Dry Creekbeds', Unpublished Memoir, 1967, John Oxley Library, MSS OM.71–23, p. 26; Rose Scott, Printed Leaflets and Newspaper Cuttings (*re*. Australian history 1902–1924), Scott Family Papers (hereafter SFP), ML MS38/66, p. 25.

107 See for instance A. Summers, *Damned Whores and God's Police*, pp. 197–289; K. Daniels, 'Women's History', in G. Osborne and W.F. Mandle (eds), *New History*, Allen & Unwin, Sydney, 1982, pp. 32–50; J.A. Allen, 'From Women's History to History of the Sexes', pp. 220–41; M. Lake, 'Gender and History', *Australian Feminist Studies*, nos 7/8, 1988, pp. 1–10; J.K. Conway, 'Gender in Australia', *Daedalus*, vol. 114, no. 2, 1985, pp. 343–68; P. Grimshaw, 'Women in History: Reconstructing the Past', in J. Goodnow and C. Pateman (eds), *Women, Social Science and Public Policy*, Allen & Unwin, Sydney, 1985, pp. 32–55, and 'Writing the History of Australian Women', in K. Offen *et.al.* (eds), *Writing Women's History*, pp. 151–70. See also N. MacKenzie, *Women in Australia*, Cheshire, Melbourne, 1962; S. Encel, *Women and Society*, Longman Cheshire, Melbourne, 1974; and I. Turner, 'Prisoners in Petticoats', in J. Rigg (ed.), *In Her Own Right*, Nelson, Melbourne, 1970, pp. 3–24.

108 H. Radi, 'Lawson, Louisa (1848–1920)', in B. Nairn and G. Serle (eds), *ADB, Vol. 10, Lat–Ner*, Melbourne University Press, Melbourne, pp. 23–5, and 'Windeyer, Mary Elizabeth (1836–1912) and Margaret (1866–1939)', in J. Ritchie (ed.), *ADB, Vol. 12, Smy–Z*, 1990, pp. 537–9; B.R. Kingston, 'Anderson, Maybanke Susannah (1845–1927)', in B. Nairn and G. Serle (eds), *ADB, Vol. 7, A–Ch*, 1979, pp. 59–60; J.N. Brownfoot, 'Goldstein, Vida Jane Mary (1869–1949)', in B. Nairn and G. Serle (eds), *ADB, Vol. 9, Gil–Las*, 1983, pp. 43–5; M. Brown, 'Cowan, Edith Dircksey (1861–1932)', in B. Nairn and G. Serle (eds), *ADB,Vol. 8, Ci–Gib*, 1981, pp. 123–4; N. Lutton, 'Rischbieth, Bessie Mabel (1874–1967)', in G. Serle (ed.), *ADB, Vol. 11, Nes–Smi*, 1988, pp. 394–6;

and P. Young, 'Miller, Emma (1839–1917)', in B. Nairn and G. Serle (eds), *ADB, Vol. 10*, pp. 509–10. See also M. Gatens, 'A Critique of the Sex/Gender Distinction', pp. 144–6 and 152–4.

109 See for instance, S. Magarey, *Unbridling the Tongues of Women*, pp. 28 and 181–94; M. Lake, 'The Politics of Respectability', pp. 116–22;
H. Golder, *Divorce in Nineteenth Century New South Wales*, University of New South Wales Press, Kensington, 1985, pp. 222–9;
B.R. Kingston, *My Wife, My Daughter and Poor Mary Ann*, Nelson, Melbourne, 1975, pp. 26–8; M. Dixson, *The Real Matilda*, Penguin, Ringwood, 1976, pp. 210–14; P. Grimshaw, 'Women and the Family in Australian History', in E. Windschuttle (ed.), *Women, Class and History*, Fontana, Melbourne, 1980, pp. 37–52; H. Radi, 'Organizing for Reform', in H. Radi (ed.), *Jessie Street*, pp. 107–17 and 'Lawson, Louisa (1848–1920)' in G. Serle (ed.), *ADB, Vol. 10, 1891–1939, Lat–Ner*, 1985, pp. 23–5;
P. Johnson, 'Nineteenth Century Australian Feminism: A Study of *The Dawn* ', *Australia 1888: A Bicentennial Bulletin*, no. 13, 1984, pp. 71–81;
S. Sheridan, 'Louisa Lawson, Miles Franklin and Feminist Writing 1888–1901', *Australian Feminist Studies*, pp. 29–31; A. Summers, *Damned Whores and God's Police*, pp. 347–78; J. Roe, 'Chivalry and Social Policy in the Antipodes', *Historical Studies*, vol. 22, no. 88, 1987, pp. 404–10;
E. Zinkhan, 'Louisa Albury Lawson: Feminist and Patriot', in D. Adelaide (ed.), *A Bright and Fiery Troop*, Penguin, Melbourne, 1988, pp. 217–32;
C. Lansbury, 'The Feminine Frontier: Women's Suffrage and Economic Reality', *Meanjin Quarterly*, vol. 31, no. 3, 1972, pp. 286–96; and J.J. Matthews, 'Feminist History', *Labour History*, no. 50, 1986, pp. 147–53.

110 P. Grimshaw, 'Women and the Family', pp. 44–5; A. Summers, *Damned Whores and God's Police*, pp. 370–3; M. Dixson, *The Real Matilda*, p. 211, and 'Gender, Class and the Women's Movements in Australia, 1890, 1880', in N. Grieve and A. Burns (eds), *Australian Women*, p. 20.

111 K. Spearritt, 'New Dawns', p. 329. See also B.R. Kingston, *Glad Confident Morning: The Oxford History of Australia, Vol. 3, 1860–1900*, Oxford University Press, Melbourne, 1988, p. 104; B. Cameron, 'The Flappers and the Feminists: A Study of Women's Emancipation in the 1920s', and K. White, 'Bessie Rischbieth, Jessie Street and the End of the First Wave of Feminism in Australia', and P. Ranald, 'Feminism and Class: The United Associations of Women and the Council for Action for Equal Pay in the Depression', in M. Bevege *et.al.* (eds), *Worth Her Salt*, Hale & Iremonger, Sydney, 1982, pp. 257–69, 270– 85 and 319–29; B. Searle, *Silk and Calico*, Hale & Iremonger, Sydney, 1988; and C. Shute, 'Heroines and Heroes: Sexual Mythology in Australia, 1914–1918', *Hecate*, vol. 1, no. 1, 1975, pp. 6–22.

112 See for instance, C.G. Heilbrun, *Writing a Woman's Life*, The Women's Press, London, 1989; The Personal Narratives Group (ed.), *Interpreting Women's Lives*, Indiana University Press, Bloomington, 1989; L. Stanley, 'Biography as Microscope or Kaleidoscope? The Case of "Power" in Hannah Cullwick's Relationship with Arthur Munby', *Women's Studies International Forum*, vol. 10, no. 1, 1987 pp. 19–31, and 'Recovering Women From Feminist Deconstruction', pp. 154–7; and K. Barry, 'The New Historical Synthesis', pp. 96–9.

Chapter 1   Generations (1847–64)

1 See essays upon these prominent women in H. Radi (ed.), *200 Australian*

Women, Women's Redress Press, Sydney, 1988; *Australian Dictionary of Biography (ADB), 1891–1939*, vols 10–12, Melbourne University Press, Melbourne, 1981, 1985 and 1990. That pattern of diversity is clear in the comparison of women like Annette Bear Crawford (1853–1899), Emma Miller (1839–1927), Mary Windeyer (1836–1912), Louisa Lawson (1848–1920), Maybanke Wolstenholme (Anderson)(1845–1927), Annie and Belle Golding (1855–1934 and 1864–1940), Louisa MacDonald (1858–1949), Vida Goldstein (1869–1949) and many others.

2 Georgianna Rusden to Saranna Scott, 25 October 1864, Saranna Scott Correspondence (SSC) ML A2268, p. 953.

3 See 'Rusden Family Tree' in Rusden Family Papers, vol. I, Newcastle Region Public Library (NRPL) LHF.929.2RUS; and C.E. Smith, 'Pioneer Priest of St. Peters', ML DOC 1067, Typescript, 1967, 3pp.

4 C.E. Smith, 'The Scott Family', ML DOC 1032, Typescript, 1967, p. 2.

5 ibid., pp. 1–2. As a woman of considerable wealth, Mrs Scott purchased the grand Sydney house Cumberland Place, originally built for Bishop Broughton. Friends and visitors to the house included artist Conrad Martens, Dr James Mitchell (1792–1869) of the staff of Sydney Hospital, and various colonial gentry sometimes dubbed 'the government house set'.

6 Patrick Scott — Power of Attorney, SFP, ML MS 38/19, n.p.

7 Helenus Scott to Augusta Maria Scott, 3 October 1822, Hellenus Scott Correspondence (HSC), ML A2264.

8 ibid., 25 September 1826.

9 ibid., 10 October 1824.

10 ibid., 16 April 1827.

11 Helenus Scott to Robert Scott, 8 August 1824, HSC, A2264.

12 Helenus Scott to Augusta Maria Scott, October 1824, HSC, A2264.

13 Robert Scott to Helenus Scott, 2 March 1830, Robert Scott Correspondence, ML A2263 n.p.

14 E. Guilford, 'The Glendon Stud of Robert and Helenus Scott and the Beginnings of the Thoroughbred Breeding Industry in the Hunter Valley', *Journal of Hunter Valley History*, vol. 1, no. 1, 1985, pp. 63–106.

15 J.C. Caldwell, 'Population' in W. Vamplew (ed.), *Australians*, Fairfax Syme & Weldon and Associates, Sydney, 1988, pp. 23–4.

16 B. Pearson, 'Wilhelm Kirchner: His Diary and Subsequent Life in Australia', Society of Australian Genealogists, 4/9472/3; and N. Grey, 'Scott, Alexander Walker', 1973. NRPL, Vertical Files, pp. 1–4.

17 N. Grey, 'Scott, Alexander Walker', p. 3.

18 Mitchell Library, Picture Copying Scheme Catalogue, 'S–Siz'.

19 For an account of the Merewether family tree, see F.C. Mowle (ed.), *A Genealogical History of Pioneer Families of Australia*, 5th ed., Rigby, Adelaide, 1978 (1st edition, 1939), pp. 257–8.

20 Helenus Scott, Business and Glendon Property Papers, SFP, 38/11, 12x and 19.

21 Helenus Scott to Augusta Maria Scott, 3 October 1922, HSC, A2264.

22 A. R. Scott Cowen, 'Across Dry Creeks', p. 4.

23 'Association for Obtaining Permission to Transport Coolies from India to New South Wales', Governor George Gipps, Dispatches [Indian Labour], 1840, ML A2029, p. 1.

24 R.W. Connell & T.H. Irving, *Class Structure in Australian History*, Longman Cheshire, Melbourne, 1980, pp. 105–35.

25 Helenus Scott to Augusta Maria Scott, 28 September 1826, HSC, A2264;

'Enquiry into the Shooting of Natives, Hunter River, 6 October 1826', Governor's Dispatches, vol. 8, ML A1197, pp. 288–415.

26 Helenus Scott to Augusta Maria Scott, 16 April 1827, HSC, A2264.
27 Edward John Eyre, 'Autobiography' ML A1806, p. 47.
28 'Robert Scott, 1838 — Presided at meeting at Patrick's Plains in support of the eleven men who had murdered blacks', Governor George Gipps, Dispatches, 1838, ML A1219, pp. 690–1; 'Leader of Deputation to Sir G. Gipps on behalf of men convicted of murdering the blacks', and 'omitted from the new Commission of the Peace on account of his actions in connection with the men who murdered the blacks', ML A1219, pp. 694–5.
29 Mitchell was a signatory to 'Petitions against the transportation of criminals to New South Wales', NSW Legislative Council, 1850 ML A285, p. 30.
30 M. Munro, '"Passionately in Earnest:" A Biography of Rose Scott', Typescript, NLA, MS 2724, p. 4.
31 ibid., p. 5.
32 A. R. Scott Cowen, 'The Scott Family', ML M3/693. There are grounds to doubt the reliability of Alice Hamilton's testimony as reported by this author, her daughter. She claims that Alice spoke French and German and that on this account Leichhardt came and spoke his native language with her at Glendon, however the Scotts sold Glendon in 1858 when Alice was only 7.
33 Robert Scott, Last Will and Testament, 17 July 1844, Robert Scott Correspondence, A2263, n.p.
34 Patrick Scott to Saranna Scott, 21 August 1847, SSC, A2268, pp. 353–6.
35 *Singleton District Pioneer Register*, Family History Society, Maitland, 1989.
36 Helenus Scott to Saranna Scott, 29 August 1844, HSC, A2264.
37 ibid., 18 August 1844
38 P. McDonald *et.al.*, 'Marriage, Fertility and Mortality' in W. Vamplew (ed.), *Australians*, p. 42.
39 George Keylock Rusden to Saranna Scott, 3 October 1840, Miscellaneous Scott and Rusden Manuscripts (MSRM), A2269, p. 239.
40 ibid., 18 May 1845, p. 253.
41 Helenus Scott to Saranna Scott, 20 November 1845, HSC, A2264.
42 ibid., 16 September 1846.
43 Anne Rusden to Saranna Scott, 11 May 1848, MSRM, A2269, p. 389.
44 ibid., 12 May 1848, p. 394.
45 George Keylock Rusden to Saranna Scott, 30 December 1847, MSRM, A2269, p. 260–1.
46 Helenus Scott to Undersecretary, NSW Department of the Attorney General, 15 March 1879, HSC, A2264.
47 Saranna Scott to Helenus Scott, 3 June 1855, HSC, A2264.
48 Rose Scott's library by 1912 was reported to Bertram Stevens, editor of *The Lone Hand*, who was undertaking a survey of the reading habits of Sydney's leading citizens. The following authors were listed as Scott's favourites: Thackeray, Arnold, Dickens, Scott, Shelley, Keats, Shakespeare, Spencer, Mill, Kipling, Plato, Rossetti, Elliot, Gaskell, Huxley, Tennyson, Ibsen, Tolstoi, Caird, Bernard Shaw, Kingsley, Mazzini, Dante, Perkins Gilman, Bebel and Galsworthy. See Bertram Stevens to RS, 4 April 1912, Rose Scott Correspondence (RSC), A2283, pp. 809–10.

49 R. Scott, 'Retirement Speech to Feminist Club' Sydney, 12 April 1921, SFP 38/27, p. 317–22.
50 For evidence of this relationship between cousins, see Merewether Estate Archives (MEA), Edward Charles Merewether Correspondence (ECMC) 1876–1893, NRPL, A1.
51 Anne Rusden to Saranna Scott, 31 July 1850, MSRM, A2269, p. 467.
52 Saranna Scott to Helenus Scott, 7 December 1850, HSC, A2264.
53 ibid., 28 December 1851.
54 ibid., 30 September 1855.
55 George Keylock Rusden to Saranna Scott, 20 January 1858, MSRM, A2269, p. 269. There is some uncertainty about what happened to Fannie Scott. The 1979 Mitchell Library guide to *The Scott Family* contains a family tree which entirely omits both her and Walker Scott, born in 1844. There is no mention of her in family correspondence after the 1850s nor in Rose Scott's extensive papers *c.* 1880–1925. Yet she is recorded as buried in Cowra cemetery in 1924 as Mrs Saranna Wensley, pre-deceased by John Wensley (1836–1919). Photographs of Saranna Wensley (née Scott) were donated to the Newcastle City Library in 1967 by her granddaughter, Florence Wensley, and there is no mistaking the Scott family resemblance. Five of the children of John Wensley are called by common Rusden and Scott names: George Arthur (b. 1861), Alice Elizabeth (b. 1862), Rose Augusta (b. 1864), Alfred Henry (b. 1867). The sixth child, Jessie, was born in 1868; and a seventh, Herbert in 1878. However, indexes to New South Wales Birth, Deaths and Marriages show no marriage between John Wensley and Saranna Scott. Instead, the marriage of John Wensley and Lucy West is recorded in 1860 and the parents' names listed for the births of all of these Wensley children are 'John' and 'Lucy'.
56 George Keylock Rusden to Saranna Scott, 4 November 1858, MSRM, A2269, p. 273.
57 RS to Alice Scott, 11 October 1858, Rose Scott Further Papers 1858–1951, ML MS 5066, Item I.
58 Georgianna Rusden to Saranna Scott, 24 November 1858, SSC, A2268, p. 855.
59 C.E. Smith, 'Five Articles Concerning Dr James Mitchell and His Family (1791–1869)', 1966, ML DOC.993.
60 Georgianna Rusden to Saranna Scott, 24 February 1862 and 16 July 1865, SSC, A2263, pp. 919, 963 and 968. It should be noted that this paucity of formal education was by no means confined to upper-middle-class and genteel families fallen on hard times. This issue has been explored particularly well in British women's history, useful examples of which are: D. Gorham, *The Victorian Girl and the Feminine Ideal*, Croom Helm, London, 1981; C. Dyhouse, *Feminism and the Family in Victorian England, 1880–1930*, Basil Blackwell, Oxford, 1989; and B. Caine, *Destined to Be Wives*. See also N. Kyle, *Her Natural Destiny*, University of New South Wales Press, Kensington, 1987.
61 Rose and Augusta Scott, 'Notebook for the Journal May 20, 1864–November 14, 1865', ML B1528.
62 Arthur Selwyn to Saranna Scott, 6 July 1861, Selwyn Family Papers, ML MS 201/1, p. 19. See also Rose Selwyn, 'Memories', unpublished typescript, 1905, ML A1616.
63 Though evidence of a marriage has not been located, it seems clear that she was no longer in residence in the Scott home.

64 See Queensland, Indexes to Registers of Marriages, 1877, Registers of Births 1878–1881, and Register of Deaths 1881; and Rose Scott, Last Will and Testament, *Australian Dictionary of Biography* File no. 77. I am indebted to Dr Chris Cuneen for copies of this will.

65 See further discussion in Chapter 2: Home Lessons (1865–90). The age difference between them and the mobility imposed by his career meant that Rose Scott had little contact with her brother, Helenus, or his wife prior to his untimely death in 1881. However, his daughter Rosie was to become very close to her aunt , and eventually was named as executrix of Rose Scott's will.

66 Anglican Diocese of Newcastle, Christ Church Cathedral, Newcastle 1858–1879 — Registers of Marriages, Baptisms and Burials, NRPL, LHQ.929. In percentage terms the majority of men who married in the Scott's Church, Christ Church Cathedral, did so before the age of 30 and the majority of women before 25.

67 Helenus Scott, Magistrate's Papers, SFP, 38/9, pp. 17–36.

Chapter 2   'Home Lessons' (1865–90)

1 Gussie Scott to Rose Scott, 4 August 1867, SFP, 38/21 252–6.

2 *Newcastle Morning Herald (NMH)*, 14 June 1892.

3 G.D. Richardson, 'Mitchell, David Scott (1836–1907)', in B. Nairn *et.al.* (eds), *ADB, vol. 4 1851–90, K–Q*, Melbourne University Press, Melbourne, 1974, pp. 260–1.

4 See H. Radi, Windeyer, Mary Elizabeth (1836–1912)' in J. Ritchie (ed.), *ADB, vol. 12. 1891–1939, Smy–Z*, pp. 537–9.

5 D.S. Mitchell, 'To Miss Emily Manning (November 1864)', Mitchell Family Papers, ML MS379/4, Item 1.

6 D.S. Mitchell to RS, 13 April, 9 July and 7 October 1865, RSP 1862–1923, ML A1437, pp. 21, 27 and 29.

7 D.S. Mitchell, To My Pipe (1866), Mitchell Family Papers, 379/4, Item 1.

8 D.S. Mitchell to RS, 1 December 1867, RSP, A1437, p. 496.

9 (Anon.) *Mutum est Pictura Poema*. Original High Art kindly Composed for and Dedicated to DSM, BA. for the Edification and special Enlightenment of His Mind During His Sojourn in Tartarius by Pitying Beings In Elysium', 19 March 1868, Mitchell Family Papers, 379/4, Item 4.

10 D.S. Mitchell to RS, 10 May 1868, RSP, A1437, p. 69b.

11 Grace Rusden to Saranna Scott, 1867, Rose Scott Further Papers 1858–1951, ML MS5066, Item 2.

12 Mitchell Library, Biographical Notes on Emily Matilda Heron (neé Manning), her family and David Scott Mitchell, 1845–1890. 1967, ML DOC.1454, 2pp.

13 C.E. Smith, 'Five Articles on Dr James Mitchell and His Family 1791–1869' and *Newcastle Chronicle*, 19 May 1869.

14 Sir William Manning to Dr James Mitchell, 27 January 1869, and Sir John Young to Augusta Mitchell, 9 September 1869, Mitchell Family Papers, 379/2, p. 293.

15 C.E. Smith, 'Five Articles on Dr James Mitchell and His Family 1791–1869'.

16 D.S. Mitchell to E.C. Merewether, 23 and 29 May 1869, ECMC, MEA, NRPL, A1 part.

17 Bertram Stevens, 'David Scott–Mitchell' Typescript, 1919. ML A1830, p. 24 and H.C.L. Anderson, Reminiscences of David Mitchell', Typescript 1922, ML A1830.

18 D.S. Mitchell to RS, 13 February 1870, RSP, A1437, p. 145.
19 D.S. Mitchell to RS, 6 March 1870, RSP, A1437, p. 152.
20 Bertram Stevens, 'David Scott Mitchell', p. 11.
21 *SMH*, March 1966.
22 D.S. Mitchell to RS, 21 March and 25 July 1875, RSP, A1437, pp. 176, 273–7 and 278–84.
23 D.S. Mitchell to Saranna Scott, 24 February 1880, SFP, 38/19, p. 315 and RS to D.S. Mitchell, 'Xmas 1892', Mitchell Family Papers, 379/4.
24 Madam Sibly, 'Phrenological Analysis of Miss Rose Scott' (25 January 1875), SFP, 38/32x, pp. 3–10.
25 Bertram Stevens, 'David Scott Mitchell', pp. 2 and 10; and D.S. Mitchell, Will, 3 October 1905. ML Safe 3/20a-b and H.C. Anderson, 'Reminiscences of David Mitchell', p. 32.
26 R. Rosenberg, *Beyond Separate Spheres*, pp. 5–12.
27 Henry Keylock Rusden to RS, 22 June 1892 and 13 August 1898, MSRM.
28 A.R. Scott Cowen, 'Across Dry Creek Beds', p. 26.
29 E.C. Merewether (ECM) to Robert Scott, 5 January 1877, MEA, ECM A1 part.
30 Anglican Diocese of Newcastle, Christ Church Cathedral, Newcastle Marriage Register, 20 February 1878, No.91; Parish Register Indexes, NRPL, LH mfm 923.3 SIN. Roll 1; and Christ Church Cathedral, Newcastle Marriage Register, 8 June 1880, No. 123.
31 ECM to Robert Scott, 23 June 1881; 7 May and 23 July 1881, MEA, ECMC, A1 Part.
32 Queensland Indexes to Births, Deaths and Marriages 1877–1881.
33 ECM to Robert Scott, 15 June 1887; 18 and 25 August, 1881; 24 August 1881; MEA, ECMC, A1 Part. 15 and 21 June and 10 August 1881. 12 February, 7 May and 27 August, 1883, MEA, ECMC, A1 Part.
34 A.R. Scott Cowen, 'Across Dry Creekbeds', pp. 90–1.
35 Saranna Scott to Patrick Scott, 23 January 1882, MSRM A2269.
36 ECM to Robert Scott, 3 February 1885, MEA, ECMC, A1 Part.
37 Aimée Ranclaud to RS, 3 February 1885, SFP 1835–1968, ML MS 1694, p. 3–4.
38 *NMH*, 25 June 1885.
39 ECM to Robert Scott, 13 February 1885; 29 June, 9 August, 15 and 29 December 1886; 9 June, 13 and 30 July, 21 October and 5 November 1887; 5 November 1886; 14 May 1881, MEA, ECMC, A1 Part.
40 A.R. Scott Cowen, 'Across Dry Creekbeds', p. 90.
41 Mary Stoddard to RS, 30 August 1884; 7 January 1885; 22 January 1890, RSC, A2282, pp. 2, 3 and 16.
42 C.A. A'Beckett to RS, 8 June 1888, SFP, 38/21, p. 233.
43 Bishop Pearson to RS, 17 May 1884, RSC, A2276.
44 F. McDonald to RS, 4 June 1888, RSC, A2282, pp. 9–10; H.K. Keylock to RS, 17 and 19 March 1888, MSRM, A2269, pp. 421 and 431.
45 See W.C. Windeyer, *Ex Parte Collins*, Government Printers, Sydney, 1888; and C.R. Stimpson, 'Are the Differences Spreading? Feminist Criticism and Postmodernism', *English Studies in Canada*, vol. 15, no. 4, 1989, pp. 373–5.
46 See M. Vicinus, *Independent Women*, Virago, London, 1985, pp. 293–4; G.A. Carmichael, *With This Ring*, Australian National University, Canberra, 1988, p. 3; P. McDonald, *Marriage and the Family in Australia*, Australian National University, Canberra, 1978, pp. 112 and 143; K. Saunders and K. Spearritt, 'Is There Life After Birth? Childbirth, Death and Danger for Settler Women in Colonial Queensland', *Journal of Australian Studies*, no. 29, pp. 122–53;

K. Spearritt, 'The Market for Marriage in Colonial Queensland', *Hecate*, vol. 16, nos 1–2, pp. 23–42; L. Faderman, *Surpassing the Love of Men*; S. Jeffreys, 'Sex Reform, and Anti-Feminism in the 1920s' in London Feminist History Group (eds), *The Sexual Dynamics of History*, pp. 175–201; M. Ramas, 'Freud's Dora, Dora's Hysteria' in J. Newton *et.al.* (eds), *Sex and Class in Women's History*, pp. 73–113; D. Hunter, 'Hysteria, Psychoanalysis and Feminism: the Case of Anna O', *Feminist Studies*, vol. 9, no. 3, 1983, pp. 465–88; C. Smith-Rosenberg, 'The Female World of Love and Ritual', pp. 73–6; and N. Cott, *The Grounding of Modern Feminism*, pp. 36–50.

47 *SMH*, 27 April 1925 and 20 April 1889.

48 Charlotte Hadfield, 'A Mental Analysis of Mr Hope Helenus Scott Wallace . . . and Miss Rose Scott, Sydney 1888' and Professor Blumenthal, 'H.H. Wallace: Phrenological and Physiognometrical Chart', 23 August 1890, SFP 38/32x, 11–41 and 61–9.

49 See B. Berg, *The Remembered Gate*, Oxford University Press, New York, 1978; and M.J. Buhle, *Women and American Socialism 1870–1930*, University of Illinois Press, Urbana, 1983.

50 Women's Literary Society (WLS), Rules, Programmes 1890–95 and Annual Report 1893.

51 M. Foley, The Women's Movement in New South Wales and Victoria 1918–1938, unpublished PhD dissertation, University of Sydney, 1985, pp. 62–6.

52 For discussions of the relationships between illegitimacy, philanthropy, temperance and feminism in both Australian and comparative contexts, see J. Godden, Philanthropy and the Woman's Sphere: Sydney 1870–1900, unpublished PhD dissertation, Macquarie University, 1981, '"The Work for Them and the Glory for Us": Sydney Women's Philanthropy 1870–1900', in R. Kennedy (ed.), *Australian Welfare History*, Critical Essays, Macmillian, Melbourne, 1982, pp. 84–102, and 'Portrait of a Lady: A Decade in the Life of Helen Fell (1849–1935)', in M. Bevege *et.al.* (eds), *Worth Her Salt*, Hale & Iremonger, Sydney, 1982, pp. 33–48; L. Brignell, Illegitimacy in New South Wales 1875–1972, unpublished PhD dissertation, University of Sydney, 1990; S.R. Garton, *Out of Luck*, Allen & Unwin, Sydney, 1990, pp. 54, 86 and 89; J.A. Allen, *Sex and Secrets*, Oxford University Press, Melbourne, 1990, p. 20; M. Lake, 'The Politics of Respectability: Identifying the Masculinist Context', pp. 116–31; A. Summers, 'A Home from Home: Women's Philanthropic Work in the Nineteenth Century', in S. Burman (ed.), *Fit Work for Women*, Croom Helm, London, 1979, pp. 33–64; J. Lewis, 'Women and Late Nineteenth Century Social Work', in C. Smart (ed.), *Regulating Womanhood*, pp. 78–99; B. Harrison-Lee, One of *Australia's Daughters*, N.J. Osborn, London, 1906; J. Ackerman, *Australia From a Woman's Point of View*, Cassell, London, 1913; P. Grimshaw, *Women's Suffrage in New Zealand*, University of Auckland Press, Auckland, 1972; A. Hyslop, 'Agents and Objects: Women and Societal Reform in Melbourne 1900–1914', in M. Bevege *et.al.* (eds), *Worth Her Salt*, pp. 230–43; A. O'Brien, *Poverty's Prison*, Melbourne University Press, Melbourne, 1988, pp. 200–24; and B. Matthews, *Louisa*, McPhee Gribble, Melbourne, 1987, pp. 159–63.

53 O. Lawson (ed.), *The First Voice of Australian Feminism*, p. 67.

54 B. Matthews, *Louisa*; J. Hagan, 'An Incident at *The Dawn*', *Labour History*, no. 8, 1965, pp. 19–21. See also O. Lawson (ed.), *The First Voice of*

Australian Feminism, pp. 53–4, 67, 72–3, 84, 89 and 91; G. O'Connor, 'The Life of Louisa Lawson', Lawson Family Papers, ML A1898, pp. 112–17. More generally see *The Dawn: 1888–90*; E. Zinkhan, 'Louisa Albury Lawson: Feminist and Patriot', in D. Adelaide (ed.), *A Bright and Fiery Troop*, pp. 217–32; H. Radi, 'Lawson, Louisa (1848–1920)', in B. Nairn & G. Serle (eds), *ADB, Vol. 10: 1891–1939, Lat–Ner*, Melbourne University Press, Melbourne, 1985, pp. 23–5; and P. Johnson, 'Nineteenth Century Australian Feminism: A Study of *The Dawn* ', *Australia 1888 Bulletin*, no. 13, 1984, pp. 71–81.

55 R. Scott, Undated Notebook, SFP, 38/22, Items 9 and 2. For contextual discussion of reproductive experiences of women before and after the contraction of childbearing see R. Howe & S. Swain, 'Fertile Grounds for Divorce: The Marital and Reproductive Imperatives', in K. Saunders and R. Evans (eds), *Gender Relations in Australia*, pp. 158–74; M. Anderson, '"A Helpmeet for Man"', pp. 101–12; P. Quiggin, *No Rising Generation*, Australian National University Press, Canberra, 1988; H. Ware, *Fertility and Family Formation in Australia*, Australian National University Press, Canberra, 1975; and M. Lake, 'Building Themselves Up with Aspros: The Pioneer Woman Reassessed', *Hecate*, vol. 7, no. 1, 1981, pp. 7–19.

56 L. Gordon & E. Dubois, '"Seeking Ecstasy on the Battlefield": Danger and Pleasure in Nineteenth Century Feminist Sexual Thought', pp. 7–26. Scott's scepticism about existing notions of consent have interesting modern reflections in C. Pateman's 'Women and Consent', *Political Theory*, vol. 8, no. 2, 1980, pp. 149–68.

57 B.R. Kingston, *My Wife, My Daughter and Poor Mary Ann*, Nelson, Melbourne, 1975, pp. 116–20.

58 N. Cott, *The Grounding of Modern Feminism*, pp. 5 and 39.

59 R. Scott, notebook entry, n.d.

Chapter 3 *'Why Women Want a Vote' (1891–96)*

1 Rose Selwyn to RS, 9 November 1892, Selwyn Family Papers, ML MS 201/3/3, pp. 36–8; Rose Selwyn, Should Women Be Jurors?, unpublished speech, 201/3/6, pp. 23–7; and Rose Selwyn to RS, 26 January 1893, SFP, 38/21, p. 73.

2 A.R. Scott Cowen, 'Across Dry Creek Beds', pp. 27 and 89.

3 G.W. Rusden to RS, 3 November 1891, MSRM, A2269, p. 315.

4 Miles Franklin to Mollye Menken, 20 July 1952, Miles Franklin Papers (MFP), ML MS 364/20, pp. 169–71.

5 A.R. Scott Cowen, 'Across Dry Creek Beds', pp. 89–90.

6 Saranna Scott to Patrick Scott, 23 January 1882, MSRM, A2269, p. 160.

7 Saranna Scott, 'My Birthday Gifts', 3 April 1891, MSRM, A2269, p. 177.

8 RS to Augusta Merewether, 1893, ECMC, A1 (part) b.

9 G.W. Rusden to RS, 7 May 1891, RSC, A2269, p. 311.

10 A.R. Scott Cowen, 'Details of My Family History', NRPL, Vertical Files, 'S'.

11 G.W. Rusden to RS, 7 May 1891, MSRM, A2269, p. 314.

12 ibid., 9 February 1896, MSRM, A2269, pp. 250–2.

13 ibid., 23 July 1896, MSRM, A2269, p. 355.

14 RS to Dowell O'Reilly, 6 September 1896, RSC, A2272, p. 127.

15 J. Roe, *Beyond Belief*, University of New South Wales Press, Kensington, 1987, pp. 34–7

16 W.C. Windeyer, 'Notes on Seances 1892', Windeyer Family Papers

(WFP), ML MS 186/12/6, pp. 3–15; and see J. Docker, *The Nervous Nineties*, Oxford University Press, Melbourne, 1991, p. 56.

17 RS, ['Notes on a Seance'] 24 March 1893, SFP, 38/32, pp. 90–2.

18 J. Roe, *Beyond Belief*, pp. 82–5.

19 Maybanke Wolstenholme to RS, 11 June 1893, RSC, A2282, p. 60.

20 G.W. Rusden to RS, 29 March 1896, MSRM, A2269, p. 353.

21 Mary Cameron to RS, 29 May 1894, RSC, A2282, p. 70.

22 The interpretation of Lane's *Workingman's Paradise* and his basic masculinism, warring with an in principle commitment to feminism, receives insightful analysis by Marilyn Lake. Bruce Scates takes issue with her emphasis on Lane's 'masculinism', the centrality of manhood for socialism of the period and with her (in his view over-) reading of Lane's text. Lake's reply to Scates accuses him of a fraternal over-identification with Lane, of humanist reading and of misrepresenting her argument. See M. Lake 'Socialism and Manhood: The Case of William Lane', *Labour History*, no. 50, May 1986, pp. 54–62, B. Scates, 'Socialism and Feminism: The Case of William Lane. A reply to Marilyn Lake' and M. Lake 'Socialism and Manhood. A Reply to Bruce Scates', *Labour History*, no. 60, May 1991, pp. 45–58 and 114–26.

23 Frank Cotton to RS, 20 June 1893, RSC, A2282, p. 51.

24 Arthur Rae to RS, 27 March 1892 and J.D. Fitzgerald to RS, 29 March 1892, RSC, A2271, pp. 26–7.

25 RS, On Socialism, unpublished speech read at the WLS, April 1893, SFP, 38/28, pp. 75–85.

26 Arthur Rae to RS, 2 April 1892, 23 December 1893 and 18 August 1892, RSC, A2271, pp. 29, 55 and 73g. For an interesting reading of some consequences of this world-view for conjugal relations, see M. Lake, 'Intimate Strangers', in V. Burgmann and J. Lee (eds), *Making A Life*, McPhee Gribble/Penguin, Fitzroy/Ringwood, 1988, pp. 152–65.

27 WLS, Annual Reports 1890–95, ML374.23/W; and 'Papers on Literature', SFP, 38/69/1 19–27.

28 [Newscuttings on the *A Doll's House* controversy], 'Papers on Literature', SFP, 38/69/1, pp. 8–56; and see D. Campbell, 'A Doll's House: The Colonial Response' in S. Dermody *et.al.* (eds), *Nellie Melba, Ginger Meggs and Friends*, Kibble Books, Melbourne, 1982, pp. 192–210.

29 See correspondence on the campaign for a Women's College, 'Women's Work and Women's Movements' Vol. 1 [a binders' title] RSC, A2276.

30 RS, Woman Suffrage, unpublished speech, March 1892, SFP, 38/38, pp. 19, 23–6, 27, 28–9, 30–1, 37, 37–8, 38, 41–4.

31 *NSWPD*, 1st Series, 1894, vol. 72, p. 465.

32 R. Scott, 'Woman Suffrage', p. 45.

33 E. Grosz, 'Feminist Theory and the Challenge to Knowledge', pp. 476–9.

34 RS, 'Woman Suffrage', pp. 1–2, 33–7, 41 and 12–14, and G. O'Connor, 'Life of Louisa Lawson', pp. 155–6.

35 R. Scott, Reply to Miss Edith Badham, unpublished speech, May 1895, SFP, 38/38, pp. 139–42. Many of Scott's rebuttals of such common arguments against woman suffrage were published in an article that year: R. Scott, 'Woman and the Franchise', *Australian Economist*, vol. 4, no. 15, 1895. See also M. Anderson, *A Citizen Who Has No Vote*, Australian Christian World, Sydney, n.d.

36 *NSWPD*, 1st Series, 1892, vol. 60, 1368–91 and 1377–9.

37 Arthur Rae to RS, 3, 9, and 15 February, 11, 18, 21 and 27 March, 2, 6,

21 and 22 April, 18 May, 18 August, 6 October, 17 November, 13
December 1892; 2 November, 20 December 1893; 17 November 1892,
RSC, A2271, pp. 12, 13, 19, 18, 23, 25, 26, 29, 31, 37, 48, 55, 59, 63, 69,
71, 73–4 and 64; Frank Cotton to RS, 21 January 1892 and n.d., RSC,
A2276, pp. 63a and 64.

38 Mary Windeyer to RS, n.d., RSC, A2284, p. 1320; Alice Wilson to RS,
24 March 1892, Georgina Edwards to RS, 17 December 1892,
N. Manning to RS, 20 January 1893, Annie Kelly to RS, 22 February
1893, and Dora Montefiore to RS, n.d., RSC, A2276, pp. 67, 69, 75, 76
and 77.

39 RS, incomplete, untitled, unpublished speech n.d. (on men and women),
SFP, 38/30, pp. 119–29.

40 RS to Bruce Smith, 17 March 1892, RSC, A2271, p. 17.

41 R. Scott, notebook entries, n.d., SFP, 38/22, Items 6, 7, 9 and 13.

42 C. Pateman, *The Sexual Contract*, Polity Press, Cambridge, 1988, pp. 193–4.

43 See H. Golder and J.A. Allen, 'Prostitution in New South Wales
1870–1932: Restructuring an Industry', *Refractory Girl*, nos 18/19, 1980,
pp. 17–24; J.A. Allen, 'The Making of A Prostitute Proletariat in Early
Twentieth Century New South Wales', in K. Daniels (ed.), *So Much Hard
Work*, Fontana, Sydney, 1984, pp. 192–232; and J.A. Allen, *Sex and
Secrets*, pp. 22–5.

44 See R. Rosen, *The Lost Sisterhood*, Johns Hopkins University Press,
Baltimore, Maryland, 1983, pp. 96–8.

45 See H. Golder, *Divorce in Nineteenth Century New South Wales*, pp. 143–8,
188–9 and 193; and P. Russell, 'For Better and for Worse: Love, Power
and Sexuality in Upper Class Marriages in Melbourne 1860–1890',
Australian Feminist Studies, nos 7/8, 1988, pp. 11–28; and U. Vogel,
'Whose Property? The Double Standard of Adultery in Nineteenth
Century Law', in C. Smart (ed.), *Regulating Womanhood*, pp. 147–65.

46 N. Cott, 'Passionlessness: An Interpretation of Victorian Sexual Ideology
1790–1850', *Signs*, vol. 4, no. 1, 1978, pp. 169–72.

47 RS, incomplete, untitled, unpublished speech, n.d. (on men and
women), SFP, 38/30, p. 97.

48 J.N. Simpson to RS, 15 April 1891, RSC, A2271, p. 3; and G. O'Connor,
'Life of Louisa Lawson', Lawson Family Papers, ML 1898, pp. 119–20.

49 JF (identity uncertain) to RS, 26 July 1896, RSC, A2282, p. 96.

50 RS to Henry Parkes, 17 October 1892, Parkes Correspondence, ML A905,
Vol. 58, pp. 680–1.

51 Louisa Lawson to RS, n.d., RSC, A2284, n.p.; Louisa Lawson to RS,
19 May 1892, RSC, A2271, p. 50; WSL, Roll book 1891–1902, SFP 38/34,
Item 1; WSL, Minutes, 22 April 1891, 16 June 1891; 10 August 1891; 1
and 15 December 1891, 15 March 1892, 19 April 1892, 6 September
1892, 4 October 1892; 21 February 1893, 1 and 9 August 1893, 5 and 9
September 1893, 3 and 11 October 1893, 21 November 1893, and 5
December 1893; 21 January 1894, SFP 38/33, pp. 4, 9, 17, 33, 35–7, 49,
55, 82, 87, 106, 136–41, 143, 146–8, 151, 153, 160, 163–5 and 165–6.

52 G. O'Connor 'Life of Louisa Lawson', pp. 127–8 and 'Louisa Lawson: Her
Life and Work', Lawson Family Papers, ML A1897, pp. 22–30; and
J. Docker, *The Nervous Nineties*, pp. 4–12.

53 RS to Henry Parkes, 17 October 1892, Parkes Correspondence, ML A905,
vol. 58, p. 682.

54 Lady Jersey to Lady Windeyer, 15 November 1891, WFP, ML MS 186/13,

p. 455.
55 O. Lawson (ed.), *The First Voice of Australian Feminism*, p. 121; *Illustrated Sydney News*, 7 May 1892.
56 RS to Henry Parkes, 22 November 1892, Parkes Correspondence, ML A905, vol. 58, p. 687.
57 Maybanke Anderson to RS, 27 October 1891, RSC, A2271, p. 10; RS to Mary Windeyer, [1892], WFP, ML MS 186/13, p. 477c.
58 Mary Lee to Mary Windeyer, 24 July 1893 and 4 January 1895, WFP, ML MS 186/14, pp. 85 and 275; RS to Mary Windeyer, July, 3 August and August n.d., WFP, 186/14, pp. 81a–87, 91–7, 109b, 127.
59 Mary Windeyer to M. Walsh, 22 September 1893, WFP, 186/14, pp. 141–9.
60 RS to Margaret Windeyer, 20 May 1894, WFP, 186/17, p. 229.
61 *The Australian Woman*, 28 March, 12 May and 23 June 1894; Annie Kelly to RS, 14 August n.d., WFP, 186/18, p. 81. WSL Minutes, 23 April 1894 and 1 September 1895, SFP, 38/33, pp. 180 and 317–19.
62 Maybanke Wolstenholme to RS, n.d. [1894?], RSC, A2271, p. 75c; L. Ashton to RS, n.d., RSC, A2284, pp. 195–6.
63 Bruce Smith to RS, 22 February 1892, p. 15; S.A. Rosa to RS, 18 September 1891, pp. 8–9; J.D. Fitzgerald to RS, 16 and 29 March 1892, pp. 22 and 27–8; Arthur Rae to RS, 11 March 1892, 5 June 1894, 17 August 1895; and T. Routley to RS, 9 August and 31 August 1895, RSC, A2271, pp. 8–9, 15, 22, 27–8, 82, 222, 222a and 223; and WSL, Minutes, 23 July, 27 August and 11 September 1895, and 28 January 1896, SFP, 38/33, pp. 308, 317, 324 and 348.
64 *NSWPD*, 1st Series, Vol. 72, 1894–95, pp. 463–515.
65 Dowell O'Reilly to RS, 21 January 1896, RSC, A2271, p. 226.

Chapter 4   Expanding the Brief (1897–1902)

1 Arthur Rae to RS, 20 February 1897, RSC, A2271, p. 255.
2 J.J. Matthews, *Good and Mad Women*, Allen & Unwin, Sydney, 1984, p. 32.
3 WSL, Minutes, 17 July 1900, p. 116; and May Tomkins to RS, 19 July 1900, RSC, A2272, p. 455.
4 See J. Mulraney, 'When Lovely Woman Stoops to Lobby', 1988, pp. 95–114; J. Roe, 'Introduction' to M. Franklin, *Some Everyday Folk and Dawn*, Virago, London, 1985, pp. vii–xix; C. Fernon, 'Women's Suffrage in Victoria', *Refractory Girl*, no. 22, 1981; S. Sheridan, 'Louisa Lawson, Miles Franklin and Feminist Writing 1888–1901', pp. 29–47; and F. Kelly, 'Vida Goldstein: Political Woman', in M. Lake and F. Kelly (eds), *Double-Time*, Penguin, Ringwood, 1985, pp. 167–78.
5 G.W. Rusden to RS (1899), MSRM, A2269, pp. 379–80.
6 M. Munro, '"Passionately in Earnest": A Biography of Rose Scott', p. 20.
7 H.K. Rusden to RS, 13 August 1898, MSRM, A2269, pp. 443–5.
8 *The World's News*, 20 October 1923.
9 Louisa MacDonald to RS, 15 December 1897, SFP, 38/20x, p. 393.
10 Frances Saul to RS, 25 May 1898, RSC, A2282, p. 148.
11 RS, 'Notes of My Visit to the Lawsons', 19 April 1899, SFP, 38/26. p. 55.
12 Henry Lawson to RS, 23 January 1898, RSC, A2270, p. 68; and H. Lawson, 'Joe Tries His Hand At A Sex Problem Story', SFP, 38/68, p. 45.
13 Frank Fox to RS, 25 March 1900, RSC, A2282, p. 189; and unidentified newscutting, 'Scott Looks Back — People of Her Salon', 23 December 1921, SFP, 38/60/1, pp. 107–8; and see Scott among correspondents of

John Farrell and with his bereaved relatives after his death in John
Farrell Papers, 1897–1904, ML MS1522.

14 RS to Miles Franklin (MF), 31 March 1902, MFP 364/8, pp. 7–8. On
Franklin's relationship with Scott see D. Modjeska, *Exiles at Home*, Sirius,
London, 1981, pp. 31–8.

15 See M. Franklin, *My Brilliant Career* [1901], Angus & Robertson, Sydney,
1966; and RS to 'Leila', n.d., SFP, 38/21.

16 RS to MF, 27 April, 22 and 27 June, 25 September and 15 December
1902, MFP, 364/8, 10, 15, 25, 51 and 52–3.

17 *Sun*, 24 March 1899.

18 See National Council of Women of New South Wales, 'Records, 1896–1958',
ML MS3739; National Council of Women of New South Wales, *The NCW of
NSW*, The Council, Sydney, n.d., and *Jubilee Report 1896–1946*, The Council,
Sydney, 1947; F.E. Hooper, *The Story of The Women's Club*, The Club, Sydney,
1964, and Women's Club, *Annual Report and Balance Sheet 1906–1939*, The
Club, Sydney 1907–40; Mary Booth to RS, 2 July 1901; Lilian Wise to RS, 7
October 1901; and 'Rules', RSC, A2276, pp. 112, 125 and 129; *Daily
Telegraph*, 21 October 1901. See also M. Anderson, *A Citizen Who Has No Vote*,
Australian Christian World, Sydney, n.d.

19 W.P. Cullen to RS, 11 February 1897, RSC, A2271, p. 249.

20 *NSWPD*, 1st Series, Vol. 108, 1900, p. 5476.

21 R. Scott, untitled, unpublished speech on federation, 1897, SFP, 38/27,
pp. 31–2 and 187.

22 RS to Commissioner of Taxation, n.d., RSC, A2271, pp. 274–5, and
W.P. Cullen to RS, 21 February 1897, RSC, A2271, p. 258.

23 *NSWPD*, 2nd Series, Vol. 1, 1901, p. 595.

24 A. Summers, *Damned Whores and God's Police*, p. 369.

25 James Ashton to RS, 27 June 1899, RSC, A2280, p. 43.

26 Edith Cowan to RS, 11 December 1901, RSC, A2277, p. 238.

27 For a historical account of various nations' participation in the National
Council of Women, see V. Strong-Boag, *The Parliament of Women* (History
Division Paper No.18), National Museum of Canada, Ottawa, 1976. See
also the official history of the foundation of the International Council of
Women and its original brief: M.W. Sewell, *The Genesis of the International
Council of Women 1888–1893*, ICW, Illinois, 1914; and for accounts of the
ICW's proceedings and work see International Council of Women, *Report
from the Quinquennial Meeting at Berlin, 1904, Toronto, 1909, Rome, 1914 and
Kristinia, 1920*, ICW, The Hague, 1921.

28 Emily Ryder to RS, 9 July 1898. RSC, A2282, p. 139; 2 August 1898, 21
February 1899, 10 November 1899, 1900 SFP, 38/57, pp. 41–4. See also
K. Mayo, *Mother India*, Jonathan Cape, London, 1927; M. Daly,
Gyn/Ecology, Beacon Press, Boston, 1978, pp. 137–43; and C. Ram,
'Sexual Violence in India', *Refractory Girl*, no. 22, 1981, pp. 2–9.

29 See National Council of Women (NCW) Papers 1896–1911 and Louisa
MacDonald to RS, 22 March 1900, RSC, A2274, pp. 13–59 and 143.

30 R. Scott, 'Arbitration versus War', unpublished speech presented to
NCW, 24 May 1898, SFP, 38/34, pp. 618–19; R. Scott, untitled,
unpublished speech on Boer War, 1900 SFP, 38/54, pp. 7–9, 9–12 and
19; E. Hobhouse, *The Brunt of War and Where It Fell*, Dent, London, 1902.

31 W. Main to RS, 17 September 1897, p. 48; Bruce Smith to RS, 3
November 1897; Dr James Julian to RS, 17 July 1898; Annie Duncan to
RS, 'Friday Evening', RSC, A2280, pp. 48, 53, 59 and 79; Annie Duncan

to RS, 20 June 1900, RSC, A2277, pp. 260–1. See also F. Gordon, 'The Conditions of Female Labour and Rates of Women's Wages in Sydney', *Australian Economist*, vol. 14, no. 12, 1894.

32 G. Jones to RS, 20 March 1901, Dora Coghlan Murphy to RS, 27 July 1899; E.W. O'Sullivan to RS, 19 December 1901; T.A. Coghlan to RS, 22 November 1901; and Harry Holland to RS, March 1901, RSC, A2277, pp. 227, 236, 237, 240 and 241. See also D. Deacon, *Managing Gender*, Oxford University Press, Melbourne, 1989, pp. 157–74.

33 For fuller discussion of the labour movement and women workers, see R. Frances, 'Never Done, But Always Done Down', in V. Burgmann and J. Lee (eds), *Making A Life*, McPhee Gribble/Penguin, Ringwood, 1988, pp. 117–32.

34 R. Scott, notebook entry [draft of letter to the editor of *SMH* re. age of consent 1901?] and untitled, unpublished speech on social life [fragment] 1897, SFP, 38/22, Item 7, 21, pp. 383–90 and Item 8, pp. 427–30; and J. Hunt to RS, 9 September 1897, RSC, A2277, p. 217.

35 RS to MF, 31 March, 19 August, 25 September and 15 December 1902, MFP, 364/8, pp. 1, 19 and 43–4; MF to RS, 19 August 1902, RSC, A2282, p. 268.

36 S. Armstrong to RS, 13 June 1900; J.W. Julian, MD to RS, 10 May 1898, RSC, A2277, pp. 217 and 230.

37 Mary Canes to RS, n.d.; Louisa MacDonald to RS, 'Wednesday'; Charlotte See to RS, 27 October 1897, J.C. Nield to RS, 21 October 1897; J.C. Nield to RS, 28 October 1898; Helen Fell to RS, 31 October 1898, John See to RS, 1 November 1898; Frances Levy to RS, n.d., Gertrude Browne to RS, 21 November 1898, RSC, A2279, pp. 5, 8–9, 13 and 15, 16, 18 and 22, 33 and 38.

38 R. Scott, The Amelioration of Women Prisoners, unpublished report, 1898, SFP, 38/56, pp. 1–15, 17–22; Frederick Neitenstein, 16 November 1898, and 10 September 1900, RSC, A2279, p. 59; and J.A. Allen, *Sex and Secrets*, p. 43.

39 For a history of this work in the United States, see E. Freedman, *Their Sisters' Keepers*, University of Michigan Press, Ann Arbor, 1983.

40 Gertrude Brown to RS, 25 November 1898; Leontine Cooper to RS, 23 October 1900; Vida Goldstein to RS, 4 July 1900; B.R. Wise to RS, 15 April 1902; Frederick Neitenstein to RS, 4 November 1901; John Hughes to RS, 13 June 1902; John Hughes to RS, 22 June 1902; RSC, A2279, pp. 439, 456, 460, 465, 469 and 471.

41 Prisoners' Aid Association, Ladies Committee: 'Petition for Raising the Age of Consent to 17 Years', n.d., SFP, 38/56, p. 181.

42 Moffitt Burns to RS, 3 November 1902, RSC, A2279, p. 72–3.

43 WPEL Minutes, 22 October 1902, SFP 38/40, p. 5; RS to editor of the *SMH*, 31 October 1902; and Edward Smithurst to editor of the *SMH*, 1 November 1902, SFP 38/57, p. 91.

44 NSW Clerk of the Peace, Supreme Court Deposition: Regina versus Ethel Herringe, Young Circuit Court, September 1902.

45 R.J. Jolley to RS, 23 January 1902, RSC, A2279, p. 81.

46 R. Scott, Why Women Need A Vote, unpublished speech, 13 March 1901, SFP, 38/41, pp. 174–5, 197, 199, 200, 196, 191–2, 213–18, 223–6 and 257; and C.E. Clarke to RS, 15 December 1900, RSC, A2272, p. 560.

47 *NSWPD*, 1st Series, Vol. 107, 1900, p. 5311; Vol. 108, 1900, pp. 5291–6, 5496, 5489; 5481, 5485, 5512, 5541, 5543, 5544, 5555, 5874–5, 5879,; and 2nd Series, Vol. 1, 1901, pp. 677, 715–17; Vol. 2, pp. 1362–3, 1556; 1st Series, Vol. 107, 1900, pp. 5287, 5300; Vol. 108, pp. 5478 and 5546;

2nd Series, Vol. 1, 1901, pp. 599 and 5873.

48 RS to Dowell O'Reilly, 4 June [1898?], O'Reilly Family Papers, 231/9, p. 119; Louisa MacDonald to RS, 23 November 1900, SFP, 38/20x, p. 395; Lilian Wise to RS, 13 June 1900; Vida Goldstein to RS, 16 December 1900; E. Woolley to RS, 11 January 1901; Vida Goldstein to RS, 29 November 1900, RSC, A2272, pp. 441, 562, 567 and 550; and B.R. Wise to RS, 7 August 1900, RSC, A2270, p. 119. For fascinating discussions of Wise's character and career, see J.D. Rickard, *Class and Politics*, Australian National University Press, Canberra, 1976, pp. 147–8; and J.A. Ryan, An Oxford Liberal in the Free Trade Party in New South Wales, MA dissertation, University of Sydney, 1965.

49 WSL, Minutes, 28 November 1900, pp. 155–6.

50 P. J. Gandon to editor of the *Evening News*, n.d., SFP, 38/35, p. 92; W.E. Gundry to RS, 19 July 1900; W.E. Gundry to RS, 30 August 1900; May Tomkins to RS, 19 July 1900, RSC A2272, pp. 454, 455 and 458; and Frank Cotton to RS, August 1901, RSC, A2282, p. 228.

51 See also WSL, Minutes, 22 April, 16 June, 10 August, 1 and 15 December 1891; 15 March, 19 April, 6 September, 4 October 1892; and 21 January, 21 February, 1–9 August, 5 and 9 September, 3 and 11 October, 21 November, and 5 December 1893, SFP 38/33, pp. 98–100, 106–9, 120–1, 170–2, 180–2, 184–6, 194–5, 218–19 and 228–9.

52 P. J. Gandon to RS, 1 October 1901, RSC, A2272, p. 665–8.

53 William Lyne to RSC, 31 July 1902, Dowell O'Reilly to RS, 18 August 1902; Frances Saul to RS, 18 August 1902, RSC, A2272, pp. 707, 717, and 718a. For accounts of aspects of the lives and work of Annie and Belle Golding and Kate Dwyer see: B.R. Kingston, 'Golding, Annie MacKenzie (1855–1934)', and 'Isabella Theresa (1864–1940)', in B. Nairn and G. Serle (eds), *ADB, 1891–1931, Vol. 9: 1891–1939, Gil-Las*, pp. 41–2; and H. Radi, 'Dwyer, Kate (1861–1949)', in H. Radi, *200 Australian Women*, Redress Press, Sydney, 1988, pp. 78–9. See also J. Atkinson, Aspects of the Developing Relationship Between Working Class Women and Feminists 1890–1917, BA (Hons) dissertation, University of Sydney, 1979; R.G. Cooper, The Women's Suffrage Movement in New South Wales 1891–1902, MA dissertation, University of Sydney, 1970; J.E. Cobbe, The Women's Movement in New South Wales 1880–1914, MA dissertation, University of New England, 1967; R. Cookson, The Role of Certain Women and Women's Organisations in New South Wales and Victoria Between 1900 and 1920, BA (Hons) dissertation, University of Sydney, 1959; and C.A. Scherer, The Golding Sisters: Annie, Kate and Belle: The Complexities of First Wave Feminism in Late Nineteenth and Early Twentieth Century Australia, MA paper, University of Sydney, 1989.

54 G. O'Connor, 'Louisa Lawson: Her Life and Work', Lawson Family Papers, ML A1897, pp. 18–34. See also G. O'Connor, 'The Genesis of Women's Suffrage', Typescript, June 1923, ML QA920.7L.

55 R. Scott, 'A Short Account of the Women Suffrage Movement in New South Wales', September 1902, SFP, 38/38, pp. 260–2 and 267–9; Mary Sanger Evans to RS, 23 May 1894, RSC, A2271, p. 80.

56 O. Lawson (ed.), *The First Voice of Australian Feminism*, p. 14.

57 *The Dawn*, 1904.

58 Frances Saul to RS, 18 August 1902, RSC, A2272, p. 718a.

59 C.H. Spence to RS, 20 September 1902, SFP, 38/21, p. 81. See also some

of Scott's social letters and cards to Spence in the first years of the century in Catherine Helen Spence Papers, 1856–1902, ML MS202.

Chapter 5   The Woman Citizen (1903–10)

1 Margaret Hodge to RS, 23 August 1902, SFP, 38/20X, p. 283.
2 WPEL Minutes, 11 February 1903, SFP, 38/40, pp. 14–15.
3 RS to MF, 11 June and 8 August 1904, MFP, 364/8, pp. 111, 113; RS to Frances Saul, October 1903, RSC, A2278, p. 64.
4 Alice Hamilton to RS, 17 August 1905, SFP, 38/2, p. 271b; and Rusden, Grace, Will, 1896, Melbourne, MSRM, A2269, p. 609.
5 RS to MF, 27 April 1903, 4 and 16 January, 13 March and 9 September 1905, MFP, 364/8, pp. 53–4, 142, 147 and 161, 163 and 169.
6 C.H. Spence to RS, 25 September 1904, SFP, 38/21, p. 127.
7 Arthur Vogan to RS, 13 and 31 August and 11 September 1903, RSC, A2282, pp. 334, 337 and 339.
8 ibid., 27 January, 8 and 12 February 1904, RSC, A2282, pp. 396, 398 and 399.
9 Dowell O'Reilly to RS, 30 October 1905, SFP, 38/21, p. 19.
10 RS to MF, 13 June 1903, MFP, 364/8, p. 69.
11 Henry Lawson, 'The Women of the Town' (1904), and Louisa Lawson, 'Life's Battles' (1906), SFP, 38/68/1 and 2, pp. 81 and 9c; and R. Scott, *On The Social Evil*, Women's Christian Temperance Union of Queensland, Brisbane, 1903.
12 RS, 'Things I've Worked For', SFP, 38/32x, p. 169.
13 *SMH*, 10 August 1909.
14 R. Scott, President's Address, Women's Political and Educational League, 1904, unpublished speech, SFP, 38/41, p. 321.
15 R. Scott, Why Women Need A Vote, unpublished speech, SFP, 38/41, pp. 323–4. See also R. Pringle, 'Octavious Beale and the Ideology of the Birthrate. The Royal Commissions of 1904 and 1905', *Refractory Girl*, no. 3, 1973, pp. 19–28; J.A. Allen, 'Octavious Beale Reconsidered: Infanticide, Babyfarming and Abortion in New South Wales 1880–1939', in Sydney Labour History Group (ed.), *What Rough Beast?*, Allen & Unwin, Sydney, 1982, pp. 111–29.
16 J.A. Allen, *Sex and Secrets*, p. 127.
17 *SMH* [undated cutting], SFP, 38/41, p. 479.
18 RS to MF, 25 September 1903, MFP, 364/8, p. 93.
19 B. Lawson, *My Henry Lawson*, Frank Johnson, Sydney, 1949, p. 144; and RS to Secretary, New South Wales State Children's Relief Board, 19 January 1909, Lawson Family Papers, 1639/6, p. 27.
20 Anna Hazelton to RS, 3 June, 11 August 1903; Robert Jolley to RS, 23 January 1903; Florence Wearne to RS, 25 August 1903; B.R. Wise to RS, 13 November 1903; RSC, A2279, pp. 85–9 and 93.
21 R. Scott, untitled, unpublished, undated speech, SFP, 38/25, p. 313.
22 Anna Hazelton to RS, 11 August 1903; and Florence Wearne to RS, 25 August 1903, RSC, A2279, pp. 86–7; and C.K. MacKellar to RS, 17 July 1903, RSC, A2278, p. 45. Scott's contempt for his pronatalism can have given MacKellar no joy, yet he was prepared to work with her on the Girls' Protection Bill and other measures. For fuller outlines of the interesting development of his public reform career see Charles MacKellar Papers 1900–23, ML MS2100; and S.R. Garton, 'Sir Charles MacKellar: Psychiatry, Eugenics and Child Welfare in New South Wales

1900–1914', *Historical Studies*, vol. 22, no. 86, 1986, pp. 21–34.

23 J.A. Allen, *Sex and Secrets*, pp. 78–9.

24 Unidentified, undated newspaper cutting, SFP, 38/61, p. 40.

25 MF to RS, 2 December 1904, RSC, A2282, pp. 370–1.

26 J.A. Allen, *Sex and Secrets*, pp. 62–3 and 78. For fuller documentation of Wise's beliefs and the development of his career, see Bernhard Ringrose Wise Papers 1872–1912, ML MS312.

27 MF to RS, 2 December 1904, A2282, p. 372; and RS to MF, n.d., MFP, 364/8, p. 119.

28 R. Scott, untitled, undated, unpublished speech, and letter to the editor of the *Daily Telegraph*, 5 August 1903; SFP 38/25, p. 7 and 61/3, p. 131.

29 R. Scott, [letter to an editor] unidentified, undated newscutting, SFP, 38/21, p. 359.

30 WPEL Minutes, 2 November 1903, p. 49.

31 R. Scott, The Social Problem, unpublished speech, 1903, SFP, 38/23, pp. 223–84 and 233–5.

32 R. Scott, undated notebook entry, SFP, 38/22, Item 7.

33 R. Scott, Peace and Arbitration, unpublished speech, 1904, delivered to NCW, SFP, 38/49, pp. 149–50. See also J.K. Conway, 'Stereotypes of Femininity in a Theory of Sexual Evolution', in M. Vicinus (ed.), *Suffer and Be Still*, Indiana University Press, Bloomington, 1972, pp. 150–3.

34 E.W. O'Sullivan to RS, 22 March 1904, RSC, A2278, pp. 135 and 137.

35 *NSWPD*, 2nd Series, Vol. 11, 1903, p. 1164.

36 Alice Henry to RS, 12 August 1903, RSC, A2278, p. 203; Catherine Helen Spence to RS, 20 September 1902 and 8 May 1906, SFP, 8/21, pp. 81, 89; and Vida Goldstein to RS, 17 July 1904, RSC, A2279, p. 189.

37 R. Scott, untitled, unpublished speech to WPEL, 1904, SFP, 38/41, p. 347. See also S. Tiffin, 'In Search of Reluctant Parents: Desertion and Non-Support Legislation in Australia and the United States 1890–1920', in Sydney Labour Group (ed.), *What Rough Beast?*, pp. 130–50.

38 R. Scott, untitled, unpublished speech to NCW of NSW, 1903, SFP, 38/50, p. 233.

39 D. Montefiore, *From A Victorian to A Modern*, Archer, London, 1927, p. 18.

40 H. Radi, 'Whose Child?', in J. Mackinolty and H. Radi (eds), *In Pursuit of Justice*, p. 120.

41 R. Scott, Laws Women Need, n.d., unpublished speech, SFP 38/49, n.p.

42 R. Scott, Poverty and Wealth, unpublished, undated speech, SFP, 38/30, pp. 47–9.

43 R. Scott, untitled, unpublished, undated speech, SFP 38/23, p. 265.

44 Bertha MacNamara to RS, 12 August 1903, RSC, A2278, p. 62.

45 L.A.G. Taylor to RS, 13 September 1903, RSC, A2279, p. 90.

46 J.H. Carruthers to RS, 4 and 9 October and 13 November 1906; 25 September 1907, RSC, A2278, pp. 251, 252 and 282.

47 Arthur Griffiths to Zara Aronson, 1907, RSC, A2274, p. 328.

48 Mary Richmond to RS, 4 June 1907, RSC, A2278, p. 286.

49 'Resolution', n.d., SFP, 38/28, pp. 53–4.

50 'An Admirer of your work' to RS, 7 July 1907, RSC, A2279, pp. 110–12.

51 Vida Goldstein to RS, 18 April 1908, RSC, A2273, p. 1012.

52 Alice Wilson to RS, 6 August 1908, RSC, A2276, p. 73.

53 Florence Wearne to RS, 10 August 1908; and C.G. Wade to RS, 14 August 1908, RSC, A2279, pp. 133 and 134.

54 W.A. Holman to RS, 12 July 1909, SFP, 38/20X, p. 305.

55 Women's Political Association of Goulburn, [letter to the editor], unidentified newscutting, 19 May 1903, SFP 38/43, pp. 47–9.

56 WPEL, Minutes, 8 September 1903, p. 45.

57 Ethel Hamilton to RS, 21 August 1904; and Rebecca Swann to RS, 29 July 1904, RSC, A2278, pp. 138e, 144b.

58 WPEL, Minutes, 12 May, 21 November 1904; 20 March 1905; 23 April, 11 May, 11 September and 19 November 1906; 15 July 1907; Item 1, pp. 75, 104, 115, 156.

59 J.D. Fitzgerald to RS, 3 April 1903; J.H. Carruthers to RS, 14 March 1904, RSC, A2278, pp. 18 and 134b; Vida Goldstein to RS, 11 August 1904; Vida Goldstein to RS, 22 August 1904; Vida Goldstein to RS, 29 May 1903, RSC, A2273, pp. 832, 969 and 974.

60 J.L. Fegan to RS, 22 September 1903, RSC, A2278, p. 96.

61 Vida Goldstein to RS, 29 May 1903; Vida Goldstein to RS, 13 and 21 January, 9 March and 29 May 1903; RSC, A2273, pp. 791, 806 and 816a and 832.

62 R. Fulford, *Votes for Women*, Faber, London, 1969, p. 112; and E. Wolstenholme–Elmy to RS, 25 May 1904, RSC, A2273, pp. 931–2.

63 Augusta Von Heinbeuld to RS, n.d., ASC, A2278, p. 194.

64 J. Mulraney, 'When Lovely Woman Stoops to Lobby', pp. 97–104.

65 MF to RS, 29 December 1904, RSC, A2282, p. 372.

66 RS to MF, 4 January 1905, MFP, 364/8, p. 151. See also V. Goldstein, *Report to the National Council of Women in New South Wales of a Conference in Washington*, Norman Bros, Melbourne, 1904.

67 Arthur Rae to RS, 1905, RSC, A2284, p. 1278.

68 J.C. Watson to RS, 15 February 1905; Bertha MacNamara to RS, 10 February 1905; Anna Hazelton to RS, 25 February 1905, RSC, A2278, pp. 169, 170, and 171.

69 Ada Holman to RS, 8 March 1905, RSC, A2283, p. 544; *Australian Women's Sphere*, Vol. V, no. 55, 5 March 1905; Alice Henry to RS, 21 March 1905, RSC, A2283, p. 541; RS letter to the editor of *The Worker* March 1905, SFP, 38/60, p. 1.

70 'Another angry letter you busy body' to RS, 16 June 1904, RSC, A2273, pp. 937–8.

71 RS to E.L. Sutherland, 17 November 1908, E.L. Sutherland to RS 'Wednesday', November 1908; E.L. Sutherland to RS, 'Friday', November 1908, RS to E.L. Sutherland, November 1908 and RS to the Committee of the Women's Club, n.d., SFP, 38/57, pp. 97–127.

72 NSW Ladies Amateur Swimming Association, Minutes, 17 January 1906, RSC, A2276, pp. 150–61.

73 Vida Goldstein to RS, 18 April 1908 and 23 April 1909, RSC, A2273 and A2274, pp. 1009 and 409; Annie R. Burrough to RS, 15 May 1910, RSC A2274, p. 728, Edith Cowan to RS, 26 April 1909, RSC, A2277, p. 296; Marian Harwood to RS, 24 November 1910, RSC, A2281, pp. 107–8; RS, letter to the editor of the *Daily Telegraph*, 8 December 1908, SFP, 38/39/2, p. 47. An early and hostile account of Goldstein's work with the WSPU was published in 1960. See N. MacKenzie, 'Vida Goldstein: The Australian Suffragette', *Australian Journal of Politics and History*, vol. 56, 1960, pp. 190–204.

74 Mary Prenter to RS, 26 September 1903, RSC, A2278, p. 97.

75 Florence Roberts to RS, 6 June 1910 and Florence Aspley to RS, 1 January 1910, RSC, A2277, pp. 340 and 344. See also M. Franklin, *Some Everyday Folk and Dawn*, [frontispiece].

76 RS to ICW Conference, Amsterdam, 4 May 1908, SFP, 38/41, p. 443.

77 Anna Gale to RS, n.d., RSC, A2278, p. 318.
78 W.E. Gundry to RS, 25 October 1908, RSC, A2273, p. 1011.
79 Louisa Lawson to RS, 1908, Lawson Family Papers, ML MS1639, 16, pp. 127–32.
80 See M. Harwood, *Peace Conferences At Home and Abroad*, Private Circulation, Sydney, 1906; *The Peace Society: Its Achievements and Its Mistakes*, Windsor and Co., Sydney, 1922; and New South Wales Branch of the London Peace Society, *Annual Reports 1907–1918*, The Society, Sydney, 1920. See also RS to Alfred Deakin, 9 and 28 January, 12 February and 2 March 1908, Deakin Papers, NLA, MS 1540/1/1844, Folder 21.
81 Charles Strong to RS, 4 and 18 March, 22 July and 2 October 1907; and S.D.K. Aitken to RS, 20 July 1909, RSC, A2281, pp. 5, 6, 8, 16 and 85.

Chapter 6   *Against the Brotherhood (1911–19)*

1   Alice Bentley to RS, 28 January 1912; Kathleen Durack to RS, 26 February 1912; Marian Harwood to RS, n.d. [1912?]; Alice Bentley to RS, 28 October 1912, RSC, A2276, pp. 181, 189, 197–8 and 208.
2   Unidentified newscutting, 4 March 1912, SFP, 38/57, p. 255.
3   W.W. Hill to RS, n.d. [1912?], RSC, A2276, p. 179.
4   Alice Bentley to RS, n.d. [1912?], RSC, A2276, p. 183.
5   N.F. Cott, *The Grounding of Modern Feminism*, pp. 20 and 35–42.
6   R. Scott, *Laws in New South Wales re Women and Children*, NCW, Sydney, 1919, p. 4.
7   See J.A. Allen, 'Contextualising Late Nineteenth Century Feminism', p. 32.
8   R. Scott, The Woman's Vote in NSW, unpublished speech, 1914, SFP, 38/38, p. 359.
9   Aletta Jacobs to RS, 27 October 1915, RSC, A2281, p. 298.
10 W.M. Hughes to RS, 1917, SFP 38/54, p. 202.
11 M. Finnane, 'The Popular Defence of Chidley', *Labour History*, no. 41, 1981, pp. 68–9.
12 MF to RS, 23 August 1913, RSC, A2283, p. 832.
13 J.D. Fitzgerald to RS, 10 May 1915 [?], RSC, A2283, p. 913.
14 J.F. Archibald to RS, 24 July 1912, RSC, A2283, p. 799; and 11 November 1911, SFP, 38/20X, p. 13.
15 Florence Clarke to RS, 20 November 1912, A2277, p. 365.
16 See S. Cooke, 'Death, Body and Soul: The Cremation Debate in New South Wales, 1863–1925', *Australian Historical Studies*, vol. 24, no. 97, October 1991, pp. 323–39.
17 D.R. Hall to RS, 13 September 1916; and Nina Murdoch to RS, 15 September 1916, RSC, A2284, pp. 944 and 951.
18 A.R. Scott Cowen, 'Across Dry Creekbeds', p. 28.
19 J.F. Archibald to RS, 11 November 1911, RSC, A2283, p. 13.
20 MF to Mollye Menken, 26 July 1952, MFP, 364/20, pp. 169–70.
21 *Brisbane Courier*, 10 October 1903.
22 A.R. Scott Cowen, 'Across Dry Creek Beds', 'Details of My Family History', and 'The Scott Family'.
23 Terrick Hamilton to Annie Rose Scott Hamilton, 1895, John Oxley Library, OM 23–71.
24 *Sun*, n.d. 1915, SFP, 38/60/1, p. 213.
25 Scott made a vast collection of newspaper clippings on international relations, catalogued as 'Newscuttings and Printed Materials', SFP, 38/66;

and RS to Dowell O'Reilly, 5 April 1918, O'Reilly Family Papers, 231/10, pp. 229–30; and RS to 'Sir', 1 April 1914, RSC, A2283, pp. 857–8. See also C. Lansbury, 'Gynaecology, Pornography and the Anti-vivisection Movement', *Victorian Studies*, vol. 28, no. 3, 1985, pp. 413–38.

26 R. Scott, 'Laws Women Need', published speech presented to NCW, SFP, 38/49, pp. 267–364, 268, 277–9 and 302.

27 ibid., pp. 267–8, 296, 309, 312.

28 Florence Aspley to RS, 5 September 1912, RSC, A2277, pp. 359–60.

29 Louisa MacDonald to RS, 23 April 1913, RSC, A2276, p. 210.

30 MF to RS, 9 December 1912, RSC, A2277, p. 370; and MF to RS, 19 June 1913, RSC, A2283, p. 828.

31 ibid., 28 December 1919, RSC, A2284, p. 999.

32 D. Montefiore, *From A Victorian to A Modern*, Archer, London, 1927, p. 138.

33 M. Dixson, *The Real Matilda*, p. 152.

34 J. Roe, 'Chivalry and Social Policy in the Antipodes', pp. 395–8.

35 See for instance R. Adam, *A Woman's Place 1910–1975*, Chatto & Windus, London, 1975, p. 47.

36 Emily Leaf to RS, 14 November 1912, RSC, A2273, pp. 1061–2; and NUWSS Circular, 15 March 1913, SFP, 38/44, pp. 269–73.

37 Marian Harwood to RS, 24 November 1910, RSC, A2281, pp. 107–8.

38 ibid., 19 May 1911, RSC, A2281, p. 120.

39 J. Mulraney, 'When Lovely Woman Stoops to Lobby', p. 100.

40 MF to RS, 19 June 1913, RSC, A2283, p. 828.

41 N.A. Martel, 'An Appeal to Australasia. . .', 26 October 1912, SFP, 38/39, p. 83.

42 Louisa MacDonald to the editor of *SMH*, 24 July 1912, SFP, 38/39, p. 85.

43 Millicent Fawcett to RS, n.d., RSC, A2273, p. 1072.

44 N.S. Absolam to RS, 23 November 1912, RSC, A2273, pp. 1063, 1064.

45 Edmund Barton to RS, 10 July 1911, SFP, 38/20X, pp. 39–41; and Marian Harwood to RS, 15 October 1914, RSC, A2281, p. 1234.

46 Agnes Murphy to RS, 26 June 1912, RSC, A2273, p. 1057–8.

47 Bessie Rischbieth to Olive Evans, 23 and 19 June 1913, Bessie Rischbieth Papers, NLA 2004/1, pp. 7–10.

48 Marian Harwood to RS, 24 November 1910, p. 108.

49 N.A. Martel, *The Women's Vote in Australia*, WSPU, London, 1913, n.p.

50 R. Fulford, *Votes for Women*, Faber, London, 1966, p. 199.

51 Adela Pankhurst to RS, 13 July 1914, RSC, A2273, p. 1078. See also A. Summers, 'The Unwritten History of Adela Pankhurst Walsh', in E. Windschuttle (ed.), *Women, Class and History*, Fontana, Melbourne, 1980, pp. 388–404; Adela Pankhurst Walsh Papers 1911–38, NLA MS2123; and also fascinating accounts of the relationship between militant suffragettes and cultural modernism in J. Lyon, 'Militant Discourse, Strange Bedfellows: Suffragettes and Vorticists Before the War', *differences*, vol. 4, no. 2, pp. 100–33; L. Tickner, *The Spectacle of Women*, Chatto, London, 1987; A. Young, '"Wild Women": The Censure of the Suffragette Movement', *International Journal of the Sociology of Law*, vol. 6, no. 2, 1988, pp. 279–93.

52 Marian Harwood to RS, 15 October 1914, RSC, A2281, pp. 1234–5.

53 E. Pankhurst, *My Own Story*, E. Nash, London, 1941; S. Pankhurst, *The Suffragette Movement*, Virago, London, 1977; and D. Montefiore, *From A Victorian to A Modern*; and unidentified newsclippings of interview with Rose Scott [1918?], SFP, 38/62/1, pp. 141–2.

54 For a splendid study of the peace movement in New South Wales in this period, see A.M. Jordens' 'Against the Tide: The Growth and Decline of a Liberal Anti-War movement', *Historical Studies*, vol. 22, no. 88, 1987, pp. 373–94.

55 RS to Alice Salomons, 5 August 1914, and RS to Anna Howard Shaw, 8 August 1914, SFP, 38/44, pp. 293 and 297. For critical accounts of women's war activities, see C. Shute, 'Heroines and Heroes: Sexual Mythology in Australia, 1918–1918', *Hecate*, vol. 1, no. 1, 1975, pp. 6–22, and 'Blood Votes and the "Bestial Boche": A Case Study in Propaganda', *Hecate*, vol. 2, no. 2, 1976, pp. 6–22; and J. Smart,'The Panacea of Prohibition: The Reaction of the Women's Christian Temperance Union of Victoria to the Great War', in S. Willis (ed.), *Women, Faith and Fetes*, Dove Publications, Melbourne, 1977, pp. 162–93.

56 Flora Timms to RS, 20 August 1915 and Emily Hobhouse to RS, 10 August 1915, pp. 281–3; Chrystal MacMillan to RS, 8 January 1916, RSC, A2275, p. 182; and Aletta Jacobs to RS, n.d., RSC, A2281, pp. 223–4. See also E.F. Hurwitz, 'The International Sisterhood', in R. Bridenthal and C. Koonz (eds), *Becoming Visible*, Houghton Mifflin, Boston, 1977, pp. 330–4; A. Wiltsher, *Most Dangerous Women*, Pandora, London, 1985; D. Kruse and C. Sowerwine, 'Feminism and Pacifism: "Women's Sphere" in Peace and War', in N. Grieve and A. Burns (eds), *Australian Women*, pp. 42–58; P. Gowland, 'The Women's Peace Army', in E. Windschuttle (ed.), *Women, Class and History*, pp. 216–34; and R. Sherrick, 'Toward Universal Sisterhood', *Women's Studies International Forum*, vol. 5, no. 6, pp. 655–61.

57 MF to RS, 8 May 1915, RSC, A2283, p. 914.

58 Madge Donohoe to RS, 22 October 1915, RSC, A2281, pp. 292–3.

59 ibid., 10 October 1919, RSC, A2281, p. 233; and Louisa MacDonald to RS, 6 June 1917, RSC, A2275, p. 212.

60 R. Scott, *Laws in NSW Re Women and Children*, National Council of Women, Sydney, 1919, pp. 1–6.

61 *NSWPD*, 2nd Series, Vol. 74, 1918, pp. 3202–3.

62 J.A. Allen, 'Breaking into the Public Sphere: The Struggle for Women's Citizenship in New South Wales 1890–1920', in J. Mackinolty and H. Radi (eds), *In Pursuit of Justice*, pp. 111 and 112–13.

63 R. Scott, *Laws in NSW*, p. 8.

64 J.A. Allen, *Sex and Secrets*, pp. 75–6, 94–5, 171. See also A. Booth, 'A Lecture on Prostitution', in Workers' Educational Association of New South Wales (ed.), *Report of a Conference on Sex Hygiene, 1916*, Government Printer, Sydney, 1917.

65 Florence Aspley to RS, 28 June, 1917, RSC, A2275, p. 225.

66 *NSWPD*, 2nd Series, Vol. 75, 1918, p. 5107.

67 For discussion of their work, see S. Jeffreys 'Sex Reform and Anti–Feminism in the 1920s', pp. 175–201; and J. Weeks, *Sexuality and Its Discontents*, RKP, London, 1985, pp. 87–99. See also J.M. Irvine, *Disorders of Desire: Sex and Gender in Modern American Sexology*, Temple University Press, Philadelphia, 1990.

68 R. Scott, *Laws in NSW*, p. 5.

69 See Feminist Club of New South Wales, Records 1914–39, ML MS1703; H. Radi, 'Introducing Jessie Street', in H. Radi (ed.), *Jessie Street*, pp. 10–15; J. Street, *Truth or Repose?*, Alpha Books, Sydney, 1972; M. Sawyer and M. Simms, *A Woman's Place*, Allen & Unwin, Sydney, 1988,

pp. 59–66; and P. Sekuless, *Jessie Street*, University of Queensland Press, St Lucia, 1978.

Chapter 7   The Modern Woman (1920–25)

1   R. Scott, Speech Upon the Occasion of Retirement from Public Life, 12 April 1921, SFP, 38/27, p. 351.
2   *SMH*, 28 December 1920.
3   RS to Nene Scott Wallace, 11 October 1903, SFP 38/79/3, p. 1.
4   RS to Elimina Sutherland, 17 November 1908, SFP, 38/57, p. 97.
5   M. Foley, The Women's Movement in New South Wales and Victoria 1918–1938, pp. 96–8; and Honorary Secretary, NCW to NCW of NSW (Open Letter), 4 November 1920, RSC, A2275, p. 368a.
6   Dumelkson to RS, 3 May 1921, RSC, A2275, p. 389.
7   Louisa MacDonald to RS, 28 November 1919, RSC, A2275, p. 404.
8   *SMH*, 28 December 1920.
9   *SMH*, 13 April 1921.
10 Rose Scott Commemoration Fund, 5 April 1921, Dr Mary Booth Papers, ML MS1329/1, p. 253; and Feminist Club of NSW—Luncheon to Honour Miss Rose Scott, Farmers, Sydney, 12 April 1921 Menu, SFP, 38/32X, p. 403.
11 M. Franklin, 'Miss Rose Scott: Some Aspects of Her Personality and Work', p. 95.
12 R. Scott, 'Speech Upon . . . Retirement', pp. 350–1.
13 W. Cooper to RS, 22 June 1921, RSC, A2281.
14 Florence Wearne to RS, 29 September 1921, A2281, p. 431.
15 Louisa MacDonald to RS, 13 November 1921, RSC, A2275, p. 398.
16 Charles Hoening to RS, 27 May 1921, RSC, A2284, p. 1042.
17 M. Franklin, 'Miss Rose Scott', p. 97.
18 A.R. Scott Cowen, 'Across Dry Creekbeds', p. 27.
19 *Evening News*, 21 November 1921.
20 L. Vickery to RS, n.d. [1920], RSC, A2275, p. 327.
21 Unidentified newscutting, SFP, 38/60, Item 1, p. 191.
22 K. Yellis, 'Prosperity's Child: Some Thoughts on the Flapper', *American Quarterly*, vol. 42, no. 3, 1967, pp. 429–32.
23 Benjamin Fuller to RS, 21 February 1922, SFP, 38/20X, p. 216; RS 'Speech on Behalf of Sir Benjamin Fuller', 21 March 1922, SFP, 38/23, pp. 201, 205 and 209; and *The Dawn*, 15 October 1924.
24 RS to Dowell O'Reilly, 8 October 1922 in O'Reilly Family Papers, 231/11, p. 57.
25 Undersecretary to the Chief Secretary of NSW to H.V. Jacques, MLA, 17 November 1922, RSC, A2284, p. 1049.
26 RS to Dr Crossle, 28 December 1922, SFP, 38/20X, pp. 126 and 127.
27 RS to Mr Lockley, 15 September 1922, SFP, 38/21, p. 335; *SMH*, 23 December 1921; and B. Lawson, *My Henry Lawson*, p. 122; and MF to RS, 2 February 1924, RSC, A2284, p. 1084.
28 See J.W. Scott, 'Deconstructing Equality versus Difference or the Uses of Poststructuralist Theory for Feminism', pp. 134–48.
29 *The Dawn*, 14 May 1925.
30 M. Foley, 'The Women's Movement . . . ', pp. 41–4, 62, 68–92, 125–33 and 210–15.
31 S.R. Garton, *Medicine and Madness*, p. 75–85. See also A. Curthoys, 'Eugenics, Feminism and Birth Control: The Case of Marion Piddington',

Hecate, vol. 15, no. 1, pp. 73–89; and K. Reiger, *The Disenchantment of the Home*, Oxford University Press, Melbourne, 1985.

32 S. Jeffreys, *Anti-Climax*, The Women's Press, London, 1990; E. Holtzman, 'The Pursuit of Married Love: Women's Attitudes Toward Sexuality and Marriage in Great Britain 1918–1939', *Journal of Social History*, vol. 16, no. 2, 1982, pp. 39–48; and E.K. Trimberger, 'Feminism, Men and Modern Love: Greenwich Village 1900–1925', in A. Snitow *et.al.* (eds), *Powers of Desire*, Review Press, New York, 1983, pp. 31–52; *Intimate Warriors*, The Feminist Press, New York, 1991, pp. 2–37; and S. Rothman, *Woman's Proper Place*, Basic Books, New York, 1978.

33 *The Dawn*, 12 April 1921; 8 February 1923; 12 August 1921; 25 September 1929; 10 April, 21 May and 20 August 1930; 19 August 1931; 18 January 1933; 24 October 1934; 21 August 1935; 17 June 1936; 18 October 1939; *The Dawn Newsletter* June 1967; and *The Dawn* 12 April 1921. See also B.M. Rischbieth, *The March of Australian Women*, Paterson Brokenshaw, Perth, 1964.

34 R. Scott, Last Will and Testament (*ADB*, F77).

35 M. Franklin, 'Miss Rose Scott', p. 99.

36 RS to Marie OReilly, 7 and 27 November, 1923; 31 December 1924; 17 February 1925; O'Reilly Family Papers, ML MS231/14, pp. 17, 33–5, 97 and 103.

37 RS to Dr Crossle, 23 March 1925, RSC, A2284, p. 382.

38 Sir John Longstaff to RS, 26 March 1925, RSC, A2284, p. 385.

39 Rose Scott's Death Certificate, ADB F77; and Nene Scott Wallace to Bertha Lawson, 27 April 1925, Lawson Family Papers, 1639/6, pp. 75–7.

40 These details are taken from the register of cremations, Rookwood Crematorium, and I am grateful to Simon Cooke for generously obtaining them for me; and M. Franklin, 'Miss Rose Scott', p. 98; and for two colour photographs of this I thank Simon Cooke.

41 *The Dawn*, 14 May 1925; 12 August 1921; and 21 August 1935.

Chapter 8   Rose Scott and Australian Feminism

1 MF to Nene Scott Wallace, 10 June 1938, MFP, 364/15, p. 351.

2 See for instance *Table Talk*, 19 March 1905; and J.L. Davidge, 'Miss Rose Scott', *Advance Australia*, December 1926.

3 See for instance, *Sun*, 22 April 1925; *SMH*, 22 April 1925; *Daily Telegraph*, 23 April 1925; *SMH*, 27 and 28 April and 2 May 1925; *The Dawn*, 14 May and 14 October 1925; *Sun*, 22 May 1985; *SMH*, 13 May and 19 June 1980; *NMH*, 24 July 1971; L. MacDonald, 'Rose Scott of Sydney', *ICW Bulletin*, vol. 8, 1930; and M. Harwood, 'Reminiscences of the Late Miss Scott', NSW Branch of the London Peace Society, *Annual Reports 1907–1918*, The Peace Society, Sydney, 1925.

4 See for instance, E. Stanford-Thomas, 'Treasures of the Mitchell and Dixson' (ABC Radio Script), 1965–6; M. Munro, ' "Passionately in Earnest": A Biography of Rose Scott'; B. Searle, *Silk and Calico*, Hale & Iremonger, Sydney, 1988; and A.M. Jordens, 'Rose Scott: Making a Beginning', in J. Walter & R. Nugent (eds), *Biographers at Work*, Institute for Modern Biography, Griffith University, Brisbane, 1984.

5 State Library of New South Wales, Dixson Gallery Catalogue: 'Rose Scott: Remarkable Woman, Remarkable Friends' [Exhibition Catalogue 20 April–December 1985]. State Library of NSW, Sydney 1985.

6   A.R. Scott Cowen, 'Across Dry Creekbeds'; and 'Details of My Family History', NRPL, Vertical Files, 'S'.

7   State Library of New South Wales, 'Rose Scott: Remarkable Woman, Remarkable Friends', p. 15.

8   M. Dixson, 'Gender, Class and the Women's Movements in Australia 1890, 1980', p. 20.

9   See for instance, R. Markey, *The Making of the Labor Party in New South Wales 1880–1900*, University of New South Wales Press, Kensington, 1988, pp. 206–8.

10 A.M. Jordens, 'Rose Scott', pp. 26 and 35. See also M. Tapper, 'Can A Feminist Be A Liberal?', *Australian Journal of Philosophy*, vol. 64, no. 1, 1986, pp. 37–47; and D. Kirkby, 'Alice Henry: Expatriate Feminist', in M. Lake and F. Kelly (eds), *Double Time*, Penguin, Ringwood, 1985, p. 209.

11 A.R. Scott Cowen, 'Details of My Family History'.

12 ibid., 'Across Dry Creekbeds', p. 75.

13 RS to MF (1905), MFP, 364/8, p. 161.

14 A.R. Scott Cowen, 'Across Dry Creekbeds', p. 76.

15 C.G. Heilbrun, *Writing a Woman's Life*, p. 49.

16 M. Franklin, 'Miss Rose Scott: Some Aspects of Her Personality and Work', p. 97.

17 Nene Scott Wallace to RS, 2 August 1925, MFP, 364/15 p. 343.

18 ibid., 29 May 1937, MFP, 364/15, p. 347.

19 ibid., 29 May 1937, p. 348.

20 ibid., 1937, MFP, 364/15, p. 355.

21 Nene Scott Wallace to MF [1938], MFP, 364/46, p. 33.

22 MF to Aileen Goldstein, 24 June 1948, MFP, 364/10, p. 61.

23 ibid., 24 June 1947, p. 57.

24 Vida Goldstein to Bessie Rischbieth, 23 December 1946, BR Papers, NLA MS, 2004/4127 (a), Box 1, Folder 1.

25 Vida Goldstein to MF, 22 June 1947, MFP, 364/10, p. 44.

26 M. Franklin, 'Rose Scott', Australian Broadcasting Commission Scripts, MFP, ML MS445/36, Item 10, pp. 251–2.

27 M. Franklin, 'Miss Rose Scott', p. 98.

28 MF to Mollye Menken, 19 December 1949, MFP, 364/20, p. 157.

29 Edna Wallace to MF, 24 February 1951; and MF to Edna Wallace, 23 March 1951, MFP, 364/20, pp. 425–7.

30 MF to Mollye Menken, 30 June 1951, MFP, 364/20, p. 163–4.

31 ibid., 26 July 1952, MFP, 364/20, p. 169.

32 ibid., 26 July 1952, MFP, 364/20, pp. 169–70.

33 MF to Aileen Goldstein, 1950, MFP, 364/10, p. 64.

34 MF to Mollye Menken, 22 November 1950, MFP, 364/20, p. 156.

35 Mollye Menken to MF, 3 March 1952, MFP, 364/20, p. 167.

36 MF to Mollye Menken, 26 July 1952, MFP, 364/20, p. 170.

37 MF to Aileen Goldstein, 29 December 1950, MFP, 364/10, p. 83.

38 ibid., 17 January 1953, MFP, 364/10, p. 91.

39 *NMH*, 24 July 1971.

40 RS, Journal, n.d. I first located and used this journal in 1977 when researching the then uncatalogued Scott Family Papers. I discussed this passage with Dr Kay Daniels who had also read it and with my honours dissertation supervisor Dr Heather Radi. As I reported in my article 'Rose Scott's Vision', published in 1988, I have been unable to relocate this journal in the now catalogued Scott Family Papers.

Select Bibliography

I. Manuscripts and Unpublished Records

Anderson, H.C. Reminiscences of David Mitchell, Typescript 1924, 41pp. Mitchell Library (ML). A1830.

Anglican Diocese of Newcastle. Christ Church Cathedral, Newcastle, Marriage Register, Baptisms and Burials 1858–1879. Newcastle and Region Public Library (NRPL). 91–123.

Australian Broadcasting Commission. Radio Talk Scripts 1955–66. ML. MS1855.

Australian Dictionary of Biography. File no. 77: Rose Scott (1847–1925).

Booth, Mary. Papers. ML. MS1329.

Cowen, Annie Rose Scott. Across Dry Creek Beds (Catalogued as 'Memoir') 1967. John Oxley Library, Brisbane. OM. 71–23.

——. Details of My Family History. NRPL. Vertical Files, 'S'.

——. The Scott Family, 1965. ML. M3/693.

Deakin, Alfred. Papers. National Library of Australia (NLA). MS1540.

Eyre, Edward John. Autobiography. ML. A1806.

Feminist Club of New South Wales. Records 1914–39. ML. MS1703.

Farrell, John. Papers 1897–1904. ML. MS1522.

Franklin, Miles. Papers 1897–1949. ML. MS364 and 445.

Gipps, Governor Sir George. Dispatches 1838–1840. ML. A2029, A219.

Grey, Nancy. Alexander Walker Scott, November 1973. NRPL. Vertical Files, 'S'.

Lawson Family. Papers, 1872–1965. ML. MS1639.

Lawson Family. Scrapbooks. ML. A1898–1899.

Lawson, Louisa. Scrapbooks. ML. A1895–1897.

MacKellar, Sir Charles Kinniard. Papers 1900–1923. ML. MS2100.

Merewether, Edward Charles. Correspondence 1876–1893. Merewether Estate Archives. NRPL, A1.

Merewether and related families, 2 vols. NRPL, LHD929. 2MER.

Mitchell Family. Papers 1818–1907. ML. MS379.

Mitchell, David Scott. Poetry and Correspondence 1862–1875. ML. A1437.

——. Will 3 October 1905. ML. Safe 3/20a-b.

Mitchell Library. Biographical Notes of Emily Matilda Heron (née Manning), Her Family and David Scott Mitchell, 1845–1890, 1967. ML. DOC. 1454.

——. The Scott Family. State Library of New South Wales, Sydney, 1979.

Munro, May. 'Passionately In Earnest': A Biography of Rose Scott. Typescript, NLA MS2724.

National Council of Women of New South Wales. Records 1895–1958. ML. MS3739.

O'Connor, Gertrude. The Genesis of Women's Suffrage, Typescript June 1923. ML. QA920.7L.

O'Reilly, Dowell. Papers 1906–1922. ML. MS231.

Parkes, Sir Henry. Correspondence 1889–1894. ML. A882.

Pearson, B. Wilhelm Kirchner: His Diary and Subsequent Life in Australia, 1976. Society of Australian Genealogists Library, Sydney (SAGL). 4/9472/3.

——. Scott Family: Miscellaneous Notes, 1986. SAGL. 4/9539.

Rischbieth, Bessie. Papers 1902–1949. NLA. MS2004.
Rusden Family. Papers 1802–1965. NRPL, LHF929. 2RUS.
Scott Family. Papers 1835–1968. ML. MS1694.
——. Papers 1838–1925. ML. MS38.
Scott, Helenus. Correspondence 1821–1897. ML. A2264.
Scott, Robert. Correspondence 1821–1844. ML. A2263.
Scott, Rose. Correspondence 1874–1925. ML. MSA2270–2284.
——. Further Papers 1858–1957. ML. MS5066.
——. Papers 1862–1923. ML. A1437.
——. Speech Upon the Unveiling of her Portrait 1922. ML. AS. 75.
——. Speech Upon Her Retirement 1921. ML. DOC. 2465.
Scott, Rose & Scott, Augusta. Notebook for the Journal 1864–1865. ML. MSB1528.
Scott, Sarah Anne. Correspondence 1840–59. ML. A2268.
Miscellaneous Scott and Rusden manuscripts. ML. A2269.
Selwyn Family. Papers 1843–99. ML. MS201.
Selwyn, Rose. Memories, 1905. ML. A1616.
Smith, C.E. Five Articles Concerning Dr. James Mitchell and His Family (1791–1869), 1966. ML. DOC. 993.
——. Pioneer Priest of St. Peters, 1967. ML. DOC. 1067.
——. The Scott Family, 1967. ML. DOC. 1032.
Spence, Catherine Helen. Papers 1856–1902. ML. MS202.
Stevens, Bertram. David Scott-Mitchell, 1919. 27pp, Typescript. ML. A1830.
Walsh, Adela Pankhurst. Papers, 1911–1938. NLA. MS2123.
Windeyer Family. Papers, 1853–48. ML. MS186.
Wise, B.R. Papers, 1872–1912. ML. MS312.

II. Newspapers and Periodicals

The Australian Woman 1894–1895.
Australian Woman's Sphere 1900–1905.
Daily Telegraph 1890–1915.
The Dawn 1888–1904 (Sydney)
The Dawn 1919–1939 (Perth)
Evening News 1900–1921.
Illustrated Sydney News 1892–1900.
The Lone Hand 1907–1915.
Newcastle Morning Herald 1870–1900.
Sun 1910–1925.
Sydney Morning Herald 1880–1970.
Table Talk 1905.
The Woman Voter 1909–1917.
The World's News 1920–1925.

III. Published Works

Ackerman, J. *Australia From A Woman's Point of View*. Cassell, London, 1913.
Adam, R. *A Woman's Place 1910–1975*. Chatto & Windus, London, 1975.
Adams, P. & Cowie, E. 'The Last Issue Between Us'. *m/f*, nos 11/12, 1986.
Adams, P. & Minson, J. 'The "Subject" of Feminism'. *m/f*, no. 2, 1978.
Allen, J.A. 'Breaking Into the Public Sphere: The Struggle for Women's Citizenship in New South Wales 1890–1920', in *In Pursuit of Justice: Australian Women and the Law 1788–1979*, eds J. Mackinolty & H. Radi. Hale &

Iremonger, Sydney, 1979.

——. 'Contextualizing Late Nineteenth Century Feminism: Problems and Comparisons'. *Journal of the Canadian Historical Association*, vol. 1, 1990.

——. 'From Women's History to A History of the Sexes', in *Australian Studies: A Survey*, ed. J.A. Walter. Oxford University Press, Melbourne, 1989.

——. 'The Making of A Prostitute Proletariat in Early Twentieth Century New South Wales', in *So Much Hard Work: Women and Prostitution in Australian History*, ed. K. Daniels. Fontana, Sydney, 1984.

——. 'Marxism and the Man Question: Some Implications of the Patriarchy Debate', in *Beyond Marxism? Interventions After Marx*, eds J.A. Allen & P. Patton. Intervention Publications, Sydney, 1983.

——. 'Octavious Beale Reconsidered: Infanticide, Babyfarming and Abortion in New South Wales 1880–1939', in *What Rough Beast? The State and Social Order in Australian History*, ed. Sydney Labour History Group. Allen & Unwin, Sydney, 1982.

——. '"Our Deeply Degraded Sex" and "The Animal in Man": Rose Scott, Feminism and Sexuality 1890–1925'. *Australian Feminist Studies*, nos 7/8, 1988.

——. 'Rose Scott (1847–1925)', in *200 Australian Women*, ed. H. Radi. Redress Press, Sydney, 1988; also in *Australian Dictionary of Biography, Vol. 11, 1891–1939, Nes–Smi*, ed. G. Serle, Melbourne University Press, Melbourne, 1991.

——. 'Rose Scott's Vision: Feminism and Masculinity 1880–1925', in *Crossing Boundaries: Feminisms and the Critique of Knowledges*, eds B. Caine *et. al.* Allen & Unwin, Sydney, 1988.

——. 'Scott, Rose (1847–1925)', in *Australian Dictionary of Biography, Vol. 11: 1891–1939, Nes-Smi*, ed. G. Serle. Melbourne University Press, Melbourne, 1988.

——. *Sex and Secrets: Crimes Involving Australian Women Since 1880*. Oxford University Press, Melbourne, 1990.

Anderson, M. *A Citizen Who Has No Vote*. Australian Christian World, Sydney, n.d..

Anderson, M. 'A Helpmeet For Man: Women in Mid-Nineteenth Century Western Australia', in *Exploring Women's Past*, ed. P. Crawford. Sisters, Carlton, Victoria, 1983.

Bacchi, C. 'Evolution, Eugenics and Women: the Impact of Scientific Theories on Attitudes Towards Women 1870–1920', in *Women, Class and History*, ed. S. Windschuttle. Fontana, Melbourne, 1980.

——. 'First Wave Feminism: History's Judgment', in *Australian Women: Feminist Perspectives*, eds N. Grieve & P. Grimshaw. Oxford University Press, Melbourne, 1981.

——. *Liberation Deferred? The Ideas of the English Canadian Suffragists 1877–1918*. University of Toronto Press, Toronto, 1982.

Baker, P. 'The Domestication of Politics: Women and American Political Society 1780–1920'. *American Historical Review*, vol. 89, no. 4, 1984.

Banks, O. *Becoming A Feminist: The Social Origins of 'First Wave' Feminism*. Wheatsheaf Books, Brighton, Sussex, 1986.

——. *Faces of Feminism: A Study of Feminism as a Social Movement*. Martin Robertson, Oxford, 1981.

Barrett, M. *Women's Oppression Today: Problems in Marxist Feminist Analysis*. Verso, London, 1980.

Barry, K. 'The New Historical Synthesis: Women's Biography'. *Journal of Women's History*, vol. 1, no. 3, 1990.

——. *Susan B. Anthony: A Biography of a Singular Feminist*. Ballantine Books, New York, 1990.

——. 'Tootsie Syndrome, or "We have met the enemy and they are us" '. *Women's Studies International Forum*, vol. 12, no. 5, 1989.

Bennett, J.M. 'Feminism and History'. *Gender and History*, vol. 1, no. 3, 1989.

Berg, B. *The Remembered Gate: The Origins of Feminism: Women and the City 1800–60*. Oxford University Press, New York, 1978.

Black, N. *Social Feminism*. Cornell University Press, Ithaca, 1989.

Bland, L. 'Marriage Laid Bare: Middle Class Women and Marital Sex c. 1880–1914', in *Labour of Love: Women's Experience of Home and Family, 1850–1940*, ed. J. Lewis. Basil Blackwell, Oxford, 1986.

——. 'The Married Woman, the "New Woman" and the Feminist Sexual Politics in the 1890s', in *Equal or Different? Women's Politics 1800–1914*, ed. J. Rendall. Basil Blackwell, Oxford, 1987.

——. 'Feminist Vigilantes of Late Victorian England', in *Regulating Womanhood: Historical Essays on Marriage, Motherhood and Sexuality*, ed. C. Smart. Routledge, London, 1992.

Booth, A. 'A Lecture on Prostitution', in *Report of a Conference on Sex Hygiene*, 1916, ed. Workers' Educational Association of New South Wales. Government Printer, Sydney, 1917.

Brandt, G. C. & Black, N. 'Il En Faut Peu: Farm Women and Feminism'. *Journal of the Canadian Historical Association*, vol. 1, 1990.

Brodribb, S. *Nothing Mat(t)ers: A Feminist Critique of Postmodernism*. Spinifex Press, North Melbourne, 1992.

Brookes, B. *et.al.* (eds). *Women in History: Essays on European Women in New Zealand*. University of Victoria Press, Wellington, 1986.

Brown, M. 'Cowan, Edith Dircksey (1861–1932)', in *Australian Dictionary of Biography, Vol. 8: 1891–1939, Cl–Gib*, eds B. Nairn & G. Serle. Melbourne University Press, Melbourne, 1981.

Brown, W. 'Feminist Hesitations, Postmodern Exposures'. *differences*, vol. 3, no. 1, 1991, pp. 63–84.

Browne, A. *The Eighteenth Century Feminist Mind*. Harvester Press, Brighton, 1987.

Brownfoot, J.N. 'Goldstein, Vida Jane Mary (1869–1949)', in *Australian Dictionary of Biography, Vol. 9: 1891–1939, Gil-Las*, eds B. Nairn & G. Serle. Melbourne University Press, Melbourne, 1983.

Buhle, M.J. *Women and American Socialism 1870–1930*. University of Illinois Press, Urbana, 1983.

Burton, A. 'The Feminist Quest for Identity: British Imperial Suffragism and Global Sisterhood 1900–1915'. *Journal of Women's History*, vol. 3, no. 2, 1991.

Butler, J. 'Contingent Foundations: Feminism and the Question of Postmodernism', *in Feminists Theorize the Political*, eds J. Butler & J.W. Scott. Routledge, New York, 1992.

Caine, B. *Destined to be Wives. The Sisters of Beatrice Webb*. Oxford University Press, Oxford, 1986.

——. 'Millicent Fawcett — A Liberal Feminist?', in *Crossing Boundaries: Feminisms and the Critique of Knowledge*, eds B. Caine *et. al.* Allen & Unwin, Sydney, 1988.

——. *Victorian Feminists*. Oxford University Press, London, 1992.

Caldwell, J.C. 'Population', in *Australians: Historical Statistics*, ed. W. Vamplew. Fairfax, Syme & Weldon and Associates, Sydney, 1988.

Cameron, B. 'The Flappers and the Feminists: A Study of Women's

Emancipation in the 1920s', in *Worth Her Salt: Women at Work in Australia*, eds
M. Bevage *et. al.* Hale & Iremonger, Sydney, 1982.

Campbell, D. 'A Doll's House: The Colonial Response', in *Nellie Melba, Ginger Meggs and Friends: Essays in Australian Cultural History*, eds S. Dermody *et. al.* Kibble Books, Melbourne, 1982.

Carmichael, G.A. *With This Ring: First Marriage Patterns and Prospects in Australia*. Australian National University, Canberra, 1988.

Connell, R.W. & Irving, T.H. *Class Structure in Australian History*. Longman Cheshire, Melbourne, 1980.

Conway, J.K. *The Female Experience in 18th and 19th Century America*. Princeton University Press, Princeton, 1982.

——. 'Gender in Australia'. *Daedalus*, vol. 114, no. 2, 1985.

——. 'Stereotypes of Femininity in a Theory of Sexual Evolution', in *Suffer and Be Still: Women in the Victorian Age*, ed. M. Vicinus. Indiana University Press, Bloomington, 1972.

Cooke, S. 'Death, Body and Soul: The Cremation Debate in New South Wales 1863–1925'. *Australian Historical Studies*, vol. 24, no. 97, 1991.

Cott, N.F. *The Bonds of Womanhood: 'Woman's Sphere' in New England, 1780–1835*. Yale University Press, New Haven, 1977.

——. 'Comment on Karen Offen's "Defining Feminism": A Comparative Historical Approach'. *Signs*, vol. 15, no. 1, 1989.

——. 'Feminist Theory and Feminist Movements: The Past Before Us', in *What Is Feminism?*, eds J. Mitchell & A. Oakley. Harvester Press, Brighton, 1986.

——. *The Grounding of Modern Feminism*. Yale University Press, New Haven, 1987.

——. 'Historical Perspectives: The Equal Rights Amendment Conflict in the 1920s', in *Conflicts in Feminism*, eds M. Hirsch & E. Fox-Keller. Routledge, New York, 1990.

——. 'Passionlessness: An Interpretation of Victorian Sexual Ideology 1790–1850'. *Signs*, vol. 4, no. 1, 1978.

——. 'What's in A Name? The Limits of "Social Feminism" or Expanding the Vocabulary of Women's History'. *Journal of American History*, vol. 76, no. 3, 1989.

——. *A Woman Making History: Mary Ritter Beard Through Her Letters*. Yale University Press, New Haven, 1991.

——. 'Women's Rights: Unspeakable Issues in the Constitution'. *Yale Review*, vol. 77, no. 3, 1988.

Curthoys, A. 'Eugenics, Feminism and Birth Control: The Case of Marion Piddington'. *Hecate*, vol. 15, no. 1, 1989.

Daly, M. *Gyn/Ecology: The Metaethics of Radical Feminism*. Beacon Press, Boston, 1978.

Dalziel, R. 'The Colonial Helpmeet: Women's Role and the Vote in Nineteenth Century New Zealand', in *Women in History*, eds B. Brookes *et. al.* Allen & Unwin, Auckland, 1986.

Daniels, K. 'Introduction', in *Women in Australia: An Annotated Guide to Records*, eds K. Daniels *et. al.*, vol. I. AGPS, Canberra, 1977.

——. 'Women's History', in *New History: Studying Australia Today*, eds G. Osborne & W.F. Mandle. Allen & Unwin, Sydney, 1982.

Davidge, J.L. 'Miss Rose Scott'. *Advance Australia*, December 1926.

Davidoff, L. 'Class and Gender in Victorian England', in *Sex and Class in Women's History*, eds J.L. Newton *et. al.* Routledge, London, 1983.

Deacon, D. *Managing Gender: The State, the New Middle Class and Women Workers 1830–1930*. Oxford University Press, Melbourne, 1989.

DeLauretis, T. 'Eccentric Subjects: Feminist Theory and Historical Consciousness'. *Feminist Studies*, vol. 16, no. 1, 1990.

Delmar, R. 'What is Feminism?', in *What Is Feminism?*, eds J. Mitchell & A. Oakley. Harvester Press, Brighton, 1986.

Dixson, M. 'Gender, Class and the Women's Movements in Australia, 1890, 1990', in *Australian Women: New Feminist Perspectives*, eds N. Grieve & A. Burns. Oxford University Press, Melbourne, 1986.

——. *The Real Matilda: Women and Identity in Australia 1788–1975*. Penguin, Ringwood, 1976.

Docker, J. *The Nervous Nineties*. Oxford University Press, Melbourne, 1991.

Dubois, E.C. 'Comment on Karen Offen's "Defining Feminism": A Comparative Historical Approach'. *Signs*, vol. 15, no. 1, 1989.

——. 'Eleanor Flexnor and the History of American Feminism'. *Gender and History*, vol. 3, no. 1, 1991.

——. *Feminism and Suffrage: The Emergence of an Independent Women's Movement in America 1848–1869*. Cornell University Press, Ithaca, 1978.

——. 'Outgrowing the Compact of the Fathers: Equal Rights, Woman Suffrage and the United States Constitution 1820–1878'. *Journal of American History*, vol. 74, no. 3, 1987.

——. 'The Radicalism of the Woman Suffrage Movement: Notes Toward the Reconstruction of Nineteenth Century Feminism' *Feminist Studies*, vol. 3, nos 1/2, 1975.

——. 'Working Women, Class Relations and Suffrage Militance: Harriet Stanton Blatch and the New York Woman Suffrage Movement, 1894–1909'. *Journal of American History*, vol. 74, no. 1, 1987.

Dubois, E.C. *et. al.* 'Politics and Culture in Women's History: A Symposium'. *Feminist Studies*, vol. 6, no. 1, 1980.

Dumaresq, D. 'Rape — Sexuality in the Law', *m/f*, nos 5/6, 1981.

Dyhouse, C. *Feminism and the Family in Victorian England, 1880–1930*. Basil Blackwell, Oxford, 1989.

Echols, A. 'The New Feminism of Ying and Yang', in *Powers of Desire: The Politics of Sexuality*, eds A. Snitow *et. al.* Monthly Review Press, New York, 1983.

Encel, S. *et. al. Women and Society: An Australian Study*. Longman Cheshire, Melbourne, 1974.

Epstein, B. *The Politics of Domesticity: Women, Evangelism and Temperance in Nineteenth–Century America*. Wesleyan University Press, Middletown, 1981.

Evans, R.J. *The Feminists: Women's Emancipation Movements in Europe, America and Australia 1840–1920*. Croom Helm, Sydney, 1977.

Evans, R. 'A Gun in the Oven: Masculinism and Gendered Violence', in *Gender Relations in Australia: Domination and Negotiation*, eds K. Saunders & R. Evans. Harcourt Brace Jovanovich, Sydney, 1992.

Faderman, L. *Surpassing the Love of Men: Romantic Love and Friendship Between Women From the Renaissance to the Present*. Holt, Rinehart & Winston, New York, 1981.

Family History Society, Maitland. *Singleton District Pioneer Register*. Family History Society, Maitland, 1989.

Fernon, C. 'Women's Suffrage in Victoria'. *Refractory Girl*, no. 22, 1981.

Finnane, M. 'The Popular Defense of Chidley'. *Labour History*, no. 41, 1981.

Firestone, S. *The Dialectic of Sex: The Case for the Sexual Revolution*. Paladin, London, 1972.

Flax, J. 'The Conflict Between Nurturance and Autonomy in Mother-Daughter Relationships and Within Feminism'. *Feminist Studies*, vol. 4, no. 2, 1978.

——. 'The End of Innocence', in *Feminists Theorize the Political*, eds J. Butler & J.W. Scott. Routledge, New York, 1992.

Fouquet, C. 'The Unavoidable Detour: Must a History of Women Begin with the History of Their Bodies?', in *Writing Women's History*, ed. M. Perrot. Basil Blackwell, Oxford, 1992.

Fox-Genovese, E. 'Culture and Consciousness in the Intellectual History of European Women'. *Signs*, vol. 12, no. 3, 1981.

——. 'Socialist Feminist, American Women's History'. *Journal of Women's History*, vol. 1, no. 3, 1990.

Fraisse, G. 'Feminist Singularity: A Critical Historiography of the History of Feminism in France', in *Writing Women's History* , ed. M. Perrott. Basil Blackwell, Oxford, 1992.

Frances, R. 'Never Done, But Always Done Down', in *Making A Life* , eds V. Burgmann & J. Lee. McPhee Gribble/Penguin, Ringwood, 1988.

Franklin, M. 'Miss Rose Scott: Some Aspects of Her Personality and Work', in *The Peaceful Army: Memoirs of Australia's Pioneer Women*, ed. F.B.S. Eldershaw [1938]. Reprinted Penguin, Ringwood, 1988.

——. *My Brilliant Career* [1901]. Reprinted Angus & Robertson, Sydney, 1966.

——. *Some Everyday Folk and Dawn* [1909]. Reprinted Virago, London, 1986.

Fraser, F. & Palmer, N. (eds). *Centenary Gift Book*. Robertson & Mullens, Melbourne, 1934.

Freedman, E. *Their Sisters' Keepers: Women's Prison Reform in America 1870–1930*. University of Michigan Press, Ann Arbor, 1983.

Frye, M. *The Politics of Reality: Essays in Feminist Theory*. The Crossing Press, Trumansburg, 1983.

Fulford, R. *Votes for Women*. Faber & Faber, London, 1966.

Gallego, V. 'Dwyer, Catherine Winifred (1861–1949)', in *Australian Dictionary of Biography,Vol. 8: 1891–1939, Cl-Gib*, eds B. Nairn & G. Serle. Melbourne University Press, Melbourne, 1981.

Garton, S.R. 'Bad or Mad: Developments in Incarceration in New South Wales 1880–1920', in *What Rough Beast? The State and Social Order in Australian History*, ed. Sydney Labour History Group. Allen and Unwin, Sydney, 1982.

——. *Medicine and Madness: A Social History of Insanity in New South Wales 1880–1940*. University of New South Wales Press, Kensington, 1988.

——. *Out of Luck: Poor Australians and Social Welfare*. Allen & Unwin, Sydney, 1990.

——. 'Sir Charles MacKellar: Psychiatry, Eugenics and Child Welfare in New South Wales 1900–1914'. *Historical Studies*. vol. 22, no. 86, 1986.

Gatens, M. 'A Critique of the Sex/Gender Distinction', in *Beyond Marxism? Interventions after Marx*, eds J.A. Allen and J. Patton. Intervention Publications, Sydney, 1983.

——. *Feminism and Philosophy: Perspectives on Difference and Equality*. Polity Press, Cambridge, 1991.

Godden, J. 'Portrait of A Lady: A Decade in the Life of Helen Fell (1849–1935)', in *Worth Her Salt: Women and Work in Australia*, ed. M. Bevege *et. al.* Hale & Iremonger, Sydney, 1982.

——. ' "The Work for Them and the Glory For Us" Sydney Women's Philanthropy 1870–1900', in *Australian Welfare History: Critical Essays*, ed. R. Kennedy. Macmillan, Melbourne, 1982.

Golder, H. *Divorce in Nineteenth Century New South Wales*. University of New South Wales Press, Kensington, NSW, 1985.

Golder, H. & Allen, J.A. 'Prostitution in New South Wales 1870–1932: Restructuring an Industry', *Refractory Girl*, nos 18/19, 1980.

Goldstein, V. *Report to the National Council of Women of New South Wales of a Conference in Washington*. Norman Bros, Melbourne, 1904.

Gordon, F. *After Winning: The Legacy of the New Jersey Suffragists 1920–1947*. Rutgers University Press, New Brunswick, 1986.

Gordon, F. 'The Conditions of Female Labour and Rates of Women's Wages in Sydney'. *Australian Economist*, vol. 14, no. 12, 1894.

Gordon, L. *Heroes of Their Own Lives: The History and Politics of Family Violence: Boston 1880–1960*. Virago, London, 1987.

——. '[Review] Joan Wallach Scott, Gender and the Politics of History'. *American Historical Review*, vol. 95, no. 4, 1990.

——. 'What's New in Women's History?', in *Feminist Studies/Critical Studies*, ed. T. De Lauretis. Indiana University Press, Bloomington, 1986.

——. 'Why Nineteenth Century Feminists Did Not Support "Birth Control" and Twentieth Century Feminists Do?: Feminism, Reproduction and the Family', in *Rethinking the Family: Some Feminist Questions*, eds B. Thorne & M. Yalom. Longman, New York, 1982.

Gordon, L. & Dubois, E.C. '"Seeking Ecstasy on the Battlefield": Danger and Pleasure in Nineteenth Century Feminist Sexual Thought'. *Feminist Studies*, vol. 9, no. 1, 1983.

Gorham, D. 'Flora McDonald Denison: Canadian Feminist', in *A Not Unreasonable Claim: Women and Reform in Canada 1880–1920s*, ed. L. Kealey. Canadian Women's Education Press, Toronto, 1979.

——. 'The "Maiden Tribute to Modern Babylon" Reconsidered: Child Prostitution and the Idea of Childhood in Late Victorian England'. *Victorian Studies*, vol. 21, no. 3, 1978.

——. *The Victorian Girl and the Feminine Ideal*. Croom Helm, London, 1981.

Gowland, P. 'The Women's Peace Army', in *Women, Class and History: Feminist Perspectives on Australia, 1788–1978*, ed. E. Windschuttle. Fontana, Melbourne, 1980.

Green, A.W. *The Necessity for Further Legislation for the Protection of Women and Children*. National Council of Women, Sydney, 1919.

Grimshaw, P. 'Man's Own Country', in *Australian Women: New Feminist Perspectives*, eds N. Grieve & A. Burns. Oxford University Press, Melbourne, 1986.

——. 'Only the Chains Have Changed', in *Staining the Wattle: A People's History of Australia*, eds V. Burgmann & V. Lee. McPhee Gribble/Penguin, Ringwood, 1988.

——. 'Women and the Family in Australian History', in *Women, Class and History*, ed. E. Windschuttle. Fontana, Melbourne, 1980.

——. 'Women in History: Reconstructing the Past', in *Women, Social Science and Public Policy*, eds J. Goodnow & C. Pateman. Allen & Unwin, Sydney, 1985.

——. *Women's Suffrage in New Zealand*. University of Auckland Press, Auckland, 1972.

——. 'Writing the History of Australian Women', in *Writing Women's History: International Perspectives*, eds K. Offen *et. al.* Indiana University Press, Bloomington, 1991.

Grosz, E.A. 'Feminist Theory and the Challenge to Knowledge'. *Women's Studies International Forum*, vol. 10, no. 5, 1987.

——. 'Notes Towards a Corporeal Feminism', in *Feminism and the Body* (Special Issue) *Australian Feminist Studies*, no. 5, 1987.

Guilford, E. 'The Glendon Stud of Robert and Helenus Scott and the

Thoroughbred Breeding Industry in the Hunter Valley'. *Journal of Hunter Valley History*, vol. 1, no. 1, 1985.

Hagan, J. 'An Incident at *The Dawn* '. *Labour History*, no. 8, 1965.

Hall, C. 'Politics, Poststructuralism and Feminist History'. *Gender and History*, vol. 3, no. 2, 1991.

Haraway, D. 'Ecce Homo, Ain't (Ar'n't) I a Woman, and Inappropriate/d Others: The Human in a Post–Humanist Landscape', in *Feminists Theorize the Political*, eds J. Butler and J.W. Scott. Routledge, New York, 1992.

Harrison-Lee, B. *One of Australia's Daughters*. N. J. Osborn, London, 1906.

Harwood, M. *Peace Conferences at Home and Abroad*. Private Circulation, Sydney, 1906.

——. *The Peace Society: Its Achievements and Its Mistakes*. Windsor & Co. Sydney, 1922.

——. 'Reminiscences of the Late Miss Scott', in NSW Branch of the London Peace Society, *Annual Reports 1907–1918*. NSW Peace Society, Sydney, 1925.

Heilbrun, C.G. *Writing A Woman's Life*. The Women's Press, London, 1989.

Hobhouse, E. *The Brunt of War and Where it Fell*. Dent, London, 1902.

Hoff, J. 'Introduction: An Overview of Women's History in the United States', in *Journal of Women's History: Guide to Periodical Literature*, eds G.V. Fischer *et. al.* Indiana University Press, Bloomington, 1992.

Holton, S.S. *Feminism and Democracy: Women's Suffrage and Reform Politics in Britain, 1860–1914*. Cambridge University Press, Cambridge, 1987.

Holtzman, E. 'The Pursuit of Married Love: Women's Attitudes Toward Sexuality and Marriage in Great Britain 1918–1939'. *Journal of Social History*, vol. 16, no. 2, 1982.

Hooper, C.A. 'Child Sexual Abuse and the Regulation of Women: Variations on a Theme', in *Regulating Womanhood: Historical Essays on Marriage, Motherhood and Sexuality*, ed. C. Smart. Routledge, London, 1992.

Hooper, F. E. *The Story of the Women's Club: The First Fifty Years*. The Club, Sydney, 1964.

Howe, R. & Swain, S. 'Fertile Grounds for Divorce: The Marital and Reproductive Imperatives', in *Gender Relations in Australia*, eds K. Saunders & R. Evans. Harcourt Brace Jovanovich, Sydney, 1992.

Huggins, J. & Blake, T. 'Protection or Persecution? Gender Relations in the Era of Race Segregation', in *Gender Relations in Australia*, eds K. Saunders & R. Evans. Harcourt Brace Jovanovich, Sydney, 1992.

Hunter, D. 'Hysteria, Psychoanalysis and Feminism: the Case of Anna O'. *Feminist Studies*, vol. 9, no. 3, 1983.

Hurwitz, E.F. 'The International Sisterhood', in *Becoming Visible: Women in European History*, eds R. Bridenthal & C. Koonz. Houghton Mifflin, Boston, 1977.

Hyslop, A. 'Agents and Objects: Women and Social Reform in Melbourne 1900 to 1914', in *Worth Her Salt: Women at Work in Australia*, eds M. Bevege *et. al.* Hale & Iremonger, Sydney, 1982.

International Council of Women. *Report from the Quinquennial Meeting at Berlin 1904, Toronto 1909, Rome 1914, and Kristinia 1920*. ICW, The Hague, 1921.

——. *Women's Position in the Laws of Nations*. G Bravnsche Hafbeench-drontkerai und Verlag, 1912.

——. *Report Concerning the Legal Position for Women for 1903–1906*. Roy, Dresden , 1908.

——. *Report for 1908–9*. Private Circulation, The Hague, May 1914.

Irvine, J.M. *Disorders of Desire: Sex and Gender in Modern American Sexology*. Temple University Press, Philadelphia, 1990.

Jackson, M. 'Sexology and the Construction of Male Sexuality (Havelock Ellis)', in *The Sexuality Papers*, eds L. Coveney *et. al.* Hutchinson, London, 1984.

Jay, N. 'Gender and Dichotomy', *Feminist Studies*, vol. 7, no. 1, 1981.

Jeffreys, S. *Anti-Climax: A Feminist View of the Sexual Revolution*. The Women's Press, London, 1990.

——. ' "Free From All Uninvited Touch of Man": Women's Campaigns Around Sexuality 1880–1914'. *Women's Studies International Forum*, vol. 5, no. 6, 1982.

——. 'Sex Reform and Anti-Feminism in the 1920s', in *The Sexual Dynamics of History*, eds London Feminist History Group. Pluto, London, 1983.

——. *The Spinster and Her Enemies: Feminism and Sexuality 1880–1930*. Pandora Press, London, 1985.

Johnson, P. 'Nineteenth Century Australian Feminism: A Study of *The Dawn* ', *Australia, 1888: A Bicentennial Bulletin*, no. 13, 1984.

Jordens, A.M. 'Against the Tide: The Growth and Decline of a Liberal Anti-War Movement'. *Historical Studies*, vol. 22, no. 88, 1987.

——. 'Rose Scott: Making a Beginning', in *Biographers at Work*, eds J. Walter & R. Nugent. Institute for Modern Biography, Griffith University, Brisbane, 1984.

Kealey, L. & Sangster, J. (eds). *Beyond the Vote: Canadian Women and Politics*. University of Toronto Press, Toronto, 1989.

Kelly, F. 'Vida Goldstein: Political Woman', in *Double-Time: Women in Victoria 150 Years*, eds M. Lake & F. Kelly. Penguin, Ringwood, 1985.

Kelly, J. *Women, History and Theory*. University of Chicago Press, Chicago, 1985.

Kent, S.K. *Sex and Suffrage in Britain, 1860–1914*. Princeton University Press, Princeton, 1987.

Kingston, B.R. 'Anderson, Maybanke Susannah (1845–1927)', in *Australian Dictionary of Biography, Vol. 7: 1891–1939, A-Cl*, eds B. Nairn & G. Serle. Melbourne University Press, Melbourne, 1979.

——. *Glad Confident Morning: The Oxford History of Australia, vol. 3: 1860–1900*. Oxford University Press, Melbourne, 1988.

——. 'Golding, Annie MacKenzie (1855–1934) and Isabella Theresa (1864–1940)', in *Australian Dictionary of Biography, Vol. 9: 1891–1939, Gil-Las*, eds B. Nairn & G. Serle. Melbourne University Press, Melbourne, 1983.

——. *My Wife, My Daughter and Poor Mary Ann: Women and Work in Australia*. Nelson, Melbourne, 1975.

Kirkby, D. 'Alice Henry: Expatriate Feminist', in *Double Time: Women in Victoria 150 Years*, eds M. Lake & F. Kelly. Penguin, Ringwood, 1985.

——. *Alice Henry: The Power of Pen and Voice: The Life of an Australian–American Labor Reformer*. Cambridge University Press, Sydney, 1991.

Kraditor, A. *The Ideas of the Woman Suffrage Movement 1890–1920*. Columbia University Press, New York, 1965.

Kruse, D. & Sowerwine, C. 'Feminism and Pacifism: "Women's Sphere" in Peace and War', in *Australian Women: New Feminist Perspectives*, eds N. Grieve & A. Burns. Oxford University Press, Melbourne, 1986.

Kyle, N. *Her Natural Destiny: The Education of Women in New South Wales*. University of New South Wales Press, Kensington, 1987.

Lake, M. 'Building Themselves Up with Aspros: The Pioneer Woman Reassessed'. *Hecate*, vol. 7, no. 1, 1981.

——. 'Female Desires: The Meaning of World War II'. *Australian Historical Studies*, vol. 24, no. 95, 1990.

——. 'Gender and History'. *Australian Feminist Studies*, nos 7/8, 1988.

——. 'Intimate Strangers', in *Making A Life: A People's History of Australia*, eds V. Burgman & J. Lee, McPhee Gribble/Penguin, Ringwood, 1988.

——. 'Jessie Street and Feminist Chauvinism', in *Jessie Street: Essays and Documents*, ed. H. Radi. Redress Press, Sydney, 1990.

——. 'The Politics of Respectability: Identifying the Masculinist Context'. *Historical Studies*, vol. 22, no. 86, 1986.

——. 'Socialism and Manhood: A Reply to Bruce Scates'. *Labour History*, no. 60, 1991.

——. 'Socialism and Manhood: The Case of William Lane'. *Labour History*, no. 50, 1986.

Lane, A.J. *To Herland and Beyond: The Life and Work of Charlotte Perkins Gilman*. Meridian Books, New York, 1991.

Lansbury, C. 'Gynaecology, Pornography and the Anti-Vivisection Movement'. *Victorian Studies*, vol. 28, no. 3, 1985.

——. 'The Feminine Frontier: Women's Suffrage and Economic Reality'. *Meanjin Quarterly*, vol. 31, no. 3, 1972.

Lawson, B. *My Henry Lawson*. Frank Johnson, Sydney, 1949.

Lawson, O. (ed.) *The First Voice of Australian Feminism*. Penguin, Ringwood, 1990.

Lawson, S. *The Archibald Paradox*. Penguin, Ringwood, 1988.

Leach, W. *True Love and Perfect Union: The Feminist Reform of Sex and Society*. Basic Books, New York, 1980.

Lerner, G. 'Reconceptualizing Differences Among Women'. *Journal of Women's History*, vol. 1, no. 3, 1990.

Levine, P. *Feminist Lives in Victorian England: Private Roles and Public Commitment*. Basil Blackwell, Oxford, 1990.

——. *Victorian Feminism*, Hutchinson, London, 1987.

Lewis, J. 'Women and Late Nineteenth Century Social Work', in *Regulating Womanhood: Historical Essays on Marriage, Motherhood and Sexuality*, ed. C. Smart. Routledge, London, 1992.

Lloyd, G. *The Man of Reason: 'Male' and 'Female' in Western Philosophy*. Methuen, London, 1984.

Loveday, P. *et. al. The Emergence of the Australian Party System*. Hale & Iremonger, Sydney, 1980.

Lutton, N. 'Rischbieth, Bessie Mabel (1874–1967)', in *Australian Dictionary of Biography, Vol. 11: 1891–1939, Nes-Smi*, ed. G. Serle. Melbourne University Press, Melbourne, 1988.

Lyon, J. 'Militant Discourse, Strange Bedfellows: Suffragettes and Vorticists Before the War'. *differences*, vol. 4, no. 2.

MacDonald, L. 'Rose Scott of Sydney 1847–1925'. *ICW Bulletin*, vol. 8, May 1930.

——. *The Women's College Within the University of Sydney*. Sydney University Press, Sydney, 1949.

Mackenzie, N. 'Vida Goldstein: The Australian Suffragette'. *Australian Journal of Politics and History*, vol. 56, 1960.

——. *Women in Australia*. Cheshire, Melbourne, 1962.

Magarey, S.M. *Unbridling the Tongues of Women: A Biography of Catherine Helen Spence*. Hale & Iremonger, Sydney, 1985.

Malone, J. 'What's Wrong With Emma? The Feminist Debate in Colonial Auckland', in *Women in History: Essays on European Women in New Zealand*, eds B. Brookes et. al. University of Victoria Press, Wellington, 1986.

Markey, R. *The Making of the Labor Party in New South Wales 1880–1900*. University of New South Wales Press, Kensington, 1988.

Martel, N. A. *The Woman's Vote in Australia.* WSPU, London, 1913.

Matthews, B. *Louisa.* McPhee Gribble/Penguin, Melbourne, 1987.

Matthews, J.J. 'Feminist History'. *Labour History*, no. 50, 1986.

——. *Good and Mad Women: The Historical Construction of Femininity in Twentieth Century Australia.* Allen & Unwin, Sydney, 1984.

Mayo, K. *Mother India.* Jonathan Cape, London, 1927.

McDonald, P. *Marriage and the Family in Australia.* Australian National University, Canberra, 1978.

——. 'Marriage, Fertility and Mortality', in *Australians: Historical Statistics*, ed. W. Vamplew. Fairfax, Syme, Weldon and Associates, Sydney 1988.

Mitchell, W. *Fifty Years of Feminist Achievement: A History of the United Associations of Women.* UAW, Sydney, 1979.

Modjeska, D. *Exiles At Home: Australian Women Writers 1925–1945.* Sirius, London, 1981.

Montefiore, D. *From A Victorian to A Modern.* Archer, London, 1927.

Morris, M. *The Pirate's Fiancée: Feminism, Reading Postmodernism.* Verso, London, 1988.

Mouffe, C. 'Feminism, Citizenship and Radical Democratic Politics', in *Feminists Theorize the Political*, eds J. Butler & J.W. Scott. Routledge, New York, 1992.

Mowle, F.C. (ed.), *A Genealogical History of Pioneer Families of Australia*, 5th ed. Rigby, Adelaide, 1978.

Mulraney, J. 'When Lovely Woman Stoops to Lobby'. *Australian Feminist Studies*, nos 7/8, 1988.

National Council of Women of New South Wales. *The NCW of NSW: History of Its Establishment with Constitution*, 26 June 1896. The Council, Sydney, n.d.

——. *Jubilee Report 1896–1946.* The Council, Sydney, 1947.

Newman, L. 'Critical Theory and the History of Women: What's at Stake in Deconstructing Women's History?'. *Journal of Women's History*, vol. 2, no. 3, 1991.

Newton, J.L. 'A Feminist Scholarship You Can Bring Home to Dad', *Journal of Women's History*, vol. 2, no. 3, 1991.

NSW, *Statistical Registers 1880–1925.*

NSW Branch of the London Peace Society, *Annual Reports 1907–1918.*

NSW Parliament, *Debates 1880–1925.*

——. *Statutes 1880–1924.*

O'Brien, A. *Poverty's Prison: The Poor in New South Wales 1880–1918.* Melbourne University Press, Melbourne, 1988.

Offen, K. 'Defining Feminism: A Comparative Historical Approach'. *Signs*, vol. 14, no. 1, 1988.

——. 'On the French Origin of the Words Feminism and Feminist'. *Feminist Issues*, vol. 8, no. 2, 1988.

——. 'A Reply to Cott', and 'A Reply to Dubois'. *Signs*, vol. 15, no. 1, 1989.

Ollif, L. *Louisa Lawson: Henry Lawson's Crusading Mother.* Rigby, Adelaide, 1978.

Pankhurst, E. *My Own Story.* E. Nash, London, 1941.

Pankhurst, S. *The Suffragette Movement: An Intimate Account of Persons and Ideals.* Virago, London, 1977.

Pateman, C. *The Sexual Contract.* Polity Press, Cambridge, 1988.

——. 'Women and Consent'. *Political Theory*, vol. 8, no. 2, 1980.

The Personal Narratives Group (ed.) *Interpreting Women's Lives: Feminist Theory and Personal Narratives.* Indiana University Press, Bloomington, 1989.

Pierson, R.R. 'Experience, Difference, Dominance and Voice in the Writing of

Canadian Women's History', in *Writing Women's History: International Perspectives*, eds K. Offen *et. al.* Indiana University Press, Bloomington, 1991.

Prentice, A. *et. al. Canadian Women: A History*. Harcourt Brace Jovanovich, Toronto, 1988.

Pringle, R. 'Octavius Beale and the Ideology of the Birthrate. The Royal Commission of 1904 and 1905', *Refractory Girl*. no. 3, 1973.

Quiggin, P. *No Rising Generation: Women and Fertility in Late Nineteenth Century Australia*. Australian National University, Canberra, 1988.

Radi,H. 'Introducing Jessie Street', in *Jessie Street: Essays and Documents*, ed. H. Radi, Women's Redress Press, Sydney, 1990.

——. 'Lawson, Louisa (1848–1920)', in *Australian Dictionary of Biography, Vol. 10: 1891–1939, Lat-Ner*, eds B. Nairn & G. Serle. Melbourne University Press, Melbourne, 1986.

——. 'Organizing for Reform', in *Jessie Street: Essays and Documents*, ed. H. Radi, Women's Redress Press, Sydney, 1990.

——. 'Whose Child?', in *In Pursuit of Justice: Australian Women and the Law 1788–1979*, eds J. Mackinolty & H. Radi. Hale & Iremonger, Sydney, 1979.

——. 'Windeyer, Mary Elizabeth (1836–1912) and Margaret (1866–1939)', in *Australian Dictionary of Biography, Vol. 12: 1891–1939, Smy-Z*, ed. J. Ritchie. Melbourne University Press, Melbourne, 1990.

——. (ed.), *200 Australian Women*. Women's Redress Press, Sydney, 1988.

Ram, C. 'Sexual Violence in India'. *Refractory Girl*, no. 22, 1981.

Ramas, M. 'Freud's Dora, Dora's Hysteria', in *Sex and Class in Women's History*, eds J.L. Newton *et. al.* Routledge & Kegan Paul, London, 1983.

Ranald, P. 'Feminism and Class: The United Associations of Women and the Council for Action for Equal Pay in the Depression', in *Worth Her Salt: Women at Work in Australia*, eds M.Bevege *et. al.* Hale & Iremonger, Sydney, 1982.

Reiger, K.M. *The Disenchantment of the Home: Modernizing the Australian Family 1880–1940*. Oxford University Press, Melbourne, 1985.

Richardson, G.D. 'Mitchell, David Scott (1836–1907)', in *Australian Dictionary of Biography, vol. 5, 1851–90, K-Q*, ed. B. Nairn *et.al.* Melbourne University Press, Melbourne, 1974.

Rickard, J. *Class and Politics—New South Wales, Victoria and the Early Commonwealth*. Australian National University Press, Canberra, 1976.

Riley, D. *'Am I That Name?' Feminism and the Category of 'Women' in History*. University of Minnesota Press, Minneapolis, 1988.

Riley, G. *Inventing the American Woman: A Perspective on Women's History*. Harlan Davidson, Inc. Arlington, Ill. 1987.

Rischbieth, B.M. *The March of Australian Women: A Record of Fifty Years of Struggle for Equal Citizenship*. Paterson Brokenshaw, Perth, 1964.

Roe, J. *Beyond Belief: Theosophy in Australia 1879–1939*. University of New South Wales Press, Kensington, 1987.

——. 'Chivalry and Social Policy in the Antipodes'. *Historical Studies*, vol. 22, no. 88, April 1987.

——. 'Introduction', in Franklin, M. *Some Everyday Folk and Dawn*. Virago, London, 1986.

Rogers, K. *Feminism in Eighteenth Century England*. University of Illinois Press, Urbana, 1980.

Rosen, R. *The Lost Sisterhood: Prostitution in America 1900–1918*. Johns Hopkins University Press, Baltimore, 1983.

Rosenberg, R. *Beyond Separate Spheres: Intellectual Roots of Modern Feminism*. Yale University Press, New Haven, 1982.

Rothman, S.M. *Women's Proper Place: A History of Changing Ideals and Practices, 1870 to the present*. Basic Books, New York, 1978.

Rowbotham, S. *Woman, Resistance and Revolution*. Penguin, Harmondsworth, 1974.

Russell, P. 'For Better and For Worse: Love, Power and Sexuality in Upper Class Marriages in Melbourne, 1860–1890'. *Australian Feminist Studies*, nos 7/8, 1988.

Ryan, M.P. 'The Power of Women's Networks', in *Sex and Class in Women's History*, eds J.L. Newton *et. al*. Routledge, London, 1983.

——. *Women in Public*. Johns Hopkins University Press, Baltimore, 1990.

Sarah, E. 'Towards a Reassessment of Feminist History'. *Women's Studies International Forum*, vol. 5, no. 6, 1982.

Saunders, K. & Spearitt, K. 'Is There Life After Birth? Childbirth, Death and Danger for Settler Women in Colonial Queensland'. *Journal of Australian Studies*.,no. 29, 1991.

Sawer, M. & Simms, M. *A Woman's Place: Women and Politics in Australia*. Allen & Unwin, Sydney, 1984.

Scates, B. 'Socialism and Feminism: The Case of William Lane: A Reply to Marilyn Lake'. *Labour History*, no. 60, 1991.

Scott, D. 'Woman Suffrage: The Movement in Australia'. *Journal of the Royal Australian Historical Society*, vol. 53, no. 4, 1967.

Scott, J.W. 'Deconstructing Equality Versus Difference or the Uses of Poststructuralist Theory for Feminism', in *Conflicts in Feminism*, eds M. Hirsch & E. Fox-Keller. Routledge, New York, 1990.

——. 'Experience', in *Feminists Theorize the Political*, eds J. Butler & J.W. Scott. Routledge, New York, 1992.

——. *Gender and the Politics of History*. Columbia University Press, New York,1988.

——. 'Reply to the *difference* Questions', in Christian, B. 'Conference Call'. *differences*, vol. 1, no. 3, 1990.

Scott, R. 'Australian Women and the Franchise'. *Australian Economist*, vol. 4, no. 15, 1895.

——. *Laws in New South Wales Re Women and Children*. National Council of Women, Sydney, 1919.

——. *On the Social Evil*. Women's Christian Temperance Union of Queensland, Brisbane, 1903.

Searle, B. *Silk and Calico: Class, Gender and the Vote in Australia*. Hale & Iremonger, Sydney, 1988.

Sekuless, P. *Jessie Street: A Rewarding But Unrewarded Life*. University of Queensland Press, St Lucia, 1978.

Sewell, M.W. *The Genesis of the International Council of Women 1888–1893*. ICW, Illinois, 1914.

Sheridan, S. 'Louisa Lawson, Miles Franklin and Feminist Writing 1888–1901'. *Australian Feminist Studies*, nos 7/8, 1988.

Sherrick, R. 'Toward Universal Sisterhood'. *Women's Studies International Forum*, vol. 5, no. 6, 1982.

Shute, C. 'Blood Votes and the Bestial Boche: A Case Study in Propaganda'. *Hecate*, vol. 2, no. 2, 1976.

——. 'Heroines and Heroes: Sexual Mythology in Australia, 1914–1918'. *Hecate*, vol. 1, no. 1, 1975.

Singer, L. 'Feminism and Postmodernism', in *Feminists Theorize the Political*, eds J. Butler & J.W. Scott. Routledge, New York, 1992.

Sklar, K.K. *Catherine Beecher: A Study in American Domesticity*. Yale University, New Haven, 1973.

Smart, J. 'The Panacea of Prohibition: The Reaction of the Women's Christian Temperance Union of Victoria to the Great War', in *Women, Faith and Fetes*, ed. J. Willis. Dove Publications, Melbourne, 1977.

Smith-Rosenberg, C. 'The Female World of Love and Ritual: Relationships Between Women in Nineteenth Century America', in Smith-Rosenberg, C. *Disorderly Conduct: Visions of Gender in Victorian America*. Oxford University Press, New York, 1985.

Spearritt, K. 'The Market for Marriage in Colonial Queensland'. *Hecate*, vol. 16, nos 1–2, 1990.

——. 'New Dawns: First Wave Feminism 1880–1914', in *Gender Relations in Australia*, eds K. Saunders & R. Evans.

Spender, D. *There's Always Been A Women's Movement This Century*. Pandora, London, 1983.

——. *Women of Ideas*. Routledge & Kegan Paul, London, 1982.

Stanford-Thomas, E. 'Treasures of the Mitchell and Dixson' (ABC Radio Script) 1965–6.

Stanley, L. 'Biography as Microscope or Kaleidoscope? The Case of "Power" in Hannah Cullwick's Relationship with Arthur Munby'. *Women's Studies International Forum*, vol. 10, no. 1, 1987.

——. 'Recovering *Women* in History from Feminist Deconstruction'. *Women's Studies International Forum*, vol. 13, nos 1/2, 1990.

Stansell, C. *City of Women: Sex and Class in New York 1789–1860*. University of Illinois, Urbana, 1987.

State Library of New South Wales, Dixson Gallery Catalogue. 'Rose Scott: Remarkable Woman, Remarkable Friends' [Exhibition Catalogue no. 20, April–December 1985]. State Library of NSW, Sydney, 1985.

Stimpson, C.R. 'Are the Differences Spreading? Feminist Criticism and Postmodernism'. *English Studies in Canada*, vol. 15, no. 4, 1989.

Street, J. *Truth or Repose?*. Alpha Books, Sydney, 1976.

Strong-Boag, V. '"Ever a Crusader": Nellie McClung, First-Wave Feminist', *in Rethinking Canada: The Promise of Women's History*, eds V. Strong-Boag & A. Fellman. Copp Clark Pittman, Toronto, 1986.

——. *The Parliament of Women: The National Council of Women of Canada 1893–1929*. National Museums of Canada, Ottawa, 1976.

Summers, A. *Damned Whores and God's Police: The Colonisation of Women in Australia*. Penguin, Ringwood, 1975.

——. 'The Unwritten History of Adela Pankhurst Walsh', in *Women, Class and History*, ed. E. Windschuttle. Fontana, Melbourne, 1980.

——. 'A Home From Home: Women's Philanthropic Work in the Nineteenth Century', in *Fit Work for Women*, ed. S. Burman. Croom Helm, London, 1979.

Tapper, M. 'Can A Feminist Be A Liberal?'. *Australian Journal of Philosophy*, vol. 64, no. 1, 1986.

Terry, J. 'Theorizing Deviant Historiography'. *differences*, vol. 3, no. 2, 1991.

Tickner, L. *The Spectacle of Women: Imagery of the Suffrage Campaign*. Chatto, London, 1987.

Tiffin, S. 'In Search of Reluctant Parents: Desertion and Non-Support Legislation in Australia and the United States 1890–1920', in *What Rough Beast? The State and Social Order in Australian History*, ed. Sydney Labour History Group. Allen and Unwin, Sydney, 1982.

Trimberger, E.K. 'Feminism, Men and Modern Love: Greenwich Vilage 1900–1925', in *Powers of Desire: The Politics of Sexuality*, eds A. Snitow *et. al.* Monthly Review Press, New York, 1983.

——. *Intimate Warriors: Portrait of a Modern Marriage, 1899–1944*. The Feminist Press, New York, 1991.

Turner. I. 'Prisoners in Petticoats: A Shocking History of Female Emancipation in Australia', in *In Her Own Right: Women of Australia*, ed. J. Rigg. Nelson, Melbourne, 1970.

Valverde, M. *The Age of Light and Soap and Water: Moral Reform in English Canada 1880–1925*. McClelland Stewart, Toronto, 1991.

——. '"When the Mother of the Race is Free": Race, Reproduction and Sexuality in First-Wave Feminism', in *Gender Conflict: New Essays in Women's History*, eds F. Iacovetta & M. Valverde. University of Toronto Press, Toronto, 1992.

Vicinus, M. *Independent Women: Work and Community for Single Women 1850–1920*. Virago, London, 1985.

Vogel, L. 'Telling Tales: Historians of Our Own Lives'. *Journal of Women's History*, vol. 2, no. 3, 1991.

Vogel, U. 'Whose Property? The Double Standard of Adultery in Nineteenth Century Law', in *Regulating Womanhood: Historical Essays on Marriage, Motherhood and Sexuality*, ed. C. Smart. Routledge, London, 1992.

Walkowitz, J.R. *City of Dreadful Delight: Narratives of Sexual Danger in Late Victorian London*. University of Chicago Press, Chicago, 1992.

——. 'Male Vice and Female Virtue: Feminism and the Politics of Prostitution in Late Nineteenth Century England', in *Powers of Desire: The Politics of Sexuality*, eds A. Snitow *et. al.* Monthly Review Press, New York, 1983.

Ware, H. *Fertility and Family Formation in Australia*. Australian National University Press, Canberra, 1975.

Ware, S. *Beyond Suffrage: Women in the New Deal*. Harvard University Press, Cambridge, 1981.

Warner, M. 'Introduction', in de Pisan, C. *The Book of the City of Ladies*. Picador, London, 1983.

Weeks, J. *Sex, Politics and Society: The Regulation of Sexuality Since 1800*. Longman, London, 1981.

——. *Sexuality and Its Discontents*. Routledge & Kegan Paul, London, 1985.

White, K. 'Bessie Rischbieth, Jessie Street and the End of First Wave Feminism in Australia', in *Worth Her Salt: Women at Work in Australia*, eds M. Bevege *et. al.* Hale & Iremonger, Sydney, 1982.

——. *Women in Australian Politics*. Allen & Unwin, Sydney, 1983.

Wiltsher, A. *Most Dangerous Women: Feminist Peace Campaigners of the Great War*. Pandora, London, 1985.

Windeyer, W.C. *Ex Parte Collins*. Government Printer, Sydney, 1888.

Wood, N. 'Prostitution and Feminism in Nineteenth Century Britain'. *m/f*, no. 7, 1982.

Womanhood Suffrage League of New South Wales. *Annual Reports 1–10 1891/2–1900/01*. WSL, Sydney.

Women's Club. *Annual Report and Balance Sheet 1906–1939*. The Club, Sydney.

Women's Literary Society. *Rules, Programmes and Annual Reports 1891–1896*. WLS, Sydney.

Wright, A. 'Jessie Street, Feminist', in *Women at Work*, eds A. Curthoys *et. al.* Society for the Study of Labour History, Canberra, 1975.

Yeatman, A. 'A Feminist Theory of Social Differentiation', in *Feminism/Postmodernism*, ed. L. Nicholson. Routledge, New York, 1990.

Yellis, K. 'Prosperity's Child: Some Thoughts on the Flapper'. *American Quarterly*, vol. 42, no. 3, 1967.

Young, A. '"Wild Women": The Censure of the Suffragette Movement'. *International Journal of the Sociology of Law*, vol. 6, no. 2, 1988.

Young, P. 'Miller, Emma (1839–1917)', in *Australian Dictionary of Biography, Vol. 10: 1891–1939, Lat-Ner*, eds B. Nairn & G. Serle. Melbourne University Press, Melbourne, 1986.

——. *Proud to Be A Rebel: The Life and Times of Emma Miller*. University of Queensland Press, St Lucia, 1991.

Zinkhan, E. 'Louisa Albury Lawson: Feminist and Patriot', in *A Bright and Fiery Troop: Australian Women Writers of the Nineteenth Century*. ed. D. Adelaide. Penguin, Ringwood, 1988.

IV. Unpublished Dissertations and Papers

Allen, J.A. Aspects of the Public Career of Rose Scott: Feminist, Social Reformer and Pacifist 1890–1925. BA (Hons) dissertation, University of Sydney, 1977.

——. Women, Crimes and Policing in New South Wales, 1880–1939. PhD dissertation, Macquarie University, 1984.

Atkinson, J. Aspects of the Developing Relationship between Working Class Women and Feminists 1890–1917. BA (Hons) dissertation, University of Sydney, 1979.

Biskup, P. The Female Suffrage Movement in Western Australia. PhD dissertation, University of Western Australia, 1959.

Brignell, L. Illegitimacy in New South Wales 1875–1972. PhD dissertation, University of Sydney, 1990.

Campbell, D. The Status of Women in New South Wales 1925–28. BA (Hons) dissertation, University of New South Wales, 1974.

Cobbe, J.E. The Women's Movement in New South Wales 1880–1914. MA dissertation, University of New England, 1967.

Cookson, R. The Role of Certain Women and Womens Organisations in New South Wales and Victoria between 1900 and 1920. BA (Hons) dissertation, University of Sydney, 1959.

Cooper, R.G. The Women's Suffrage Movement in New South Wales 1891–1902. MA dissertation, University of Sydney, 1970.

Coward, D. The Impact of War on New South Wales: Some Aspects of Political and Social History 1914–17. PhD dissertation, Australian National University, 1974.

Cowden, V. 'Mothers As a Rule, Do Not Know . . .' : Mothercraft Campaigns in the Inner Suburbs of Sydney 1904–15. BA (Hons) dissertation, University of Sydney, 1980.

Fitzsimons, T. Childbirth and the Professions in New South Wales 1890–1930. BA (Hons) dissertation, University of Sydney, 1981.

Foley, M. The Women's Movement in New South Wales and Victoria 1918–38. PhD dissertation, University of Sydney, 1985.

Godden, J. Philanthropy and the Women's Sphere, Sydney 1870–1900. PhD dissertation, Macquarie University, 1983.

Ryan, D. Women's Employment in New South Wales During the First World War. BA (Hons) dissertation, University of Sydney, 1979.

Ryan, J.A. B.R. Wise: An Oxford Liberal in the Free Trade Party in New South Wales. MA dissertation, University of Sydney, 1965.

Scherer, C.A. The Golding Sisters: Annie, Kate and Belle: The Complexities of First Wave Feminism in Late Nineteenth and Early Twentieth Century Australia. MA paper, University of Sydney, 1989.

Smith, E.F. Millicent Preston Stanley: A Feminist in Politics. BA (Hons) dissertation, University of Sydney, 1977.

Young, P. The Struggle for Woman Suffrage in Queensland. Women and Labour Conference Papers, Melbourne, 1980.

Index